CULTURAL HERITAGE AND THE FUTURE

Cultural Heritage and the Future brings together an international group of scholars and experts to consider the relationship between cultural heritage and the future.

Drawing on case studies from around the world, the contributing authors insist that cultural heritage and the future are intimately linked and that the development of futures thinking should be a priority for academics, students and those working in the wider professional heritage sector. Until recently, the future has never attracted substantial research and debate within heritage studies and heritage management, and this book addresses this gap by offering a balance of theoretical and empirical content that will stimulate multidisciplinary debate in the burgeoning field of critical heritage studies.

Cultural Heritage and the Future questions the role of heritage in future-making and will be of great relevance to academics and students working in the fields of museum and heritage studies, archaeology, anthropology, architecture, conservation studies, sociology, history and geography. Those working in the heritage professions will also find much to interest them within the pages of this book.

Cornelius Holtorf is Professor of Archaeology and holds a UNESCO Chair on Heritage Futures at Linnaeus University in Kalmar, Sweden, where he is also directing the Graduate School in Contract Archaeology (GRASCA). In his research, he is particularly interested in contemporary archaeology, heritage theory, and heritage futures, with numerous international publications in these areas. He also likes sailing.

Anders Högberg is Professor of Archaeology at Linnaeus University and Associated Researcher at the University of Johannesburg, South Africa. He has broad research interests, and is currently working with projects on heritage futures, migration and cognitive evolution.

CULTURAL HERITAGE AND THE FUTURE

Edited by Cornelius Holtorf and Anders Högberg

LONDON AND NEW YORK

United Nations Educational, Scientific and Cultural Organization · UNESCO Chair on Heritage Futures, Linnæus University, Sweden

First published 2021
by Routledge
2 Park Square, Milton Park, Abingdon, Oxon OX14 4RN

and by Routledge
52 Vanderbilt Avenue, New York, NY 10017

Routledge is an imprint of the Taylor & Francis Group, an informa business

British Library Cataloguing-in-Publication Data
A catalogue record for this book is available from the British Library

Library of Congress Cataloging-in-Publication Data
Names: Holtorf, Cornelius, 1968- editor. | Högberg, Anders, editor.
Title: Cultural Heritage and the Future / edited by Cornelius Holtorf and Anders Högberg.
Description: London ; New York, NY : Routledge/Taylor & Francis Group, 2021. | Series: Key issues in cultural heritage | Includes bibliographical references and index.
Identifiers: LCCN 2020024716 (print) | LCCN 2020024717 (ebook)
Subjects: LCSH: Cultural property--Protection--Case studies. | Cultural property--Protection--Planning. | Historic preservation--Case studies. | Historic preservation--Planning. | Cultural policy--Case studies.
Classification: LCC CC135 .C824 2021 (print) | LCC CC135 (ebook) | DDC 363.6/9--dc23
LC record available at https://lccn.loc.gov/2020024716
LC ebook record available at https://lccn.loc.gov/2020024717

ISBN: 978-1-138-82900-8 (hbk)
ISBN: 978-1-138-82901-5 (pbk)
ISBN: 978-1-315-64461-5 (ebk)

Typeset in Bembo
by Deanta Global Publishing Services, Chennai, India

CONTENTS

SECTION 1
The future in heritage studies and heritage management

FIGURES

TABLES

CONTRIBUTORS

Erica Avrami, PhD, is the James Marston Fitch Assistant Professor of Historic Preservation at Columbia University's Graduate School of Architecture, Planning and Preservation and a Research Affiliate at the Center for Sustainable Urban Development – Earth Institute.

Marcos Buser is a geologist and social scientist. He has been working in the field of nuclear energy and the disposal of chemotoxic hazardous waste for over 40 years. He managed large waste projects in Switzerland and was chairman/member of expert commissions, such as the EKRA Expert Commission for the Swiss Repository Concept and the Federal Commission for Nuclear Safety. Since 2008, Marcos Buser has published several studies on preservation of records, knowledge and memory across generations and the consequences of toxic waste disposal for future societies.

May Cassar is the Director of the UCL Institute for Sustainable Heritage and the Bartlett Vice Dean (Public Policy). May's research interests lie at the confluence of preventive conservation, climate change and public policy. As the Director of the Arts and Humanities Research Council/Engineering and Physical Sciences Research Council's Science and Heritage Programme (2007–2014) and as Special Adviser to the House of Lords Science and Technology Committee Inquiry on Science and Heritage (2005–2006), May has led the establishment of heritage science research activity in the UK over the last two decades for which she was recognized by the Royal Warrant Holders' Association with the award of the Plowden Gold Medal in 2012.

Caitlin DeSilvey is Professor of Cultural Geography, based at the University of Exeter's Cornwall campus, where she is Associate Director for Transdisciplinary

Research in the Environment and Sustainability Institute. Her research into the cultural significance of material change has involved extensive collaboration with heritage practitioners, archaeologists, ecologists, artists and others. From 2015 to 2019 she was co-investigator on the Heritage Futures project (funded by the Arts and Humanities Research Council), and in 2016–2017 she was a fellow at the Centre for Advanced Study, Oslo. Her publications include *Anticipatory History* (2011, with Simon Naylor and Colin Sackett) and *Visible Mending* (2013, with Steven Bond and James R. Ryan). *Curated Decay: Heritage Beyond Saving* (2017) received the University of Mary Washington's Center for Historic Preservation 2018 Book Prize, awarded each year to an author whose book has a positive impact on preservation in the United States.

James Dixon is a contemporary archaeologist with work and interests covering historic buildings, contemporary buildings and landscapes, archaeology and art and public archaeology. He is co-editor of the journal *Post-Medieval Archaeology* and a co-organizer of the Public Archaeology Twitter Conference series.

Alfredo González-Ruibal is an archaeologist specializing in the archaeology of the contemporary past. His research focuses on the darker side of modernity (conflict, dictatorship, colonialism). He is the author of two recent books: *An Archaeology of the Contemporary Era* (2019) and *The Archaeology of the Contemporary Past* (2020), both with Routledge.

Alice Gorman is an internationally recognized leader in the field of space archaeology. Her research focuses on the archaeology and heritage of space exploration, including space junk, planetary landing sites, off-earth mining, rocket launch pads and antennas. Gorman demonstrated that the Burra Charter heritage principles could be applied to space heritage, and developed cultural landscape approaches to the space environment. She is currently working on an archaeology of the International Space Station. Gorman is an Associate Professor at Flinders University and a member of the Advisory Council of the Space Industry Association of Australia. In 2017, she won the Bragg University of New South Wales Press Prize for Science Writing. Her book *Dr Space Junk vs the Universe: Archaeology and the Future*, published in 2019, was shortlisted for the Queensland Literary Award and won the NIB Literary Award People's Choice in November 2019. She tweets as @drspacejunk and blogs at Space Age Archaeology.

Paul Graves-Brown. I am a recovering prehistorian, who turned to modern material culture after an enlightening year with CNRS (*Centre National de la Recherche Scientifique*) in Paris. I have researched car culture, shopping centres, the internet, the AK47, music technology, the economics of artefacts and written fairly extensively on popular music heritage. I have edited three books, but never managed a monograph of my own. I now want to spend more time writing fiction (if indeed my earlier work is not as such). I live in west Wales with my partner and four greyhounds. I am finally trying to learn Welsh. Oh, and I am a vegan.

Rodney Harrison is Professor of Heritage Studies at the University College London Institute of Archaeology and Arts and Humanities Research Council (AHRC) Heritage Priority Area Leadership Fellow (2017–2020). He has experience working in, teaching and researching natural and cultural heritage conservation, management and preservation in the UK, Europe, Australia, North America and South America. He is the (co)author or (co)editor of 17 books and guest-edited journal volumes and over 80 peer-reviewed journal articles and book chapters and is the founding editor of the *Journal of Contemporary Archaeology*. Between 2015 and 2019 he was principal investigator on the AHRC funded Heritage Futures research programme, www.heritage-futures.org. His research has been funded by AHRC, Global Challenges Research Fund/UK Research and Innovation, British Academy, Wenner-Gren Foundation, Australian Research Council, Australian Institute of Aboriginal and Torres Strait Islander Studies and the European Commission. His latest books include *Deterritorializing the Future: Heritage in, of and after the Anthropocene* (co-edited with Colin Sterling, OHP, 2020); and *Heritage Futures: Comparative Approaches to Natural and Cultural Heritage Practices* (co-authored, UCL Press, 2020).

Anders Högberg is a Professor of Archaeology at Linnaeus University and Associated Researcher at the University of Johannesburg. He has broad research interests, currently working with projects on heritage futures, migration and cognitive evolution.

Cornelius Holtorf is Professor of Archaeology and holds a UNESCO Chair on Heritage Futures at Linnaeus University in Kalmar, Sweden. He is also directing the Graduate School in Contract Archaeology at his university. In his research, he is particularly interested in contemporary archaeology, heritage theory and heritage futures, with numerous international publications in these areas. He also likes sailing.

Rosemary A. Joyce is Professor of Anthropology at the University of California, Berkeley. A field archaeologist with over 30 years of experience in research in Honduras, and a museum anthropologist who has conducted research in museums throughout North America and Europe, her work is centrally concerned with issues of materiality and understanding human social relations with and through things.

Abraham Van Luik (†2016) earned a bachelor's degree in chemistry, and both master's and doctorate degrees from Utah State University. His dissertation involved modelling heavy metal solubility in Utah's Great Salt Lake, an evaporating brine. His career began at Argonne National Laboratory in Illinois and continued with the Pacific Northwest National Laboratory in nuclear waste repository siting investigations in the 1970s and 1980s. He then joined the US Department of Energy in Nevada, where he oversaw the science and engineering side of the Yucca Mountain Project licence application. He served as Senior

Policy Adviser for Performance Assessment as well as the manager of international programmes in the Las Vegas office. In 2010, he moved to the Department of Energy Waste Isolation Pilot Plant in New Mexico to set up cooperation between US repository programmes and other international agencies pursuing deep geologic disposal of radioactive waste. Abraham Van Luik passed away in 2016.

Luo Li is an Assistant Professor in Law at Coventry Law School. Dr Li's research includes intellectual property and its application to culture, cultural heritage, fashion design and information technology. Prior to joining Coventry Law School, Dr Li worked at the Law and Legislative Advice Division of the World Intellectual Property Organization. Dr Li was an Associate Editor of *Queen Mary Journal of Intellectual Property* in 2015–2017 and is currently the journal's article reviewer. Dr Li is also a grant reviewer of the National Social Science Academy in Poland.

Sarah May is a Senior Lecturer in Public History and Heritage at Swansea University in South Wales. She has researched heritage in the private sector, the public sector and academia. Her research interests are broad following the myriad ways that heritage is used to support contemporary power struggles. In addition to her work on children and on the future, she has ongoing work on toxic heritage and games as a communication method in heritage practice.

Robert Charlotte Maxwell is an Australian contemporary archaeologist based in Sydney. They are currently completing a PhD exploring the relationship between ideology and materiality in episodes of 20th-century settlement decline and abandonment. Their other research interests include the heritage and material culture of satanism, occultism and new religious movements, horror studies, quantum archaeology and the archaeologies of non-humans.

Roger Nelson has almost 50 years of experience in management and conducting environmental programmes for both public and private sector projects. In the 1970s, he primarily worked on commercial environmental monitoring programmes. The 1980s found him managing the clean-up across the US of uranium mill tailings left over from the early days of the Cold War. In the early 1990s, he began working at the US Department of Energy Waste Isolation Pilot Plant (WIPP) in New Mexico. As the Chief Scientist for WIPP from 2000 to 2016, he served as the principal scientific adviser focused on the development of innovative, cost-effective radioactive and hazardous waste handling, treatment, characterization, packaging, transportation and disposal technologies. Now retired, he continues to promote the use of the unique underground environment at WIPP for use as a laboratory for basic science experiments requiring extremely low dose rate background radiation.

Richard Sandford is Professor of Heritage Evidence, Foresight and Policy at University College London's Institute for Sustainable Heritage, where his research explores future contexts for heritage, future forms of heritage and the work of heritage in future societies, drawing on sociological and philosophical perspectives on time and change. Previously, Richard led horizon-scanning teams in the UK Civil Service providing strategic analysis for ministers and senior civil servants. Before joining the UK Civil Service, Richard was based in Singapore, where he designed and facilitated foresight workshops across Asia, the US and Europe for groups including UNESCO, the British Council and Singapore policy groups.

PREFACE

There are multiple possible futures ahead of us. What these futures, more than anything else, have in common is that they differ from the present. Cultural heritage and the future is a field of research and practice that has been developing over the past few years. Today's heritage practitioners need the ability to understand and navigate in a world of uncertainty and fast change. That is why we need to build global capacity for future thinking among professionals, both in heritage studies and in heritage management.

The present volume was originally devised in 2012, related to a session on the same topic which we co-organized for the First Conference of the Association of Critical Heritage Studies in Gothenburg, Sweden. Between 2015 and 2019, some of the contributors, including the co-editors, were involved in, and stimulated by, the Heritage Futures research programme, led by Rodney Harrison and based at University College London.

The volume contains a wide range of contributions discussing examples from many parts of the world that raise important issues about the interrelations between cultural heritage and the future. Taken as a whole, we believe that the book will contribute significantly to building capacity in futures thinking and futures literacy among researchers and practitioners throughout the heritage sector.

Since 2017, we have both been involved in the UNESCO Chair on Heritage Futures at Linnaeus University. Heritage futures are concerned with the roles of heritage in managing the relations between present and future societies, e.g., through anticipation and planning. The Chair develops tools for creative and critical futures thinking among heritage professionals, e.g., concerning how cultural heritage might help future generations to solve important challenges. This volume on *Cultural Heritage and the Future* and its contributions were conceived and written in different contexts, but we believe that they will make an important contribution to this general ambition too.

Cornelius Holtorf
Anders Högberg
UNESCO Chair on Heritage Futures

1

INTRODUCTION

Cultural heritage as a futuristic field

Cornelius Holtorf and Anders Högberg

Insisting that we need to preserve the remains of the past for the benefit of future generations is common in heritage policy and legislation around the world, from the goals of local heritage projects all the way to global policy (Spennemann 2007a). Article 4 of the UNESCO World Heritage Convention is a good example. "The duty" of each state party to the Convention is described as 'the identification, protection, conservation, presentation and transmission to future generations of the cultural and natural heritage... situated on its territory' (UNESCO 1972). The idea of preservation for the future is axiomatic. It is frequently used and so deeply ingrained in the way we think today about cultural and natural heritage that it seems self-evident. This became clear in an empirical study we conducted (Högberg et al. 2017). Based on interviews with heritage managers and international experts in cultural heritage from several countries, we found that almost all of them recognized the heritage motto of preserving the past for the future. At the same time, few of the interviewees had ever properly considered, or could explicitly articulate, how heritage actually will be beneficial to future societies.

The ways in which people think and act are bound to particular cultural contexts and are therefore specific in time and place. Given that the cultural heritage sector (of all sectors!) should appreciate this, it is somewhat ironic that the need to preserve the heritage for the future is widely taken for granted, both in the heritage sector itself and society at large. The desire to transmit heritage as a human legacy to future generations is often treated like an unproblematic and nearly universal principle. Queries about the prospects of actual future benefits resulting from policies of preservation are often not only deemed to be unnecessary but also unthinkable (but see Willems 2012; Karl 2015; 2018). A lack of concern with developments and changes over time and actual needs of the future is prevalent, even though the future motivates preservation and conservation in the first place. That is why François Hartog (2015) suspected that the contemporary heritage sector remains caught in the logic of that particular "regime of historicity" that he calls presentism. That regime is so strong that even the emerging discourse about heritage and sustainable development hardly considers anything else than benefits of heritage in our present, addressing the challenges of our own time, and hoping that the outcomes will carry forward into the future (e.g. Auclair and Fairclough 2015; Albert et al. 2017; Larsen and Logan 2018).

To us, the future rhetoric tied to heritage and its various practices is both intriguing and frustrating. As researchers, we are captivated by the task to analyze the underlying logic of preservation and its limitations. Why is the future nearly always present when heritage is considered, but so rarely inspires knowledgeable agendas on how, in practice, to provide actual benefits for the future? At the same time, it is frustrating to see opportunities to make a difference to future societies being lost in a pre-occupation with present-day heritage processes and practices. Could this be changed? Could the heritage sector improve its capacity to think the future? The book you are reading presents ways of applying future thinking to heritage. By "future thinking" we mean the way people anticipate what lies several years or even decades ahead, informing how they act today. By "heritage" we mean what reminds people of the past, tangible or intangible, predominantly cultural but also natural. Although there is personal and family heritage, in this volume, we focus mostly on collective heritage in communities and societies.

Cultural Heritage and the Future explores heritage futures, which are concerned with the roles of heritage in managing the relations between present and future societies. The contributing authors not only insist that cultural heritage and the future are deeply and inherently linked but also that the development of future thinking deserves the full attention of both heritage studies and the professional heritage sector (see also the outcomes of the Heritage Futures Research Programme,[1] especially Harrison et al. 2020). We have tried to present a truly global perspective in this volume. The case studies and examples discuss future thinking in various parts of Europe as well as China, Japan, North America, South Africa, Australia, and outer space. However, significant parts of the world are not adequately represented and appear only in passing if at all. This is a shortcoming we are unhappy about, but the topic is new, many papers are mostly theoretical in nature, and we have been unable to commission papers of high quality from additional world regions. We will have to agree with critics that future work on this topic must rectify this omission and add global nuances to the picture we present in this volume.

Historical futures

The concept of the future is itself historical. Societies have different ways of engaging with uncertainty and managing change over time (Adam and Groves 2007). Before the beginning of the Neolithic some 10,000 years ago, people in

Europe did not commonly invest in building permanent structures that could survive as visible monuments a long time into the future. From then onwards, they built numerous impressive monuments that may have been intended as memorials to influence the way in which future generations looked back at the past (Holtorf 1996). During the Middle Ages, the future was ordained and predictable, as deduced from the Bible (Lowenthal 1995: 387). The contemporary concept of the future did not emerge until the early modern period, as described in a classic study of *The Discovery of the Future* by the German historian Lucian Hölscher (1999) and contextualized in Barbara Adam and Chris Groves' account of *Future Matters* (2007). As Paul Graves-Brown (chapter 15, this volume) discusses, there were alternatives. One example is early 20th-century Futurism that formulated the future as a sharp rejection of the past. In its purest form, this ideology involved no past at all.

Futures are not given but mutable, and one may say that ultimately, "nothing is less likely than a plausible future" (Lowenthal 1995: 393). The British sociologist Steve Fuller (2013) brought this insight down to Earth: "you can be sure that if a model says the world will end in 50 years, the model itself will be gone in 25."

As shown in historical studies about the future until our own time (e.g. Corn and Horrigan 1996; Rosenberg and Harding 2005; Andersson and Rindzevičiūtė 2015), perceived futures have in many ways been socially negotiated and played out in everyday social realities. Among the most influential 20th-century future visions around the world are the architect and town planner Le Corbusier's ideas about *The City of Tomorrow and its Planning* (1929) and films such as Fritz Lang's *Metropolis* (1926), Ishirō Honda's *Godzilla* (1954), and Ridley Scott's *Blade Runner* (1982). Ironically, more often than not, the history of the future turned out to be "a history of people attempting to project the values of past and present into an idealized future," as argued by Joseph J. Corn and Brian Horrigan in their account of *Yesterday's Tomorrows* (1996: 135). They go on to suggest that the history of past futures "is a history of conservative actions in the guise of newness."

We are not aware of documented expectations of future futures. However, history definitely features episodes of nostalgia for past futures (Figure 1.1). In the mid-1970s, there were plans for a new themed land for Disneyland called Discovery Bay based on a celebration of utopian retro futures. Although these plans were in the end never realized, Victorian steampunk, linked to the stories of Jules Verne and H. G. Wells, was considered popular because it evoked a widely appealing 19th-century belief, now vanishing, in technological progress and a glorious future. According to the plans, Disneyland's original Nautilus ride based on Verne's *20,000 Leagues Under the Sea* was supposed to be moved from an increasingly outdated Tomorrowland to a nostalgic Discovery Bay. In the end, Tomorrowland itself was updated by making it more retro-futuristic and thus avoiding the impression it was out of date. Retro futures had effectively replaced present futures (Mittermeier 2017).

Urban ruins can reflect past futures. For example, abandoned building projects that were stopped as a result of the economic crisis of 2008 are historic

FIGURE 1.1 Birthplace of James T. Kirk, Captain of the USS *Enterprise*: present-day future-making in a traditional format. Will this marker contribute to shaping the future, if only by nostalgically evoking a future that never was? Image taken from https://en.wikipedia.org/wiki/Riverside,_Iowa#/media/File: Future_Birthplace_of_Captain_James_T_Kirk.jpg CC BY-SA 2.0

monuments manifesting past futures that have been prevented from being realized. Such incomplete and decaying structures may be seen as "suspended futures" that never fulfilled their intended purposes but to some extent, still express the spirit in which they were planned (Dobraszczyk 2017). Arguably, the "spectre of non-completion" and the possibility of alternative futures is relevant to all buildings and a significant part of their cultural heritage too, deserving more attention (see Dixon, chapter 7 this volume).

Lucian Hölscher (1999: 233–236) argued that concepts of the future are important and must be taken seriously throughout historical studies because they can integrate the power of fiction into the analysis of historical processes. Widely shared imagined or expected futures place specific present-day processes and events into far larger historical perspectives, which effectively become historical forces themselves. For example, even though German unification was a political minefield and had seemed unthinkable to ever occur in people's lifetimes as late as spring 1989, after the fall of the Berlin Wall on 9 November 1989, it was politically realized in less than one year. The events, as they unfolded, were immediately perceived in the context of imagined larger historical processes, connecting past and future, about the unity of the German people and an emerging new world order after the end of the Cold War. By the same token, the preservation of natural and to some extent cultural heritage gained considerable momentum in society as soon as it became linked to our need to care for our planet and the needs of future generations (see also Harrison, chapter 2 this volume).

The experiences of two world wars, destructive post-war development, the nuclear threat during the Cold War, and increasing awareness of the depletion of non-renewable natural resources led to a growing awareness during the 1950s and 1960s of the precariousness of human life on planet Earth. A sense of endangerment and risk of future loss spread across a wide range of fields, from ecologists worrying about biodiversity to anthropologists representing indigenous cultures and from economists warning about running out of finite resources to archaeologists and architects saving cultural heritage (Vidal and Dias 2015; see also Maxwell, chapter 8 this volume). This trend culminated in 1972 when the Club of Rome simulated the future consequences of human exploitation of the Earth and famously warned of the limits of growth; their report was translated into 30 different languages, sold more than 30 million copies, and became the best-selling environmental book in history (according to Wikipedia). In the same year, the spacecraft Pioneer 10 was launched with an eternal message about humanity, to which we will return (see also Gorman and May, chapter 9 this volume). Most importantly for the heritage sector, in 1972, UNESCO also adopted the Convention Concerning the Protection of the World Cultural and Natural Heritage (1972), which was motivated by the insight that cultural and natural heritage is "unique and irreplaceable property" but "increasingly threatened with destruction" and thus in need of being safeguarded for the future "as part of the world heritage of mankind as a whole." As Jenny Andersson and Sibylle Duhautois (2016) argued, between the 1950s and the 1970s, the idea of a common world future mobilized utopian energies and became subject to global management processes. Another important trend that emerged at about the same time is "strategic foresight." This kind of forecasting and simulating trends for the future, often using scenarios, was adopted especially by governments and corporations for the purposes of planning (see Sandford and Cassan, chapter 16 this volume).

These processes ultimately led in the late 1970s to the emergence and subsequent establishment of the environmental movement, which has since then turned increasing attention to the threat of future climate change and the need for society to develop sustainably. Gro Harlem Brundtland's UN World Commission on Environment and Development published in 1987 a report entitled *Our Common Future*, which contains in paragraph 27 a definition of sustainable development as "development that meets the needs of the present without compromising the ability of future generations to meet their own needs," still a common definition. In the heritage sector, sustainable development according to this definition is often taken to mean that we need to preserve natural and cultural heritage for future generations who will value it as much and depend on it to the same extent as we do (see also Avrami, chapter 13 this volume).

Presentism in the heritage sector

Detailed discussions of the future in the literature about heritage are few and those that take place are often about ensuring continuity of the present rather than preparing for future change. Future generations are often imagined as if they were small children for whom we need to create the best future conditions possible and who will eventually be grateful to us, although they do not realize the sense in all we do for them (yet) (see also May, chapter 3 this volume). This has been expressed succinctly by Neville Agnew (2006: 1) who stated that "Conservation is a futuristic activity vested in the belief that we, who have the power today to safeguard or degrade what is of value to society, should strive to be good ancestors for future generations," with the term "ancestors" being almost interchangeable with "parents."

A good example is the recent initiative of US ICOMOS, which on the occasion of the 50th anniversary of the US National Historic Preservation Act invited submissions of short essays on the question "What can and should U.S. preservation law and federal programs look like for the next 50 years?" (Figure 1.2).

FIGURE 1.2 Should the heritage preserved today from the past be our legacy for the future? Copyright: Preservation50, http://preservation50.org

The eight submissions published on the internet[2] reflect what was very much intended: the essays describe promising ideas that are already working in practice and make sense to us today. Visions of how historic preservation might actually work in a world 50 years ahead, that likely will be very different from the present, were not on the agenda.

By the same token, a report entitled "Collections for the Future" published by the Museums Association in the UK fails to address the future explicitly (Museums Association 2005). In the report, recommendations are given about knowledge management and digitization of collections. It also contains guidance on how to develop museum collections actively by strategic acquisition and disposal. Indeed, there is considerable worry in the museum sector about the problem of profusion, i.e. the lack of resources to continue collecting and maintaining collections and a need to de-collect (Morgan and Macdonald 2018). To create better museums for the future, the Museums Association suggests strengthening the museum sector through increased collaboration and development, requiring, also, additional knowledge about the existing collections. While pertinently addressing issues of how to make museum collections more open, accessible, and useful to the public, none of the recommendations presented in the report actually address in what ways a future society may benefit from improved museum collections.

In the same way, a majority of studies presented in the book with the title *Curating the Future* (Newell et al. 2017) address the future merely implicitly, i.e. as possible effects of present-day museum practices such as conservation initiatives, policymaking, and outreach. There is far too little explicit, critical discussion on the intended consequences of conservation, the likely outcomes of specific policies, or the societal impact of outreach in the future (see also Lindsay 2005/2006).

In contrast, the Center for the Future of Museums, an initiative of the American Alliance of Museums, explores visible trends in order to help museums navigate the future. The Center publishes TrendsWatch, which is an annual forecasting report addressing issues such as how to future-proof museums, alternative business models for future museums, and the implications for museums of new trends and developments in society (Center for the Future of Museums 2018). Even though some of the activities launched by the Center deal more with the future of museums than how museums actually can contribute in meaningful ways to future societies, several interesting initiatives are presented on how museums can find ways to engage directly with future issues overcoming presentism.

Archives often aspire to preserve items in their collections "forever," or as long as possible, but a recent study found that, in practice, the archivists' temporal depth is not longer than that of people in general (Rydén 2019). UNESCO's archival programme entitled Memory of the World, for example, considers that the significance of some documentary heritage "is deemed to transcend the boundaries of time and culture." The programme aims, therefore at preservation in the ambitious sense of ensuring "the permanent accessibility – forever – of documentary heritage" to all peoples of the world (UNESCO 2002: 5, 12).[3] However, it remains unclear what this aspiration means for concrete practice. In our view, the term "forever" needs some sort of specification in order to avoid the impression of an assumed timelessness of the significance of heritage.

The underlying belief in universal transcendence of cultural significance may hide an unwillingness to create or adapt to new conditions and innovate social practices. Earlier, we referred to the assessment by Corn and Horrigan (1996: 135) that the history of the future is "a history of conservative actions in the guise of newness." This is certainly the case in relation to many future visions of heritage, and not only as far as the future significance of archive collections is concerned. In Christopher Nolan's science-fiction movie *Interstellar* (2014), everything is visionary and futuristic except the heritage that looks even more traditional and less inspiring than in our own present. Why do many expect such approaches to heritage to be sustained into the far future?

When heritage institutions commission foresight studies, their time frame tends to be short, their aim is to support the status quo in heritage policy, and their content usually limited to describing what is already the case. For example, Historic England's study on *Facing the Future: Foresight and the Historic Environment* (2015) anticipates threats and opportunities for the historic environment beyond the normal planning cycle of three to five years. Many of the trends described are relevant in the long term, but all the report considers is how the sector can maintain its present ambitions in managing the historic environment under changing circumstances. There is no analysis of how future generations might relate to and be affected by heritage in different ways than today, requiring new ambitions for managing what we call today the historic environment. Similarly, the report *Trends in Time 2010–2015* (RAÄ 2012) by the Swedish National Heritage Board is limited to an analysis of the current situation. Acknowledging changing conditions and new demands, the lesson learned is a new need to find ways of collaborating, in part, with new partners, and to communicate more successfully so as to succeed in continuing with the organization's current ambitions.

The most informative study of this kind, though also the oldest of the ones discussed here, is the Swedish National Heritage Board's study *Towards Future Heritage Management* (RAÄ 2006). Its aim was to determine which trends would likely have an impact on the uses of heritage in society and how managing cultural heritage up until 2015 will have to change to better meet these trends. Much of the content remains relevant for the future even at our time of writing (more than a decade after the study was published). This is actually one of the best documents on heritage work in relation to the future we have come across. However, not much of its content made an impact on the Swedish heritage sector, and few heritage actors have been referring to it in their daily work (Högberg 2013).

The recent Swedish *2030 Vision for Working with the Historic Environment* (RAÄ 2016) acknowledges an increasing diversity in its ambition that "everyone, regardless of background, feels that they have a claim on the cultural heritage which formed Sweden." But this vision fails to go beyond the established view that cultural heritage is about tangible and intangible traces of collective origins on a given territory, accessible to all. It does not consider how, much more generally, the past is (or could be) meaningful to people in creating collective futures – which, in a diverse Swedish society, may not be restricted to Swedish or other traditions or collections in museums and thus requires a very different vision for cultural heritage.

Even at the highest international level, a potentially different significance of heritage in the future, compared with the present, is seldom considered. The UNESCO Declaration on the Responsibilities of the Present Generations Towards Future Generations (1997), which is little known in the heritage sector, even within UNESCO, asserts the importance of protecting the needs and interests of future generations. The possible significance of appropriate uses of heritage to respond to the declaration's concern for "the fate of future generations in the face of the vital challenges of the next millennium" has, however, to date not been comprehensively investigated (Högberg et al. 2017). This is possibly changing, as UNESCO's World Heritage and Sustainable Development Policy (2015) calls for more attention to such issues (see e.g. Larsen and Logan 2018). It is, however, not clear yet how exactly the implementation of this policy will lead to informed future thinking in heritage management.

At the same time, there is any number of studies addressing "the future of heritage" (e.g. Silberman and Liuzza, 2007) but they never actually have much to say about the future to come and the role heritage may come to play in that future. Invariably, they indulge instead in varieties of presentism that often take the form of expressed desires of what the future should be like if the authors were to decide themselves. Other studies take the value of heritage largely for granted and risk reducing questions about the future of heritage to questions of accessibility of that heritage (e.g. Hollmann and Schüller-Zwierlein 2014).

In her book-length discussion of international law, common patrimony, and intergenerational equity, the American legal scholar Edith Brown Weiss simply asserts that cultural heritage is "essential to the well-being of future generations," citing that it provides them "with a sense of ongoing community with the past, with a rich resource base upon which to build and to continue their societies, with knowledge essential for living in and using natural systems, and with artistic pleasures" (Brown Weiss 1989: 257–258). This argument is timeless and therefore essentially presentist, as it is built on the thesis that "each generation receives a natural and cultural legacy in trust from previous generations and holds it in trust for future generations" (Brown Weiss 1989: 2). On one level, a community's sense of historical continuity is able to evoke certainty in an uncertain world and hence helps individuals to create a secure position from which to act in the interest of a collective agenda that stretches both backward and forward into time (Reicher 2008). But on another level, in a long-term historical perspective, such continuity is clearly imaginary, as human communities have been changing drastically over time and still do, while frequently disagreeing about the value of specific traditions and legacies. Cultural change and social conflict have been at least as normal as cultural continuity, and there is no reason why this should not continue. Surely, we should avoid any "temporal bias" (Taylor 2013). Different future generations will have different needs, may require different resources and knowledge, and will gain pleasures in different ways than we do today (see also Spennemann 2007b).

Given the inevitability, in the long term, of future change, whether we want it or not, and the contingency of contemporary heritage processes, we have two ways open to us. We can accept that serving the future is impossible and that we should, therefore, concentrate on serving the present rather than any future generations, as advocated by the English museum expert Kevin Moore as long ago as 1997 (p. 31) but still relevant:

> How do we know that they will be grateful for all, some or even any of the material culture we have so graciously preserved for their benefit? After all, we are not entirely delighted with what we have inherited from our forebears.

One of the main challenges of museums and other collections in our age may be that they keep too many things of the wrong kind for the future but find it difficult to manage their possessions in the present (Morgan and Macdonald 2018).

Critical observers like the Australian cultural heritage expert Dirk Spennemann (2007a) have long concluded that the claim that the past is to be preserved for the future is often nothing but an empty cliché lacking a truly futurist strategy. Instead, it tends to be based on the belief that "[t]he past is deemed valuable for its own sake and thus worthy of protection and transmission to the future" (Spennemann 2007a: 13). This belief ignores, however, that the meaning and significance of the past and heritage are different in different societies and change over time – which, ironically, historical experts and heritage specialists know better than anybody else. Unfortunately, the rhetorical reference to an apparent responsibility to preserve the heritage for the future can easily become an excuse of heritage authorities for not accepting full responsibility for their own decisions in critically evaluating, selectively preserving, and creatively forming our surroundings in the present (Rüsch 2004). This challenge is however embraced by others, such as international heritage experts Britta Rudolff and Kristal Buckley who conclude their discussion of the future of the World Heritage Convention by expressing that "[t]he present is challenging, important, and endlessly engaging, and the future – as is always the case – will take care of itself" (Rudolff and Buckley 2016: 535). From our research, we know that many experts in the heritage sector feel the same (Högberg et al. 2017). Looking at the multiple challenges facing future society, may they be environmental, social, demographic, or economic (Steffen et al. 2015), we believe that heritage managers cannot afford to think in such terms and instead will need to create policies for long-term preservation and management in a more professional way (Holtorf and Högberg 2014).

An alternative way to go is to plan better for a future that is different from the present and will keep changing over time. Surely, it is true that "to correctly conserve the past we need to anticipate the future" (Ceccarelli 2017: 6). What we know best about the future is that it will differ from the present. Perhaps there will be no need at all for formally managing any cultural heritage as we do today but have not been doing for much longer than about two centuries (Boccardi 2015). This may involve some fundamental changes:

> The traditional view that heritage conservation carries a treasured past into a well-understood future must be rejected. A new view of heritage, serving society in times of rapid climate change, embraces loss, alternative forms of knowledge and uncertain futures.
>
> *(Harvey and Perry 2015: 3)*

But how can we professionally approach and prepare for a future in which many of the efforts taken in the heritage sector today may be ignored or even undone?

In principle, we see two main possibilities for future-proofing heritage (inspired by Miller, 2009). They are non-exclusive and can be combined with each other too, for example, in relation to different time scales. The first possibility is that we improve our work using scenarios of change, for example by basing decisions on what may be beneficial in several or all scenarios rather than just one in which we may uncritically believe. Such scenarios may be framed as risks threatening the status quo (e.g. sea-level rises) or as opportunities for creative exploration of new potentials (e.g. digitization). The key question for such direct planning is how future generations, under different conditions, would be able to benefit most through heritage. Alternatively, we create or optimize processes and principles of decision-making so that they can best adjust to changing conditions of the future. That means we plan indirectly, by establishing and maintaining certain values and ways of proceeding that are desirable irrespective of the specific outcomes regarding the heritage to which their application may lead. Ideas of equality and democracy, linked to practices of equal opportunities and participation, for example, have proven powerful and beneficial, even though they have been implemented in very different ways and lead to a wide range of decisions that could initially not have been foreseen. This means we need to ask which principle(s) should govern heritage processes so as to benefit future generations the most? Note that none of these two suggested ways of working is about predicting the future or dictating what future humans ought to think or do. They are ways of enabling us to future-proof heritage from an informed perspective of today.

The future in related disciplines

Heritage studies is a multidisciplinary field with relevant perspectives drawing on a range of academic fields. Our own perspective on heritage futures is coloured by our backgrounds in the discipline of archaeology (see also Holtorf and Högberg 2018). A brief look at related disciplines provides additional perspectives on relations between cultural heritage and the future. In conservation, intergenerational benefits are inherently central but what exactly is meant by future generations and what we can know about their needs and desires is usually taken for granted – much as in the rest of the heritage sector. The Spanish conservator Salvador Muñoz Viñas (2005) provided a critical discussion of many aspects of the theory of conservation and conservation science, but he too failed to problematize the relationship between conservation and future generations. He assumed instead, like most of his colleagues, that future users of conserved objects will appreciate them most with minimal change and only reversible interventions carried out by us (Muñoz Viñas 2005: 194–197).

In a unique study of time perspectives in collections care, the British conservator William Lindsay (2005/2006: 53) established that "[c]onservation, and collection-care in general, has no agreed philosophical temporal framework." This lack of framework is very unfortunate, as Lindsay (2005/2006: 60) explains:

> While there must be some notion of future in our decisions for the appropriate treatment for a collection, it appears as a poorly defined horizon against which risks are assessed, towards which object utility is extended, and by which material behavior is judged acceptable.

Moreover, conservation theorist Joel Taylor (2013) argued that it is extremely difficult in conservation practice to answer important questions such as: when has a given generation saved enough? How do we understand the needs of future generations that are not concurrent with our own? Is heritage that, at some point, cannot be conserved any longer ever substitutable? Such discussions are still largely new territory for collection care and conservation science.

As mentioned earlier, historians have begun to study the history of how people perceived the future and what, rightly or wrongly, they expected to happen at any given moment in time (e.g. Corn and Horrigan 1996; Hölscher 1999; Rosenberg and Harding 2005). The American historian David Staley (2002) argued that historical thinking can equally be applied to the future as to the past without requiring specific predictions and instead focusing on creating scenarios of what might happen. His model of a "history of the future" is still based on evidence: "surviving evidence from the past provides only a trace of what was; evidence in the present provides possible precursors of what might be" (Staley 2002: 84). Past and future are both equally material and elusive, real and imagined. Indeed, they are not polar opposites but closely connected: the very idea of change implies a future that is different from a past (Simon 2018). There are many differences between studying the future and writing history but also many similarities (Männikkö 2017). And yet, historians have hardly begun to give attention to what is still to come in human history.

There are also studies in the didactics of history on the significance of studying the past for future-making in the present. Historical consciousness, which is an established concept in the didactics of history, refers to the underlying thought structures that generate meaning when a particular historical perspective is given significance, with certain consequences for the way we see the present and the future in the light of the past (Rüsen 2004). Similar thought structures can also generate meaning when particular perspectives on the future are given significance, with consequences for how we see the past and the present in the light of the future (see Holtorf and Högberg, chapter 10 this volume). When shifting attention from the past in the present to the future in the present, historical consciousness turns into future consciousness. Just as it is possible to analyze historical consciousness from the way it manifests itself in uses of the past, future consciousness can be analyzed from the way it manifests itself in perceptions and uses of the future. This is a way of thinking that moves away from an approach that infers what will happen in the future from an analysis of what happened in the past, as, for example, in Freudian psychoanalysis where conflicts unresolved in the distant past affect people's future or biological predictions of behaviour determined by evolution. Instead, a perspective of "navigating into the future" gives significance to the human ability of prospection and imagining possible futures (Seligman et al. 2013).

In human geography, Ben Anderson at the University of Durham discussed anticipatory action in relation to future geographies opening up the challenge "to understand how geographies are lived and made as futures are prophesized, imagined, deterred, regularized, invested in, hoped for and so on" (Anderson 2010: 778). Similar questions have begun to be asked in anthropology. The American anthropologist Arjun Appadurai (2013: 292) argued that "the future is a part of how societies shape their practices" and thus not a blank space but a "cultural fact" to be studied by anthropologists. Accordingly, his colleague Samuel Collins (2008) discussed anthropological engagements with the future exploring, among other things, the possibility of encountering extraterrestrial alien cultures in the future. Given the prevalence of the idea of aliens in Western popular culture, Collins argues that our way of life, and how we imagine the future, has already been affected by imagined aliens, "never mind that they may never have been there to begin with" (Collins 2008: 69). Indeed, such imagined aliens have already become part of the heritage discourse too, and thus influence even how we imagine the past (Figure 1.3). Perceptions of the future and anticipations of the unknown are affecting society and people's lives in various ways and under different circumstances, which is what a recent anthropological volume on emerging and uncertain worlds is exploring too (Salazar et al. 2017). This agenda is linked to the claim made in a volume co-edited by anthropologists Limor Samimian-Darash and Paul Rabinow (2015) that we need to study in much more detail how people and societies engage with the problem (and opportunity) of uncertainty, which goes beyond the challenge of dealing with any specific risks or indeed with risk as such.

Anthropologists, like sociologists, understand that futures are always situated in specific contexts. The academic conceptualization of future studies is very much framed in science and a linear way of understanding time (Bell 1997). In this view, the past lies behind us, the present is where we are, and the future is ahead of us. As cognitive linguist Sarah Duffy (2018) showed, this linear

(a)

(b)

FIGURE 1.3 (a) In June 1947, a flying disc claimed to have crashed outside the town Roswell in New Mexico, USA. The UFO and alien bodies travelling with it are said to have been confiscated by the US government. The International UFO Museum and Research Center in Roswell is dedicated to informing the public about what has become known as The Roswell Incident. Photograph by Anders Högberg. (b) According to an eye witness, a UFO landed in a small forest in the suburb of the town Ängelholm in south Sweden, May 1946. Today the site holds the Ängelholm UFO Memorial, listed as a heritage site by the Swedish National Heritage Board, site number RAÄ Strövelstorp 47:1. Photograph by Anders Högberg.

conceptualization of time is not universal. There are other ways to talk about time. Duffy gives an example of a person from the Yupno community of Papua New Guinea that looks up a mountain, to the spring of a stream, when talking about the future and when talking about the past points towards the river (that started with the spring in the mountain) and its estuary by the sea. Here, past and future become embedded in the present landscape in a way that differs from how, say, a majority of heritage managers conceptualize time today (Smith 2006). The British sociologist John Urry (2016) discussed how in our society too, futures are of huge significance but always specific, contextual, and therefore multiple.

Taking a larger perspective of how societies relate to the future, the British sociologists Barbara Adam and Chris Groves (2007; 2011) questioned long-standing and dominant concepts of the future and called for a new way to manage change and uncertainty over time. They suggested that as human beings, we need an understanding of ethical responsibilities towards the future in terms of care, embracing our dependency on the forgiveness of future generations for the unknown consequences of our action. In this perspective, the future we all should care about most is the future of care itself. A rather different argument has been made by sociologist Steve Fuller (2012; 2013) regarding policymaking in society. He suggested that the prevalent precautionary principle risks preventing likely future progress in science and therefore renders future generations worse off than would otherwise be the case. The precautionary position effectively prevents us "from making the sort of radical experiments that in the past had resulted in major leaps in knowledge that enabled us to overcome our natural limits" (Fuller 2013). Fuller advocates instead an alternative, proactionary principle that promotes calculated risk-taking allowing us to seize opportunities in the interest of human progress (for further sociological approaches to the future see Sandford and Cassan, chapter 16 this volume).

Preserving good causes for the long term

In practice, heritage is preserved for the future in a variety of ways. Although the means of transmission may be uncertain and the exact purposes of the heritage we want to preserve for the future may be unclear, the causes it is meant to serve are often worthwhile and profound (see also Holtorf and Högberg, chapter 4 this volume).

On a personal level, heritage can serve individuals' desires to find meaning in their lives and thus make their own future worthwhile. Individuals who are getting actively involved in preservation not only save the heritage but to some extent also themselves (Holtorf and Ortman 2008: 83–87). In a different sense, a group of craftspeople has been creating a future for themselves in Guédelon, central France. They are part of a unique 25-year-long project to build from scratch a castle on a reimagined 13th-century construction site, which has given them not only employment but also a sense of purpose in their lives (Minard and Folcher 2003).

Other projects that invest in heritage to make futures may serve broader causes and often evoke a much longer future too. The human legacy in deep time is a field that has attracted a number of high-profile initiatives that resonate widely in society (Benford 1999). The question of responsibly taking care of radioactive nuclear waste for up to one million years into the future has been engaging not only academics but also politicians, journalists, and the population at large for several decades. Creating final repositories of nuclear waste for the long term raises issues of how best to discharge our ethical responsibility for the health and safety of all future generations of human beings on planet Earth (see also Holtorf and Högberg, chapter 10; Joyce, chapter 11; Buser et al., chapter 12; this volume).

An even longer time frame is associated with messages sent on spacecraft into deep space. The space probes Pioneer 10 and 11 (launched in 1972 and 1973, respectively), Voyager 1 and 2 (launched in 1977), and New Horizons (launched in 2006) are the only five human-made objects ever to have left the solar system. All carry messages on board that may very well still travel through the universe when life, as we know it, has ceased to exist on planet Earth. These messages are designed as greetings to extraterrestrial audiences, of which we know nothing. They represent, in one way or another, the human legacy in the universe. Voyager's golden record contains pictures, spoken greetings, and music from Earth, i.e. a selection of the heritage of Earth representing what it meant to be human according to a small group of experts in 1977 (Sagan et al. 1978). At the time of writing, a digital message is being prepared to be beamed up to the New Horizons spacecraft before we will lose all contact. This time, the heritage of Earth will be selected more democratically through a crowdsourcing process.[4]

Less temporarily ambitious but possibly even more useful to people on Earth are projects to conserve species and maintain biodiversity through dedicated archives. Such long-term archives include frozen zoos and other gene banks. The Svalbard seed vault stores duplicate seeds of crops that are considered important to humanity, in particular for food security and sustainable agriculture (Harrison 2017 and chapter 2, this volume).[5] Planned from the early 1980s onwards, the storage facility opened in 2008 and is funded by the Norwegian government, although its content belongs to the respective owners, which include public and private institutions around the world. In this potentially largest collection of seeds in the world, up to 4.5 million seed samples will be stored permanently in permafrost conditions at −18°C. When some seeds lose the ability to germinate after a few decades, they will need to be planted and then replaced by their owners with the new seeds. Although the facility could last forever, it was designed with a life expectancy of 200 years. A similar facility for historical documents is the Barbarastollen in southern Germany where since 1975, more than 30 km of microfilm are providing a back-up of German historical documents.[6]

The idea to preserve valuable information for the long-term future resonates in many contexts. An archive that does not exist yet but would be much-needed preserves knowledge of the exact locations of long-lasting and potentially lethal landmines. Landmines are a legacy of 20th- and 21st-century wars. It is estimated that currently there are 110 million landmines in the ground, which may take more than 1,000 years to remove,[7] but there is no archive preserving the knowledge of their locations. Preserving such memory could prevent much unnecessary future harm to people.

There have been numerous time capsule initiatives around the world, among the best known being the Oglethorpe Crypt of Civilization in Atlanta, USA (see also Maxwell, chapter 8 this volume). Time capsules may be exciting not because "of the message a time capsule *contains* but of the message a time capsule *is*" (Durrans 2014: 185, original emphasis). Here we are thinking beyond the immediate present and often even beyond our own lifetimes! A particularly interesting project in this context is the Memory of Mankind initiative in Hallstatt, Austria (see also Holtorf and Högberg, chapter 4 this volume).[8] This particular storage facility is open for contributions of content from everybody, which it promises to preserve on glazed tiles for the far future. Another repository of information about humanity is being prepared by the Beyond the Earth foundation. This library consists of an archive of human cultural heritage, to be self-selected by each participating cultural group, micro-etched onto small nickel discs, and then launched aboard satellites into permanent orbits around Earth. Its purpose is to provide a future human or extraterrestrial discoverer with an introductory guide to human life on Earth.[9]

A novel approach to long-term thinking using tangible heritage was realized by two art projects. Completed in 1996 in Ylöjärvi, central Finland, and dedicated by the President of Finland, Agnes Denes' Tree Mountain is a huge artificial mountain covered by 11,000 trees that were planted by 11,000 people from around the world.[10] Her idea was that in 400 years, a complete ecosystem will have emerged. For now, the monument is designed to remind us of the need to restore environmental damage on Earth and work for the future wellbeing of all life on Earth. The 10,000 Year Clock of the Long Now Foundation has an even longer time perspective but is similarly motivated (Brand 1999).[11] This huge clock is funded by Jeff Bezos, the founder of Amazon, and is currently being built inside a mountain in western Texas. Its hands advance once every century, driven by an ingenious technology powered by natural energy. The point is to make people aware of long-term continuities and the need to maintain our civilization on Earth in the long term, too.

Similarly important may be the unforgetting of some of the darkest sides of 20th-century history, both out of respect for the victims but also as a warning for future generations on what once occurred in Nazi Germany but might occur again somewhere else. At the site of Auschwitz in what is now Poland, therefore, there is a lot of emphasis on "never forgetting" the 1.5 million human beings murdered here. One of the local memorials starts with the words: "For ever let this place be a cry of despair and a warning for humanity." On one level, the memory of the Holocaust, as a legacy of the 20th century, will indeed need to be preserved forever. But on another level, as the last survivors pass away and the remains themselves age, the meaning of the preserved site and artefacts will become more ambiguous. The Dutch historian, Robert Jan van Pelt argued that once the last survivor has died, the site ought to be closed and peacefully left to decay rather than attracting millions of visitors every year (BBC News 2009). The forms of remembrance of the Holocaust are now changing. According to media reports, some grandchildren of former Auschwitz inmates who had their prisoner numbers tattooed on their bodies have had the same number tattooed on their own bodies in order to pass on the legacy of the Holocaust to future generations (Rubin 2012). Consequently, the meaning of the tattoos has begun to change from a historical trace of the Holocaust to a personal token of kinship. This raises the problem of what a realistic time frame might be of preserving heritage for the future without changes of meaning questioning its very significance. Space messages are forever, and more or less immediately after launch, out of human reach; nuclear waste remains radioactive for up to one million years, but whether at some point in the future it will stop to be considered as waste and a health risk, we do not know; the 10,000 Year Clock lets its name speak but may never last so long anyway; microfiche slides will remain readable for a minimum of 500 years, but their content may not be valued in the same way for as long.

So, what is the adequate scope of future thinking for remembering the historical legacies of human cultures?

Future-making through heritage

The future is not only a temporal space to be anticipated, investigated, planned for, and furnished with legacies. It is also a set of practices, to the extent that human communities contribute to shaping and bringing it into being in the first place. Many communities continue to practice and value what they associate with their own cultural heritage because their members prefer to have a future of precisely such continuity based on memory. When such a future may appear to be in conflict with other communities' aspirations or as a result of changing circumstances outside the community, for example in the environment or in society at large, future-making can be problematic and needs co-ordination or indeed re-invention. Such processes are at work in Sub-Saharan Africa, where heritage is currently renegotiated in postcolonial settings (Peterson et al. 2015).

The British anthropologist Johanna Zetterström-Sharp showed, with reference to Sierra Leone, how heritage choices determine specific agendas for development and social transformation. Heritage is significant in society because of its capacity to contribute to "the making and shaping of collective futures rather than preserving collective pasts" (Zetterström-Sharp 2015: 612). A similar point is made by the British political scientist Joanie Willett (2018: 79) who argued that the "future needs to be consistent and congruent with the stories that are told about the past and present." That is why it is important in telling stories about the past to consider even what kinds of futures they make possible or impossible (see also González-Ruibal, chapter 6 this volume).

Uses of cultural heritage in future-making processes were observed by the American archaeologist Trinidad Rico in Banda Aceh, Indonesia. A decade after a tsunami had devastated the city, so-called tsunami boats that remained on rooftops and other witnesses of this turning point in the recent history of the area had begun to form a new kind of narrative about the regional past. In Rico's analysis, the emerging heritage of destruction "mobilizes destruction as a tool for carving a space in which the conversation about the future of Aceh can carry on less burdened by the past" (Rico 2016: 39) and it can thus bring local populations together in their efforts to overcome loss and plan for a better future.

Similar thinking, though with a global scope, lies behind the work of the International Coalition of Sites of Conscience. Sites of Conscience support the memory of difficult and traumatic events in the past with the intention for visitors to connect past and present, reflect about them in the context of human rights, and ultimately "ensure a more just and humane future."[12] Although not formally associated with the Coalition, the Hiroshima Peace Memorial shares related aims and is very clear about its role concerning the future. In the many buildings and monuments at the memorial site, remembrance is not primarily aimed at unforgetting past trauma but bringing about future world peace, as the name already makes clear. This intention is particularly succinctly expressed in the inscription of the monument commemorating John Paul II's visit to Hiroshima on 25 February 1981. It states: "To remember the past is to commit oneself to the future. To remember Hiroshima is to abhor nuclear war. To remember Hiroshima is to commit oneself to peace." As future-oriented as this message is, what they do not appear to have considered is how this message will be transmitted reliably into the future, given that there is no permanent marker, the entire memorial ages, and some local residents (according to text on display in the Hiroshima Peace Memorial Museum in 2013) perceive the famous Dome to be shrinking every year because of an increasing number of modern buildings dominating the skyline. Arguably, this message about world peace is even more important for humanity to be kept alive into very distant futures than the location of nuclear waste contained deep below the surface.

Elsewhere, conservation efforts make very specific contributions to the future. One example is the Svalbard Global Seed Vault, which we already mentioned. Its efforts at providing back-up for the world's seed banks can be seen as a specific future-making practice contributing to increased heterogeneity in future global agrobiodiversity (Harrison 2017). Another example is the war memorial recently built in the new town of Bradley Stoke, Gloucestershire, UK. Its slogan "We Will Remember Them" serves future social cohesion by offering a collective focal point for future remembrance ceremonies, as in other towns. It hardly seems to matter that Bradley Stoke was green fields and farmlands during the two world wars, whose dead are the ones traditionally remembered in ceremonies like this, or that for now the plaque is still empty, as the moment when the first resident dies in military action has not yet come. Many other worthwhile causes for future societies might be addressed by heritage too (Holtorf and Högberg 2014; Holtorf 2020).

Sometimes our efforts at making favourable futures can be more complicated than we think, though. For example, the British human geographer Caitlin DeSilvey (2017) argued that prevailing narratives advocating long term conservation for an indefinite future will inevitably fall short in the light of drastic landscape transformations, as they may result, for example, from coastal erosion. Conservation narratives will therefore not be able to succeed unless they embrace dynamic processes of transformation in "postpreservation" practices that reach "beyond saving" and may even include "palliative curation" (DeSilvey 2017 and chapter 14, this volume). Indeed, in some cases, outright destruction may be the way to make favourable futures, given that even in relation to heritage, less can be more (Holtorf 2015). In our endeavours to investigate and develop appropriate new ways of thinking of conservation that are better at accommodating change and transformation over time, we may want to look outside Western ways of thinking. We may, for example, turn to Buddhist thought that values fluidity and processes of meaning-making over the preservation of fixed objects and their values (Kimball 2016).

As we noted earlier, sometimes conservation campaigns serve the interest of the campaigners, who want to do good and make a future for themselves, more than what they say they strive to save for the future (Holtorf and Ortman 2008). David Lowenthal suggested that the concern for future generations in heritage management is first and foremost "a matter of enriching our own life with depth and purpose" (Lowenthal 2005: 33). This is possibly the Achilles heel of future-making: it can be difficult to distinguish in specific cases between gestures expressing the will to do good in the present and professional preparations for better human lives in the future.

The Dutch social anthropologist Paul Richards (1992) cautioned us in an insightful paper that, in some cases, conservationists campaigning to save the rainforest fail to understand that local communities consider the forest, in fact, to be protecting *them*. To reverse that relation between the people and the forest as part of a conservation campaign will not lead to securing continuity of the community into the future but rather creating profound insecurity as their previous patron to which they could turn for support becomes a client in need of help. In cases such as this, additional strategies will need to be found in order to "make" and "invent" futures that suit everybody.

On a planetary scale, the design of space messages, like those we mentioned earlier, can be either beneficial or harmful for our future on Earth. Are they the ultimate expression of some humans' hubris, possibly attracting unwanted attention, or do they prompt us to focus on what all human beings share and need to survive together on Earth? The task requires us to consider past, present, and future of the human species: how do we see ourselves, and how is this perception reflected in human actions? How do we think others will see us and be reflected in their actions? And will we ever be able to agree on the answers to such questions – or will the decision-making process reveal and deepen already existing cultural, social, political, or ethical differences?

These examples illustrate why future-making is of considerable relevance to cultural heritage and should not be taken lightly but requires extensive research and critical thinking. Cultural heritage is a futuristic field!

The volume in brief

The present volume is divided into four sections. The first section deals with notions of the future in heritage studies and heritage management. Rodney Harrison asks what it means to speak of heritage practices as "future-making" processes. Focusing on the example of the Svalbard Global Seed Vault and how it secures crop diversity for the future, he argues that understanding specific conservation practices in a comparative perspective can help us learn how to contribute to designing common human futures. As Sarah May discusses in the following paper, heritage discourse often evokes children as placeholders of the future. Commonly, heritage is considered to be a precious gift from the past that must be preserved for the benefit of our children. But, she asks, how can we be sure that in the future, the heritage we preserve will not be seen as a burden and an unwanted gift, standing in the way for our children to assert their own independent agency? According to May's analysis, we have to re-think the way we are using heritage to domesticate the future through strategies of infantilization. Cornelius Holtorf and Anders Högberg argue in their chapter that the long-term accessibility of cultural heritage actually relies to a great extent on specific perceptions of the future as they are articulated in particular strategies of preservation. Studying specific examples connected to the Austrian town of Hallstatt, they show that expectations that changes in the future to some extent are manageable, for example, by political decisions or wills, do not necessarily create the best prospects of maintaining accessibility over long periods into the future. In the final paper of this section, Luo Li discusses how evolving notions of the "future" are influencing legislation and the management of intangible cultural heritage in China. She argues that a discernible trend to consider intangible heritage as something that is not maintained unchanged but continuously re-adapted to changing circumstances in society allows for misappropriation, for example in the form of commodification, but it also enables traditional culture to develop, adapt, and thus stay relevant today and for the future.

The second section explores the future as it is reflected in tangible cultural heritage. Drawing on examples from folk art environments in Spain and elsewhere, Alfredo González-Ruibal argues that unlike official monuments and other hegemonic forms of heritage that are seemingly frozen in time, living folk art and architecture visibly embrace much more open and organically growing futures. They can thus interrogate established notions of time in heritage management and propose more imaginative ways of dealing with heritage for the present and the future. Addressing the "spectre of non-completion," James Dixon explores how all buildings relate to the future at a particular moment in their life-spans and what that means as buildings age and become potential heritage assets. In his assessment, the uncertainty of construction work connects every building in human history and relates to the lives of all human beings; it, therefore, deserves more attention in a heritage context too. In another rendering of uncertainty, Robert Charlotte Maxwell demonstrates, in their contribution, how sites associated with the Church of Scientology express a fear of nuclear annihilation. This particular heritage was a built insurance against a threatening future and tells the story of the "nuclear armageddonism" of their builders and followers. The section ends with a dialogue between Alice Gorman and Sarah May exploring the significance of outer space and space technology as a location of utopias and dystopias for the future. Among other topics, they discuss how the tangible heritage of humankind in space not only represents perceived departures to new shores elsewhere in the universe but also their entanglement with the politics and various problematic legacies of human life on Earth.

In the third section, authors are re-thinking heritage future by engaging in some detail with the case of nuclear waste. Cornelius Holtorf and Anders Högberg start us off by introducing how repositories of long-lived nuclear waste, as material remains, are part of the human legacy of the 20th and 21st centuries and will become a very particular part of the cultural heritage of the future. Introducing the concept of "future consciousness," they are focusing, on the one hand, on the present-day challenge of how to inform intelligent beings thousands of years in the future about the content of these repositories and, on the other hand, specific lessons to be learned for the heritage sector that likewise aspires today to preserve human legacies for future generations. Rosemary Joyce looks at the discussion about long-term markers for the Waste Isolation Pilot Plant in Carlsbad, New Mexico, USA, questioning the common-sense assumption that long-lasting monuments are necessarily intended to communicate specific meanings to the future. Instead, she maintains that built monuments, including World Heritage sites, will create unintended effects in future social contexts that always exceed and often also subvert original expectations. Finally, Marcos Buser, Abraham Van Luik†, Roger Nelson, and Cornelius Holtorf explore in their conversation convergences between cultural heritage, toxic waste, and a legacy of risk imposed on future generations. From an applied perspective, they discuss specific challenges of legacy management, including nuclear semiotics and concrete attempts of the industry to transmit information across very long time periods, while agreeing on the significance of open-minded engagement and dialogue across existing borders.

The fourth and last section of the book explores some specific relations between cultural heritage and future-making. Erica Avrami asks in her chapter how heritage conservation can empower future generations to be agents of change rather than stewards of the past. Pursuing this ambition, she argues, means to refocus conservation on heritage as process, so as to promote collective agency and engender civic engagement, now and in the future. Referring to the increasing precariousness of the Orfordness Lighthouse located near the fast-eroding coast of Suffolk, UK, Caitlin DeSilvey, too, questions the wisdom of a desire to preserve the tangible heritage by all means. She suggests that we could instead practice "palliative curation" referring to a process of giving care while letting go, with the structure eventually not being entirely lost but persisting into the future in various forms of reproduction and memory. Paul Graves-Brown reflects on the future as heritage. To him, the future is a particular set of ideas associated primarily with the period from the late 19th century to the 1970s and linked to phenomena like Futurism, modernist planning, the notion of an affluent society, and space exploration. By now, the future may very well be over and has been replaced by an era of "atemporality" that is dominated by an endless now obsessively archiving and recycling the past. According to Graves-Brown, eventually, the discourse of the future lapsed into a bricolage of the past. Richard Sandford and May Cassar conclude the section with a treatise of "strategic foresight" and "critical futures" relating to their understanding of heritage as an anticipatory practice. They are advocating for a futures-literate heritage sector that is better equipped than at present to imagine, describe, research, and manage issues that arise from present futures.

The volume concludes with some final reflections by the co-editors. We point to the apparent need to critically understand the roles of cultural heritage in managing the relations between present and future societies and to build professional strategies addressing the future in heritage management. Fifty years ahead, will there be much concern at all with what many of us today appreciate as cultural heritage? Should there be? It is time to think outside the box. Throughout the cultural heritage sector, we may have to change the present in order to create heritage futures that perhaps we did not imagine before.

Acknowledgements

We are very grateful to the many people we have been collaborating with over the last decade for inspiring our work on cultural heritage and the future, especially Sarah May and the other members of the AHRC-funded Heritage Futures Research Programme (directed by Rodney Harrison) as well as Claudio Pescatore and our main collaborators at the Swedish Nuclear Fuel and Waste Management Company (SKB), Sofie Tunbrant and Erik Setzman. We have benefitted from critical comments made on a penultimate draft by William Logan and Laurajane Smith.

Notes

1 https://heritage-futures.org
2 http://www.usicomos.org/about/wwhsr/
3 https://en.unesco.org/programme/mow
4 http://oneearthmessage.org
5 http://www.seedvault.no
6 https://www.bbk.bund.de/DE/AufgabenundAusstattung/Kulturgutschutz/Zent ralerBergungsort/zentralerbergungsort_node.html

7 http://www.landminefree.org/2017/index.php/support/facts-about-landmines, updated 2018, accessed April 2018
8 https://www.memory-of-mankind.com
9 https://www.beyondtheearth.org
10 http://www.agnesdenesstudio.com/works4.html
11 http://longnow.org/clock/
12 http://www.sitesofconscience.org/en/who-we-are/about-us/

References

Adam, B. and Groves, C., 2007. *Future Matters. Action, Knowledge, Ethics*. Leiden and Boston: Brill.
Adam, B. and Groves, C., 2011. Futures Tended: Care and Future-Oriented Responsibility. *Bulletin of Science, Technology and Society* 31(1), 17–27.
Agnew, N., 2006. Introduction. In: N. Agnew and J. Bridgland, eds. *Of the Past, for the Future: Integrating Archaeology and Conservation*. Los Angeles: Getty Conservation Institute, pp. 1–2.
Albert, M.-T., Bandarin, F. and Pereira Roders, A. (eds.)., 2017. *Going Beyond – Perceptions of Sustainability in Heritage Studies No. 2*. Cham: Springer.
Anderson, B., 2010. Preemption, Precaution, Preparedness: Anticipatory Action and Future Geographies. *Progress in Human Geography* 34(6), 777–798.
Andersson, J. and Duhautois, S., 2016. Futures of Mankind. The Emergence of the Global Future. In: R. van Munster and C. Sylvest, eds. *The Politics of Globality Since 1945. Assembling the Planet*. London and New York: Routledge, pp. 106–125.
Andersson, J. and Rindzevičiūtė, E. (eds.)., 2015. *The Struggle for the Long-Term in Transnational Science and Politics*. London and New York: Routledge.
Appadurai, A., 2013. *The Future as Cultural Fact*. London and New York: Verso.
Auclair, E. and Fairclough, G. (eds.)., 2015. *Theory and Practice in Heritage and Sustainability*. London and New York: Routledge.
BBC News, 2009. Cash Crisis Threat to Auschwitz Be Left to Decay? Available at http://news.bbc.co.uk/2/hi/7827534.stm (accessed 11 February 2018).
Bell, W., 1997. *Foundations of Future Studies. Human Science for a New Era*, vols 1–2. New Brunswick & London: Transaction Publishers.
Benford, G., 1999. *Deep Time. How Humanity Communicates Across Millennia*. New York: Avons.
Boccardi, G., 2015. From Mitigation to Adaptation: A New Heritage Paradigm for the Anthropocene. In: M.-T. Albert, ed. *Perceptions of Sustainability in Heritage Studies*. Berlin and Boston: De Gruyter, pp. 87–97.
Brand, S., 1999. *The Clock of the Long Now. Time and Responsibility*. New York: Basic.
Brown Weiss, E., 1989. *In Fairness to Future Generations: International Law, Common Patrimony, and Intergenerational Equity*. Tokyo: United Nations University/New York: Transnational Publishers.
Ceccarelli, P., 2017. Past Is Not a Frozen Concept: Considerations about Heritage Conservation in a Fast Changing World. *Built Heritage* 1(3), 1–12.
Center for the Future of Museums, 2018. Available at https://www.aam-us.org/programs/center-for-the-future-of-museums/ (accessed 22 July 2018).
Club of Rome, 1972. *The Limits of Growth*. New York: Universe.
Collins, S.G., 2008. *All Tomorrow's Cultures. Anthropological Engagements with the Future*. New York and Oxford: Berghahn.

Corn, J.J. and Horrigan, B., 1996. *Yesterday's Tomorrows. Past Visions of the American Future* [1984]. Baltimore and London: Johns Hopkins University Press.

DeSilvey, C., 2017. *Curated Decay: Heritage Beyond Saving*. Minneapolis and London: University of Minnesota Press.

Dobraszczyk, P., 2017. *The Dead City. Urban Ruins and the Spectacle of Decay*. London and New York: Tauris.

Duffy, S., 2018. How Our Minds Construct the Past, Present and Future Depends on Our Relationship with Time. *The Conversation*, January 3, 2018. Available at https://the conversation.com/how-our-minds-construct-the-past-present-and-future-depends-on-our-relationship-with-time-89253 (accessed 25 April 2018).

Durrans, B., 2014. Time Capsules as Extreme Collecting. In: G. Were and J. C. H. King, eds. *Extreme Collecting. Challenging Practices for 21st Century Museums*. New York and Oxford: Berghahn, pp. 181–202.

Fuller, S., 2012. Precautionary and Proactionary as the New Right and the New Left of the Twenty-First Century Ideological Spectrum. *International Journal of Politics, Culture and Sociology* 25(4), 157–174.

Fuller, S., 2013. Beyond the Precautionary Principle. *The Guardian*, 10 July 2013. Available at https://www.theguardian.com/science/political-science/2013/jul/10/beyond-precautionary-principle (accessed 18 March 2018).

Harrison, R., 2017. Freezing Seeds and Making Futures: Endangerment, Hope, Security, and Time in Agrobiodiversity Conservation Practices. *Culture, Agriculture, Food and Environment* 39(2): 80–89.

Harrison, R., DeSilvey, C., Holtorf, C., Macdonald, S., Bartolini, N., Breithoff, E., Fredheim, H., Lyons, A., May, S., Morgan, J. and Penrose, S., 2020. *Heritage Futures. Comparative Approaches to Natural and Cultural Heritage Practices*. London: UCL Press.

Hartog, F., 2015. *Regimes of Historicity. Presentism and Experiences of Time* [first published in French in 2003]. New York: Columbia University Press.

Harvey, D.C. and Perry, J., 2015. Heritage and Climate Change. The Future Is Not the Past. In: D. C. Harvey and J. Perry, eds. *The Future of Heritage as Climates Change. Loss Adaptation and Creativity*. London and New York: Routledge; pp. 3–21.

Historic England, 2015. Facing the Future: Foresight and the Historic Environment. Available at https://historicengland.org.uk/images-books/publications/facing-the-future/ (accessed 26 March 2016).

Högberg, A., 2013. *Mångfaldsfrågor i kulturmiljövården. Tankar, kunskaper och processer 2002–2012*. Lund: Nordic Academic Press.

Högberg, A., Holtorf, C., May, S. and Wollentz, G., 2017. No Future in Archaeological Heritage Management? *World Archaeology* 49(5). doi:10.1080/00438243.2017.140 6398.

Hollmann, M. and Schüller-Zwierlein, A. (eds.)., 2014. *Diachrone Zugänglichkeit als Prozess. Kulturelle Überlieferung in systematischer Sicht*. Berlin etc: De Gruyter.

Hölscher, L., 1999. *Die Entdeckung der Zukunft*. Frankfurt/M.: Fischer.

Holtorf, C., 1996. Towards a Chronology of Megaliths: Understanding Monumental Time and Cultural Memory. *Journal of European Archaeology* 4(1), 119–152.

Holtorf, C., 2015. Averting Loss Aversion in Cultural Heritage. *International Journal of Heritage Studies* 21(4), 405–421.

Holtorf, C., 2020. An archaeology for the future: from developing contract archaeology to imagining post-corona archaeology. *Post-Classical Archaeologies* 10, 57–72. Available at http://www.postclassical.it/PCA_Vol.10_files/PCA10_Holtorf.pdf (accessed 1 September 2020).

Holtorf, C. and Högberg, A., 2014. Communicating with Future Generations: What Are the Benefits of Preserving for Future Generations? Nuclear Power and Beyond. *European Journal of Post-Classical Archaeologies* 4, 315–330. Available at http://www. postclassical.it/PCA_vol.4_files/PCA%204_Holtorf-Hogberg-1.pdf (accessed 1 September 2020).

Holtorf, C. and Högberg, A., 2018. Archaeology and the Future. In: C. Smith, ed. *Encyclopedia of Global Archaeology*. Cham: Springer. doi:10.1007/978-3-319-51726-1_2792-1.

Holtorf, C. and Ortman, O., 2008. Endangerment and Conservation Ethos in Natural and Cultural Heritage: The Case of Zoos and Archaeological Sites. *International Journal of Heritage Studies* 14(1), 74–90.

Karl, R., 2015. Every Sherd Is Sacred. Compulsive Hoarding in Archaeology. In: G. Sayeh, D. Henson and Y. F. Willumsen, eds. *Managing the Archaeological Heritage: Public Archaeology in Europe*. Kristiansand: Vest-Agder-Museet, pp. 24–37.

Karl, R., 2018. Against Retention In Situ. How to Best Preserve Archaeology for 'Future Generations'? Archäologische Denkmalpflege Blog. Available at https://archdenk. blogspot.se/2018/02/against-retention-in-situ.html (accessed 15 March 2018).

Kimball, M., 2016. Our Heritage Is Already Broken: Meditations on a Regenerative Conservation for Cultural and Natural Heritage. *Human Ecology Review* 22(2), 47–76.

Larsen, P.B. and Logan, W. (eds.)., 2018. *World Heritage and Sustainable Development. New Directions in World Heritage Management*. London and New York: Routledge.

Lindsay, W., 2005/2006. Time Perspectives: What 'the Future' Means to Museum Professionals in Collections-Care. *The Conservator* 29(1), 51–61.

Lowenthal, D., 1995. The Forfeit of the Future. *Futures* 27(4), 385–395.

Lowenthal, D., 2005. Stewarding the Future. *CRM: The Journal of Heritage Stewardship* 2(2), 20–39. Available at https://www.nps.gov/crmjournal/Summer2005/view2.pdf (accessed 26 March 2018).

Männikkö, M., 2017. Studying the Future and Writing History. In: Sirkka Heinonen, Osmo Kuusi and Hazel Salminen, eds. *How Do We Explore Our Futures? Methods of Futures Research*. Helsinki: Finnish Society for Futures Studies, pp. 28–39.

Miller, R., 2009. The Future of the Future: The Role of Anticipation in a Universe of Fundamental Indeterminacy. Conference presentation, London. Available at http:// futures.research.southwales.ac.uk/media/files/documents/2009-07-29/Futures_ Seminar_-_Riel_Miller.pdf (accessed 18 March 2018).

Minard, P. and Folcher, F., 2003. *Guédelon. Fanatics for a Fortress*. Geneva: Aubanel.

Mittermeier, S., 2017. Utopia, Nostalgia, and Our Struggle with the Present. Time Travelling through Discovery Bay. In: F. Carlà-Uhink, F. Freitag, S. Mittermeier and A. Schwarz, eds. *Time and Temporality in Theme Parks*. Hanover: Wehrhahn, pp. 171–187.

Moore, Kevin, 1997. *Museums and Popular Culture*. London: Cassel.

Morgan, J. and Macdonald, S., 2018. De-Growing Museum Collections for New Heritage Futures. *International Journal of Heritage Studies*. doi:10.1080/13527258.201 8.1530289.

Muñoz Viñas, S., 2005. *Contemporary Theory of Conservation*. Burlington: Elsevier.

Museum Association, 2005. Collections for the Future. Available at https://www. museumsassociation.org/download?id=11121 (Accessed 22 July 2018).

Newell, J., Robin, L. and Wehner, K., 2017. *Curating the Future. Museums, Communities and Climate Change*. London and New York: Routledge.

Peterson, D.R., Gavua, K. and Rassool, C. (eds.)., 2015. *The Politics of Heritage in Africa. Economies, Histories, and Infrastructures*. Cambridge: Cambridge University Press.

RAÄ, 2006. Towards Future Heritage Management. The Swedish National Heritage Board's Environmental Scanning Report. Stockholm: Riksantikvarieämbetet. Available at http://www.raa.se/publicerat/9789172094581.pdf (accessed 11 February 2018).

RAÄ, 2012. Trender i tiden (Trends in Time. Riksantikvarieämbetets omvärldsanalys). pp. 2010–2015. Stockholm: Riksantikvarieämbetet. Available in Swedish at: http://www.raa.se/app/uploads/2012/08/Trender-i-tiden-2012-2015-9789172096011.pdf (accessed 9 February 2018).

RAÄ, 2016. Vision för kulturmiljöarbetet Till 2030 (Vision for Working with the Historic Environment.). Stockholm: Riksantikvarieämbetet. Available in Swedish at: https://www.raa.se/app/uploads/2017/08/Visionsrapport_vlslutversion_med-bilaga.pdf (accessed 9 February 2018).

Reicher, S., 2008. Making a Past Fit for the Future. The Political and Ontological Dimensions of Historical Continuity. In: F. Sani, ed. *Self Continuity. Individual and Collective Perspectives*. New York and Hove: Psychology Press, pp. 145–157.

Richards, P., 1992. Saving the Rain Forest? Contested Futures in Conservation. In: S. Wallman, ed. *Contemporary Futures: Perspectives from Social Anthropology*. London and New York: Routledge, pp. 145–157.

Rico, T., 2016. *Constructing Destruction. Heritage Narratives in the Tsunami City*. London and New York: Routledge.

Rosenberg, D. and Harding, S. (eds.)., 2005. *Histories of the Futures*. Durham, NC: Duke University Press.

Rubin, E., 2012. Passing on Holocaust Tattoos. *Deutsche Welle*. Available at http://dw.de/p/16ngf (accessed 11 February 2018).

Rudolff, B. and Buckley, K., 2016. World Heritage: Alternative Futures. In: W. Logan, M. Nic Craith and U. Kockel, eds. *A Companion to Heritage Studies*. Chichester: Wiley Blackwell, pp. 522–540.

Rüsch, E., 2004. Vergangenheitsfalle oder Zukunftsentsorgung? Folgen einer Denkmalpflege ohne Gegenwartsbewusstsein, *Kunsttexte.de* 1/2004. Available at http://edoc.hu-berlin.de/kunsttexte/download/denk/sym3-ruesch-v.pdf (Accessed 9 February 2018).

Rüsen, J., 2004. Historical Consciousness: Narrative Structure, Moral Function, and Ontogenetic Development. In: P. Seixas, ed. *Theorizing Historical Consciousness*. Toronto etc.: University of Toronto Press, pp. 63–85.

Rydén, R., 2019. Archivists and Time: Conceptions of Time and Long-Term Information Preservation among Archivists. *Journal of Contemporary Archival Studies* 6(1), Article 6. Available at https://elischolar.library.yale.edu/jcas/vol6/iss1/6

Sagan, C., Drake, F.D., Druyan, A., Ferris, T., Lomberg, J. and Sagan, L.S., 1978. *Murmurs of Earth. The Voyager Interstellar Record*. New York: Random House.

Salazar, J.F., Pink, S., Irving, A. and Sjöberg, J. (eds.)., 2017. *Anthropologies and Futures. Researching Emerging and Uncertain Worlds*. London etc.: Bloomsbury.

Saminian-Darash, L. and Rabinow, P. (eds.)., 2015. *Modes of Uncertainty. Anthropological Cases*. Chicago and London: University of Chicago Press.

Seligman, M.E.P., Railton, P., Baumeister, R.F. and Sripada, C., 2013. Navigating Into the Future or Driven by the Past. *Perspectives on Psychological Science: A Journal of the Association for Psychological Science* 8(2), 119–141.

Silberman, N. and Liuzza, C., 2007. *The Future of Heritage. Changing Visions, Attitudes and Contexts in the 21st Century. Interpreting the Past*, vol. V, part I. Brussels: Ename Center for Public Archaeology and Heritage Interpretation.

Simon, Z.B., 2018. History Begins in the Future. On Historical Sensibility in the Age of Technology. In: S. Helgesson and J. Svenungsson, eds. *The Ethos of History: Time and Responsibility*. Oxford and New York: Berghahn, pp. 192–209.

Smith, L., 2006. *Uses of Heritage*. London: Routledge.

Spennemann, D.H.R., 2007a. The Futurist Stance of Historical Societies: An Analysis of Position Statements. *International Journal of Arts Management* 9(2), 4–15.

Spennemann, D.H.R., 2007b. Of Great Apes and Robots: Considering the Future(S) of Cultural Heritage. *Futures* 39(7), 861–877.

Staley, D.J., 2002. A History of the Future. *History and Theory* 41(4), 72–89.

Steffen, W., Richardson, K., Rockström, J., Cornell, S.E., Fetzer, I., Bennett, E.M., Biggs, R., Carpenter, S.R., de Vries, W., de Wit, C.A., Folke, C., Gerten, D., Heinke, J., Mace, G.M., Persson, L.M., Ramanathan, V., Reyers, B. and Sörlin, S., 2015. Sustainability. Planetary Boundaries: Guiding Human Development on a Changing Planet. *Science* 347(6223): 1259855.

Taylor, J., 2013. Intergenerational Justice: A Useful Perspective for Heritage Conservation. *CeROArt (Online)*. Available at http://ceroart.revues.org/3510 (accessed 10 February 2018).

Vidal, F. and Dias, N. (eds.)., 2015. *Endangerment, Biodiversity and Culture*. London and New York: Routledge.

UNESCO, 1972. *Convention Concerning the Protection of the World Cultural and Natural Heritage*. Paris: UNESCO. Available at http://whc.unesco.org/en/conventiontext/ (accessed 2 October 2019).

UNESCO, 1997. *Declaration on the Responsibilities of the Present Generations Towards Future Generations*. Paris: UNESCO General Conference.

UNESCO, 2002. *Memory of the World. General Guidelines to Safeguard Documentary Heritage*. Revised 2nd edition prepared by Edmondson, R. Paris: UNESCO. Available at http://unesdoc.unesco.org/images/0012/001256/125637e.pdf (accessed 2 October 2019).

UNESCO, 2015. *World Heritage and Sustainable Development Policy*. Paris: UNESCO Available at https://whc.unesco.org/document/139747 (accessed 2 October 2019).

United Nations, 1987. *Report of the World Commission on Environment and Development: Our Common Future*. New York. Available: http://www.un-documents.net/our-common-future.pdf (accessed 8 February 2018).

Urry, J., 2016. *What Is the Future?* Cambridge and Malden: Polity.

Willems, W.J.H., 2012. Problems with Preservation In Situ. In: C. Bakels and H. Kamermans, eds. *The End of Our Firth Decade*. Leiden: Leiden University, pp. 1–8.

Zetterström-Sharp, J., 2015. Heritage as Future-Making: Aspiration and Common Destiny in Sierra Leone. *International Journal of Heritage Studies* 21(6), 609–627.

2

HERITAGE PRACTICES AS FUTURE-MAKING PRACTICES

Rodney Harrison

Introduction

What does it mean to speak of heritage practices as "worlding" or "future-making" practices? While it is conventional to think about heritage as a series of practical fields oriented towards preserving and managing what remains of biological and cultural diversity from the *past*, it is perhaps less often the case that we reflect on the role of heritage in assembling and making *futures*, despite ubiquitous claims that the aim of such procedures is the preservation of objects, places and practices *for future generations*. If we begin to seriously probe these future orientations, then it becomes possible to think of heritage as a series of activities that are intimately concerned with *assembling*, *building* and *designing* future worlds. In this chapter, I focus empirically on crop diversity conservation practices and the work of the Svalbard Global Seed Vault (SGSV), as an example of the ways in which heritage practices might be productively reframed as "worlding" or "future making" practices, and how such a framework might suggest productive new lines of inquiry for critical heritage studies more generally.

What are "futures" and how are they "made"?

The "future" has a long history as a concept in both the popular and scientific imaginary (e.g. Jameson 2007) and is part of the same modern set of concepts that undergirds contemporary understandings of heritage (e.g. Harrison 2013a). And yet the sudden deluge of scholarly publication relating to futures would suggest that it is having a bit of a "moment". This is perhaps nowhere more apparent than in the fields of anthropology and design studies, where the meeting of these two disciplines has received significant recent attention (e.g. Ehn, Nilsson and Topgaard 2014; Smith et al. 2016). As the late John Urry notes in his recent synthetic review of future studies in the social sciences, particular futures tend to be produced by the same anticipatory systems that have been built to plan for and predict them (2016: 9; see also Law and Urry 2004). This is not only because the power to realise certain futures is unequally distributed and prioritises those futures which benefit certain powerful actors and institutions, but also because specific planning and management systems themselves enact and produce specific futures.

To speak of "futures" as "enacted" and "made" seems to contradict the idea of the future as a "reality", a specific temporal and spatial zone of material and social experience. Here we confront a central problematic of the contemporary social sciences – how can we speak of something as simultaneously "real" and also "constructed"? And how can we talk about *multiple* real, co-existent constructed realities? The work of Michel Callon and Fabien Muniesa (e.g. Callon 1998, 2005; Callon and Muniesa 2005; Muniesa 2014; Muniesa and Callon 2007), which examines the ways in which the economy is simultaneously real and produced by the intervention of the same economists who claim to observe it (see also Hertz 2000), addresses this question directly. As Muniesa notes:

> reality is indeed constructed, but it is so in the engineer's sense: the scientific fact stands objectively in the laboratory as the bridge stands firmly over the water, that is, insofar as it undergoes a laborious process of material assemblage. But that is not, alas, quite a common view. For constructivism to mean realism it has first to emancipate from the idea of "social construction" that is often found in the social sciences and according to which reality would be located not in things but in what we think of them. And for realism to mean constructivism it has to avoid the temptation of considering reality as something that just stands there without taking the trouble to happen.
>
> *(Muniesa 2014: 32)*

Perhaps the most important finding to emerge from the history and sociology of the natural and social sciences over the past decades is that *observation* is always itself a form of *intervention* (e.g. see Barad 2007; Daston and Galison 2010; Latour 1987, 2013; Stengers 2000). My reference to the example of the economy here is not arbitrary – this is the very context in which "futures" are "traded", and in doing so, *assembled* and *produced* (see also Urry 2016: 8). And like the economy, heritage is defined by its management practices, practices that are intended to identify, define and secure the existence of its conservation object into the future, and which thus intervene in, and contribute directly to, the assembling of specific future worlds (see also Harrison 2017; Breithoff and Harrison 2018, 2020; Breithoff 2020; Harrison and Sterling 2020; Harrison et al. 2020).

Heritage: assembling, building and designing future worlds

Recent approaches to heritage studies have drawn on assemblage and actor-network approaches to show the value of seeing heritage as a series of strategic socio-technical and/or biopolitical assemblages composed of various people, institutions, apparatuses (*dispositifs*) and the relations between them (e.g. Macdonald 2009; Harrison 2013a, 2013b; Bennett et al. 2017). Thinking of heritage in this way not only helps us to understand how it operates at the level of both material and social relations but also helps us to focus our attention on the particular constellation of power/knowledge effects that it facilitates, that is, the relationship between heritage and governmentality (see also Smith 2006).

Jane Bennett's (2010) discussion of assemblage theory shows how human and nonhuman agents of change cannot be separated from the ways in which they are arranged and the affordances of the various socio-technical assemblages in which they are entangled. Thinking of heritage as an assemblage (or *agencement*) means paying attention not only to individuals and corporations and the discourses they promulgate or resist but also to the specific arrangements of materials, equipment, texts and technologies, both "ancient" and "modern", by which heritage is produced in conversation with them. These specific arrangements of materials might include not only the "historic" fabric of a heritage site itself, along with the assortment of artefacts and "scars" that represent its patina of age and authenticity, but also the various technologies of tourism and display by which it is exhibited and made "visitable" (c.f. Dicks 2004) as a heritage site. We might think of the governmental capacities of these various socio-technical components, which together make up the heritage *agencement*, in relation to the concept of an apparatus or *dispositif*, as developed by Michel Foucault in his work on governmentality.

Paul Rabinow (2003: 49ff) has shown how Michel Foucault defined an apparatus as a device or technology that specifies (and hence helps to create) a subject so that it might control, distribute and/or manage it. Agamben further defines an apparatus as "anything that has in some way the capacity to capture, orient, determine, intercept, model, control, or secure the gestures, behaviours, opinions, or discourses of living beings" (2009: 14) (and indeed, the system of relations between them). We might think here of the governmental capacities of the various modern and historic material interventions at heritage sites – conservation methods and equipment, crowd-controlling devices, infrastructure associated with movement around a site, the various interpretive appliances that have been introduced alongside the affordances of the material that forms the heritage site itself and the texts and discourses that give each of them their authority to control behaviour in specific ways. These devices and texts are arranged and assembled in precise and identifiable ways, the study of which allows their capacity to control and regulate behaviour, and the various networks of agency in which they are distributed, to be better understood.

So what is the "world-making" work of heritage? Elsewhere I have shown how heritage registers and lists of many different forms might be seen to act "at a distance" to direct and constrain the management of both intangible and tangible forms of cultural heritage (see Harrison 2016). One of the key outcomes of heritage practices is the material and semiotic transformation of ruined and redundant objects, places and practices in a process by which they are given a "second life" (c.f. Kirshenblatt-Gimblett 1998, 2006). But this transformation is not only discursive. The work of heritage transforms not only the objects themselves (by way of conservation processes, for example, which may chemically or physically alter and transform the object into a piece of "heritage") but also the landscapes in which they are situated. We tend to think of heritage as something that is pre-existing and thus incorporated passively into the design of rural and urban landscapes, but the decision to conserve and incorporate what had previously existed as merely a "ruin" into a new development and to label it as "heritage" is one which transforms the material world in particular ways. What I mean here is that a decision to build "around", "within", "above" or "below" is also a decision to build "with" something – an archaeological site, part of a ruined building, a former factory – and this is also a process of creating something new out of fragments (see also Shanks 2012).

In thinking of heritage as an assemblage, we are forced to dissolve the boundaries between that which is "old" and that which is "new" to consider each as part of the physical infrastructure that constitutes a piece of "heritage" (see Harrison 2013c). In this sense, we need to look beyond the remains of the heritage sites themselves which are conserved, to simultaneously consider the vast material infrastructure relating to conservation and visitor management and the production of the heritage "experience" that work together to "create" the heritage site. We might think of these as the "technologies" of heritage – the various mechanisms and apparatuses by which the heritage experience is created. At the same time as this increasing mechanisation of the technologies of heritage, we are seeing a vast global increase in the number of places that are classified and managed as heritage sites (Harrison 2013a). Even in the case of natural and so-called "intangible" heritage, these landscapes and cultural practices are increasingly being linked to sites of consumption (and their associated technologies of heritage experience) where they are staged and reframed for exhibition and consumption. The globalisation and expansion of particular definitions of heritage throughout the 20th and early 21st century have had important material implications that have rarely been considered alongside their discursive consequences. However, both are equally important and work together in intervening within, transforming and making future worlds.

Towards an ecology of heritage practices

If we are to see heritage practices of various kinds as enacting new realities through contingent practices of assembling and reassembling bodies, techniques, technologies, materials, values, temporalities and spaces in particular ways, what does it mean to speak of "futures", "realities" and "worlds" in the plural?

> This is how I produced what I would call my first step towards an ecology of practice, the demand that no practice be defined as "like any other", just

as no living species is like any other. Approaching a practice then means approaching it as it diverges, that is, feeling its borders, experimenting with the questions which practitioners may accept as relevant, even if they are not their own questions, rather than posing insulting questions that would lead them to mobilise and transform the border into a defence against their outside.

(Stengers 2005: 184)

Invoking Isabelle Stenger's notion of ecologies of practices, I want to draw attention to the relative *autonomy* of different domains of heritage practices, with each of these domains specifying *particular* objects of conservation and *specific* accompanying methods of management. Examples of such domains include the fields of biodiversity conservation, built heritage conservation, and endangered language preservation, each of which identifies a specific risk (respectively, loss of biological diversity, loss of cultural patrimony and loss of language and "culture") and an endangered object ("biodiversity", "built heritage" and "language diversity"). Each of these domains applies its own specific techniques for identifying, collecting, conserving, and managing the endangered object and the factors that are perceived to threaten it (see Harrison 2015; see also Vidal and Dias 2016). In so far as heritage is generally tasked with preserving its endangered object for the "future", and each of these domains is concerned with establishing its respective conservation targets as both objects of knowledge and fields of intervention, these different heritage domains can be said to be actively engaged in the work of assembling and caring for the future. Central here is a plural notion of heritage ontologies understood as the world making, future assembling capacities of heritage practices of different kinds, and the ways in which different heritage practices might be seen to enact different realities and hence to assemble radically different futures (Harrison 2015; see also Holtorf and Högberg 2015). I will explore these different future-making practices by looking in detail at the futures that are generated in the work of the Svalbard Global Seed Vault (SGSV) and considering how these might diverge from other fields of heritage practices.

The Svalbard Global Seed Vault

Established in 2008 in partnership between the Royal Norwegian Ministry of Agriculture and Food; the Global Crop Diversity Trust (GCDT), an independent international organisation based in Germany, which was itself established as a partnership between the United Nations Food and Agriculture Organization (FAO) and the Consultative Group on International Agricultural Research (CGIAR); and the Nordic Genetic Resource Centre (NordGen), SGSV is currently the world's largest secure seed storage facility. At the cost of US$ 9 million to the Norwegian government, the construction of the SGSV began in 2005 as a result of the recommendations of the 2004 International Treaty on Plant Genetic Resources for Food and Agriculture, which created a global ex-situ system for the conservation of agricultural plant genetic resource diversity. Situated on the remote island of Spitsbergen in the Norwegian Svalbard archipelago, high in the Arctic north, it received its first deposits of seeds in 2008. NordGen, which is responsible for the day-to-day operations of the facility and maintains its public database of samples, reports that (at the time of writing) it holds approximately 850,000 "accessions" and 54.7 million seeds from 233 countries and 69 depositor institutes in its frozen repository (NordGen 2017). Each accession represents an individual crop phenotype and is usually made up of approximately 500 individual seeds. The seed accessions are dried by depositing institutions to limit their moisture content to 5% to 6% and are then sealed inside an individual airtight aluminium bag. These bags are packed into standard-sized crates and stacked on shelving racks within one of the three separate, identical storage vaults, each measuring approximately 9.5 × 27 metres, which are refrigerated to maintain a constant temperature of −18 degrees Celsius (Figure 2.1). These vaults have been excavated approximately 120 metres into the side of a sandstone mountain at the height of 130 metres above sea level; entry to the vaults is via a 100-metre entrance tunnel (Figure 2.2). Equal parts bunker and frozen "ark", its dramatic façade (Figure 2.3) includes a commissioned artwork, *Perpetual Repercussion* by Dyveke Sanne, which "renders the building visible from far off both day and night, using highly reflective stainless steel triangles of various sizes" (Government of Norway 2015). Cold climate and permafrost ensure that even if power is lost, the storage vaults will remain frozen for a significant period of time, even taking into account the possible effects of climate and sea-level changes. "Designed for [a] virtually infinite lifetime", it is perceived to be "robustly secured against external hazards and climate change effects" (Government of Norway 2015).

The SGSV is not a conventional seedbank, but was conceived as part of a global system to facilitate the secure storage of a duplicate "back up" of seeds from national and regional repositories.

> Worldwide, more than 1,700 genebanks hold collections of food crops for safekeeping, yet many of these are vulnerable, exposed not only to natural catastrophes and war, but also to avoidable disasters, such as lack of funding or poor management. Something as mundane as a poorly functioning freezer can ruin an entire collection. And the loss of a crop variety is as irreversible as the extinction of a dinosaur, animal or any form of life.
>
> *(Crop Trust 2016a)*

These backed-up copies of seeds are stored free of charge and are held as part of an international agreement in which the seeds remain the property of the depositing institution and are available for withdrawal by the depositing institution (and only that depositing institution) at any time. It is thus not an active genebank, but a literal "vault" containing a secure stock of duplicate seeds that can be used if seed stocks from the depositing institution become depleted or lost. The requirement for such a facility seemed to be clearly demonstrated when,

FIGURE 2.1   Interior of the central of three storage vaults at SGSV showing standard-ised storage crates on shelving units. Each box is individually barcoded and registered on the SGSV database. Currently, only this one of the three vaults is in use. The SGSV has the capacity to store 4.5 million seed samples or 2.25 billion seeds, which would account for over double the world's current estimated crop diversity held in the existing system of regional, national and international seedbanks. Photograph by the author.

in September 2015, scientists from the International Centre for Agricultural Research in Dry Areas (ICARDA) who had lost access to their genebank facility in Aleppo, Syria, requested the return of duplicate samples of seed that had been sent to the SGSV to reconstruct their collection in a new facility in Lebanon. This first withdrawal of seed samples from the SGSV as a result of the ongoing conflict in Syria was reported widely in the media and seemed to indicate clearly that the SGSV was already fulfilling a purpose that it had previously been assumed would arise in a more distant future, justifying the significant investment in this global "insurance policy". The manager of the new genebank facility in Terbol, Bekaa, was reported to have said of the withdrawal of seed samples,

FIGURE 2.2 The "Svalbard tube" – the long entrance tunnel leading from the external concrete portal building into the mountainside to the three identical vaults. The insulated (heated) service building, containing foyer, office and toilet facilities, is visible in the foreground of the photograph. Photograph by the author.

> It [SGSV] was not expected to be opened for 150 or 200 years ... It would only open in the case of major crises but then we soon discovered that, with this crisis at a country level, we needed to open it.
>
> *(Alabaster 2015)*

Banking diversity, making futures, securing hope

In articulating the need for such a repository, the SGSV's mission is framed within what we might see as a fairly conventional articulation of the endangerment sensibility (c.f. Vidal and Dias 2016) and its accompanying entropic view of the relationship between diversity and time (see further discussion in Harrison 2017). The GCDT, as the charitable organisation responsible for funding the ongoing operations of the SGSV and the preparation and shipment of seed from developing countries, perhaps articulates this most clearly in its explanation of the SGSV's purpose.

> The purpose of the Svalbard Global Seed Vault is to provide insurance against both incremental and catastrophic loss of crop diversity held in

FIGURE 2.3   The SGSV's dramatic concrete portal building and façade, including the artwork, *Perpetual Repercussion* by Dyveke Sanne, commissioned and produced by Public Art Norway (KORO). The access tunnel and the vault itself are located entirely within drill- and blast-excavated sandstone within the mountain. Photograph by the author.

traditional seed banks around the world. The Seed Vault offers "fail-safe" protection for one of the most important natural resources on earth.

It continues,

> Crop diversity is the resource to which plant breeders must turn to develop varieties that can withstand pests, diseases, and remain productive in the face of changing climates. It will therefore underpin the world food supply … the Seed Vault will ensure that unique diversity held in genebanks in developing countries is not lost forever if an accident occurs.
>
> *(Crop Trust 2016b)*

In these statements, we see all of the conventional articulations of an entropic view of the relationship between diversity, including the potential loss of diversity through catastrophic incidents and the need to build resilience in the face of such changes.

However, the situation becomes somewhat more complicated when we consider the operation of the SGSV in relation to the global system of crop diversity conservation and in particular, the relationship of the materials stored in the SGSV to the specific conservation targets of crop diversity conservation practices. As Sara Peres (2016) shows, seed banks were developed as part of a strategy to ensure the maintenance of crop genetic diversity as a result of the widespread adoption of a small number of high yielding crop monocultures during the course of the 20th century. This was itself an outcome of the industrialisation and modernisation of global agricultural crop production over this same period. The freezing of seeds would enable the maintenance of crop diversity without the need for ongoing cultivation of old crop varieties, resulting in an "archive" of the evolutionary histories of crop varieties that might be of use to future generations of agricultural scientists and farmers. Nikolai Valilov's important work in the first part of the 20th century on the concepts of "centres of origin" and "genetic erosion" underpin this system. He suggested that both wild and domestic genetic diversity was fundamental to food security. "Landraces", localised genetic variants of crop species that are the result of both cultural and natural selection processes, were seen to represent a bank of genetic diversity that held potential for future crop improvement to mediate the effects of future climate change and assist with the development of new crops that are resilient to possible emergent diseases in the future (e.g. see discussion in Hummer 2015). Peres (2016) notes that the present system of genebanks is the outcome of debates in the 1960s and 1970s surrounding the most appropriate methods of crop diversity conservation – in situ or ex situ – in which the frozen seeds held in seedbanks across the world have come to act as "proxies" for crops. These debates were closely related to, and indeed stimulated, the development of broader technologies of cryogenic and other frozen preservation across a large number of different fields of conservation (see Radin 2016, 2017; chapters in Radin and Kowal 2017). As objects that naturally store genetic records, the seeds would facilitate future retrieval of the histories of local agricultural experimentation and selection present in landraces and other cultivars, alongside the genetic diversity of wild crop seed. Holding these seeds at low temperatures would potentially halt the genetic erosion that might occur in situ through a combination of natural and cultural processes, thus providing a frozen archive of genetic material which could be "recalled" in the future (see also Bowker 2005).

> Seed banks can therefore be imagined as repositories that enabled the "recall" of genetic diversity, both by committing it to memory and by allowing it to be recovered from cold storage for use. By evoking both these meanings, the concept of recall conveys how the conservation of old landraces is entangled with concerns regarding their future use. Seed banks thus function as archives that make records of the past of crops accessible in the future.
>
> *(Peres 2016: 102)*

This view of seedbanks as archives of past natural and cultural processes is significant in motivating the work of the SGSV. The seeds hold within their genetic material records of localised crop experimentation and natural and cultural selection that archive histories of agricultural activity, which extend back in time to ancient Mesopotamia. In relation to the ICARDA accession withdrawal, the genebank manager was again quoted as saying

> When you trace back the history of these seeds, [you think of] the tradition and the heritage that they captured … They were maintained by local farmers from generation to generation, from father to son and then all the way to ICARDA's gene bank and from there to the Global Seed Vault in Svalbard.
>
> *(Alabaster 2015)*

In freezing crop seeds as archives that map global genetic diversity from different points in time, each of which contains echoes or fragments of the diversity of past natural and cultural processes, the SGSV intervenes in the normative, entropic decay of diversity, "banking" a record of past genetic diversity in frozen, arrested time. Thus, in conjunction with ongoing processes of in situ crop diversity maintenance, themselves subject to continuous processes of natural and cultural selection that alter contemporary global crop diversity, the vault's collection reverses the entropic process of diversity decay by increasing crop genetic diversity. In this sense, the values of its collection also increase with time. Its role in securing and making futures is articulated clearly by GCDT.

> The Vault is the ultimate insurance policy for the world's food supply, offering options for future generations to overcome the challenges of climate change and population growth. It will secure, for centuries, millions of seeds representing every important crop variety available in the world today. It is the final back up.
>
> *(Crop Trust 2016a)*

It is perhaps no coincidence that the conservation target of such activity is the seed. It acts here both as a physical container for genetic material but also a poignant symbol of latent potential and hope in securing uncertain futures by intervening directly in "natural" processes of entropic diversity decay, offering "options" to future generations in responding to climate and population change by providing "fail-safe" protection for "one of the most important natural resources on earth" (Crop Trust 2016b). In doing so, the seed appears as a silent witness to political processes, its strength and resilience a result of its apolitical internationalism, just like the global system of which it has become a part.

> The power of seed can be explosive. Not just because it can force its way through rock-hard soil to reach the sunlight, but also because it is at the

centre of many political processes. The rights relating to the genetic material of plants, animals and micro-organisms have been a key issue of contention between industrial and developing countries.

(Statsbygg 2008: 8)

Ghassan Hage's (2003) analysis of the state's capacity to distribute hope as a form
of governmental power is significant in pointing to the ways in which, in offering a sense of hope and security against uncertain global futures, banking crop
diversity is also a practice that is caught up in processes of the generation and
differential distribution of forms of power. The biopolitical concerns articulated
in these processes contribute to the management of heritage risk (see Rico 2015)
and future uncertainty by establishing certain frameworks for intervening in and
shaping that future through the maintenance and development of a "bank" of
genetic materials, which might form the basis for future crop experimentation
and thus future forms of life. While the global system, of which the SGSV is a
part, is one in which there are significant regulatory frameworks for the sharing of plant genetic resources for food and agriculture, it is nonetheless one in
which the authority to determine access to those resources is vested in national
governments. It seems significant then that the SGSV, due to prohibitions under
Norwegian law on the import of and research on genetically modified organ-
isms, cannot store genetically modified seeds, while at the same time contributing to a system that might facilitate such research elsewhere.

On heritage practices and their multiple divergent futures: discussion and conclusion

In looking at the work of the SGSV as a form of future making, I have been keen
to emphasise the extent to which its specific material and temporal practices
are oriented towards the production of a distinctive future. This future is not a
generic outcome of heritage or even biodiversity conservation but arises from
the specific material and discursive practices that are enacted in the work of this
global crop diversity conservation programme – *specific* practices that work with
particular materials, gathering together *specific* human and nonhuman agents in
a *precise* time and at a *particular* place. Quite different futures emerge from the
work of other conservation agencies and practices – futures which may diverge
significantly, or even oppose, those future worlds which are made within the
operations of the SGSV.

An example of the rise and fall of practices oriented towards the assembling of
one such alternative future world could be inferred from Nesbitt and Cornish's
(2016; see also Drayton 2000; Endersby 2008) analysis of the Economic Botany
Collection at Kew. Like the SGSV, it also contains seeds amongst other potentially economically "useful" plant materials. Its development, like the botanical
and ethnographic collections between which its "biocultural" (see also Salick,
Konchar and Nesbitt 2014) assemblages ultimately came to be divided, is closely

linked to the history of (in this case, the British) Empire, in moments when it seemed that the world could be collected, assembled, ordered and governed at a distance and in miniature through such institutions (see also Bennett et al. 2017). For a time, its collections blended together unmodified plant materials with objects of manufacture and craft from across the British Empire as part of the production of a world that was ordered and valued according to its latency and potential for human exploitation. The widespread closure and dispersal of economic botany collections from the 1960s to 1980s coincides historically with the development and emergence of the concept of "biodiversity" (Takacs 1996) and reflects changing notions of "nature" and "culture" in which plant species came to be increasingly viewed as having forms of "existence" value, which were independent from their potential usefulness to humans (e.g. Calicott 1986) and "ethnographic" collections increasingly reconfigured (more or less) non-hierarchically as museums of world cultures. These reorganisations of collections reflect, and at the same time helped produce, new worlds with new potentialities and divergent latent futures.

What actions might flow from this recognition that certain heritage domains build their own distinct worlds and their own particular futures? I would argue that it is only in taking a comparative approach to understand specific fields of heritage practices that we might reflect on and explore the possibilities inherent in reaching across these different fields of practice to work towards the assembling of common or shared futures. By reframing heritage as future-making practice – and rethinking the relationships between these various modes of future making or worlding practices – I suggest that these various practices of assembling and caring for the future might be creatively redeployed to generate innovation, foster resilience, encourage sustainability and facilitate the building of "common worlds" (Latour 2014) between and across them. As Arjun Appadurai (2013: 3) has recently noted, "the future is ours to design, if we are attuned to the right risks, the right speculations, and the right understanding of the material world we both inherit and shape". It is only in developing a shared and comprehensive understanding of the ways in which current speculations regarding what (and how) to conserve in the present actively shapes our material, ecological and social futures that we will be able to actively and consciously do so.

Acknowledgements

This empirical material presented in this chapter draws on field visits, interviews and ongoing collaborations with SGSV and NordGen staff undertaken by the author and Sefryn Penrose as part of a broader comparative study of natural and cultural diversity conservation practices, one of four major areas of thematic foci for the Heritage Futures research programme. Heritage Futures is funded by a UK Arts and Humanities Research Council (AHRC) "Care for the Future: Thinking Forward through the Past" Theme Large Grant (AH/M004376/1), awarded to Rodney Harrison (as principal investigator), Caitlin DeSilvey, Cornelius Holtorf,

Sharon Macdonald (as co-investigators), Antony Lyons (as senior creative fellow), Martha Fleming (as senior postdoctoral researcher), Nadia Bartolini, Sarah May, Jennie Morgan and Sefryn Penrose (as named postdoctoral researchers). Three PhD students were additionally funded as in-kind support for the research programme by their respective host universities – Kyle Lee-Crossett (University College London), Bryony Prestidge (University of York) and Robyn Raxworthy (University of Exeter). The team of researchers was subsequently joined by Esther Breithoff (as postdoctoral researcher) and by Hannah Williams (as administrative assistant and events coordinator, a role which was in turn later filled by Kyle Lee-Crossett) and, in its final year, by Harald Fredheim (as postdoctoral researcher). It also received generous additional support from its host universities and partner organisations. See www.heritage-futures.org for further information. Since this chapter was completed and submitted in 2016, an alternative version has been published as Rodney Harrison (2017) "Freezing seeds and making futures: endangerment, hope, security, and time in agrobiodiversity conservation practices", *Culture, Agriculture, Food and Environment* 39(2): 80–89, and the ideas expanded upon in Esther Breithoff and Rodney Harrison (2018) "From ark to bank: extinction, proxies and biocapitals in ex-situ biodiversity conservation practices", *International Journal of Heritage Studies*, DOI: 10.1080/13527258.2018.1512146; Esther Breithoff and Rodney Harrison (2020) Making futures in end times: nature conservation in the Anthropocene. In Rodney Harrison and Colin Sterling (eds.) *Deterritorializing the Future: Heritage in, of, and after the Anthropocene*. London: Open Humanities Publishing; and in Harrison, R., DeSilvey, C., Holtorf, C., Macdonald, S., Bartolini, N., Breithoff, E., Fredheim, H., Lyons, A., May, S., Morgan, J. and Penrose, S. (2020) *Heritage Futures: Comparative Approaches to Natural and Cultural Heritage Practices*. London: UCL Press.

References

Agamben, G., 2009. *What Is an Apparatus? And Other Essays*. Stanford: Stanford University Press.

Alabaster, O., 2015. Syrian civil war: Svalbard "Doomsday" Seeds Transferred to Lebanon to Preserve Syria's Crop Heritage. *The Independent Newspaper*, 10th October 2015. http://www.independent.co.uk/news/world/middle-east/syrian-civil-war-svalbard-doomsday-seeds-transferred-to-lebanon-to-preserve-syrias-crop-heritage-a6689421.html (Accessed 15th August 2016).

Appadurai, A., 2013. *The Future as Cultural Fact: Essays on the Global Condition*. London and New York: Verso.

Bennett, T., Cameron, F., Dias, N., Dibley, B., Harrison, R., Jacknis, I. and McCarthy, C., 2017. *Collecting, Ordering, Governing: Anthropology, Museums and Liberal Government*. Durham and New York: Duke University Press.

Barad, K., 2007. *Meeting the University Halfway: Quantum Physics and the Entanglement of Matter and Meaning*. Durham and London: Duke University Press.

Bennett, J., 2010. *Vibrant Matter: A Political Ecology of Things*. Durham and London: Duke University Press.

Bowker, G. C., 2005. *Memory Practices in the Sciences*. Cambridge: MIT Press.

Breithoff, E., 2020. *Conflict, Heritage and World-Making in the Chaco: War at the End of the Worlds?* London: UCL Press.

Breithoff, E. and Harrison, R., 2018. From Ark to Bank: Extinction, Proxies and Biocapitals in Ex-Situ Biodiversity Conservation Practices. *International Journal of Heritage Studies.* doi:10.1080/13527258.2018.1512146.

Breithoff, E. and Harrison, R., 2020. Making Futures in End Times: Nature Conservation in the Anthropocene. In: R. Harrison and C. Sterling, eds. *Deterritorializing the Future: Heritage in, of, and after the Anthropocene.* London: Open Humanities Publishing.

Callicott, J. B., 1986. On the Intrinsic Value of Nonhuman Species. In: B.G. Norton, ed. *The Preservation of Species: The Value of Biological Diversity.* Princeton, NJ: Princeton University Press; pp 138–172.

Callon, M. (ed.)., 1998. *The Laws of the Markets.* London: Blackwell Publishers.

Callon, M., 2005. Why Virtualism Paves the Way to Political Impotence. A Reply to Daniel Miller's Critique of the Laws of the Markets. *Economic Sociology: European Electronic Newsletter* 6, 3–20.

Callon, M. and Muniesa, F., 2005. Economic Markets as Calculative Collective Devices. *Organization Studies* 26(8), 1229–1250.

Crop Trust, 2016a. Svalbard Global Seed Vault. https://www.croptrust.org/what-we-do/svalbard-global-seed-vault/ (Accessed 15th August 2016).

Crop Trust, 2016b. FAQ About the Seed Vault. https://www.croptrust.org/what-we-do/svalbard-global-secd-vault/faq-about-the-vault/ (Accessed 15th August 2016).

Daston, L. and Galison, P., 2010. *Objectivity.* Brooklyn: Zone books.

Dicks, B., 2004. *Culture on Display: The Production of Contemporary Visibility.* Milton Keynes: Open University Press.

Drayton, R., 2000. *Nature's Government: Science, Imperial Britain and the "Improvement" of the World.* New Haven, CT and London: Yale University Press.

Endersby, J., 2008. *Imperial Nature: Joseph Hooker and the Practices of Victorian Science.* Chicago: University of Chicago Press.

Ehn, P., Nilsson, E. and Topgaard, R. (eds.)., 2014. *Making Futures: Marginal Notes on Innovation, Design, and Democracy.* Cambridge and London: MIT Press.

Foucault, M., 1980. The Confession of the Flesh (1977) interview. In: C. Gordon (ed.). *Power/Knowledge Selected Interviews and Other Writings.* New York: Pantheon Books; pp. 194–228.

Government of Norway, 2015. Svalbard Global Seed Vault: More about the Physical Plant. https://www.regjeringen.no/en/topics/food-fisheries-and-agriculture/landbruk/svalbard-global-seed-vault/mer-om-det-fysiske-anlegget/id2365142/ (Last updated 23rd February 2015).

Hage, G., 2003. *Against Paranoid Nationalism. Searching for Hope in a Shrinking Society.* Annandale: Pluto Press.

Harrison, R., 2013a. *Heritage: Critical Approaches.* Abingdon and New York: Routledge.

Harrison, R., 2013b. Reassembling Ethnographic Museum Collections. In: R. Harrison, S. Byrne, and A. Clarke, eds. *Reassembling the Collection: Ethnographic Museums and Indigenous Agency.* Santa Fe: School for Advanced Research Press; pp. 3–35.

Harrison, R., 2013c. Heritage. In: P. Graves-Brown, R. Harrison, and A. Piccini, eds. *The Oxford Handbook of the Archaeology of the Contemporary World.* Oxford: Oxford University Press; pp 273–288.

Harrison, R., 2015. Beyond "Natural" and "Cultural" Heritage: Toward an Onto-logical Politics of Heritage in the Age of Anthropocene. *Heritage and Society* 8(1), 24–42.

Harrison, R., 2016. World Heritage Listing and the Globalization of the Endangerment Sensibility. In: F. Vidal and N. Dias, eds. *Endangerment, Biodiversity and Culture*. Abingdon and New York: Routledge; pp 195–217.

Harrison, R., 2017. Freezing Seeds and Making Futures: Endangerment, Hope, Security, and Time in Crop Diversity Conservation Practices. *Culture, Agriculture, Food and Environment* 39(2), 80–89.

Harrison, R. and Sterling, C. (eds.)., 2020. *Deterritorializing the Future: Heritage in, of and after the Anthropocene*. London: Open Humanities Publishing.

Harrison, R., DeSilvey, C., Holtorf, C., Macdonald, S., Bartolini, N., Breithoff, E., Fredheim, H., Lyons, A., May, S., Morgan, J. and Penrose, S., 2020. *Heritage Futures: Comparative Approaches to Natural and Cultural Heritage Practices*. London: UCL Press.

Hertz, E., 2000. Stock Markets as "Simulacra": Observation That Participates. *Tsantsa* 5, 40–50.

Holtorf, C. and Högberg, A., 2015. Contemporary Heritage and the Future. In: E. Waterton and S. Watson, eds. *The Palgrave Handbook of Contemporary Heritage Research*. London: Palgrave; pp 509–523.

Hummer, K. E., 2015. In the Footsteps of Valivov: Plant Diversity Then and Now. *Horticultural Science* 50(6), 784–788.

Jameson, F., 2007. *Archaeologies of the Future: The Desire Called Utopia and Other Science Fictions*. London and New York: Verso.

Kirshenblatt-Gimblett, B., 1998. *Destination Culture: Tourism, Museums, and Heritage*. Berkeley and Los Angeles: University of California Press.

Kirshenblatt-Gimblett, B., 2006. World Heritage and Cultural Economics. In: I. Karp, C.A. Kratz, L. Szwaja, and T. Ybarra-Frausto, eds. *Museum Frictions: Public Cultures/Global Transformations*. Durham and London: Duke University Press; pp 161–202.

Latour, B., 1987. *Science in Action*. Cambridge, MA: Harvard University Press.

Latour, B., 2013. *An Inquiry into Modes of Existence: An Anthropology of the Moderns*. Cambridge, MA Harvard University Press.

Latour, B., 2014. Another Way to Compose the Common World. *HAU: Journal of Ethnographic Theory* 4(1), 301–307.

Law, J. and Urry, J., 2004. Enacting the Social. *Economy and Society* 33(3), 390–410.

Macdonald, S., 2009. Reassembling Nuremberg, Reassembling Heritage. *Journal of Cultural Economy* 2(1–2), 117–134.

Muniesa, F. and Callon, M., 2007. Economic Experiments and the Construction of Markets. In: D. Mackenzie, F. Muniesa, and L. Siu, eds. *Do Economists Make Markets? On the Performativity of Economics*. Princeton: Princeton University Press; pp 163–189.

Muniesa, Fabian, 2014. *The Provoked Economy. Economic Reality and the Performative Turn*. London: Routledge.

Nesbitt, M. and Cornish, C., 2016. Seeds of Industry and Empire: Economic Botany Collections between Nature and Culture. *Journal of Museum Ethnography* 29, 53–70.

Nordgen, 2017. Search Seed Portal. https://www.nordgen.org/en/global-seed-vault/search-seed-vault (Accessed 30th June 2017).

Peres, S., 2016. Saving the Gene Pool for the Future: Seed Banks as Archives. *Studies in History and Philosophy of Biological and Biomedical Sciences* 55, 96–104.

Rabinow, P., 2003. *Anthropos Today: Reflections on Modern Equipment*. Princeton: Princeton University Press.

Radin, J., 2016. Planning for the Past: Cryopreservation at the Farm, Zoo, and Museum. In: F. Vidal and N. Dias, eds. *Endangerment, Biodiversity and Culture*. Abingdon and New York: Routledge; pp 218–238.

Radin, J., 2017. *Life on Ice: A History of New Uses for Cold Blood.* Chicago and London: University of Chicago Press.

Radin, J. and Kowal, E. (eds.)., 2017. *Cryopolitics: Frozen Life in a Melting World.* Cambridge, MA: MIT Press.

Rico, T., 2015. Heritage at Risk: The Authority and Autonomy of a Dominant Preservation Framework. In: K. Lafrenz Samuels and T. Rico, eds. *Heritage Keywords: Rhetoric and Redescription in Cultural Heritage.* Boulder: University Press of Colorado; pp. 147–162.

Salick, J., Konchar, K. and Nesbitt, M. (eds.)., 2014. *Curating biocultural Collections: A Handbook.* Kew: Royal Botanic Gardens.

Shanks, M., 2012. *"Let Me Tell You About Hadrian's Wall..." Heritage, Performance, Design.* Amsterdam: Reinwardt Academy.

Smith, L., 2006. *Uses of Heritage.* Abingdon and New York: Routledge.

Smith, R. C., Tang Vangkilde, K., Gislev Kjaersgaard, M., Otto, T., Halse, J. and Binder, T. (eds.)., 2016. *Design Anthropological Futures.* London and New York: Bloomsbury.

Statsbygg, 2008. *Svalbard Global Seed Vault, Longyearbyen, Svalbard: New Construction.* Oslo: Statsbygg.

Stengers, I., 2000. *The Invention of Modern Science* D.W. Smith (trans.). Minneapolis: University of Minnesota Press.

Stengers, I., 2005. Introductory Notes on an Ecology of Practices. *Cultural Studies Review* 11(1), 183–196.

Takacs, D., 1996. *The Idea of Biodiversity: Philosophies of Paradise.* Baltimore: Johns Hopkins University Press.

Urry, J., 2016. *What Is the Future?* Cambridge and Malden: Polity Press.

Vidal, F. and Dias, N., 2016. Introduction: The Endangerment Sensibility. In: F. Vidal and N. Dias, eds. *Endangerment, Biodiversity and Culture.* Abingdon and New York: Routledge; pp 1–38.

3

HERITAGE, THRIFT, AND OUR CHILDREN'S CHILDREN

Sarah May

Everyone talks about the future; what do they mean?

Heritage is commonly claimed to preserve things from the past for future generations. What does the word 'generations' do in that phrase? It reminds us of children so that the phrase becomes analogous to 'for our children, and our children's children'. Of course, the children of today are the adults of tomorrow, so what is at stake when we use this formulation? This paper will explore the role of children in heritage discourse as placeholders of the future. It will examine how this role exerts a domesticating force for the future, which twins with the rescuing of the past to avoid anxieties about the present.

The future is important to heritage; after all, we conserve the past for the future. This is reflected in government policy documents with names like 'A force for our future' (English Heritage 2000). The newly formed Historic Environment Scotland released its corporate plan, entitled *For All Our Futures* (Historic Environment Scotland 2016). But when we examine these documents, we find very little about this future we are working for. What challenges does it face? What demographics does it have? How far in the future is it? What relationship does it have with us? Considering that it is the stated beneficiary of our work, we know remarkably little about it. In this paper, I will look at how and why heritage uses the concept of 'future generations' in explaining the importance of our work. I will critically examine how this positions us in relation to children, and I will explore how transgenerational gifts can be burdens as well as assets.

Serious consideration of futures and future making is just beginning in heritage studies, and this volume is an important corrective to that (though, see Harrison 2015; Holtorf and Högberg 2015). In this paper, I will consider the work of sociologists such as Adams and Groves (2007, 2011), and social psychologists such as

Reicher (2008), who have made considerable progress in understanding the role of future making in contemporary society, which in turn gives us a context for why it is important to heritage.

Dirk Spennemann has studied the rise of 'the future' in the slogans and rhetoric of Historical Societies in the United States. He argues that the future is so vague in heritage discourse because it is rhetorical. It is an *excuse*, an explanation for the importance of heritage that cannot be refuted because it cannot be known (2007). He argues that the appeal to the future in heritage discourse coincided with the rise of concern about environmental degradation. As Figure 3.1 shows, the relationship between 'future generations' and heritage is broader than in the slogans of American historical societies. The two concepts have similar fortunes in the corpus of books searched by Google Ngrams and are both on the rise.

But Spennemann cautions that this sloganeering, while increasing relevance for concerned communities,

> also raises the expectation that the historic preservation organizations have the interest and intellectual capacity to apply strategic foresight and actively manage not only the extent heritage, but also have strategies in place to deal with the issues of emergent and future heritage.
>
> *(Spennemann 2007, 98)*

Can we engage meaningfully with the future that we rely on for relevance? Historic England, the body with statutory responsibility for England's heritage did establish a 'foresight' team, but their remit was primarily to 'future-proof'

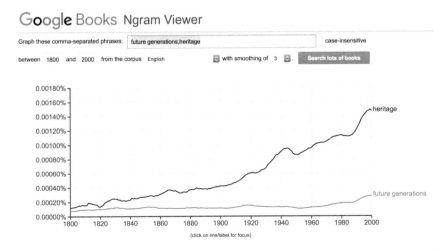

FIGURE 3.1   If we look at the use of the term 'future generations' across the corpus of English language books catalogued by Google Books, we see a sharp rise from the mid-1980s that correspond with an even sharper rise in the term 'heritage' (Michel et al. 2011; http://books.google.com/ngrams).

heritage, rather than to ensure that the future benefitted from our work (Historic England 2015).

But it is not only heritage policies that rely on the future. It is not just a rhetorical device. I conducted fieldwork for the Heritage Futures project, examining future-making practices in the Lake District of England. My participants did include heritage professionals working with the World Heritage bid for the area, but they also included shepherds, regulators, entrepreneurs, astronomers, and engineers with responsibility for nuclear waste. All of these people have concern or responsibility for futures well beyond their lifespans. While some of them have never unpicked what motivates them to do so or what they mean when they work for these futures, they are sincere in their practice. The heritage manager who balances academic and community values in a consultation hopes that their work will make life better in the future. The shepherd who builds their flock reaching for an ideal of a breed that matches the landscape is not only thinking of the present. These practices point to something more than Spennemann's dismissal of the future as an excuse in heritage discourse. The fieldwork describes their practices and compares how these construct different long-term futures. In this paper, I lay out the conceptual frame that guides that empirical work. I argue for present-focused future making.

Heritage as a link between past and future

There are, of course, no shortage of people predicting the future, from climate modelling to technological fixes and catastrophes. However, when we say that heritage is a future-making practice, we do not mean that it attempts to predict the future, but rather that it seeks to influence it. Though the materials we use may have been with us for many generations, this is no less creative or politically powerful than seeking to influence the future with new technology or new modes of working. In order to assess whether the future-focused policies and slogans mentioned above are effective, it is useful to understand what the overall project of future making does for the present day.

The social psychologist Reicher studies how people and societies establish self-continuity, a key aspect of emotional wellbeing. Being future-focused is often equated with a positive attitude. But while futures of technological revolution may present as optimistic, heritage draws on a different aspect of wellbeing. Establishing an identity that can form the past and extend into the future is one of the ways that people deal with change and challenges throughout life. Reicher gives a psychological explanation of the power of heritage as something people use in self-construction so that it is powerful in the establishment of social control. 'One of the critical ways people contest future directions of a group is by arguing over whether it represents continuity or rupture with the past' (Reicher 2008, 151). He also argues that the same structures are key in establishing futures. 'The very fact that human beings are able to gaze ahead, to imagine their own future, and create their own destiny renders the topic of history of fundamental importance' (Reicher 2008, 170). Do heritage policies that speak of future generations work within this framework?

The sociologists Adam and Groves have examined how different future positionings do different work in the present, contrasting empty futures with lived futures. They consider empty futures as being blank slates that can be used for technological and economic abstractions, pointing to practices such as discounting costs as modellers move further into the future. 'Neoclassical economics constructs the future as an empty, quantifiable medium and uses it to construct tools for assessing the costs and benefits of different actions in the present' (Adam and Groves 2011, 20). Lived futures, by contrast, stem from relationships of care, with specific people and things that we appreciate for their dynamic and ongoing value. Following this argument, heritage can be the bridge that allows an ethical perspective of care to continue past the lifespans of individuals into the deep future. Adam and Groves believe that this gives moral force to our actions as 'constructing our own futures through imagination and action forges novel connections that in turn unleash living futures that far outlive us' (2011, 25). This certainly supports the self-continuity that Reicher argues is necessary for our present wellbeing.

But this is not what the 'future generations' framing does. We do not extend our living care into an integrated future. We imagine a future which itself is in need of our care, and that is figured as our descendant, our child. In so doing, heritage contributes to filling the blank slates of the empty future(s) and therefore becomes an enormously powerful use of the past – no longer the innocent positioning of humble historical societies, but a future-making practice, an identification of the most valuable elements of the past, and a positioning of those actively construct the future. As Adam and Groves argue,

> when we extend ourselves into the future through imagination and through action, we make and take futures. Because this is the case, there is a basic inequality of power between present and future that does not exist between living contemporaries.
>
> *(2011, 21)*

Heritage, a gift from the past to the future

The 'future generations' model figures heritage as a gift, which we received from our parents and will give to our children. 'The cultural and natural heritage of every nation is a priceless possession, a precious gift that has been inherited from the past and is to be kept in trust by the present generation for generations yet to come' (von Droste zu Hülshoff 2006, 389). As with other heirlooms like watches and china, we should take good care of them, use them more carefully than we do things we have made or bought ourselves, and pass them on to our children for them to treasure and treat in the same fashion. 'Any loss or serious impairment of this heritage is a tragedy, because these gifts are irreplaceable' (von Droste zu Hülshoff 2006, 389).

There are two problems with this vision. Firstly, it overlooks our own role in the creation of heritage. Very little of what we perceive as heritage was 'given' to us. The majority could at most be said to be salvaged, while some of it has been created by our own efforts from materials that our forbearers neglected or even deliberately tried to get rid of (Holtorf 2015).

Secondly, it overlooks the fact that not all gifts are well received and an unwanted gift can be a burden (Daniels 2009). The gift is a central and complex feature of most if not all cultures and anthropologists have long made it a subject of particular study. There is considerable discussion concerning the centrality of reciprocity, but most authors agree that gifts and gift-giving practice create and regulate social relations and usually social obligations (Sigaud 2002, Skykes 2004). If we are to consider heritage management as a gift-giving practice, then we need to examine the social relations it is entangled in, as I am beginning to do in this paper.

Won't somebody think of the children?

Using the phrase 'future generations' leads us to associate the future with children. The anthropologist Miller has looked at the intergenerational relationships managed through gift-giving in his account of shopping in North London. He identifies thrift as an unquestionable virtue in his respondents, regardless of whether their budgets were restricted or not. He suggests that this desire for thrift is associated with intergenerational devotion – the desire to leave wealth for our children. He links this to a phenomenon he refers to as 'the cult of the infant', an aspect of contemporary Western society where children have replaced adult males as the devotional focus of the household (Miller 2013, 123–125).

This devotion, in sacralising children, also has the effect of constraining them as I have argued elsewhere (May 2013, 717). Sacred beings are not fully human; they have a responsibility to embody our better nature. Devotion particularly constrains their relationship with material culture. Sacred children are less and less involved in production and disposal, while their acquisition of objects is endlessly scrutinised. This constraint is further tightened by the 'future generations' formulation. If we believe that 'children are the future' this undermines the importance of their lives and their agency today.

The Queer Theorist Lee Edelman has argued that the child who is figured as the future in this way is nothing to do with the real cared-for children that will carry our care into the future in Adam and Groves' lived futures. The child who is present in this discourse:

> has come to embody for us the Telos of the social order and come to be seen as the one for whom that order is held in perpetual trust ... In its coercive universalization, however, the image of the Child, not to be confused with the lived experiences of any historical children, serves

to regulate political discourse – to prescribe what will *count* as political discourse.

(Edelman 2004, 11)

The 'future generations' formulation calls on the 'our children's children' trope. What of the future generations who are the recipients of our bounty? They are dependent on us as our children and are not adults with equal agency. They are endangered; our carelessness with their inheritance will leave them impoverished. They can neither produce their own sense of place and self nor use fragments in the way that we have. They must be given our past so that they can have a future. But these future generations will grow up just as we have. The future is not the domain of children needing our care, but of independent agents with their own concerns and competencies.

Gift or sacrifice?

If heritage is a gift, what do we expect the people of the future to give us in return? Of course, the concept of legacy sidesteps the question, but the formulation that von Droste zu Hülshoff used above was not legacy but gift. I believe that what we ask for from future generations is *forgiveness*. The rise of futurist rhetoric as identified by Spennemann is also associated with a rise in the practice of apologising to the future for mistakes we have made, especially for the destruction of ecosystems, extinctions, and climate change (Figure 3.2). This trend is trackable in the increase in the use of the phrase 'future generations', which has risen steadily since the 1960s and is exemplified in the spoken-word

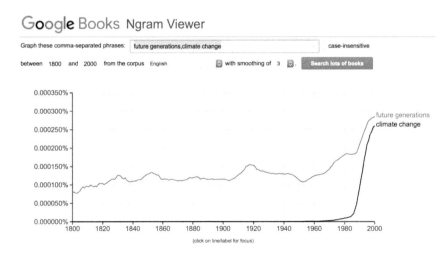

FIGURE 3.2   Just as with the term 'heritage', the use of the phrase 'future generations' rises in the same time frame as the more dramatic rise in the phrase 'climate change' (Michel et al. 2011; http://books.google.com/ngrams).

piece 'Dear Future Generations: Sorry' (Prince Ea n.d). In this widely shared video, the artist enumerates our failures and apologises for the subsequent losses that future generations have suffered. With phrases like 'You probably know it as the Amazon Desert', he describes an impoverished future. Of course, the real audience for the piece is the present day; he hopes to change behaviour, not just apologise for it. He invokes the future as judge, but it is a powerless and imperilled judge.

Of course, if we return to Miller's notion of the cult of the infant, we remember that children are placeholders of the divine. Gifts to the gods are neither gifts nor legacies, but sacrifices. How would it be to consider heritage as a sacrifice to future generations? This removes the need for us to gain benefit from it; indeed, the less benefit we have, the greater the sacrifice. This may underpin some of the resistance to the economic use of heritage sites. It also modifies the question of whether these sacrifices will be valuable to the people of the future. What the gods like about sacrifice is that we have forgone benefit, not that they will use it.

Nonetheless, heritage policymakers such as von Droste zu Hülshoff (see above), do not speak of sacrifice, they speak of gifts. This vision of heritage as a gift to the future bolsters a fantasy of intergenerational harmony at odds with our own experiences. This disconnect is so strong that we need to look at what the fantasy does as a social force in the present.

It's the thought that counts

If heritage is a gift to the future that we give with sincerity, then we need to consider how the gift will be received. Simply the fact that it comes from the past should not be assumed sufficient justification for its use in making a future. Gift exchange, especially unequal gift exchange, creates and maintains social obligations and hierarchies. The fact of receiving a gift is valuable beyond the value of the gift because it establishes and maintains relationships. In a useful exploration of the current understanding of the gift in anthropology, Skyes asks: 'Why should I receive a gift with the understanding that it is the thought that counts, except to acknowledge that I do not necessarily like or need what I receive in order to be glad for it' (Sykes 2004, 2). When we treat heritage as valuable because of its status as a gift, rather than for the pleasure it brings, we emphasise the social relations it enacts.

The gift of heritage is complex and assembles a particularly powerful set of relations. As Gradén has shown in the analysis of a gift of heritage materials from Sweden to Minneapolis, the gift contain[s] and enact[s] multiple performances that simultaneously create and recreate the idea of gift-giving in its role as an activity that binds people together' (Gradén 2010). It is the gifting that makes the materials' heritage, and gives them value in the new context. Swedish and North American communities are bound together.

The giving of gifts to children is part of their socialisation. Through receiving gifts we want them to learn about who cares for them and how, and how to be grateful. Especially for younger children, the gifts are also often educational in a broad sense, meant to create the conditions for the child to become the adult we want them to be. The inappropriate reactions of children to the overwhelming number of gifts some of them receive is the source of considerable moral panic. A recent study on materialism and wellbeing cites broken boxes and toys strewn over the floor at Christmas as signs that gifts have not been properly received (Nairn and Ipsos Mori 2011, 4). So through this socialisation, we learn how to receive gifts, even those we do not want. Does this include the gift of heritage?

China is a traditional gift for the establishment of a home, a wedding gift, and then an inheritance, sometimes both. China companies traded on this model for most of the 20th century, but changing domestic patterns undermined the value of china (Blaszczyk 2000). Combined with changing labour markets, this rendered high-status china companies such as Wedgwood, unsustainable in Britain. While aspects of design and marketing are maintained here, porcelain production is now based in China (Morgan 2009). Coincidentally, this was received as a loss of heritage by many in the UK, but a Chinese perspective sees it as a return of the historical dominance for China (Lin 2013).

But what does this mean for the status of china as a gift? I received my grandmother's china when she died, but I do not use it. I keep it safe, well packed, I would not consider getting rid of it. But I keep it as a social obligation to her, not because it brings me joy or even because it has happy memories of her. I have other objects that do those things, but the china is a gift, a legacy, an inheritance that I am responsible for. My care for the china validates my grandmother as having lived a good life. It is a fairly small requirement, but a larger gift may be more difficult to manage (Figure 3.3).

My father was a keen sailor and wooden boat owner (Figure 3.4). He sailed both the Atlantic and the Pacific and moved on retirement to a house where his boat could be docked at the end of his drive for much of the year. He loved the boat as much as the sailing. He was very proud of her and spent much of his free time and his free money repairing her. When he died, he left the boat jointly to his five children in hopes that we would enjoy her too. But none of us had free time or free money. A wooden boat requires constant care. The repairs and other costs mounted and soon her costs outweighed her value. Could we find someone else with more free time and free money to take her on? No. We loved the remembrance of our father contained in the boat, but we could not continue to care for her. She was broken up, and we each took a part to remember her (or was it my father?) by.

Both of these examples are things that were valuable within one life, and given to the next generation for the joy they could bring. But their main value was as heritage. We honoured them as gifts, as links to previous generations. While we did not love them in the same way our parents and grandparents did, we saw them as reminders of good lives. But not all heritage has that pleasant function. Heritage often preserves reminders of more complex pasts, even atrocities. When we give a gift like that, the burden may extend beyond the cost of

FIGURE 3.3 My grandmother's china in use at a family Christmas gathering. Holding on to the china bears witness to these events, her hospitality and care. We use our own plates at Christmas now.

FIGURE 3.4 My father's boat, *The Gay Goose*. He sailed her around the world, but we could not preserve his adventures by preserving the boat.

care. Of course, such reminders serve useful functions for us and may do for future generations. But when they come in the wrapper of heritage, we and they may feel an obligation to keep them no matter what they do.

A good example of this can been seen in the 'Rhodes must fall' campaigns at the University of Cape Town in South Africa and at Oxford in England. Cecil Rhodes gave a substantial amount of money to both universities and was honoured with statues in both places. In 2015 students and staff at the University of Cape Town drew attention to the way that the statue continued aspects of white supremacy and colonial thinking that had not been overturned with apartheid. They called for the removal of the statue as part of a programme of decolonisation of the university (Kros 2015). Inspired by their example, and recently reminded of the role that Rhodes played in imperialist narratives, a mirror movement in Oxford called for the removal of their statue. The main argument against the removal was that it was heritage, that to remove the statue was to erase history. 'A healthy culture does not cease to remember those with whom it has come to disagree. Rather, with the help of historians, it endlessly debates and revises its assessment of them' (Lemon 2016). According to those critical of the 'Rhodes must fall' campaigns, this endless debate clearly cannot include removing memorials to people we no longer admire.

It could be argued that, in providing a focus for decolonising thought, the statues serve a useful function beyond the intention of the original gift to the future. Certainly, neither the activists in South Africa nor those in Oxford are the future generations that Rhodes, or his sculptor, had in mind. But the response to the Oxford activism, that removing the statue is an attempt to whitewash the past, also shows how our gifts can be successful in holding social relations in place, forestalling critical appraisal.

Beyond cynicism

So far in this paper, I have argued that future generations hold an unreasonable burden in heritage discourse. In attempting to save the past for future generations we may be avoiding responsibilities to our own generation and creating further problems for those we paint as our benefactors. Earlier, I posited the work of future-gifting as a work of apology and atonement and suggested the possibility for moving beyond our current construction of *future generations*. It is tempting at this point to agree with Hocquenghem who writes in the same tradition as Edelman, discussed above:

> We do not intend a new politics, a better society, a brighter tomorrow, since all of these fantasies reproduce the past, through displacement in the form of the future. We choose, instead, not to choose the Child, as disciplinary image of the Imaginary past or as site of a projective identification with an always impossible future.
>
> *(Hocquenghem 1993, 138)*

Hocquenghem does not construct the removal of the child from future discourse as an act of social revolution, but as a reality-check, an act of reflection on the hubris of future-building. He calls on us to base our work on caring for those people and places we live with now.

Refusing to choose the child and refusing to create a gift for future generations neither requires nor allows a selfish or trivial approach to heritage. While the fantasies of future generations may be poorly examined, they are sincere sources of inspiration for many people trying to live a good life. They give moral structure to complex and worrying circumstances. As Adam and Groves (2011, 22) state, 'the continual reaching beyond what we are to explore what we might become is the dynamic that generates the narrative structure of our lives, giving them a kind of unity over time and, with it, overall ethical significance.' The present must project itself into the future for the sake of its own story-arc. Being curious and careful of the future and its people is enriching to us, but it requires that we perform acts of care in the present.

The anthropologist Robbins has recently laid out a challenge to study an anthropology of the good life (Robbins 2013). He asks us to focus our attention on how people understand and construct lives that they are proud of. Heritage future-making practice, broadly conceived, may be part of such a good life. While recognising, as Spennemann does, that the future can be an excuse for our relevance and that the future generations formulation can be corrosive, as I have argued here, that does not mean that we should dismiss heritage as future-making practice. Recognising that futures are multiple and complex supports these practices, rather than simply pulling the rug from under them.

Many pasts, many futures

I have argued here that the future should not be imagined as grateful recipient of the heritage that we preserve today. It is not just that people want different things from the future but that futures are created in the present just as pasts are. We have been properly concerned with the morality of our actions in the present in relation to how they may create different futures, but we have paid less attention to how future-making practice acts as a political force in the present. There are many reasons that people consider the future as an honourable beneficiary of our efforts. One of these is because transgenerational devotion functions as a focus for moral action. Caring for children is seen as more important than caring for other adults. Heritage envisioned as a gift to the future generations is a gift to children. We should remember that gifts create obligation, and transgenerational gifts can be received as burdens. This infantilisation of the future is partly a domestication tactic. Facing into the uncertainty of the future is less frightening if we focus on our need to care.

Heritage policy that seeks to preserve things for future generations is only one aspect of heritage future-making practice. The rhetoric itself may be used without serious consideration. It sounds good, and it captures a sense of care and longevity that motivates many people to engage with heritage. If we look beyond this rhetoric to the practices it draws from, we may find a richer, more useful sense of the future.

Acknowledgements

This paper was originally presented at the 2012 conference of the Association of Critical Heritage Studies. It was completed as part of my work for the AHRC-funded Heritage Futures project. Heritage Futures is funded by a UK Arts and Humanities Research Council (AHRC) "Care for the Future: Thinking Forward through the Past" Theme Large Grant (AH/M004376/1), awarded to Rodney Harrison (Principal Investigator), Caitlin DeSilvey, Cornelius Holtorf, Sharon Macdonald (Co-Investigators), Martha Fleming (Senior Researcher), Antony Lyons (Senior Creative Fellow), Nadia Bartolini, Sarah May, Jennie Morgan and Sefryn Penrose (Postdoctoral Researchers). It receives generous additional support from its host universities and partner organisations. The work has benefitted through conversations with all project members, but particularly with Sefryn Penrose and Cornelius Holtorf, both of whom commented on earlier drafts.

References

Adam, B. and Groves, C., 2007. *Future Matters: Action, Knowledge, Ethics*. Leiden & Boston: BRILL.

Adam, B. and Groves, C., 2011. Futures tended: Care and future-oriented responsibility. *Bulletin of Science, Technology & Society* 31(1), 17–27. doi:10.1177/0270467610391237.

Blaszczyk, R.L., 2000. *Imagining Consumers: Design and Innovation from Wedgwood to Corning*. Baltimore: JHU Press.

Daniels, I., 2009. The `social death' of unused gifts surplus and value in contemporary Japan. *Journal of Material Culture* 14(3), 385–408. doi:10.1177/1359183509106426.

Edelman, L., 2004. *No Future: Queer Theory and the Death Drive*. Durham: Duke University Press.

English Heritage, 2000. *Power of Place: The Future of the Historic Environment*. London: Her Majesty's Stationary Office.

Gradén, L., 2010. Performing a present from the: The Varmland heritage gift, materialized emotions and cultural connectivity. *Ethnologia Europaea* 40, 29–46.

Harrison, R., 2015. Beyond "Natural" and "cultural" heritage: Toward an ontological politics of heritage in the age of Anthropocene. *Heritage & Society* 8(1), 24–42. doi:10.1179/2159032X15Z.00000000036.

Historic England, 2015. *Facing the Future: Foresight and the Historic Environment*. London: Historic England.

Historic Environment Scotland, 2016. *For all Our Futures (Corporate Plan)*. Edinburgh: Historic Environment Scotland.

Hocquenghem, G., 1993. *Homosexual Desire*. Durham: Duke University Press.

Holtorf, C., 2015. Averting loss aversion in cultural heritage. *International Journal of Heritage Studies* 21(4), 405–421. doi:10.1080/13527258.2014.938766.

Holtorf, C. and Högberg, A., 2015. Contemporary heritage and the future. In: E. Waterton and S. Watson, eds. *The Palgrave Handbook of Contemporary Heritage Research.* New York: Palgrave; pp. 509–523.

Kros, C., 2015. Rhodes Must fall: Archives and counter-archives. *Critical Arts* 29(sup1), 150–165. doi:10.1080/02560046.2015.1102270.

Lemon, A., 2016. 'Rhodes Must Fall': The dangers of Re-writing history. *The Round Table* 105(2), 217–219. doi:10.1080/00358533.2016.1154669.

Lin, S., 2013. Fate of the cycle: The past and present of high-end porcelain brands. *The Science Education Article Collects* 9, 123.

May, S., 2013. The contemporary material culture of the cult of the infant: Constructing children as desiring subjects. In: P. Graves-Brown, R. Harrison and A. Piccini, eds. *The Oxford Handbook of the Archaeology of the Contemporary World.* Oxford: Oxford University Press; pp. 713–727.

Michel, J.B., Shen, Y.K., Aiden, A.P., Veres, A., Gray, M.K., Pickett, J.P., Hoiberg, D., Clancy, D., Norvig, P., Orwant, J. and Pinker, S., 2011. Quantitative analysis of culture using millions of digitized books. *Science* 331(6014), 176–182.

Miller, D., 2013. *A Theory of Shopping.* Hoboken: John Wiley & Sons.

Morgan, T., 2009. The sad legacy of Wedgwood. *The Independent.* http://www.inde pendent.co.uk/news/business/analysis-and-features/the-sad-legacy-of-wedgwood-1226638.html (accessed 21/9/16).

Nairn, A. and Ipsos, M., 2011. *Children's Well-Being in UK, Sweden and Spain: The Role of Inequality and Materialism.* York: UNICEF.

Prince, Ea. Dear future generations: Sorry - YouTube [WWW Document]. https://www. youtube.com/watch?v=eRLJscAlk1M (accessed 4/8/16).

Reicher, S., 2008. Making a past fit for the future: The political and ontological dimensions of historical continuity. In: F. Sani, ed. *Self Continuity: Individual and Collective Perspectives.* London: Psychology Press; pp. 145–174.

Robbins, J., 2013. Beyond the suffering subject: Toward an anthropology of the good. *Journal of the Royal Anthropological Institute* 19(3), 447–462. doi:10.1111/1467-9655.12044.

Sigaud, L., 2002. The vicissitudes of the Gift. *Social Anthropology* 10, 335–358. doi:10.1111/j.1469-8676.2002.tb00063.x.

Spennemann, D.H.R., 2007. Futurist rhetoric in us historic preservation: A review of current practice. *Int Rev on Public Marketing* 4, 91–99. doi:10.1007/BF03180757.

Sykes, K., 2004. *Arguing with Anthropology: An Introduction to Critical Theories of the Gift.* London: Routledge.

von Droste zu Hülshoff, B., 2006. A gift from the past to the future: Natural and cultural world heritage. *SIXTY Years of Science at UNESCO 1945–2005*, 389–400.

4

PERCEPTIONS OF THE FUTURE IN PRESERVATION STRATEGIES

(Or: why Eyssl von Eysselsberg's body is no longer taken across the lake)

Cornelius Holtorf and Anders Högberg

The very idea of preserving cultural heritage for future generations presupposes that this heritage will be accessible in the future. In this chapter, we argue that the long-term accessibility of heritage relies to a great extent on perceptions of the future that are articulated in specific strategies of preservation. The way we preserve something is influenced by the way we imagine the future – in other words, the future past depends on the present future.

All the examples we will be using to elaborate on this argument are connected with the village of Hallstatt in Austria's Salzkammergut region. Here, different perceptions of the future interact in a single locale and, through their concrete preservation strategies, result in divergent forms and degrees of long-term accessibility.

Our argument addresses three perceptions of the future: one that assumes ongoing continuity, one that assumes controllable transformation, and one that assumes an eventual break in continuity. At first sight, it might seem that the reliability of preservation strategies, and the consequent accessibility of heritage in the long term, should increase in line with the weakness of expectations that things will stay as they are and with the strength of expectations that things will change. Yet this, as our discussion shows, is not necessarily the case.

A quite different question would, of course, be why a particular piece of heritage should be preserved for the future at all, and what use it can or will have in the future – but that is not the topic of the present chapter and is discussed elsewhere in the present volume (see also Holtorf and Högberg 2014).

Continuity

We first present three examples from Hallstatt that illustrate how a continuity-oriented perception of the future can facilitate accessibility over several centuries.

Archaeological finds and analyses document the life and work of prehistoric people in the Hallstatt high valley from the Neolithic period onwards, with organized salt mining documented since the Middle Bronze Age. Near the mines is the famous Hallstatt cemetery, dating from the Early Iron Age, that gave rise to the well-established, archaeological term "Hallstatt period." In 1846, the mines inspector Johann Georg Ramsauer began the first systematic excavations of the large Iron Age cemetery, and others have continued excavating both there and in the salt mines ever since. The salt mine finds are most notable for the site's extraordinary preservation conditions that have enabled even wood, pelts, skin, tree bast, grass, wool, thread, excrements, and food scraps to survive for thousands of years. The cemetery is celebrated especially for the wealth of metal objects, jewellery, and ceramic vessels found there. Since 1960, a group of researchers from the prehistory department of the Natural History Museum in Vienna, currently led by Anton Kern and Hans Reschreiter, has been working in Hallstatt (see Kern et al. 2008). The archaeological research and its findings are presented to the general public at the excavation sites up in the high valley and the Hallstatt Museum in the village below.

Whereas archaeological finds and their documentation are preserved for future generations of researchers in scholarly collections and archives, safeguarding published archaeological research for the future in academic publications is the responsibility of research libraries. Scholarship is a cumulative endeavour: every generation of researchers builds upon the findings of the foregoing generation and picks up where it left off – usually from a critical perspective and not necessarily implying an acceptance of earlier results. This unbroken chain depends on the accessibility of previous work. In archaeology, even today it is still perfectly normal to cite relevant publications from as far back as the 19th century. The accessibility of scholarly information in this form can endure for as long as there are research libraries that preserve academic publications and make them available. The ascendancy of the printed book, then the expansion of universities and university libraries, contributed to what we may certainly regard as a continuity in the preservation and application of scholarship in archaeological publications from at least the early 19th century, though the oldest libraries go back much further than that. Today, all the indications are (and this accords with the currently prevailing perception of the future among academic researchers) that the proud tradition of scholarly endeavour will continue unbroken for at least several more centuries.

Our second example is to be found in the Chapel of St Michael, next to the Catholic church in Hallstatt village. Under the chapel is a crypt with an ossuary that has existed since the 12th century. It holds around 1,200 skulls and the long bones belonging to them (Figure 4.1). According to information available locally, a special religious tradition has survived here since 1720, and remains vibrant today even if it is no longer practised to any real extent: the ossuary contains 610 skulls, arranged by family, that are painted with their former owners' names and dates of death and with various floral wreaths, crucifixes, and so on. This local tradition appears to

FIGURE 4.1 Painted skulls carrying historical information in the Hallstatt Ossuary.
Photograph: Cornelius Holtorf 2013. Reproduced by permission of Pfarre
Hallstatt.

have sprung from the paucity of space in the neighbouring graveyard, which made
it necessary to reopen graves after just 10–15 years and accommodate the majority
of each skeleton elsewhere. The skulls were cleaned, bleached in the sun, and then
painted by artists, in most cases the sextons. For a long time, this religious tradition
was practised in Hallstatt on such a large scale that today there are painted skulls
going back for many generations of some local families. Although a steep rise in
the number of cremations has now resolved the shortage of space in the graveyard,
in principle the deceased can still find their eternal peace in the ossuary, if this is
requested in their last will and testament. The most recent skull is that of a woman
who died in 1983. Her wish to be interred in the ossuary was fulfilled in 1995.

The Hallstatt Ossuary, then, passes down the names and death dates of 610
inhabitants. The accessibility of that information across a period of up to three
centuries depends wholly on the lasting preservation of the skulls that are kept in
the crypt. The ossuary has regular opening times, and for a small fee, any visitor can step in and study the skulls and other bones close up. For as long as the
crypt continues to exist in this form and the skulls are preserved, the information painted on them will survive. The growing secularization of society and
the fact that no more skulls appear to have been added to the ossuary since 1995
are reason to doubt the continuation of this tradition. Nevertheless, the ossuary

FIGURE 4.2   Preserving Hallstatt in Austria by copying in China. Photograph of the Austrian Hallstatt by Cornelius Holtorf 2013.

shows that a thriving faith in the continuity of preservation in the chapel crypt has already been able to preserve this tradition for up to 300 years.

A third example of preservation with a continuity-based perception of the future concerns the Chinese culture of copying as a preservation strategy. In summer 2012, the international press picked up the news that a copy of the centre of the Austrian village of Hallstatt (Figure 4.2) was being constructed in the southern Chinese province of Guangdong on an area of one square kilometre, complete with a lake, market square, fountain, and church (Bosker 2013, 47). The copy was built very fast, by the China Minmetals Corporation, as a luxury housing development in the 800,000-inhabitant county of Boluo. According to press reports, the mayor of Hallstatt, Alexander Scheutz, told journalists at its opening: "You can see right away: this is Hallstatt." Initial reactions in Hallstatt had been less enthusiastic, however:

> Around a year ago, when the Chinese plans became known in the original Hallstatt, there was uproar in the popular Austrian tourist destination. Feelings ran high among village officials and local residents over the fact that no one had informed them of the project. They watched suspiciously as Chinese guests wandered the narrow alleyways, capturing every picturesque detail with their cameras and sketchbooks.
>
> *(Focus 2012)*

Far from being an isolated case, the Chinese copy of Hallstatt exemplifies a whole series of copies of foreign architecture and urban planning in China (see Bosker 2013). From a European point of view, constructions of this kind are easy to dismiss as imitations or counterfeits – the exact reverse of strategies to preserve original cultural monuments. Instead of protecting the genuine Hallstatt and keeping it accessible, a commercial copy was produced at a different location and with a different purpose. Yet from a Chinese perspective, historicizing copies are not necessarily less valuable than historical originals. Instead, as Bianca Bosker points out (2013, chap. 2), in China the ability to produce a good copy for new ends has long been regarded as proof of both technical and cultural superiority. The practice has enabled certain cultural forms to survive for many centuries in China, and the culture of copying must consequently be regarded as a successful preservation strategy. Copies are not made in order to invent a past for oneself, but rather to give typically Chinese expression to the enduring power of one's own culture into the future. In this sense, the Chinese Hallstatt need not be regarded as a short-lived, cheap commercial imitation of the historical place in Austria; on the contrary, it could be seen as the manifestation of a long and still viable tradition of preservation. After all, as long as the likeness of Hallstatt seems attractive to Chinese people and continues to be actualized afresh on the same or a different site in the future, accessibility to this particular heritage is guaranteed.

Controllable transformation

We now turn from a perception of the future marked by continuity to one that is marked by an assumption of constant change, but change that seems possible to control by means of political agreements or other methods (for example through a will). Again using three examples from Hallstatt, we ask whether preservation strategies that assume controllable transformation in the future deliver more lasting accessibility of heritage than those that assume continuity and content themselves with preservation for a few centuries.

Since 1997, the cultural landscape of Hallstatt-Dachstein/Salzkammergut has been recognized by UNESCO as one of currently around one thousand World Heritage sites. The World Heritage Convention of 1972 arose from the belief "that parts of the cultural or natural heritage are of outstanding interest and therefore need to be preserved as part of the world heritage of mankind as a whole" (UNESCO 1972, preamble). In the convention's crucial Article 4, the signatories agree that they have a duty to ensure "the identification, protection, conservation, presentation and transmission to future generations of the cultural and natural heritage" on their territory (ibid., Art. 4). The World Heritage Convention is an attempt to assure, through international agreement and voluntary commitments by the now 193 signatory states, that the selected heritage sites are preserved far into the future and therefore, among other benefits, remain accessible. Here, the implied perception of the future is not one of a straightforward continuity. It is assumed instead that there will be change, but that such change will be amenable to political influence and that it will be possible to safeguard the world's cultural property through the efforts of cultural heritage preservation.

The continued existence of the World Heritage sites is not an end in itself; it is a means of affecting, and thus at least partially controlling, the future. In the case of Hallstatt, the region's designation as a World Heritage site serves not only to express an already existing preservation process but to promote a process of change that is regarded as politically desirable and necessary. As visitors are informed by a prominently placed panel greeting pedestrians above the village (Figure 4.3), the award of UNESCO World Heritage site status demonstrates "that this is an enduring region, not a fossil or a relic, and one where a process of change continues to take place."

UNESCO World Heritage status thus preserves heritage through political agreement and as a political resource. The aim is to have a hand in shaping the future – even if, or precisely because, that future is characterized by mutability. The irony is, of course, that this strategy itself is very vulnerable to political change, and can only survive for as long as it enjoys a political majority. UNESCO has no way of forcing signatory states to comply with the World Heritage Convention. It is also easy for a state to leave the convention and to seriously erode the role of cultural heritage preservation through its own cultural policies; no more than a national political majority in the relevant forums

FIGURE 4.3 Information board, World Heritage site, Hallstatt. Photograph: Cornelius Holtorf 2013.

is required. The convention has now been in place for almost five decades, and will most probably continue to exist for at least a few more.

Closely related to this preservation strategy, with similar motivations and fundamentally the same problems of permanence, is the 1954 Hague Convention for the Protection of Cultural Property in the Event of Armed Conflict. Designating important cultural property with the familiar blue-and-white shield symbol, this international treaty aims to protect it from destruction, damage, theft, looting, and other forms of unlawful appropriation during a war or armed conflict. The Lutheran church in Hallstatt village is one such protected cultural site; another is the Rudolfsturm castle in the high valley. A second protocol to the Hague Convention, which came into effect in 1999, has made it possible to prosecute certain violations, but membership of the convention is not compulsory. At present, only 64 states have acceded to the convention and its two protocols.

A second and very different attempt of long-term preservation of heritage in a future considered mutable, yet at least partially controllable, is driven not by a political process but by a religious legacy. When the rich and powerful salt mine administrator Christoph Eyssl von Eysselsberg died in 1668, he was laid to rest in a chapel endowed especially for this purpose, below Hallstatt's Catholic parish church (Figure 4.4). To ensure that his memory remained alive far into the future, Eyssl von Eysselsberg's last will and testament laid down a ritual that was to be carried out every 50 years on the anniversary of his death. On that day, his

FIGURE 4.4   The grave of Eyssl von Eysselsberg (†1668) below Hallstatt's Catholic parish church. Photograph: Cornelius Holtorf 2013.

coffin was to be retrieved from the crypt, carried once around the church, and then taken by boat across Lake Hallstatt to his former property, Grub Castle, and back. According to information on the internet, this ritual was indeed observed until the middle of the 19th century, that is, up to four times. If this is true, such longevity must certainly be attributed in part to the religious context, which as we know has conserved a large number of traditions and rituals in the past. It may also be due to the commemorative power of ritual performances (Connerton 1989). Today, the salt mine official's curious legacy is not quite forgotten, but it is no longer practised. The tomb as such survives, and it preserves Christoph Eyssl von Eysselsberg's name and mortal remains.

This case reflects a perception of the future based on continuity, which relies primarily on the continued existence of the associated chapel. But Eyssl von Eysselsberg did not place all his trust in that preservation strategy. He also determined that every two generations, a particular and rather complicated ritual be performed in order to keep his memory alive even in times of change. As it turns out, the tomb is still preserved at its original site, whereas the ritual has long since ceased to be performed. Ultimately, therefore, the efficacy of the will endured for a shorter time than that of the chapel and its crypt. Over the decades and centuries, even in a religious context, and even though requested in a will, a ritual that is no longer really understood will hardly be considered binding. After a few generations, the testament was no longer respected, and the ritual was abandoned.

Broken continuity

Our last case exemplifies a third perception of the future, one that assumes neither continuity nor controllable transformation, but uncontrollable change and a break in continuity. When the future is imagined in this way, the inference is that eventually – whether sooner or later and for whatever reason – preservation will fail and accessibility of heritage will have to be re-established.

For some years now, the Austrian ceramicist Martin Kunze has been planning to store a "Memory of Mankind" in the Hallstatt salt mines (Lyons and Holtorf 2020).[1] He asserts: "In a few decades, every trace of our digital photos, emails and blogs will have faded and in a few centuries nobody will any longer know who we were or how we lived and what we lived for" (Kunze 2013). The Memory of Mankind project thus preserves a record of our time from possible oblivion caused by the consequences of ecological, economic, or other processes leading to the loss of electronic data. Based on this logic, the Memory of Mankind aims to establish an analogue archive, in a cavern of the former Hallstatt salt mine, where anyone can have information printed onto stoneware ceramic tablets, particularly durable ceramic data carriers, to be stored for one million years (Figure 4.5). Kunze has managed to win support for his project from several prestigious institutions, including the Natural History Museum and the Art History Museum in Vienna and the University of Vienna, which have immortalized

FIGURE 4.5   Martin Kunze being filmed while working with the *Memory of Mankind* inside the Hallstatt salt mine. Photograph: Cornelius Holtorf 2013.

images and descriptions of parts of their collections on the ceramic tablets. He has also been discussing with the nuclear waste industry the possibility of storing on such tablets information about nuclear waste repositories in order to keep it accessible in the future even when continuity should get lost.

The accessibility of the Memory of Mankind in the distant future is assured on the one hand by the durability and flexibility of the salt seams, which over the years will gradually seal up the ceramic plates completely and safely, and on the other hand by a large number of small ceramic plaques, or tokens, that describe the exact location of the storage vault (Figure 4.6). These plaques will be distributed across the world's surface. Because the locator tokens require the future user to correctly decipher the geographical information they contain, then to find and excavate the archives in a salt mountain cavern sealed up over the centuries, a future society will only be able to access the preserved information if it is capable of understanding that information. Certainly, it is an open question how future generations of humans will be able to judge whether the time has come to open the archives – for the holdings cannot easily be returned to their original slumber. Opening the Memory of Mankind too soon will jeopardize precisely the permanence of the information it holds since it will not necessarily be possible to close the archives again securely and effectively after viewing.

FIGURE 4.6 A double-sided token indicates the location of the Memory of Mankind with an accuracy of some ten metres. Everyone who deposits a ceramic tablet will receive one such token measuring 6.5 cm in diameter. Photograph: Cornelius Holtorf 2013.

Unlike the previous examples, in this case, the idea is not to keep heritage accessible continuously, but rather to store it safely for a later point in time. In this sense, Kunze's vision of the future may seem somewhat dystopian: the Memory of Mankind is intended to sustain information, if necessary, through an extreme societal crisis, even for a situation where humanity has been reduced to a few thousand individuals, and much important knowledge has been lost. Kunze refers to a "back-up" of selected present-day information, placed for safekeeping in the salt mine so that it can be restored in the distant future, even after a break in continuity, with the help of the locator tokens. Whether this will be successful and the information will then really be both accessible and adequately intelligible – all this is uncertain but perfectly possible, even if the moment does not come for some hundreds of thousands of years. In this example, the planning period is extremely long. But the longer the timeframe, the more likely it becomes that continuity will indeed break down.

Discussion

Through the case of Hallstatt, our examples have shown how several different perceptions of the future can converge at a single location and result in very different strategies for the preservation of heritage (Table 4.1). The examples of research libraries, the ossuary, and the Chinese copy of Hallstatt show that

TABLE 4.1 Preservation strategies, perceptions of the future, and long-term accessibility of heritage for various examples in Hallstatt

	Preservation strategy	Perception of the future	Long-term accessibility	Time in years
Archaeological debate	Scholarly publications in libraries	**Continuity**	As long as libraries exist	200+, continuing
Ossuary	Display of painted skulls	**Continuity**	As long as the ossuary exists	300, continuing
Copy of Hallstatt in China	Copying	**Continuity**	As long as copies are made	100s, continuing
World Heritage, Hague Convention	Political resolution, heritage protection	**Controllable transformation**	As long as political will continues	40+, continuing
Tomb in chapel	Ritual laid down in testament	**Controllable transformation**	As long as testament is respected	max. 200, finished
Memory of Mankind	Storage in salt mine, locator tablets	**Broken continuity**	Uncertain; after the rupture	1,000,000+, planned

living traditions based on an assumption of social and cultural continuity may well survive for several centuries. Information embedded in appropriate, living practices can remain accessible for at least several generations. If such continuity is not assumed, as in the case of the Memory of Mankind, and a kind of dormant tradition is created in a secure location to be reawakened at some future time, in principle, the heritage can be expected to remain accessible for many millennia, even after a civilizational disaster. In this case, long-term accessibility is assured precisely by the absence of short-term accessibility.

An interesting conclusion to be drawn from our deliberations is that a perfectly realistic perception of the future – one assuming that the future can be controlled or influenced at least to a certain extent – generates perhaps the least favourable prospects for durable access to heritage. The examples of World Heritage protection, the Hague Convention, and wills show that the general acceptance of particular resolutions regarding the future will not necessarily remain in place for long. Indeed, an acceptance lasting as long as two centuries appears quite unusual.

Of course, these findings cannot be generalized without reservations. Certain information conserved in apparently safely stored time capsules will, for various reasons, probably not be transmitted into the distant future. Not all living traditions survive for centuries without any essential change. In turn, there may be political decisions and testamentary dispositions that do endure for longer than two centuries. In the light of our limited discussion of the Hallstatt examples, at any rate, the preservation strategies with the best chance of ensuring the long-term accessibility of heritage appear to be those that either assumes the continuity of a lively and proud tradition – even a simple one (such as the ossuary) – or predict a radical breach in continuity and therefore archive information very inaccessibly (in this case inside a mountain). While the former strategies may be sustained over a few centuries, the latter ones may still be functioning many millennia later, even if they are unknown or unintelligible. It would be interesting to examine the robustness of these conclusions further through more extensive analyses and different case studies.

In this chapter, we have shown the intimate connection of strategies for the long-term preservation of heritage with particular perceptions of the future. What is pivotal for the choice of a preservation strategy is not the particular processes or events of the *past* that are to be remembered, nor the importance that we attach to those memories *today*, but rather the particular notion of the *future* that we hold in the present. This insight underlines the hitherto neglected significance of perceptions of the future for cultural heritage preservation.

This chapter has identified three categories of perceptions of the future that impact crucially on the long-term accessibility of heritage. A perception of the future shaped by the expectation of continuity entails preservation strategies that mesh directly with living traditions of the present and may well endure for several centuries. If, in contrast, the assumption is that continuity will break down sooner or later, there will be a preference for preservation strategies that sustain heritage less accessibly, but more securely and for much longer periods of time. Between these two poles lie preservation strategies that assume controllable change in the future and rely on political resolutions, wills, or other forms of agreements. Although the level of determination and commitment to preservation is high in these cases, the outcomes are not necessarily reliable. Clearly, there is no one-size-fits-all response to the question of which preservation strategy or combination of strategies will work best for which particular situation. Our most important concern in this chapter has been to encourage closer attention to the perception of the future that so decisively shapes every preservation strategy.

Acknowledgements

An earlier version of this text was originally published as part of a chapter entitled "Zukunftsbilder in Erhaltungsstrategien" in the volume *Diachrone Zugänglichkeit als Prozess. Kulturelle Überlieferung in systematischer Sicht*, edited by M. Hollmann and A. Schüller-Zwierlein (Berlin etc., de Gruyter 2014). The current text is based on a translation into English by Kate Sturge. For assistance during a visit in Hallstatt and advice on an earlier draft we are obliged to Hans Reschreiter, Kerstin Kowarik, and Martin Kunze.

Note

1 See https://www.memory-of-mankind.com

References

Bosker, B., 2013. *Original Copies. Architectural Mimicry in Contemporary China*. Honolulu: University of Hawai'i Press.
Connerton, P., 1989. *How Societies Remember*. Cambridge: Cambridge University Press.
Focus, 2012. Kopie mit kleinen Fehlern: Hallstatt in China. *Online Focus*, 3. Juni 2012. http://www.focus.de/panorama/welt/tourismus-kopie-mit-kleinen-fehlern-hallstatt-in-china_ aid_761918.html (accessed 5 May 17).
Holtorf, C. and Högberg, A., 2014. Communicating with Future Generations: What Are the Benefits of Preserving for Future Generations? Nuclear Power and Beyond. *European Journal of Post-Classical Archaeologies* 4, 315–330.
Kern, A. et al. (eds.)., 2008. *Salz-Reich. 7000 Jahre Hallstatt*. Veröffentlichungen der Prähistorischen Abteilung, 2. Wien: Naturhistorisches Museum.
Kunze, M., 2013. Memory of Mankind: A Breath of Immortality for Everybody. Information Leaflet Distributed in 2013.
Lyons, A. and Holtorf, C., 2020. The one-million-year time capsule. In: R. Harrison, C. DeSilvey, C. Holtorf, S. Macdonald, N. Bartolini, E. Breithoff, H. Fredheim, A. Lyons, S. May, J. Morgan and S. Penrose, *Heritage Futures. Comparative Approaches to Natural and Cultural Heritage Practices*. London: UCL Press, pp. 325–335.
UNESCO, 1972. Convention Concerning the Protection of the World Cultural and Natural Heritage. http://whc.unesco.org/en/conventiontext/ (accessed 5 May 17).

5

THE FUTURE AND MANAGEMENT OF ICH IN CHINA FROM A LEGAL PERSPECTIVE

Luo Li

Background

The film *The Song of the Phoenix* was released in China in May 2016. It shows the current situation in which Chinese traditional music is receiving less appreciation and recognition in modern society because it seems to no longer fit modern lifestyles and values. Although two generations of folk artists have kept their faith in passing on such a tradition, its survival depends on government relief, which is a huge four-tier management system for intangible cultural heritage (ICH) called the representative ICH work and representative inheritor system. Such a system was established through a series of administrative regulations and the law of the People's Republic of China on Intangible Cultural Heritage (simplified as ICH Law) in 2011. It was the first legislation on ICH protection from the perspective of public law. This film shows the reality that strict adherence to tradition is difficult to maintain in modern society, although the Chinese government's four-tier management system could artificially help to maintain such "adherence".

The truth is that human beings never stopped using wisdom in developing their culture, values and spirits to deepen their understanding of themselves and strengthen their self-recognition, though some of that wisdom might be wrong. Cultural heritage refers to a historical tradition that highlights the good parts of culture rather than the bad (Kang, 2006). But how to determine whether a culture is bad or not was an issue in China. During the Cultural Revolution, all "past" culture, whether tangible or intangible cultural heritage, folk beliefs, customs or traditions, faced destruction because it fell into the "Four Olds"[1] defined by the ultra-left trend of thought, and thereby should be abandoned. At that time, Buddhist music and Taoist music was equivalent to cultural rubbish without meaning and value, so it faced destruction. It is perhaps worth paying attention to such identification of a culture through a perspective of ideology and political views. This is because to do so would be an unpredictable disaster for any culture. A good culture may refer to a culture "with typical significance and value for history, arts, ethnology, folklore, sociology, anthropology, linguistics and literature" (Interim Measures for Evaluation of National Intangible Cultural Heritage Representative Work, 2005). This is communally recognised in Chinese academia (Wu, 2013, p. 172). Contemporary values and modern scientific knowledge, according to the law, play the main role in determining bad or good ICH and thereby determines the spirit that the "current we" expect to transmit to the "future us". Therefore, the ICH, born due to humanity's limited understanding of the world in that historical stage, conflicting with such modern values and knowledge, is not suitable for use in today's social life (Liao, 2008). For instance, some traditional Chinese customs, such as the foot-binding[2] and brazier jumping,[3] refer to typical gender discrimination (to women) from a perspective of contemporary values recognised by laws. Keeping such customs "alive" results in backwardness to our society because it breaches our common recognised values that developed following social progress. It also breaches laws structured by such values, such as the Convention on the Elimination of all Forms of Discrimination Against Women (1979) made by the United Nations and the White Paper on Gender Equality and Women's Development in China made by the State Council in China (White Paper: Gender Equality and Women's Development in China, 2015). Therefore, such ICH may be preserved through documentation and digital recordings as they are valuable for research purposes, but a modern Chinese person would not believe that those who deny foot-binding are committing a serious breach of tradition and inheritance. No Chinese person believes that such folk customs should be transmitted and inherited in future. In fact, the change in value of considering what was once thought to be a legitimate folk custom in the past to be a "bad" one today is typical evidence of a development, a change or a creative understanding of the culture.

This paper discusses different notions of the "future" and their influence on Chinese ICH management and development through a series of laws and regulations. In particular, this paper traces the changes in understanding ICH from something to be inherited largely without change and thus remain stable in the future to something to be alive and continuously re-adapted to a society changing over time. Such a living heritage is, however, problematic to the extent that it can be misappropriated, e.g. in the form of commodification. The paper concludes with an outlook on the significance of ICH for a younger generation of Chinese people that arguably are the future.

Understanding intangible cultural heritage

The term "intangible cultural heritage" was first used by the United Nations Educational, Scientific and Cultural Organisation (UNESCO) in the Convention for the Safeguarding of the Intangible Cultural Heritage (2003). Before this term was formally entered into official Chinese documents, the terms "*minzu minjian chuantong wenhua*" (traditionally ethnic and folk culture) or "*minzu minjian wenhua*" (ethnic and folk culture) were commonly used by Chinese officials and in the civil society to point to ICH (Regulations on the Protection of Traditional Ethnic and Folk Culture of the Province of Yunnan, 2000; Regulations on the Protection of Ethnic and Folk Culture of the Province of Guizhou, 2002). The ICH law in 2011 officially replaced the above terms with the term "ICH". The definition of the term "ICH" in Chinese ICH law is similar to that made by UNESCO, which is to define ICH as:

> various traditional cultural manifestations which are handed down by the people of all ethnicities from generation to generation and regarded as a constituent part of their cultural heritage, and physical objects and premises related to the traditional cultural manifestations, including: (1) Traditional oral literature and the language as a carrier thereof; (2) Traditional fine arts, calligraphy, music, dance, drama, folk art and acrobatics; (3) Traditional artistry, medicine and calendar; (4) Traditional rituals, festivals and other folk customs; (5) Traditional sports and entertainment; and (6) Other intangible cultural heritage.
>
> *(Law of the People's Republic of China on Intangible Cultural Heritage, 2011, art. 2)*

It is evident from the above definitions that ICH has two unique characteristics: the first is that it is "living heritage". ICH is an intellectual product branding certain community's identity and its unique spirit, which not only embraces literature and the arts but also includes lifestyles, value systems, traditions and beliefs. It can be said that ICH means life. ICH is an attitude of a certain community in response to different phenomena in its life (Duan and Xu, 2016, p. 175). During such a response, that literature and arts, lifestyles, value systems, traditions and beliefs are transmitted from generation to generation. However, no response remains unchanged because of changes in the external environment, so no kind of inheritance remains completely the same (Zhen, 2014, p. 64). It always absorbs change and creation from its later generations. ICH's inheritance is a "living" process that must incorporate a person's daily life, that embraces both succession and innovation. The second characteristic is ICH's inheritance and development that relies on the participation of thousands of people in a certain community or ethnic group. Its inheritance and development is the group's communal behaviour, with an element of collectivity. Those participating members of that community or ethnic group are all creators and inheritors of their ICH.

Changing futures of ICH: from stability to change

In the 20th century, the management model of ICH taken by the Chinese government was to maintain a stable inheritance. The Regulations on Protection of Traditional Arts and Crafts (1997) treats traditional arts and crafts, as part of ICH, as cultural relics for the purpose of protection. Inheritance of ICH stays at the level of "tangible transmission" because the meaning of the word "future" links only with maintaining skills and goods for future generations' appreciation. A narrow understating of the "future" results in too much attention to the formal protection of ICH, e.g. inheriting skills with which to craft rather than paying attention to the substantive nature of ICH, e.g. transmission of cultural identity, beliefs and faith.

Since UNESCO awarded the Chinese Kunqu Opera the Masterpieces of the Oral and Intangible Heritage of Humanity title in 2001 (Kun Qu Opera, 2008), Chinese ICH protection and management has gone through a process of change from fixed protection to living heritage. This is the result of changes in the way ICH is understood in relation to its "future".

Stability or change

There was fierce debate in Chinese academia before and after the four-tier management system was adopted. Those people who emphasised "preserving inheritance" are called conservatives, (Ma, 2010;Zhao, 2015) whereas those who encourage commercialisation of ICH are called radicals (Wang and Liao, 2008, pp. 107–112). For example, a representative of the radicals, Mr Qianbin Li, curator of the Guizhou Provincial Museum, said commercialisation is the sole way to save and protect ICH[4] (Save Folk Culture through Utilisation of Commercialisation, 2007). Such an opinion – treating ICH as a pure resource to target economic benefits – has encountered strong opposition from the conservatives. The conservatives' opinion dominated the early stages of ICH protection in China and largely influenced Chinese legislation. The early administration regulations (Measures for the Protection of World Cultural Heritage, 2006; Interim Measures for the Protection and Administration of National Intangible Cultural Heritage, 2006) emphasised "authenticity", "integrity" and "inheritance" in relation to the way in which ICH should be managed for the future. The literal meaning of these three words indicates "no change" and "stability". But the question is, what should remain stable and without change? Conservatives have a preference for maintaining all relevant ICH the same, including traditional lifestyles, traditional production methods, traditional core values and culture, because they believe that only through this way can ICH maintain its authenticity, integrity and inheritance. Conservatives understand the viability of ICH as maintaining its authenticity and nature "in the raw". They even believe that making ICH into a tangible heritage is the best way to maintain such authenticity, integrity and inheritance. This resulted in administrative regulations announced that emphasised "salvaging first and protection priority": on the one hand, translating ICH into a tangible heritage, such as collections and records, through either digital technology or traditional recording approach and on the other hand, ensuring a stable environment in which ICH can survive through the construction of an ecological reserve or eco-museum so as to safeguard the viability of the ICH.

However, such protection requires large financial support from governments. More importantly, such protection is likely to require, to use one analogy, a continuous blood transfusion while never developing one's self-recovery system. This is because ICH could only survive in an ecological reserve and eco-museum, like tropical plants living in a greenhouse, outside of modern society. As discussed before, ICH is alive. Its inheritance relies on the participation of its community members in response to nature, society and the environment. Where there is a change in nature, society or the environment, there is an interactive response to that change. At the same time, those spiritual and cultural beliefs, traditions and faiths are inherited during such an interactive response. Such an interactive response is the primary motivation for ICH to be passed on and developed. Without maintaining this interactive response status, ICH is a vegetative state unable to be "alive" without outside support. The conservatives' opinions reflect a worry or even a fear for the future that traditional Chinese culture and values may be completely destroyed by this cultural risk coming from modern civilisation. Such fear is combined with the modern Chinese values of "honesty", "wisdom" and "kindness", the essence of the traditionally humanistic spirit when conservatives realise that humanity's instinctive reactions and brutish nature are not noticeably lessened following the development of economics and technology (Li, 2007, p. 128). However, this does not lead to the idea of returning such values to society when considering saving ICH but alternatively forms an opinion that to save ICH is to save its "raw" status. Therefore, those traditional lifestyles, modes of production, and other ICH manifestations, as long as they satisfy the concept of "rawness", should be fully maintained. There is a need to prevent any possible change to the use of ICH to save such "rawness". Obviously, ICH's internal meaning of "living" inheritance and its values to the whole of society are misunderstood. This accelerates a dilution of cultural awareness and cultural recognition for younger generations, with a continual cultural shock. The truth is younger generations are reluctant to inherit those "raw" cultures from their older generations. Thus, a lack of younger inheritors has become an urgent issue in today's China.

Besides, those older generations are, in fact, "forced" to maintain "raw" lifestyles for the purpose of maintaining authenticity, integrity and inheritance. They have no choice to choose their desired life in the area that they live. Therefore, the conservatives' opinions definitely ignore the community's right to choose their lifestyle and right to develop (Song, 2012, p. 1). A typical example is the following: in the past, workers who towed a big boat on the Yangzi River sang a folk song called "*chuanjiang haozi*". Its rhymes and slogan had the power to encourage workers to maintain high morale as well as help them to march in step. The song reflects an optimistic and positive spirit in a tough environment of the working class at the bottom of society. Such an optimistic and positive spirit is worthy of transmission as it teaches every generation to face all the challenges in their lives with a smile and a tolerant attitude. Following the invention of machines that replaced this labour, this folk song is naturally no longer sung.

It is absolutely unrealistic to maintain towing labour in current society for the purpose of so-called inheritance. The truth is the concept of an eco-museum and its protections does not originate from local residents' self-consciousness and passion, but a pure desire from officials and academics who do not belong to the local community (Du, 2011).

Conservatives' one-sided understanding of "alive" and "save for the future" encounters radical opposition. Radicals argue that the viability of ICH originates from its adaptability to a changing nature and environment, and they are concerned with ICH's "changeability" and "living" characteristics (Song, 2012). Nevertheless, their understanding mainly focuses on ICH's development and creation as over-commercialisation, which breaches UNESCO's aim of inheritance. Later, a neutral opinion was provided in China, which promotes so-called "productive protection". It was first mentioned by Mr Wenzhang Wang, the vice minister of culture, in 2006 (Wang, 2006, p. 22).

Productive protection

Productive protection means translating ICH, through such methods as production, distribution and sales, into productivity and goods that can have an economic impact and promote the development of relevant industries (Deng, 2016, p. 87). It seems to be a new and brave exploration on the road of saving ICH, that has a more realistic attitude. It treats ICH as a valuable cultural resource, using an economic ecosystem to achieve a positive interaction between ICH's protection in an economic society and its balanced development (Deng, 2016). This opinion realises that saving ICH is connected to issues in modern-day China and the main risks for future China. These are environmental pollution, cultural conflicts, employment and other social issues in the Chinese countryside. Such a viewpoint believes that productive protection of ICH could bring huge benefits to the future from the perspectives of the ecological environment, society, culture and arts. In 2011, ICH law was highly impacted by such a viewpoint, which emphasised a balanced goal of respecting ICH (Law of the People's Republic of China on Intangible Cultural Heritage, 2011, art. 5) as well as its rational utilisation (art. 38). However, ICH law does not provide a clear definition of the word "respect", and there is no further explanation for "rational". This results in the difficulty of distinguishing rational use from misappropriation, which I will discuss shortly.

In 2012, the Ministry of Culture released guidance in regard to strengthening the productive protection of ICH, which emphasised "living" inheritance; in particular, it refused to randomly change the traditional mode of production, traditional process of traditional arts and crafts, and core skills[5] (Ministry of Culture's Guidance on Strengthening Productive Protection of Intangible Cultural Heritage, 2012). In practice, however, many "productive protection" measures face such confusion that it turns out to be a trap in which traditional culture is detached, broken down and reproduced by misappropriation due to substantive commercialisation. An example is traditional regional operas. Some local governments try to connect ICH protection with tourism and business. In Taining, with the powerful support of the tourism industry, Meilin Opera is inherited through performances for tourism. A good economic return provides the financial support to attract talent, train talent and maintain this traditional opera. However, under the tourism industry, singers perform this opera in Mandarin in commercial performances so that non-regional tourists can understand it (Ma, 2008). The problem is this: traditional Chinese regional operas have a close relationship with dialect. Dialect, as part of a language, is closely linked to the special cultural identity of any nation or community in a particular region. A community's beliefs, faiths, traditions and even temper and personality could be completely shown and felt through dialect. Dialect is the soul of all regional operas, being born based on the dialect. Therefore, such a performance in Mandarin rather than the traditional regional dialect typically breaches the authenticity of the opera, distorts its expressions of an internal cultural meaning and spirit, separates its integrity from the local culture and tradition and therefore would result in its substantive disappearance. Therefore, the success of productive protection is doubted by academia with regards to its core purpose of protection (Ma, 2008).

The question of misappropriation

The term "misappropriation" means to appropriate something wrongly. The word "appropriation" means "to take something for one's own … Appropriation happens all the time as people borrow ideas from each other to create new forms of art and symbolic expressions of culturally meaningful concepts" (Salle, 2014). *Black's Law Dictionary* defines misappropriation as:

> the common-law tort of using the non-copyrightable information or ideas that an organization collects and disseminates for a profit to compete unfairly against that organization, or copying a work whose creator has not yet claimed or been granted exclusive rights in the work.
>
> *(Graner, 2004, p. 1019)*

In the context of ICH, appropriation happens when meaningful cultural expressions such as designs and styles are "copied by someone from a different culture and/or used for a different purpose than originally intended" (Salle, 2014). Misappropriation refers to any appropriation being "contrary to indigenous customary law, offensive and even harmful", (Salle, 2014) in particular, "when the appropriated form is spiritually significant or its intended use is contradicted or threatened" (Salle, 2014). A document made by the World Intellectual Property Organisation (WIPO) defines misappropriation as:

> (i) acquisition, appropriation or use of traditional knowledge in violation of the provisions of this Act, (ii) deriving benefits from acquisition,

appropriation or use of traditional knowledge where the person who acquires, appropriates or uses traditional knowledge is aware of, or could not have been unaware of, or is negligent to become aware of the fact that the traditional knowledge was acquired, appropriated or used by any unfair means and (iii) any commercial activity contrary to honest practices that results in unfair or inequitable benefits from traditional knowledge.

> *(Glossary of Key Terms Related to Intellectual Property*
> *and Genetic Resources, Traditional Knowledge and*
> *Traditional Cultural Expressions, 2016)*

Misappropriation is closely connected with commodification. In the ICH context, commodification means to transform those intangible expressions and knowledge into products for purely commercial purposes and then sell those transformed products on the market for profit. Acknowledging consumer taste and modern appreciation is the key to obtain a successful market during commodification. Therefore, a common opinion is that respect of the internal value of heritage, and its cultural spirit is abandoned due to commodification. Those inappropriate or offensive appropriations, through misuse and distortion, cause harmful feelings of losing one's heritage and control over one's culture, (Salle, 2014) followed by the disappearance of a diversified culture.

Legal boundaries to misappropriation

Although there are no laws defining the term "misappropriation" in China, it is not difficult to trace its meaning by analysing the relevant laws. In fact, the determination of what constitutes misappropriation in law indicates an interpretation of saving ICH for the future in the Chinese context.

An early statement made by the State Council in regard to ICH protection established China's work guidelines as "taking protection as priority, rescue as primacy, rational utilisation, and inheritance for development" (Opinions on Strengthening the Protection of Intangible Cultural Heritage, 2005, sec. II). It requires the correct treatment of the relationship between protection and utilisation, asks for adherence to the authenticity and integrity of ICH protection and prevents the misunderstanding, distortion or misuse of ICH. A concept of "rational utilization on the premise of effective protection" is promoted in this statement. ICH law follows such a concept in Article 5 that "[t]he form and content of the [ICH] shall be respected when using the [ICH]. The use … in a distorted or derogatory way is prohibited" (Law of the People's Republic of China on Intangible Cultural Heritage, 2011, art. 5). Article 37 says that

> [t]he State encourages and supports the leveraging of the special advantages of [ICH] resources and the reasonable utilization of the representative items of [ICH] to develop cultural products and cultural services with local

and ethnical features and market potential on the basis of effective protection of those items.

(Law of the People's Republic of China on Intangible Cultural Heritage, 2011)

It is evident that rational utilisation does not exclude commodification; in contrast, the Chinese government encourages the development of cultural products and cultural services transformed by ICH. From this point of view, ICH is recognised as a valuable cultural resource. However, a condition of "effective protection" tries to limit uses from disrespect, distortion and misuse that are connected with misappropriation. Rational utilisation and misappropriation are two sides of "use" that are distinguished by the condition of "effective protection". According to ICH law, effective protection can be understood as focusing on ICH's authenticity, integrity and inheritance (art. 4) of "strengthening the recognition of the culture of the Chinese nation, maintaining the unification of the country and the unity of the nation and promoting social harmony and sustainable development" (art. 4). In other words, any efforts to destroy authenticity, integrity and inheritance is connected to misappropriation.

Where public law sets out what constitutes misappropriation, Chinese private law gives a more detailed explanation of what misappropriation of ICH is. In 2014, the Copyright Administration in China announced its Draft Regulations on Copyright Protection of Folk Literary and Artistic Works (hereafter Draft Regulation) for public comments, after more than ten years of discussion about the utilisation of intellectual property (IP) tools to protect ICH at both international (Duffield, 2003; Janke, 2003; Tlhapi, 2007; Lewinski, 2008) and national levels (He, 2002; Guye, 2007; Zhang, 2007; Huang, 2008; Ni and Ou, 2012). The Draft Regulation is a resource for understanding what misappropriation is in the Chinese context. On the one hand, it confirms that the rights-holders of traditional cultural expressions (TCEs) are specific nations, ethnic groups or communities, (Draft Regulations on Copyright Protection of Folk Literary and Artistic Works, 2014, art. 5) whose rights include "acknowledgement; prevention of distortion or misrepresentation of these works; use of these works by way of reproduction, distribution, performances, adaptations and disseminations, etc." (art. 6). This actually indicates that if a non-rights-holder reproduces, distributes, performs, adapts or disseminates TCEs, then they infringe upon the rights-holder's rights and are misappropriating TCEs. On the other hand, the Draft Regulation requires that the utilisation of TCEs requires prior informed consent from and remuneration to the rights-holder (art. 8) except where the use of TCEs are open to the public in some exceptional situations. Exceptional situations include use for the purposes of the user's own personal study or research; use for the purposes of education or research; use for reporting events or introducing or commenting; use in libraries, archives, memorial halls, museums or art galleries for the purpose of recording or preservation; use by an organ of the State for the purpose of fulfilling its official duties; and other uses under the regulation by other laws (art. 14). However, a member of a specific nation, ethnic group or community may use TCEs without fulfilling the above requirement, where traditional or customary use is for the purpose of cultural transmission and inheritance (art. 8). The Draft Regulation also prevents the production, sale or dissemination of TCEs through counterfeiting (art. 18). Any use breaching the above rules falls into misappropriation because it would destroy the TCE's authenticity, integrity and inheritance and thereby breach the "purpose of encouraging TCEs' inheritance and development" (art. 1).

Into the future

The IP protection of ICH focuses on authorising legal rights to a community that holds and developed its ICH over time so as to prevent misappropriation issues. Its concept is to respect the community's wishes with regards to the self-determination of their culture. However, issues from the productive protection experiment, form a more cautious view regarding various uses of ICH, resulting in an expansion of misappropriation.

The Draft Regulation for TCEs requires that any use of TCEs needs authorisation from the copyright holder, except if communities engage in traditional or customary use for the purposes of cultural transmission and inheritance (art. 8). Here, a copyright holder is a certain ethnic group or community who holds TCEs in its history. Ethnic groups and communities are both abstract concepts, so it is not possible to manage IP rights in practice. Because Chinese ethnic groups and communities have no traditional committee since the Cultural Revolution, there is a problem choosing a suitable representative for ethnic groups or communities to manage such rights. The Draft Regulation sets a special authority appointed by the copyright administration department of the State Council to manage the ethnic groups' or communities' rights, including authorisation (art. 8). However, there is no further explanation about such a special authority. Nevertheless, it can be imagined that, with such an over-cautious attitude to ICH utilisation, the special authority appointed by the central government may be very sensitive to those uses referring to creation and development.

In fact, such a sensitive approach even extends to the community's customary and traditional uses. At an international level, traditional context is

> understood as the way of using an expression of folklore in its proper artistic framework according to continuous usage by the community. For instance, to use a ritual dance in its traditional context means to perform it in the actual framework of the rite.
>
> *(Model Provisions for National Laws on the Protection*
> *of Expressions of Folklore against Illicit Exploitation*
> *and other Forms of Prejudicial Action, 1982)*

Customary context refers to "the utilization of [TCEs] in accordance with the practices of everyday life of the community, such as, for instance, usual ways of selling copies of tangible [expressions of folklore] by local craftsmen" (Model

Provisions for National Laws on the Protection of Expressions of Folklore against Illicit Exploitation and other Forms of Prejudicial Action 1982, pt. III, para. 42). "Customary use" in South Pacific Model Law is defined as "the use of [TK] or expressions of culture in accordance with the customary laws and practices of the traditional owners" (Model Law for the Protection of Traditional Knowledge and Expressions of Culture, 2002, s. 4). The Draft Regulation gives an even more strict limitation to such uses. A requirement in Article 8 about the purposes of cultural transmission and inheritance (Draft Regulations on Copyright Protection of Folk Literary and Artistic Works, 2014, art. 8) may result in usual selling behaviour falling outside of customary use. This is because community members sell copies of tangible ICHs for the purpose of financial support to their family rather than any purpose of transmission and inheritance. The community's communal awareness and recognition of their culture are formed through a long-term communal response to the same nature, environment and history. Those traditional values and spirits are naturally inherited and strengthened through "eating", "wearing", "living" and "travelling", reflecting their attitude to their lives. These traditional/customary uses are not originally born from an intention of cultural transmission and inheritance. Obviously, this over-sensitive attitude has led to anxiety at both official and academic levels which uses the larger crime of misappropriation to prevent normal inheritance.

Such anxiety at both official level and academic level leads to negative feelings about ICH's development but a safer feeling if it remains unchanged. It ignores the voices from younger generations of communities seeking change and development in their culture. With the fast urbanisation progress in China, many remote areas are no longer isolated. Compared with their older parents, younger generations have more opportunities for education in a modern education system. They have a broader vision of cultural development from surfing the internet and communicating with anyone in the world through social media platforms, and they have even more inspiration and passion impacted by fast-developing technologies. However, modern civilisation cannot really separate younger generations from their unique cultural identity. They are still deeply influenced by their older generations since they are children. The biggest advantages of these younger generations are that they have inherited a kind of cultural spirit, faith and belief from their elders but at the same time, they bring their own understandings to such culture, and they have sufficient capacity to create and develop this culture, so as to make old traditions, new faiths and beliefs become new traditions, new faith and new beliefs, which results in a new cultural awareness and recognition. From this point of view, they are the future.

Conclusion

Culture is the spiritual result of human intellectual creation. Through a series of activities, including producing goods, inventing technologies and creating tangible goods and intellectual goods, Chinese people devote their values, ideals and understandings of "honesty", "wisdom" and "kindness" to those tangible and intellectual goods that reflect their life experiences (Li, 2007, p. 126). Through such activities, Chinese people change their nature as well as their self-understanding of their nature. These beliefs, faith, lifestyles and modes of production are inherited and developed during such aforesaid activities, in which values and spirits are internal essences, whereas lifestyles and modes of production are external manifestations. Therefore, saving ICH should never be restricted to following certain lifestyles or modes of production, but its values and cultural spirit should be transmitted. More importantly, it is necessary to recognise the importance of development and creation to the culture, in particular, where a social system on which a culture relies has fundamentally changed. Historically, Chinese civilisation is an agricultural civilisation. Traditional values, beliefs, faith, lifestyles and ways of thinking all originate from the mode of production of a farming society. They form a traditional Chinese value system that regulates Chinese people's behaviours and largely impacts on the traditional Chinese social system. ICH is attached to such a traditional value system and social system. When any new culture comes from outside, it is quickly absorbed by this powerful system of traditional culture and values under a stable social system. At the same time, traditional values and culture are always being re-constructed and continually developed through such cultural communication and integration. However, modern industrialisation has resulted in the overturning of this social system in China. Farming civilisation is replaced by industrialised civilisation. Industrial society brings with it a modern social system and modern values. In this case, such traditional agricultural modes of protection and lifestyle, together with a traditional value system, face difficulty in surviving in an industrial society. However, China's industrialisation process was completed through artificial promotion by outsiders' aggression rather than a natural social development process. Therefore, Chinese society and its people's acceptance of modern values and an industrialised civilisation happened in a semi-forced situation. Where such modern values were not rooted in Chinese society, ten years of the Cultural Revolution further destroyed the traditional value system and its culture. The past 30 years of development in China is a miracle to the world. However, the large progress in Chinese economics over the past 30 years has not resulted in a new established mainstream value system. This results in the excessive pursuit of material comforts. Whether a person is successful or not does not rely on kindness, justice, wisdom or loyalty being part of traditional values but is determined based on wealth only. Therefore, more Chinese people are missing tradition, and they believe that traditional humanistic spirit and values could cure these over-materialistic desires – an illness of modernisation – and return them to a harmonious society pursuing honesty, justice, love, respect and justice. Therefore, this intangible cultural heritage, embracing the traditional humanistic spirit and values, seems to be the best medicine. That is why China's passion for ICH protection and inheritance is far more positive than that of other countries. Nevertheless, pursuing a return of the humanistic spirit and values is not simply a reversion back to past lifestyles, modes of protection and skills. Rather, an over-cautious view of how to treat ICH creation and development is substantively destroying it because such a view breaks up the relationship between the inheritance of a culture and its development. Perhaps a good start is to re-build self-confidence in traditional culture and have faith in the wisdom of the next generation in developing such a culture.

Notes

1 "Four Olds" refers to old ideas, old culture, old customs and old habits. The ultra-left trend of thought believes that the Four Olds are connected to heavy feudalistic ideas and values and should not exist anymore in a communist country.
2 Foot-binding is a custom in Chinese history in which young girls are required to bind their feet painfully and tightly so as to prevent further growth. It results in women suffering disabilities. Foot-binding is done to garner male appreciation, which indicates a social value that males are higher in status than females.
3 Brazier jumping is part of a traditional Chinese marriage custom that requires the bride to jump a brazier so as to remove her evil spirit before entering the groom's home. Such a custom also indicates a typical discrimination of the female.
4 *Yong chanyehua yunzong qiangjiu minjian wenhua guibao.*
5 Wenhuabu guanyu jiaqiang feiwuzhi wenhua yichan shengchanxing baohu de zhidao yijian.

References

Convention for the Safeguarding of the Intangible Cultural Heritage, adopted on 17 October, 2003, entered into force 20 April 2006.
Convention on the Elimination of all Forms of Discrimination Against Women, adopted on 18 December, 1979, enter into force 3 September 1981.
Deng, J., 2016. Productive Experience of and Reflection on Intangible Cultural Heritage of Traditional Handicraft Category – Taking Zigong Colourful Lantern as an Example. *Journal of Sichuan University of Science and Engineering (Social Science Edition)* 31(1), 87.
Draft Regulations on Copyright Protection of Folk Literary and Artistic Works 2014. Available at: http://www.ncac.gov.cn/chinacopyright/contents/483/225066.html (Accessed 5 November 2019).
Du, Z.J., 2011. Shuilai Baohu "Houshenyi Shiqi" De Wenhua Yichan (Who Protect Cultural Heritage at "Post Application of Representative Works of Intangible Cultural Heritage"). Zhongguo Minzu Bao (China Ethnic News), 4 November, 9.
Duan, J. and Xu, P.Q., 2016. Analysis on the Protection of Intangible Cultural Heritage in Zhangjiakou. *Learning Weekly* 16, 175.
Duffield, G., 2003. *Protection Traditional Knowledge and Folklore: A Review of Progress in Diplomacy and Policy Formulation* [Online]. Available at: http://www.ictsd.org/sites/default/files/research/2008/06/cs_dutfield.pdf (Accessed 31 July 2016).
Glossary of Key Terms Related to Intellectual Property and Genetic Resources, Traditional Knowledge and Traditional Cultural Expressions. WIPO/GRTKF/IC/31/INF/7, anx; 26. Available at: https://www.wipo.int/meetings/en/doc_details.jsp?doc_id=338437 (Accessed 1 November 2019).
Graner, A.B. (eds.)., 2004. *Black's Law Dictionary*, 8th edition. p. 1019. St Paul: Thomson West.

Guizhou Sheng Minzu Minjian Wenhua Baohu Tiaoli (Regulations on the Protection of Ethnic and Folk Culture of the Province of Guizhou) 2002, Art 2. Available at: http://www.ihchina. cn/show/feiyiweb/html/com.tjopen.define.pojo.feiyiwangzhan.FaGuiWenJian. faguiwenjianMore.html (Accessed 1 August 2016).

Guye, T.P., 2007. The Gap Between Indigenous Peoples' Demands and WIPO's Framework on Traditional Knowledge. Available at: http://www.wipo.int/export/sites/ www/tk/en/igc/ngo/ciel_gap.pdf (Accessed 31 July 2016).

He, Y.W., 2002. baohu minzu minjian wenhua de lifa moshi sisuo (Exploration of Legal Model for Protection of Folklore). In: C.S. Zheng, ed. *zhishi chanquan wencong (Paper Series on Intellectual Property) vol.8.* Beijing: China Fangzheng Press; 295–318.

Huang, Y.Y., 2008. *minjian wenxue yishu de falvbaohu (Legal Protection of Folklore).* Beijing: Intellectual Property Publishing House.

Interim Measures for Evaluation of National Intangible Cultural Heritage Representative Work 2005. Art 6. Available at: http://www.wipo.int/wipolex/en/details.jsp?id=14905 (Accessed 5 November 2019).

Interim Measures for the Protection and Administration of National Intangible Cultural Heritage 2006. Available at: http://www.lawinfochina.com/display.aspx?lib=law&id= 5940&CGid= (Accessed 28 October 2016).

Janke, T., 2003. *Minding Culture: Case Studies on Intellectual Property and Traditional Cultural Expressions* [Online]. Available at: http://www.wipo.int/edocs/pubdocs/en/tk/781/ wipo_pub_781.pdf (Accessed 31 July 2016).

Kang, B.C., 2006. *Intangible Cultural Heritage Protection Is a Strategy Issue.* Available at: http://www.nipso.cn/onews.asp?id=11812 (Accessed 9 August 2016).

Kun Qu Opera. 2008. Available at: http://www.unesco.org/culture/ich/en/RL/kun-qu-opera-00004 (Accessed 27 July 2016).

Law of the People's Republic of China on Intangible Cultural Heritage 2011. Available at: http:// www.wipo.int/wipolex/en/details.jsp?id=8939 (Accessed 5 November 2019).

Lewinski, S.V., (ed.)., 2008. *Indigenous Heritage and Intellectual Property: Genetic Resources, Traditional Knowledge and Folklore,* 2nd edition. Alphen aan den Rijn: Kluwer Law International.

Li, D.F., 2007. Legal Protection of the Human Resources of West China Area – Represented by the Legal Protection of Intangible Cultural Heritage. *Tribune of Political Science and Law (Journal of China University of Political Science and Law)* 4, 128.

Liao, B., 2008. Zhongguo feiwuzhi wenhua yichan de texing (Special Characters of Chinese Intangible Cultural Heritages) [Online]. Available at: http://www.npc.gov. cn/npc/xinwen/rdlt/sd/2008-11/13/content_1458333.htm (Accessed 12 August 2016).

Ma, J.H., 2008. An Analysis on Existing Status of Intangible Cultural Heritage Projects in Fujian. *Fujian Arts* 6, 21–28.

Ma, Z.Y., 2010. Feiyi Baohu De Kunhuo Yu Tansuo (Confusions and Explorations in Safeguarding the Intangible Heritage). *Folklore Studies,* 4 [online]. Available at: http:// www.chinesefolklore.org.cn/web/index.php?NewsID=8405 (Accessed 27 July 2016).

Measures for the Protection of World Cultural Heritage (Promulgated by Order No. 41 of the Ministry of Culture of The People's Republic of China) 2006. Available at: http://www. wipo.int/wipolex/en/details.jsp?id=15261 (Accessed 1 November 2019).

Model Law for the Protection of Traditional Knowledge and Expressions of Culture 2002, s 4. Available at: https://www.wipo.int/edocs/lexdocs/laws/en/spc/spc002en.pdf (Accessed 1 November 2019).

Model Provisions for National Laws on the Protection of Expressions of Folklore against Illicit Exploitation and Other Forms of Prejudicial Action 1982, pt III, para 42. Available at: https://www.wipo. int/edocs/lexdocs/laws/en/unesco/unesco001en.pdf (Accessed 1 November 2019).

Ni, C.X. and Ou, Y.G., 2012. Cong "Zhognguo Wenyilei Feiwuzhi Wenhua Yichan Baohu Weiquan Diyian" Shuo Qi (Discussion from the Frist Case to Claim Rights in Protection of Literary and Artistic Category of Chinese Intangible Cultural Heritage). *Cultural Heritage* 4, 38–45.

Opinions on Strengthening the Protection of Intangible Cultural Heritage 2005, sec. II. Available at: http://en.pkulaw.cn/display.aspx?cgid=61b114f1964886aebdfb&lib=law (Assessed 1 November 2019).

Regulations on Protection of Traditional Arts and Crafts 1997. Available at: http://www.wipo. int/wipolex/en/text.jsp?file_id=198447 (Accessed 5 November 2019).

Salle, L.M. 2014. *Appropriation and Commodification of Cultural Heritage: Ethical and IP Issues to Consider.* [Online]. Available at: http://www.sfu.ca/ipinch/sites/default/files/ resources/fact_sheets/ipinch_commodificationfactsheet_final.pdf (Accessed 3 August 2016).

Song, J.H., 2012. 'wenhua shengchan yu feiwuzhi wenhua yichan shenchanxing baohu' (Culture Production and Productive Protection of Intangible Cultural Heritage'). *Cultural Heritage* 1, 1.

Wang, S.H. and Liao, R., 2008. chanyehua shijiao xia de feiwuzhi wenhua yichan baohu (Protection of Intangible Cultural Heritages from a Perspective of Commercialisation). *Journal of Tongji University (Social Science Section)* 19(1), 107–112.

Wang, W.Z. (ed.)., 2006. *Feiwuzhi Wenhua Yichan Gailun (an Introduction to the Intangible Cultural Heritage).* China: Culture and Art Publishing House.

Wenhuabu guanyu jiaqiang feiwuzhi wenhua yichan shengchanxing baohu de zhidao yijian (Ministry of Culture's Guidance on Strengthening Productive Protection of Intangible Cultural Heritage), 2012. Available at: http://www.ihchina.cn/show/feiyiweb/html/com. tjopen.define.pojo.feiyiwangzhan.FaGuiWenJian.faguiwenjianMore.html (Accessed 20 August 2016).

White Paper: Gender Equality and Women's Development in China, 2015. Available at: http:// www.china.org.cn/chinese/2015-09/22/content_36651056.htm (Accessed 10 August 2016).

Wu, S.Q., 2013. woguo feiwuzhi wenhua yichan falv baohu de xin tansuo' (New Exploitation in Legal Protection of Intangible Cultural Heritage in China'). *Lanzhou Xuekan (Lanzhou Study Journal)* 12, 172.

Yong Chanyehua Yunzong Qiangjiu Minjian Wenhua Guibao (Save Folk Culture through Utilisation of Commercialisation), 2007. Available at: http://www.sznews.com/zhuanti/ content/2007-05/20/content_1141749.htm (Accessed 27 July 2016).

Yunnan Sheng Minzu Minjian Chuantong Wenhua Baohu Tiaoli (Regulations on the Protection of Traditional Ethnic and Folk Culture of the Province of Yunnan) 2000, Art 2. Available at: http:// www.ihchina.cn/show/feiyiweb/html/com.tjopen.define.pojo.feiyiwangzhan. FaGuiWenJian.faguiwenjianMore.html (Accessed 1 August 2016).

Zhang, G., 2007. *Minjian Wenxue Yishu De Zhishi Chanquan Baohu Yanjiu (Research on Intellectual Property Protection of Folklore).* Beijing: Law Press China.

Zhao, Y.Y., 2015. Shouzhu Chuantong Wenhua De DNA – Qingtian Weiyuan Tan Feiwuzhi Wenhua Yichan Baohu (Maintaining Traditional Culture's DNA – Speech on Intangible Cultural Heritage Protection Made by Tian Qing, Member of the National Committee of Chinese People's Political Consultative Conference) [Online]. Available at: http://www.rmzxb.com.cn/zt/2015qglh/yc/464689.shtml (Accessed 1 November 2019).

Zhen, Y.J., 2014. feiwuzhi wenhua yichan falv baohu de eryuan moshi chutan (Analysis of a Dural-Mode in Regard to Legal Protection of Intangible Cultural Heritage). *Journal of Hubei Institute for Nationalities (Philosophy and Social Sciences)* 3, 64.

6

DECOLONIZING THE FUTURE

Folk art environments and the temporality of heritage

Alfredo González-Ruibal

Introduction

In this chapter, I would like to examine folk art environments from the point of view of heritage. Folk environments are built spaces created by non-professional artists or architects, often peculiar characters living in the margins of society (Beardsley 1995; Ramírez, 2004a; Umberger 2007). They occur in many places, but some of the most famous examples come from the United States, Western Europe and India. To create such spaces, the artists make lavish use of recycled materials, including modern construction materials (concrete is a staple), broken artefacts (such as glass bottles and pottery), cheap decorations (i.e., porcelain and plaster figurines) and objects in varying states of decay. Although there are several historical precedents, folk art environments seem to have developed mostly from the late 19th century onwards and can be considered, in many ways, a by-product of modernity, democratization and the industrial revolution. Thus, materials are often industrial and related to mass consumption. The idea of the artist as an individual and a free spirit is very much associated with modernity, and the fact that people from the lower classes without a formal education feel entitled to engage in artistic work is in keeping with democratic values. These works have received myriad names, none of them satisfactory: *naïve*, *brut*, primitive, marginal, outsider, visionary and vernacular art or architecture, among others. The term "architecture" itself is inadequate since these works often mix building, landscaping, painting and sculpture—thus the name "sculptectures" proposed by one critic (Ramírez 2004a).

I would argue that the logic of folk art environments has much to tell archaeologists and heritage practitioners about value, emotion and temporality, which are all fundamental principles in the production of heritage. These spaces are all guided by similar utopian ideas and free creativity. Unlike most buildings, official monuments and hegemonic forms of heritage, however, the promoters of popular architecture build for an undetermined future, have no precise plan on how the building will evolve, are open to changes in the fabric and the project, do not envisage a definite ending and ignore whether the building will be ever considered heritage or simply demolished. Folk art buildings are usually intertwined with the builders' biography and continue to be under construction for the entire life of the artist. This would be a perfect example of heritage for the future (and only for the future), but at the same time, the unfolding, unfinished project in itself can be considered a form of heritage, at least as interesting as the finished structure itself (if it ever is). Folk art reverses the unilinear temporality of hegemonic heritage sites by blurring the divide between construction site, ruin, monument and dump. They exemplify at best what James Dixon (this volume) notes, that every building bears within it "the potential to have never existed in the complete form we know today", among other things because they can rarely be conceived as complete; non-completion is their more typical mode of existence. At the same time, by living astride modernity and tradition, they problematize both, including the notion of heritage itself—a creature of modernity.

I will argue that folk art environments are useful both for interrogating assumed concepts of past, present and future in heritage studies and for proposing novel and more imaginative ways of dealing with heritage. This is particularly the case with the legacy of the contemporary past, which often challenges traditional assumptions about heritage (such as uniqueness, age and aesthetic value) and asks for more active and creative interventions (Palsson 2012; Pétursdóttir 2013; Kobiałka 2014). What folk buildings and works of art propose are open, indeterminate futures, not bound and inalterable. In that, they follow premodern traditions (Glassie 2000) in which things (houses, monuments, burials, statues) continually change, as organic beings, by accretion, removal and renewal—of material elements and memories. If we embrace these open futures in our management of recent heritage without prejudices and creatively (that is, in the spirit of folk artists), we might be better prepared to imagine open pasts as well. Seeing the past as open means to be ready to accept that past and present are not separated by an impassable barrier, and it allows us to look at history more critically, not as something that is passively inherited, but something we help to co-create and therefore to change for the future. From this point of view, heritage stops being a distant entity, frozen in time that has to be accepted as a given and treated with reverence and more something with which we can interact creatively, even altering its very fabric. From this perspective, the temporality of heritage changes: it is no longer something that has to be just transferred to the future, but something that has to be reworked to shape the future: open pasts lead to open futures.

Heritage for the future

In temporal terms, we immediately associate the concept of heritage with the past. The word itself is related to inheritance, which implies a relationship with what existed before us: a legacy bequeathed by our parents or grandparents. In the case of cultural heritage, the temporal dimension goes well beyond the individual inheritance of property. As with personal inheritance, we can receive a legacy from the recent past, but a large part of what constitutes cultural heritage (including archaeological sites, languages, crafts and cuisines) belongs to remote eras; we "inherit" both the Ruhr factories from the early 20th century and the Laetoli footprints, which are 3.8 million years old. The focus on the past, which has important legal implications, has made us forget what heritage is really about, the future. The National Historic Preservation Act of the United States, passed in 1966, for instance, clearly states that its purpose is to "ensure future generations a genuine opportunity to appreciate and enjoy the rich heritage of our Nation". Unlike in the case of private inheritance, the concept of the future is more important than the concept of the past in cultural heritage.

In fact, the past has become less and less relevant in the definition of heritage, with the increasing heritagization of the very recent and the present itself (e.g. Bradley et al. 2004; Penrose 2007)—what François Hartog (2005) calls "presentism". Everything can become heritage, and the processes of heritage-making affect ever more recent times. Hartog (2005: 14) sees this as the result of the politics of time in the 20th century, the era that "has most invoked the future, the most constructed and massacred in its name" and also the era that has given more importance to the present: "a massive, overwhelming, omnipresent present, that has no horizon other than itself, daily creating the past and the future that, day after day, it needs".

However, the conscious production of heritage elements in the present (as opposed to the reception of heritage from the past) has existed for a long time, at least in the realm of the arts and the monumental. Thus, memorials and art museums displaying the work of contemporary artists already existed in the 19th century, and they were created with the clear purpose of them becoming heritage immediately after completion. The production of heritage with elements from the present is not necessarily a strategy pursued by modern institutions or corporations only, but also by communities. Byrne (2014: 103–106) notes that the rebuilding (rather than conservation) of popular temples in China is a future-oriented rather than past-oriented practice; people are not so much reinstating the past as rebuilding local communities left in disarray by the centralized communist state. In turn, there is the concept in Japan of "living national treasure"; this title has been granted, since 1950, to an artist or artisan as a "keeper of important intangible cultural heritage" (Hartog 2005: 11). It protects the present of his or her knowledge and skills and aims to transmit it to the future. We can do without the past, then, but we cannot do without the future.

In the case of modern societies, the relationship between heritage and the future can be understood in relation to the construction of the modern self, only that heritage is associated with the making of collective, rather than individual, selves. Anthony Giddens has argued that controlling the future has become one of the trademarks of social experience in late modernity. In a situation where alternative options are more and more abundant, strategic life-planning has achieved greater relevance (Giddens 1991: 85). What is true for each of us is also true for us as a collective. Modern societies tend to plan more and organize time more thoroughly, and life-planning is as much about preparing for the future as about reinterpreting the past. Giddens (1991: 86) considers life-planning as part of a more general phenomenon that he terms the "colonisation of the future". According to Giddens, in modernity,

> while the future is recognised to be intrinsically unknowable, and as it is increasingly severed from the past, that future becomes a new terrain—a territory of counterfactual possibility. Once thus established, that terrain lends itself to colonial invasion through counterfactual thought and risk calculation.
>
> *(Giddens 1991: 111)*

Heritage management is a perfect example of the strategies developed by late modern societies to colonize the future. In its more conventional manifestation, it is an attempt at reversing entropy, freezing time and averting loss (Holtorf 2015), thus making the future exactly as the present is—and therefore knowable and under control.

Against this obsession with colonizing the future, some practitioners suggest that we should be less wary with the past and the future and instead try to create open spaces for the needs of the present (Holtorf 2006; see Holtorf 2015: 7 for other references). This implies, at times, letting heritage go, to be destroyed or modified, subtracted or accreted (Kobiałka 2014). This fluid concept of heritage is akin to new ideas developed by both artists and architects.

Organic utopias

Folk environments are both nonmodern and dependent on modernity. The first clear examples appear in a very particular historical moment, the late 19th century. They cannot be understood without the Second Industrial Revolution, serial production, mass consumerism and the popularization of modern materials (such as glass and concrete) and techniques (such as montage and *pique assiette*). Yet the principles that guide these architectures have more in common with purely nonmodern principles (such as organicism and accretion) than with modernity. At the same time, to describe them as vernacular architecture, as some do (e.g. Russell 2001), is misleading; they do not comply with any tradition whatsoever, and they evince impulses of self-realization and utopia that are absent in proper vernacular styles.

Louis-Ferdinand Cheval is considered the first naive architect. A postman by trade and with no artistic qualifications, he started construction in his *Palais Ideal* next to Lyon in 1879 when he was 43 (Figure 6.1). He spent all his life and savings on building an ever-growing structure made with pebbles to the astonishment of his neighbours, who considered him crazy. Cheval reunites many of the characteristics that would define these visionary artists from then on and that

FIGURE 6.1   The *Palais Ideal* (France). Photo by Benoît Prieur—CC-BY-SA. Image released by author on the open domain through Wikimedia Commons: https://commons.wikimedia.org/wiki/File:Palais_Id%C3%A9al_-_mai _2014_-_5.JPG

would appear in different parts of the globe. These visionary artists are amateurs who work outside any recognized artistic tradition and weave together life and work. Today, folk art environments are particularly well known in the United States, but it is difficult to determine whether this is because they have received greater public and scholarly attention or because there is indeed a higher propor- tion of outsider artists in that country. The truth is that other parts of the world do have significant examples of this kind of art too, from India (Umberger 2007: 319–343) to Spain (Ramírez 2004a).

I am particularly interested in the temporal dimension of folk art environ- ments. In my opinion, these works manage to bypass some modern dualisms that are still present in many heritage practices by blending past and present, time and materiality, nature and culture, self and work. In the following section, I will explore folk art environments through five themes that are common to all of them and that directly impinge on the question of temporality regarding recycling and montage, biography, maintenance and care, organic growth, and entropy.

Recycling and montage

A first, basic element of the open temporality of these sites can be discerned in the use of discarded objects (what professional artists would call *objets trouvés*) such as glass bottles, driftwood or leftovers from construction material. The use of recycled materials is similar to the technique of montage, assemblage and collage used by contemporary artists. Montage, according to Didi-Huberman (2007: 5), "escapes teleologies, makes survivals visible, as well as anachronisms, encounters of contradictory temporalities which affect each object, each event, each person, each gesture". Folk artists are not concerned—unlike many heritage practitioners or archaeologists—with purifying time and stripping it of its supposed incoherences. In that, they follow the complex multitemporality of vernacular architecture; they both "tick with many clocks" (Glassie 2000: 70). Interestingly, montage and assemblage have been associated with an archaeological sensibility. Juhani Pallasmaa (2000: 80) argues that collage and assemblage "enable an archaeological density and a non-linear narrative through the juxtaposition of images deriving from irreconcilable origins", whereas Didi-Huberman (2008: 4) equates archaeology and montage and notes that "to do an archaeology is always to risk putting together fragments of surviving things, which are necessarily heterogeneous and anachronistic, because they come from separate places and times disjointed by gaps". The chronopolitics of folk art environments are not historicist (see Witmore 2013), but open to the mixture of events and matters. Everything can come together in the project, the old and the new, the industrial and the pre-industrial. In fact, through repeated acts of incorporation, objects can no longer be considered anachronistic; they belong to the unique time of the work.

Recycling is present in almost any folk art environment, including some of the most famous, such as the *Watts Towers*. These are 17 fretwork structures, some of which as tall as 30 metres, made primarily of concrete. They were constructed by an Italian immigrant, Simon Rodia, between 1921 and 1954 in a low-class neighbourhood of Los Angeles. Rodia embedded fragments of glazed tiles, seashells, glass bottles and shards of china in the structure, following a technique known as *pique assiette*, which is a staple of naive structures (Figure 6.2). Heterochrony is more clearly seen, however, in a much less known work, *El Pasatiempo*, in the small town of Betanzos (Spain). This work was developed between the late 19th and early 20th century by a wealthy emigrant, Juan García Naveira, returned from Brazil, where he made his riches. *El Pasatiempo* was a sort of theme park *avant la lettre* (Cabano Vázquez et al., 1991), made of gardens, terraces, sculptures, fountains and artificial caves. As in many works of this kind, it is mostly made of concrete. The heterochronic element here is not to be found in the recycling of materials, which is not present (except for seashells), but in the haphazard juxtaposition of icons associated with different eras (Villasol 2001: 441): the pyramids of Giza, dinosaurs, classic statues, items from the independence of the American colonies of Spain, the Panama Canal or an airplane, among other things (Figure 6.3). Released from historicist anxieties, folk art environments create their own time.

Biography

That folk environments inhabit a particular temporality, which is not that of modernity (unilinear and accelerated), is seen in the many decades that they take

FIGURE 6.2 *Watts Towers* (California, USA). Photo by author.

to be built. They evince a lack of concern with the future that is at odds with the construction of modern subjectivities, as we have seen. Most works only come to an end with the death of the artist or their inability to continue working. The "cathedral" of Mejorada del Campo or the *Watts Towers* are good examples of this slow architecture. The "cathedral" of Mejorada, a colossal church made basically with leftovers from construction work, was started by Justo Gallego, a former monk with no qualifications, in 1963 near Madrid (Figure 6.4). He has been working, mostly alone, on the building ever since (Rosa-Armengol 2004; García Muñoz 2012). This is something that can be traced back to early folk artists. Thus, Ferdinand Cheval worked on his palace for 33 years, between 1879 and 1912, the same amount of time that took Simon Rodia to finish his towers (Platt 1996: 18–19). It can be argued that there is nothing new in this: medieval cathedrals are in fact famous for their protracted time of construction. What is new is that this slow time, with no apparent concern for the future, coexists with the accelerated time of late modernity and its obsession with colonizing the future.

This biographical link between work and artist has important consequences for the survival of the work. Many environments are disassembled or destroyed as soon as the creator or promoter dies. Thus, *El Pasatiempo* started to decay when Juan García Naveira passed away in 1933 (Villasol 2001: 433). The best example of the intertwining of artists lives and their works' lives, though, was perhaps Man's installation in Camelle (in Galicia, the same region of Spain where *El Pasatiempo*

FIGURE 6.3 An airplane flying over the pyramids of Giza in *El Pasatiempo* (Spain). Photo by author.

was built). Man's real name was Manfred Gnädinger—a German citizen who emigrated to a small village in northern Galicia as a young man (Sobrino 2004). He had studied art, but apparently only started developing his art environment after the woman he was in love with married another man. Around his house, in front of the ocean, he erected intriguing sculptures made with pebbles glued with concrete and different sorts of debris brought by the sea (Figure 6.5). The work and his own life came to an end in December 2002, when the sculptures were badly damaged by the oil spill of *The Prestige*, a tanker that sunk off the coast of Galicia. He died some days after the spill, apparently due to the immense sadness of seeing the damage caused by the disaster to his work and his beloved coast, which for him were part of the same whole. Left to its own devices, what remained of the installation was finally destroyed by a storm eight years after the death of Man. In the meantime, nobody took care of his legacy, despite many projects and ideas. Probably, the only way the environment could have survived would have been through continuous work of maintenance and modification.

Maintenance and care

This makes clear that what enables the survival of these sites is continuous maintenance, not passive conservation, but active creation. One can hypothesize that

FIGURE 6.4 The unfinished "cathedral" of Mejorada del Campo (Madrid, Spain). Photograph by José Javier Martín Espartosa. Image released by author on the open domain through Flickr: https://www.flickr.com/photos/druid abruxux/40057571202

FIGURE 6.5 Man's installations in Camelle (Spain). Photo by Luis Miguel Bugallo Sánchez (Lmbuga). Image released by the author on the open domain through Wikimedia Commons: https://commons.wikimedia.org/wiki/File:2016._Obra_de_Man._Camelle._Galiza.jpg

the drive that leads artists to keep adding features to their works is the realization that as soon as they stop doing it, they (the works and perhaps themselves) will die. Conservation, in the conventional sense, is not enough. In a way, it could be said that when environments are finished, they are dead. Their spirit is inevitably associated with the act of making, and therefore they are more alive as a "ruin in progress" than as sanctified monuments. This brings to mind some ideas brought about by historians and archaeologists in relation to maintenance. In heritage management, the aim is usually to conceal maintenance activities, that is, to leave the original creation as unaltered as possible through preservation. This emphasis on creation as opposed to maintenance is, however, a very modernist notion, which, at the same time, misrepresents how modern societies actually work. Instead, historian David Edgerton (2006: 75–102) showed how maintenance is at least as important in modern technology as design. "Maintenance has lived in a twilight world, hardly visible in the formal accounts societies make of themselves" (Edgerton 2006: 79). Spanish feminist archaeologists, in turn, have called attention to the gendered practices of care, such as domestic tasks or child-rearing, that are, in fact, maintenance activities (Montón-Subías and Sánchez-Romero 2008). The oblivion of these activities, they argue, is due to the fact that they are typically assigned to women and other subaltern groups. It is perhaps not surprising that folk artists come from subaltern classes, too as they are mostly workers, emigrants, marginalized people and those with mental health problems.

A perfect example of the importance of care is *Salvation Mountain* in Niland, California (Figure 6.6). This is an artificial elevation made in the middle of the

FIGURE 6.6   *Salvation Mountain* (California, USA). Photo by Society Sunday. Image released by author on the open domain through Pixabay (free for commercial use, no attribution required): https://pixabay.com/photos/salvatio n-mountain-california-art-4037179

desert near a squatter colony by Leonard Knight (1931–2014) with mud, straw and tonnes of industrial paint that he received as donations (Yust, 1999). The 15-metre high "mountain" is painted in bright industrial colours and has flowers, trees, hearts, religious messages and wishes of peace and love. Because of the very nature of the materials employed and the local environmental conditions, the work can only survive if it is continuously worked on, painted and repainted; a continued lack of care would lead to the destruction of the entire work in a very short period of time. Indeed, after Knight died, the deterioration of the work advanced fast until maintenance work was resumed by a collective.

Maintenance always implies continuous reworking and creative refashioning of the art environment, that is, not keeping intact what there is; it is more about creating the future than conserving the past. It also implies more than simply working with things but encouraging people to participate in the work. Guided visits and entertaining guests are crucial elements in the work of artists so distant as Man in Spain and Knight in the United States (Umberger 2007: 343; Sobrino 2004: 208; Yust 1999). One of the first artists, if not the first, Ferdinand Cheval also encouraged the participation of visitors (including writing graffiti!) in the making of his *Palais Ideal* (Ramírez 2004b: 32). Folk art environments then are more open to socialization and interaction than many heritage sites, and this socialization is regarded as part of the maintenance of the work.

Organic growth

Folk environments rarely follow an established programme. Justo Gallego—the constructor of the "cathedral" of Mejorada del Campo (Madrid)—has not used any plans whatsoever. In fact, this artist-architect cannot draw, and the forms travel directly from his head to his hands and back, thus explaining the many asymmetries and irregularities of the building (Rosa-Armengol 2004: 223), which give it, as in many other cases, an organic appearance. Furthermore, Gallego has rejected the use of plans proposed by a committee that would have legalized the construction, for fear of his work being distorted (Rosa-Armengol 2004: 227). Simon Rodia is reported saying: "A million times I don't know what to do myself" (cited in Platt 1996: 30), a sentence one would hardly expect in a professional architect and perhaps not many artists. Plans, like maps and calendars, are tools for colonizing the future; they prevent risk and uncertainty, but also channel experience and restrict the possibilities of the real.

Folk art environments give the impression of being alive—at least when their makers are also alive. They seem to be "constantly growing and changing structure" (Platt 1996: 22). This is much more than we can say of many official heritage sites. In part, this impression is the result of the way folk environments grow, organically and, as we have seen, without a plan. Unlike professional architecture, their unfinished state is not a problem because it is part of their nature. Rosa-Armengol (2004: 227), referring to the "cathedral" of Mejorada del Campo, notes that it is a living process, whose forms evolve along the way, and concludes that its beauty lies in its unfinished presence. The idea of growth and life is sometimes explicitly present in the work of some artists. Man interspersed sculptures and plants in Camelle and saw its work as evolving naturally with the coast (Sobrino 2004: 206). His installations were not conceived to be finished at any particular point, they kept evolving through the years, and photographs taken at different times by visitors show that some elements disappeared during the life of the artist or changed radically.

Entropy

Organic growth is intrinsically linked to the problem of entropy. Being alive means decaying and eventually dying. This is something that we all know very well, and experience, as humans. However, when it comes to heritage, we try to stop entropic processes at all costs, even if it means transforming a site or work into a pastiche—a process that is redolent of human bodies that undergo plastic surgery. Laurent Olivier (2001: 181–184) has critically examined what this attempt at freezing the past means in contemporary places of trauma, such as Oradour-sur-Glane and Auschwitz. Restoration implies to change their nature and divert their evolution. He argues that in these cases "to try to fix the remains of the past in this ideal state of the past is effectively to destroy those very remains" (Olivier 2001: 184). Interestingly, the title of a work on the preservation of folk architecture is *Fixing Dreams* (Platt 1996). Actually, the title could be used to refer to conservation work on any kind of heritage site. The difference in the case of naive environments is that they evolved explicitly as material dreams.

The truth is that folk artists seem to accept entropy with a nonchalance that is rare among heritage practitioners. It is not that they conceive their work as entropic machines that will be consumed by time, as some professional artists do. It is simply that they have learned to live with decay. Entropy is, of course, kept at bay through maintenance, as we have seen, but its trace is not necessarily concealed. For much of their existence, naive architectures exist in a mode of indeterminacy between work in progress, monument and ruin. The label "ruins in reverse" coined by Robert Smithson suits them nicely. According to the artist, they are the "opposite of the 'romantic ruin' because the buildings don't *fall* into ruin *after* they are built but rather rise into ruin before they are built" (Smithson 2011: 49, emphasis in the original).

Two examples illustrate this attitude: Tyree Guyton's *Heidelberg Project* in Detroit and Man's installations in Camelle. These artists are not the best representatives of folk art, since both have artistic training, but their work fits visionary architectures perfectly, both in their materiality (expansive, accretionary, detrital) and their utopian vision. The *Heidelberg Project* began in 1986 in one of the many Detroit neighbourhoods affected by urban blight since the 1967 riots. Guyton's project was a form of dealing with the decay and destruction of his hometown. He started painting abandoned buildings with bright colours and making installations with *objets trouvés* from the derelict neighbourhood.

According to the site's description, the artist "uses everyday, discarded objects to create a two block area full of color, symbolism, and intrigue".[1] This is, however, only part of the story. The two blocks are also full of derelict and burnt buildings, piles of corroding junk and all sorts of artefacts (from toys to shoes) in varying states of decay (Figure 6.7), as well as tools used for creating the environment. Some of the houses that were made as part of the project have been victim to arson or been demolished by the town council—the logic of visionary art challenging the modernist logic of urban planning. However, Guyton continues working on his installations and in a way accepting the entropic processes of the city that seep into his art. Although allegedly a vital statement against the ruin of the city, the environment seems to partake in the blight—creatively.

If the entropic character of Guyton's work is an effect of the interaction between the art environment and the urban environment, in the case of Man's environment in Camelle, the strong entropic element was the product of the work's location on the ocean's shore, an entropic space by definition; the sea brought cultural and natural detritus (industrial rubbish, animal bones and driftwood) that Man reused in his work and at the same time the sea, rain, wind and salt continuously altered the sculptures, the garden and the rugged coast itself. Entropy, in fact, was at the heart of Man's art, because degrading agents were incorporated from the beginning: beach sand to make concrete, low-quality paintings, rusted iron, etc. The end of his work came in two phases, first by a

FIGURE 6.7 Reused waste, ruined building and clocks painted by the artist in the *Heidelberg Project* (Detroit, USA). Photo by author.

cultural process of degradation (the oil spill) and then a natural one (the storm), and this sums up the entropic forces that were continuously at work in his site. Interestingly, one of the problems that restorers face today is the difficulty in distinguishing between the remains of Man's work and rubbish thrown by people or the sea.

Conclusion: anti-heroic heritage

There is much to be learned from folk art environments, and the lessons are pertinent to architects, archaeologists and heritage managers. Architect Juhani Pallasmaa (2000: 78) has criticized the "tendency of technological culture to standardize environmental conditions and make the environment entirely predictable". Modernist architecture, too, is a tool for colonizing the future, against which Pallasmaa offers a fragile architecture open to the sensuousness of matter, ageing, weathering and decay.

The fluid heritage of folk art environments is also anti-heroic, a sort of counter-monument. Because it has a human scale, it accepts decay and ephemerality, and is made in almost all cases by marginal individuals, often belonging to the subaltern classes. As it has been criticized, the lofty ideals of hegemonic heritage isolate monuments and sites, cutting the links between communities and places (Meskell 2011; Byrne 2014). The main reason behind these attitudes is the future, the command to preserve sites for generations to come, even at the expense of the present generations.

I am aware that the lesson of folk architecture cannot be used indiscriminately in any kind of heritage; strategies of colonization of the future are still needed in many cases. It is also important to remember that much of the concern with excessive heritage and over-planning makes sense in places like the United Kingdom or Scandinavian countries with a long tradition of highly curated and sanitized heritage spaces and an obsession with listing more and more sites. In many other countries, from Mali to China, the rapid annihilation of all kinds of cultural legacy through war, capitalist development and systematic looting is a much more pressing worry than finding creative ways of dealing with a potential proliferation of heritage sites or their deactivation by routine management practices.

Yet there are millions of heritage places in the world, and in some countries, they indeed grow faster than they disappear (Holtorf 2006). It should not be anathema to deal with some, especially the most recent in an open way, inspired by the attitude of folk artists—that is, allowing processes of decay and transformation and putting more emphasis on maintenance through interaction than on pristine creation and fossilization through conservation. Recent sites are particularly amenable to more creative and flexible forms of engagement (Kobiałka 2014) as those practised by folk artists for at least three reasons: they are often extremely abundant, such as factories or bunkers, they are produced serially by industrial methods and therefore are not unique, unlike a painting by Vermeer, for instance, and because the same or similar structures are still being made. An open and fluid treatment, however, can be applied to heritage that is abundant irrespective of its age. Certainly, to curate in a creative way an Iron Age hillfort or a few Neolithic mounds might enhance rather than damage our knowledge of these structures. What would happen if we accept accretion, recycling, entropy or modification as a legitimate way of interacting with herit-age sites? To start with, it would change our perception of their temporality; we would be co-creating their future and not just simply bequeathing a supposedly untouched past to later generations. Thinking and acting as folk artists means, then, relinquishing our pressing sense of obligation to generations to come and caring less for eternity and more for the present lives of heritage. It is time to start the decolonization of the future.

Note

1 http://www.heidelberg.org/

References

Beardsley, J.I., 1995. *Gardens of Revelation: Environments by Visionary Artists*. New York: Abbeville Press.

Bradley, A., Buchli, V., Fairclough, G., Hicks, D., Miller, J., and Schofield, J., 2004. *Change and Creation. Historic Landscape Character 1950–2000*. Swindon: English Heritage.

Byrne, D., 2014. *Counterheritage: Critical Perspectives on Heritage Conservation in Asia*. Abingdon: Routledge. doi:10.4324/9781315813189.

Cabano Vázquez, I., Pato Iglesias, Mª.L., and Souza Jiménez, X., 1991. *El Pasatiempo: o capricho dun indiano*. Cadernos do seminario de Sargadelos 53. Sada: Ediciós do castro.

Didi-Huberman, G., 2007. *Cuando las imágenes tocan lo real*. Madrid: Círculo de Bellas Artes.

Didi-Huberman, G., 2008. *Cuando las imágenes toman posición*, Translators by I.B. Fernández. Madrid: Antonio Machado Libros.

Edgerton, D., 2006. *The Shock of the Old. Technology and Global History Since 1900*. Oxford: Oxford University Press.

García Muñoz, G., 2012. Aquí no hay milagros. La Catedral de Justo Gallego cincuenta años después. *Revista Sans Soleil* 4, 315–319.

Giddens, A., 1991. *Modernity and Self-Identity*. Stanford: Stanford University Press.

Glassie, H., 2000. *Vernacular Architecture*. Bloomington: Indiana University Press.

Hartog, F., 2005. Time and heritage. *Museum International* 57(3), 7–18. doi:10.1111/j.1468-0033.2005.00525.x.

Holtorf, C., 2006. Can less be more? Heritage in the Age of Terrorism. *Public Archaeology* 5(2), 101–109. doi:10.1179/pua.2006.5.2.101.

Holtorf, C., 2015. Averting loss aversion in cultural heritage. *International Journal of Heritage Studies* 21(4), 405–421. doi:10.1080/13527258.2014.938766.

Kobiałka, D., 2014. Let heritage die! The ruins of trams at Depot No. 5 in Wrocław, Poland. *Journal of Contemporary Archaeology* 1(2), 351–368. doi:10.1558/jca.v1i2.18438.

Meskell, L., 2011. *The Nature of Heritage: The New South Africa.* Oxford: Wiley-Blackwell.

Montón-Subías, S., and Sánchez-Romero, M. (eds.)., 2008. *Engendering Social Dynamics: The Archaeology of Maintenance Activities.* BAR International 1862. Oxford: Archaeopress.

Olivier, L., 2001. The archaeology of the contemporary past. In: V. Buchli & G. Lucas, eds. *Archaeologies of the Contemporary Past.* Abingdon: Routledge; pp. 175–188.

Pálsson, G., 2012. These are not old ruins: A heritage of the Hrun. *International Journal of Historical Archaeology* 16(3), 559–576.

Pallasmaa, J., 2000. Hapticity and time. Notes on fragile architecture. *Architectural Review* 207, 78–84.

Penrose, S. (ed.)., 2007. *Images of Change: An Archaeology of England's Contemporary Landscape.* Swindon: English Heritage.

Pétursdóttir, Þ., 2013. Concrete matters: Ruins of modernity and the things called heritage. *Journal of Social Archaeology* 13(1), 31–53. doi:10.1177/1469605312456342.

Platt, J.L., 1996. *Fixing Dreams: Preserving America's Folk Art Environments.* MA Thesis, Graduate Program in Historic Preservation, University of Pennsylvania.

Ramírez, J.A. (ed.)., 2004a. *Escultecturas margivagantes: La arquitectura fantástica en España.* Madrid: Siruela.

Ramírez, J.A., 2004b. Introducción: Sinceridad y brutalidad de los creadores margivagantes. In: J.A. Ramírez, ed. *Escultecturas margivagantes: La arquitectura fantástica en España.* Madrid: Siruela; pp. 19–42.

Rosa-Armengol, L., 2004. La Catedral inconclusa de Mejorada del Campo (Madrid). In: J.A. Ramírez, ed. *Escultecturas margivagantes. La arquitectura fantástica en España.* Madrid: Ediciones Siruela-Fundación Duques de Soria; pp. 215–225.

Russell, C. (ed.)., 2001. *Self-Taught Art: The Culture and Aesthetics of American Vernacular Art.* Jackson: University Press of Mississippi.

Smithson, R., 2011 [1967]. A tour of the monuments of Passaic, New Jersey. In: B. Dillon, ed. *Ruins.* London/Cambridge, MA: Whitechapel Gallery/The MIT Press; pp. 46–51.

Sobrino, M.L., 2004. El Mundo límite de Man en Camelle (A Coruña). In: J.A. Ramírez, ed. *Escultecturas margivagantes: La arquitectura fantástica en España.* Madrid: Siruela; pp. 204–211.

Umberger, L., (ed.)., 2007. *Sublime Spaces and Visionary Worlds: Built Environments of Vernacular Artists.* Princeton: Princeton Architectural Press.

Villasol, C.L., 2001. Dos sueños de piedra: A Quinta da Regaleira y el Parque del Pasatiempo. *Anuario brigantino* 24, 431–448.

Witmore, C., 2013. Which archaeology? A question of chronopolitics. In: A. González-Ruibal, ed. *Reclaiming Archaeology: Beyond the Tropes of Modernity.* London: Routledge; pp. 130–144. doi:0.4324/9780203068632

Yust, L., 1999. The interactive mountain of Leonard Knight. *Folk Art Messenger* 12(3). https://folkart.org/mag/leonard-knight.

7

THE SPECTRE OF NON-COMPLETION

An archaeological approach to half-built buildings

James Dixon

Introduction

This chapter concerns all buildings, how they relate to the future at a particular moment in their lifespans and what that means as buildings age and become potential heritage assets. A building is a lot of things. Firstly, it is an object, a structure created to fulfil a purpose. Secondly, it is the life, human and non-human, in and around that structure. Any building is most meaningfully thought of as the complete accretion of things, people, thoughts and more that occurs in relation to the physical structure. It would be a fallacy to reduce what a building is to all of those things that happen in and around it. The structure is important. It would be equally fallacious however to give primacy to the physical structure as no building is intended to be a pure object. Increasingly, architects consider themselves to be working at the intersection of buildings, real people and the natural world (see Dixon, 2015). We need only look to the idea of buildings as ecological landscapes espoused by Kongjian Yu of Turenscape (Kongjian and Padua, 2007; Saunders, 2012) or at the people-centred, post-industrial urban design of Jan Gehl Architects (Gehl, 2010; 2011) to see this in practice. The social sciences too recognise this interrelationship in analysis. Tim Ingold, for instance, has written persuasively on the intersections of 'the four As', architecture, art, archaeology and anthropology (Ingold, 2013). The ideas presented here recognise the importance of this position to understanding buildings of all periods, not merely the new buildings consciously created with these ideas in mind.

This paper arises from within buildings archaeology and its relationship to built heritage and the understanding and manipulation of historic buildings and built landscapes in relation to perceived heritage values and significance. Further, it aims to contribute to debates surrounding the conservation of historic buildings and other structural remains. It is prompted in part by an awareness of the limitations of the field as practised commercially. In the UK, all guidance on the production of high standard buildings archaeology reports is focussed on the recording of the structure as intended by its architect and alterations to that 'original' building between its existence and abandonment or any point of major change to its form (see for instance Historic England (formerly English Heritage) 2016 for an example of recording philosophy and guidance). With relatively few exceptions, a formal archaeological standing building report records the structure with reference to the architectural context surrounding its creation and subsequent alterations to it. There are obvious reasons for a primary focus on 'original' form, not least that the structure itself is often the most immediately precarious thing by the time archaeologists are involved with a building and that commercial budgets do not always allow archaeologists to expand beyond the minimum standards outlined by various organisations. Whatever the reasons for the current situation however, we are left with a field in which a great many of the contexts and perspectives that contribute meaningfully to what a building is (again, whether in the present or in the past) are routinely factored out of analysis. This chapter will examine one of these 'ignored' contexts, a building's construction period, and try to come to some conclusions as to why this period of a building's life is so important.

The 'spectre of non-completion' is common to all buildings and is demonstrably one of the most important things built heritage researchers and professionals never discuss. Appreciation of the spectre of non-completion arises from taking a multi-disciplinary approach to built heritage centred on the concept of ecology, the interrelation of a building and its environment in the widest sense. Much writing exists on the ecology of buildings, with a large portion of it situating itself within geography. Writers including Tim Edensor, Paul Dobraszczyk and J-D Dewsbury have firmly·established in the social sciences the idea of buildings as ongoing processes that do not end with de-occupation, but continue in all kinds of interesting, unintended ways (see, for instance, Dobraszczyk, 2010; Edensor, 2011; Thrift and Dewsbury, 2000).

Much of this work stems from investigations of ruins. Looking at what happens to a building in the final stages of its physical existence, it is natural enough to come to the conclusion that those processes began as soon as a building was standing and so the continual process of a building can be appreciated, whether or not you want to think of this as a building's 'life' (Cairns and Jacobs, 2014; 11–15). This chapter will challenge that perspective by moving to a different end of that life and considering buildings being created. First, it will consider in more detail exactly what a building is and highlight how different disciplinary perspectives on this point reflect researchers' different temporal points of entry into a building's existence. Then the paper will look at non-completion in the contemporary built environment and outline some of the ways in which approaching buildings in this way has a potential to reveal interesting and useful aspects of building and buildings that are not available by examining any other point in time after the construction period. Lastly, three short case studies will be presented, each of which examines public art projects focussed on the creation of new buildings and highlight potential new ways of working for archaeologists wishing to understand the spectre of non-completion and allowing archaeologists to factor consideration of it into their analysis of buildings. In conclusion, the paper will turn to what this different understanding of buildings in the present and past – as applied to all buildings – means for built heritage in the future. The point here is a fairly simple one. If we think that the spectre of non-completion is important, and if we can agree that it is a phenomenon applicable to all buildings, is there a case for rethinking or widening the ways in which the buildings of today become the formalised built heritage of tomorrow?

Incorporating the spectre of non-completion is important for the future of built heritage and buildings archaeology because it introduces a new level of understanding to the world around us, making use of standing buildings, arguably the most visible and accessible artefact type available to archaeologists and one that is used to provide the evidence base for a range of different kinds of archaeology beyond those more formally focussed on architecture (see for instance McAtackney, 2008; Pétursdóttir and Olsen, 2014). Current commercial practice in built heritage and buildings archaeology deals largely with certainty, with known intentions of architects, known forms of inhabited buildings and set forms of recording and reporting. However, the spectre of non-completion is everywhere, in all buildings, and recognition of this fact allows us to turn from this position to one of extreme precariousness wherein every single building bears within it, at least equal to any other later meaning that can be ascribed to it, the potential to have never existed *in the complete form we know today*. How we carry this past and present of multi-potentiality, vulnerability, hope and fear into the future should be a prime concern of archaeology and heritage.

What is a building?

The term 'non-complete' suggests an opposition to or a stage on the way towards 'complete'. However, there is no such thing as a complete building. Any building has meaningful existence from the point at which a need for it arises until the moment it is both forgotten by people and no longer has any physical signature in the world. A lot of different things can happen between those two theoretical points in time, and these encompass a complex set of interrelated pasts, presents and futures and tangible and intangible expressions of what that building is. Rather than a thing, a building is a process, a series of creative enterprises that result in a number of different physical forms. Each of these is independently worthy of consideration within the broad fields of buildings archaeology and built heritage.

What we should remember here is that this process of moving from being one potential future solution to a particular need at a certain point in time to being post-existent involves a series of stages that are more-or-less codified, either through disciplinary tradition and practice or through being written into legislation and policy. By understanding these set stages, we can move on from a general appreciation of a building as an ongoing process to one in which that ongoing, messy, complicated set of things and ideas is nevertheless punctuated by points at which a building is popularly or legally recognised to be a particular thing, despite the likelihood that this will never be the whole story. We also, however, see the creation of a large number of unbuilt buildings along the way.

Thus, we might imagine that a building begins its existence as a potential solution to a problem, whether or not this is realised and put into words and images by humans. At some point, the building will be conceived as a potential form, creating a series of unbuilt buildings as certain other solutions to the problem are rejected (e.g., designating an area for housing rather than retail). Thereafter, a building or number of alternative buildings will be designed, taking a variety of drawn, digital and textual forms, and one or more of those designs adopted as a potential building, leaving again more unbuilt buildings behind. This design will become a planning application that may receive permission to be built. If not, it is, for now, unbuilt. Thereafter, construction will begin. At some point, it will end. If the building has not achieved the form intended when construction began, the building is unbuilt. If the construction process ends satisfactorily, the building has reached what is probably the most widely recognised form, the built building. It will then be occupied, altered, occupied and altered again and again by multiple formal and informal tenants, and finally become disused, demolished, forgotten and, last of all, post-existent, as not even archaeologists or archivists can suspect it was ever there (in many cases, this will be in a distant future!). This paper is concerned with a very particular part of that process, the point at which construction of a building has begun, but has not yet ended. It is one of the most widely observable 'in-between' stages in the process outlined here; it can be seen all around us. The building is, at this stage, 'half-built'; a phrase here taken to denote the entire time between the beginning and end of planned construction (we might, in deeper analysis go even further to discuss how different a third-built building is from one of three-quarters). It has never been half-built before and will never be half-built again. It is also clearly not unbuilt while cranes still hover and bricklayers work. This is a very distinct moment within the past, present and future of the building when the building is active, on-the-way, but not yet popularly considered to exist. It is in this sense that we open it to interpretation.

There are a number of reasons why this period is of particular interest to archaeology and heritage. Firstly, this stage of a building is the point at which it will, or has the ability to, become part of heritage discourse. In most programmes of heritage designation or preservation, the existence of the physical structure is necessary; the structure has, and accrues, values over time that contribute when required to the assessment of relative significance necessary for formal designation as a 'heritage asset'. The second reason is disciplinary. There are many different disciplines that have interests in buildings; archaeology, heritage studies, art history and architecture are only the most obvious – in the context of this paper – among almost countless others including politics, economics, engineering and physics. What differentiates them, however, is that they all have a different perspective on the building process, a different starting point for engagement. Art history, for instance, will, in general, situate itself fairly firmly at the architectural design stage of a building, with knowledge of the physical building used to demonstrate the ideas of the architect in a 'real world' context. Likewise, in mitigation archaeology, that form of the discipline that undertakes fieldwork to record built forms about to be irretrievably lost, the start point is generally the end of occupation, with that point in time related back to the earliest stages of the built building, and research into stages before that taking the form of historical research to answer specific questions. With the exception of those taking part in the process, the stage at which a building has been started but not finished is rarely considered in its own right.

There is a large body of work dedicated to the unbuilt from a number of different temporal perspectives. There are frequent exhibitions of unrealised architectural designs (for instance *Unbuilt Helsinki* at the Museum of Finnish Architecture in 2012 or *Mackintosh Architecture* at the Hunterian Gallery, Glasgow, in 2014–2015) for reasons ranging from consideration of the bodies of work of individual architects or practices through to the past-future conception of the contemporary relevance of historic, unrealised design. The unbuilt is also considered regularly by artists. Neville Gabie, artist-in-residence for the London 2012 Olympic Park development, produced a piece of work in 2012 titled *Greatest Possible Distance* in which he spent the day of the opening ceremony on what would have been the site of the Paris 2012 Olympic Games had that city been successful in its bid. The work considers what the site has become in the absence of the buildings it was once hoped it would contain and as well as being a piece of work about contemporary Paris; it is very much about the unbuilt Paris Olympics. Archaeologists have also highlighted the importance of understanding the process of enabling that takes place during the legislated planning process (Dixon, 2013), another stage in the process of building that has unbuilt buildings as a regular by-product.

Non-completion is different. A half-built building is *not yet* part of any one temporal trajectory. In the same way in which Doreen Massey discusses space as the holder of multiple trajectories, 'a simultaneity of stories so far' (Massey, 2005: 9), we can discern in the half-built building the last point in time at which it has physical form as a building, but still remains part of the largest possible number of different narratives. As the construction finishes and the building becomes inhabited it will, though still retaining multiple identities, be part of far fewer trajectories than before it was widely accessible in its intended form. I argue that what is unique to this particular point in time is the spectre of non-completion, the potential for that accessibility and intended form to never be realised. There are many different reasons for which this may happen, and it certainly does happen as can be seen by the numerous *never-finished* buildings dotted around the globe such as the unfinished luxury apartment buildings at Skúlagata in

FIGURE 7.1 Unfinished Elizabethan house Lyveden New Bield. Kokai (CC BY-SA 2.0, http://creativecommons.org/licenses/by-sa/2.0) via Wikimedia Commons.

central Reykjavik and the well-known incomplete Nazi holiday complex Prora on Reugen in the Baltic, both of which drew media attention for attempts to re-use the part-completed structures, or even England's Lyveden New Bield, a grade I listed unfinished Elizabethan house (Figure 7.1).

However, at the point in the life of a building with which we are concerned, a future as non-complete exists only as one potential alongside countless others. The word 'spectre' implies haunting, a ghostly presence. This is intentional. Not only is a future as non-complete an important potential trajectory for a half-built building, it is perhaps *the* potential future against which all others must be judged as it is arguably the most dramatically opposed to what might be expected at the outset of construction. The spectre of non-completion, the potential for a half-built building to never become built, is one of the defining phenomena of the built environment.

The spectre of non-completion is so important because it is a phenomenon common to every single building that exists, has existed and will exist. Understanding what it might mean, or at least appreciating its comprehensive presence, enables an alternative mode of thought that can be applied to the whole of the built environment wherein historical multi-potentiality is afforded as much consideration as the actuality of the earliest completed form. This is central to buildings archaeology as it makes clear that in recording solely the building-as-intended we miss an extremely important part of the process in which many different potential trajectories centre on the construction. The future both pours into and radiates out from the half-built building. It exists here in a way in which it never will when the official construction period is deemed to be ended and is central to what a building means. This importance extends to heritage. If we can find a way to record, or at least to regularly acknowledge, the presence of the spectre of non-completion in the half-built building, we can move on to seeing its importance in all built buildings. As heritage designation and preservation fix points in past time and insert into the past nodes of relative certainty, taking the perspective presented here allows us to counter that certainty with an all-pervading uncertainty wherein we cease to take for granted that any building exists in the first place. As we move into the future, and as the majority of these buildings cease to be and those that remain become designated as heritage assets worthy of protection, we may appreciate that it is also their former potential non-completion that is being preserved. The potential for any future listed building to have, at one point in its past, never been completed is part of its identity. Those wider contexts of creation, almost limitless but represented here by non-completion, should become part of heritage discourse if we are not to over-privilege the power that is so often behind a building existing rather than not.

As this applies to the individual building, so it also applies to the built environment as a whole. Intentionally incorporating this extreme precarity into how we popularly understand the built environment, we cease to take the existence of anything for granted. The physical object carries with it its entire creative context, all of the hopes and fears, the intentions of the architect and the resistance of the dispossessed, and of course, the possibility of non-completion, feared by some, wished for by many others. Temporal uncertainty, not knowing what tomorrow will bring, is a key feature of contemporary life. The built environment, as it becomes built heritage, embodies this.

Non-completion in the built environment

Half-built buildings and non-complete building projects create their own specific networks of material culture movement, enabled by the construction or development process, yet rarely visible from either physically outside of the development or chronologically, before or after the construction period has taken place. The *Prospection* project, created by Nina Pope and Karen Guthrie as part of the North West Cambridge Art Programme in February 2014, investigated this very phenomenon. Through fieldwork on two related sites, the site hut of Oxford Archaeology Unit (OAU) excavating on the site and the site office of the site's developers Skanska, the multi-disciplinary group of investigators brought together by the project uncovered a wide range of forgotten, ignored or overlooked aspects of a project of that kind, at the construction stage, that is of use to future-thinking archaeology and heritage.

Of particular interest are the material networks enabled by construction, but not widely known, in some cases even to the people taking part in their enactment. The material network of the archaeological dig is well understood; in time before the present, formal and informal networks resulted in material being brought into and taken away from a site. Mirroring this, during the archaeological excavation (a formally, scientifically-designated 'present') the import and export of all kinds of material culture and environmental samples occurs again, with some overlaps, but also with its own distinct character. This, however, is fairly well known (see for instance Lucas, 2001: 64–106). Of more pertinent interest are the material networks created by the 'other side' of the development, the early stages of construction. Some of these are easy to trace, and indeed rather obvious such as the import of Scandinavian hardwood for construction or the sourcing of a certain kind of brick. Where investigation becomes more directly useful is in looking at material leaving the site. Here, we can see an immediate dissonance between the official and unofficial accounts. In this instance, the developer is consciously environmentally friendly and states that all material leaving the site is accounted for. Indeed as much as possible is recycled on-site, whether this is the moving around of soil for landscaping or the re-use of unwanted trees in the construction of a children's playground. However, question this, and a different story emerges. We see, for instance, that personal waste leaving the site is dealt with by a national waste contractor and the Cambridge developers do not know exactly where it ends up, immediately connecting the unfinished site to national and international networks of waste disposal in a way that is not part of the official narrative. At a micro level, we see tiny amounts of soil and other organic material travelling from Cambridge to Yorkshire every Friday as the specialist piling workers return home for the weekend. Lastly, although there are official uses for the large and medium pieces of waste wood, smaller pieces are sold to passers-by as firewood. It is a simple example, but enough to see that the processes of construction create their own material networks that are not necessarily known to those people active in the construction itself, but that are also unacknowledged as part of the official narrative of the site's creation, either before or after the fact. As Rathje concluded long ago in his pioneering studies of modern material culture, there is usually a difference between what people say they do and what their refuse tells us they actually do. Here we see that discrepancy in action (Rathje, 1979: 10–13; Rathje, Shanks and Witmore, 2013: 365–367). Returning to half-built buildings, the analogy of the investigation of the active building site gives us a clear example of how a single development, with attendant marketing literature and company policies relating to environmentally sustainable construction, can be seen to be somewhat different in practice, albeit at a relatively microscopic level. Before construction has begun, we have only intention. When the development is completed, and as we move ever further from the construction phase,

TABLE 7.1 Competing future trajectories

Future	Who?	Expectation
Ideal future	Developer, architect, owners, local authority	Building represents what it was intended to represent
Future present	Local authority, ecologists, local residents in favour of development	Building enacts site-specificity over time, gradually 'merging' into its local context
Uncertain future	Local residents not in favour of development, those aware but not actively concerned	Building may not be completed, building may never be accepted, building may be completed and accepted
Inhabited future	Protestors, activists, local residents actively concerned	Contested site actively reclaimed by local people and context

that intention becomes a fixed narrative of past action as marketing literature becomes documentary evidence. Only the investigation of the site being made reveals the alternative story, the uncertainty as to the material network being enacted.

During construction, the half-built building belongs to an endless number of different, cohabiting trajectories. Each is different, and we can take it down to the level of individual perceptions. Here, it will suffice to broadly locate these trajectories within four future-thinking themes (Table 7.1).

Firstly, we can see in the half-built building, the potential for an ideal future. The ideal future is that which is intended by a building's architects, developers, builders and owners and is the one that will see the building represent what it was intended to represent in perpetuity. This particular meme is the initial focus of art historical approaches to the built environment and is the start point for much contemporary buildings archaeology. Related to this, we have those trajectories that, in the present moment, relate to future presents and the belief that a new building will come to enact its site-specific identity over time. Although this perspective is very close to that of the ideal future, it is messier and acknowledges more fundamentally the interrelationship of buildings, people and the environment. Whereas an ideal future requires imagining time after now in the context of now, thinking in terms of future presents allows the likelihood that those contexts will be different in a later time, partially due to the changes in the built environment being enacted in the present. This future is that of the ecologically aware, those taking long-term perspectives on social, environmental and economic sustainability.

Third is the uncertain future, of which the spectre of non-completion is part. Here, completion and non-completion are equally possible, but both physically manifested in the half-built building. It is with this step that we can perhaps introduce popular feelings of melancholy, pessimism, excitement and ongoing change into what the building means. It is also this trajectory that comes to include ruins and the perspectives on buildings derived from within cultural geographies such as those of Edensor, Dobraszczyk and Dewsbury. Lastly, we can discern trajectories that relate to the inhabited future. In this form of future thinking, people's intentions to claim (or reclaim) buildings or built places on behalf of narratives that do not form part of the ideal future are brought to the fore. It is the future as represented by protest in the present, or by acts of occupation, both of which explicitly refute certain imposed narratives.

In part, these four different kinds of future thinking relate to the 'four stages of public art' as described by Mark Hutchinson (2002: 430–435). Hutchinson sees a four-stage dialectic process that occurs with the creation of any piece of public art (Table 7.2). First is non-unity, as a piece of art is placed in a public space. It is an un-reflexive position. Second is negation, where the implications of that artwork are realised by people and acted upon. The negation Hutchinson describes is equally of the alienation caused by the artwork, cultural divisions that the work implies, and the 'autonomy of art' expressed in the artwork's placement (Hutchinson, 2002). Next is totality, where the work exists both as the artist intended and as the public has appropriated it. Finally, totality develops its own agency and changes what public art might be in the future.

Hutchinson sees these four stages of public art as happening in sequence, and it is a highly persuasive argument that they will do so with any building too, with perhaps greater visibility the more prominent the development. Also though, these four stages can be seen in any present moment as different potential futures. That is to say that Hutchinson's four stages do not simply happen in turn, they have been happening concurrently all along, and it is merely the ability or need for each to be widely expressed that happens sequentially. If these have all been happening together, then there is some level of equality between them, or at least they are all interconnected and cannot be realised in isolation. Realising this, it becomes less and less acceptable to create meaning around built heritage with reference only, or even primarily, to the ideal future, the building as intended by its architects and builders. Each of these other perspectives will come to fruition in some form, and all are there together as part of what the half-built building means. Considering the future – time after now – how this multiplicity

TABLE 7.2 Mark Hutchinson's four stages of public art and their relation to competing futures

Stage	Manifestation	Related future trajectory
Non-unity	Art object placed in public place	Ideal future, uncertain future
Negation	Implications of art object realised and acted upon	Inhabited future, uncertain future
Totality	Art object exists both as intended and as it has been appropriated	Future present, uncertain future
Agency	The nature of 'totality' changes what public art might be in the future	(None, but this is the space of social scientific analysis)

of potentials, both simultaneous and sequential, is retained within heritage discourse is a prime concern if we are to understand built heritage in ways that do more than the current tendency to privilege the ideal and to ignore the dissonant.

The art and archaeology of non-completion

Marie-Jeanne Hoffner's work as part of the *BS1* residency series in 2008, itself part of the *Cabot Circus Public Art Scheme* in Bristol, explicitly focussed on the idea of non-completion and the particular material signatures of the half-built building. Hoffner's key work was the photography of some of the residential units within the wider shopping centre development mid-way through their construction. These photographs were then printed at large scale and placed within the spaces they depicted, shortly to be covered by plasterboard (Figure 7.2).

Hoffner's work here, partly a comment on the aesthetics of construction, serves also to take that present moment of non-completion and project it into the future. The photographs will only be seen again as a result of demolition or decay, and thus the work directly connects two moments of great change either side of the ideal building as intended by its developers. With Hoffner's photographs set behind its walls, the spectre of non-completion remains with the building for the course of its inhabited life, in a very literal sense. Hoffner developed the work out of initial research around the bombing during the Second World War of the area in which that particular building was being built. Noticing a visual similarity between construction sites and ruins, buildings going up and buildings coming down, she developed this work to intentionally connect those two moments of uncertainty. As the work is invisible at any point at which the building would be thought 'complete' by its builders, it forces us to look past the inhabited building and focus instead on the precarity of construction (and demolition) and foregrounds the spectre of non-completion as inherent in the ideal form.

Within the context of Hoffner's wider body of work, this photo installation gains even greater relevance to the idea of the importance of the spectre

FIGURE 7.2 *Two States*, Marie-Jeanne Hoffner, 2008. (Reproduced with permission from the artist.)

FIGURE 7.3 *Perspectives*, Marie-Jeanne Hoffner, 2005. (Reproduced with permission from the artist.)

of non-completion. Much of her work deals with perceptions of buildings and architectural space. Work produced for the Maison de la Culture in Amiens in 2005 (later repeated) for instance saw the installation within rooms of perspective drawings of those rooms mid-way across them (Figure 7.3).

These drawings contained holes for visitors to pass through, forcing them to physically enter a depiction of the architectural space to get access to the whole of the space proper. Her piece *Landscape vs Architecture* saw the photography of tracings of cities on acetates photographed within building-free landscapes (Figure 7.4).

The work is provocative. It is partly about the potential of uninhabited space to become inhabited, but it also gives rise to the familiar set of perspectives discussed above. For some, the images will simply be a juxtaposition of two different – perhaps competing – visions of the contemporary world. It is possible to see the pictures as a warning about encroachment into nature, or maybe even an aspiration. In short, this work takes us back to the multiplicity of future trajectories outlined above. What Hoffner's work, particularly that at Cabot Circus, reinforces is the notion of duality of meaning, the interconnection of present and future without necessarily having to pass through any idealised stage of completion, and that buildings are primarily about experience and perception rather than anything more easily demonstrable.

FIGURE 7.4   *Landscape vs Architecture* (part), Marie-Jeanne Hoffner, 2007. (Reproduced
with permission from the artist.)

Also of interest here, again in relation to the construction period of Cabot
Circus, but repeated elsewhere, is the work of Dan Perjovschi. Perjovschi's
work, usually the result of walking investigations of places and sites, is highly
political, often focussing on inherent contradictions in development and politics.
Significantly, his work for *BS1* in 2008 made much reference to the construction period of the shopping centre and was displayed inside the workers' canteen
within the development site. The installation was an important piece of public
art firstly for its inaccessibility to the wider public and its acceptance of the site
workers as a public for the work (Figure 7.5).

An exhibition dedicated to precarity and duality of meaning at times of change
with access solely to those enacting that change makes an interesting contribution
to debates around engagement with these issues as it is, in part, communicating
directly with those whose perspectives (and careers) revolve around the delivery
of an ideal form, regardless of whether they then leave immediately and try to do
the same thing somewhere else. Once again, we see in this work a depiction of
construction in terms of its instability and all of those things that happen around,
beneath and in opposition to the notion of completion. The spectre of non-completion, that construction period precarity common to all buildings, is constructed
in part from political perspectives like those of Dan Perjovschi, developed over

FIGURE 7.5 Site canteen drawings by Dan Perjovschi, 2008. Photo by Neville Gabie. (Reproduced with permission from Neville Gabie.)

years struggling to get by as an artist in communist Romania (Stiles, 2007) and investigating the survival of artistic autonomy within a repressive regime.

The last body of work from Cabot Circus to mention here is that of Neville Gabie, the artist-in-residence for the Cabot Circus project, mentioned earlier in connection to his work on the unrealised Paris Olympic park. Gabie was in residence for the duration of the construction period, notionally finishing his residency on the shopping centre's opening day. Thus, the work he produced was wholly focussed on aspects of the half-built building, and one particular strand of it is worth highlighting here. In *Cabot Circus Cantata* and *Canteen*, Gabie used songs and recipes, respectively, to highlight the individual people from nearly 60 countries present on the site during the construction period (Gabie, 2008; Ogden and Gabie, 2008). In collecting songs and recipes from around the world and performing/cooking them for wider audiences, Gabie sought to investigate the nature of this transient community, resident in the city for three years, yet virtually unknown to those outside the boundaries of the development. Three years is as long as most students come to a city for and they are a group who routinely receive a great deal of attention from local and national politicians, landlords, retailers and more. Not so the varied workers of a long-term construction site. Is then the spectre of non-completion partially concerned with the subaltern narratives of building? It must be. It is not just the multiple trajectories of buildings' half-built states that are written out of their interpretation as they move to the future and become heritage assets, it is also the many individuals who enact or represent these trajectories. It is rarely possible to identify individuals; indeed, it may be a fool's errand to try. It is, however, important from a future perspective on the past to at least acknowledge the presence in the past of those anonymous individual humans bound up in the spectre of non-completion. They create the counter-narratives to the ideals of the developers and of the city as a whole.

Conclusion

What this exploration of the spectre of non-completion has attempted to show is that the potential for any building to not be finished after it has been started is a phenomenon that ties together every building that has ever been built and ever will be built, but that is rarely considered in analysis. Whether in archaeological, heritage, or other disciplinary frameworks, that commonality, certainly one of the things, but perhaps the most important, that ties together the entire built environment of past, present and future, is routinely passed over in favour of work on inhabited (including previously inhabited, i.e., de-occupied) built buildings. There are many reasons for this. In part, the spectre of non-completion is a disciplinary blind spot, ignored because it is invisible from the different points of time in the process of a building around which different disciplines' interpretive frameworks have been constructed over generations. It is also difficult to access, highly visible in shape, size and mass, but with the detail obscured by hoardings and scaffolding. Hopefully, however, the usefulness of beginning to investigate and understand this phenomenon can be seen to be of importance in developing even deeper understandings of the built environment.

For instance, we might begin to investigate whether the nature of the spectre of non-completion itself has chronological and geographical variation. Do buildings embody greater certainty in the London of 2019 than in, say, Neolithic Skara Brae or Frankish Aachen? I suspect that despite its ubiquity, the spectre of non-completion is highly context-specific in its manifestations. I also suspect that more work is needed on less formal building traditions outside many countries' formal planning processes, as demonstrated by Alfredo González-Ruibal's paper in this volume (chapter 6) on how understanding 'folk architecture' can change how we understand and work with temporality, or in Robert Mellin's amazing study of the architectural tradition of invention, innovation and imaginative re-use in the village of Tilting in Newfoundland (Mellin, 2003). All this means, of course, is that we have a differently nuanced understanding to add to every building of every time in every place. No small task! But we can begin with an acknowledgement of the phenomenon and its importance. It is a perspective that should certainly become a regular part of analysis and interpretation in formalised archaeological and heritage contexts as consideration of the spectre of non-completion brings with it a whole series of suppressed narratives (and suppressed people) and enacted material networks that will be of general interest, beyond academic debate.

We live surrounded by buildings that have been designated as heritage assets and many more that have not been. Many of those buildings that are not yet formally recognised as heritage assets will come to be in the future, whether through the as-yet unrecognised significance of values they already hold, through associations and actions that have not yet been enacted or through mere longevity. If the spectre of non-completion is as important as it appears, going some way to represent the agglomeration of unofficial narratives surrounding a building as it moves between past and future and between virtual and physical forms, it is surely right that we work to ensure that what from the present moment becomes heritage in the future reflects that. This is not to say – perhaps – that heritage assemblages ought always to represent uncertainty, merely that uncertainty is a constant reality of daily life and that to ignore it in the ways we often do, embodied in legislation and disciplinary traditions, does a great disservice to the majority of our fellow citizens, for whom the conscious evocation of uncertainty is a tool for survival in an unfair world.

The spectre of non-completion is a real thing; it connects every building in human history and future, and therefore nearly every human too. It deserves more attention.

References

Cairns, S. and Jacobs, J., 2014. *Buildings Must Die: A Perverse View of Architecture*. Cambridge: The MIT Press.

Dalglish, C. (ed.), 2013. *Archaeology, the Public and the Recent Past*. Woodbridge: Boydell & Brewer.

Dixon, J., 2013. Archaeology, politics and politicians, or: Small p in a big P world. In: C. Dalglish, ed. *Archaeology, the Public and the Recent Past*. Woodbridge: Boydell & Brewer; 111–123.

Dixon, J., 2015. Human-environment relations in built heritage and urban places, past and present. In: G. Verdiani, P. Cornell, and P. Rodriguez-Navarro, ed. *Architecture, Archaeology and Contemporary City Planning: 'State of Knowledge in the Digital Age*. Florence: Giorgio Verdiani; 61–68.

Dobraszczyk, P., 2010. Petrified Ruin: Chernobyl, Pripyat and the death of the city. *City* 14(4), 370–389.

Edensor, T., 2011. Entangled agencies, material networks and repair in a building assemblage: The mutable stone of St Ann's Church, Manchester. *Transactions of the Institute of British Geographers*, 36(2), 238–252.

Gabie, N., 2008. *Canteen: A Building site Cookbook*. London: In-Site Arts.

Gehl, J., 2010. *Cities for People*. Washington, DC: Island Press

Gehl, J., 2011. *Life Between Buildings: Using Public Space*. Washington, DC: Island Press.

Historic England (formerly English Heritage), 2006. *Understanding Historic Buildings; a Guide to Good Recording Practice*. London: English Heritage.

Hutchinson, M., 2002. Four stages of public art. *Third Text* 16(4), 429–438.

Ingold, T., 2013. *Making: Anthropology, Archaeology, Art and Architecture*. London: Routledge.

Kongjian, Y. and Padua, M., 2007. *The Art of Survival: Recovering Landscape Architecture*. Mulgrave: Images Publishing Group.

Lucas, G., 2001. *Critical Approaches to Fieldwork: Contemporary and Historical Archaeological Practice*. London: Routledge.

Massey, D., 2005. *For Space*. London: Sage Publications Ltd.

McAtackney, L., 2008. Experiencing the Maze: Official and unofficial interactions with place in post-conflict Northern Ireland. In: F. Vanclay, M. Higgins, and A. Blackshaw, ed. *Making Sense of Place: Exploring Concepts and Expressions of Place through Different Senses and Lenses*. Canberra: National Museum of Australia Press; p 191–198.

Mellin, R., 2003. *Tilting: House Launching, Slide Hauling, Potato Trenching, and Other Tales from a Newfoundland Fishing Village*. New York: Princeton Architectural Press.

Ogden, D. and Gabie, N., 2008. *Cabot Circus Cantata*. London: In-Site Arts.

Pétursdóttir, Þ. and Olsen, B., 2014. Imagining modern decay: The aesthetics of ruin photography. *Journal of Contemporary Archaeology* 1(1), 7–56.

Rathje, W.L., 1979. Modern material culture studies. *Advances in Archaeological Method and Theory* 2, 1–37.

Rathje, W.L., Shanks, M. and Witmore, C. (eds.)., 2013. *Archaeology in the Making: Conversations through a Discipline*. Oxford: Routledge.

Saunders, W. (ed.)., 2012. *Designed Ecologies: The Landscape Architecture of Kongjian Yu*. Basel: Birkhäuser Verlag AG.

Stiles, K. (ed.)., 2007. *States of mind: Dan and Lia Perjovschi*. Durham, NC: Nasher Museum of Art, Duke University.

Thrift, N. and Dewsbury, J.D., 2000. Dead geographies – And how to make them live. *Environment and Planning D: Society and Space* 18(4), 411–432.

8

AN ARCHAEOLOGY OF COLD WAR ARMAGEDDONISM THROUGH THE LENS OF SCIENTOLOGY

Robert Charlotte Maxwell

The hot Cold War

During the Cold War of the 20th century, many people feared the approaching end of the world as they knew it. This led to a flourishing of new religious movements (NRMs, or 'cults' in the popular vernacular). These NRMs, being a product of the 20th-century experience, and a reaction to the *perceived experience* of the 20th century, contained a notable enculturation of armageddonism and total social collapse. At times, this focus on impending destruction and an end to society took the form of a nuclear catalyst, an exchange of nuclear warheads between Soviet and US superpowers. That was, of course, a rational fear to hold, and history proves that on at least two occasions, the US and USSR came to the brink of nuclear exchange (Zoellner, 2009).

Physical management of death, panic and disorder in the wake of a cataclysmic event became a matter for public health and safety during the Cold War. National governments issued television and radio broadcasts and booklets offering advice to the homeowner on how to survive a nuclear strike, how to construct a fallout shelter, and what to do in case of a radiological emergency. These 'preparedness guides', radiological emergency medication kits, 'nuclear survival' goods (i.e., canned water and foodstuffs) and many other consumer-oriented, non-military items, as well as the ubiquity of fallout shelters in the US landscape (and stockpiling of radiological survival goods in the USSR) reflect this real and imminent danger (Maxwell, 2015; 2016).

Mental preparedness and the psychological impact of the potential of a radiological death, however, were less well managed. Fears of attack could arguably work in favour of a government, as fear allowed the population to be highly controllable and amenable to ideological and political suggestion. In the survival guides of the period, the individual is often reduced to an agent of very simple change, managing a small group such as a household, in order to ensure biological survival for as many people as possible. Death and contamination would become a grim reality of daily life in a nuclear future. Little, if any attention, it seems, was given to the enormous emotional burden this 'preparedness' would create.

This is true for the USA as much as it is for the USSR and bears no relationship to political ideology per se. It is based entirely on the philosophy of Nuclear Fundamentalism. Whoever can control the atom can control the world (Maxwell, 2016). It is a physical expression of a behavioural and psychological need for safety. When the safety of the very fabric of matter around you is at stake, one can forgive the observer for feeling frightened, and it is certainly true for the then-adolescent author of this piece that the experience of nuclear preparedness and the enculturation of nuclear disaster can and do produce serious states of anxiety and foreboding death, even in Australia, a country recognised as relatively 'safe' in films and media of the time, being further from potential sites of conflict and bearing only one established and well known soviet target (the Pine Gap military-industrial complex) (Cooksey, 1968). Images of flames and screaming, sirens and burned humans in tattered clothing were, quite simply put, overwhelming.

New armageddons – the supernaturalisation of Cold War fears

It is the aim of this chapter to introduce contemporary sites and assemblages related to our fears of nuclear annihilation, what I call nuclear armageddonism, although it could equally be termed nuclear eschatology or any other equivalency. I posit that sites exist that exemplify the way we inherited a perceived 'future' in the contemporary past, with specific attention to the impact the threat of nuclear war had on concurrent NRMs. It is, to the author's knowledge, the first published study of nuclear armageddonism in NRMs.

The niche that the heritage of nuclear armageddonism inhabits is, to be frank, relatively unexplored territory. If shelters, communal traditions and resource security systems of the 20th century are considered as epiphenomenon of other, over-arching processes of organisation (such as the heritage study of warfare, or urbanism, or economics, for example), then the field of scholarly enquiry increases dramatically in size.

In a very real sense, an enculturation of nuclear death by NRMs is an understandable act of mental hygiene for those affected, a way to access, uptake and excrete information in an ordered and patterned way, thus allowing the individual to, in theory, *survive* in a totally and forever-altered landscape. It was an attempt by the population to control their own responses to and fears of nuclear annihilation. Religious, philosophical and 'self-help'–related groups profligated during the Cold War (being the period beginning with the end of WWII and ending with the fall of the Iron Curtain; for the purposes of this chapter delineated as between 1946 and 1991), the absolute principal and primary example of these being Scientology.

The Church of Scientology (CoS), as well as a great many other assorted NRMs and collectives, has historically embraced an eschatological orientation at some point. For some, the outcomes were relatively benign: structures remain in the landscape, yet people have moved on to other lives outside the organisation with little effect upon them.

Themes of nuclear science, nuclear warfare and nuclear apocalypse appear in the works of the author of this chapter, and several others (Maxwell, 2015; 2016; Cocroft and Thomas, 2004; Zoellner, 2009; Harvey, 2005; Jacobs, 2010; Arnold, 1992; Boyer, 1985). Cocroft and Thomas' *Cold War: Building for Nuclear Confrontation 1946–1989* is a seminal work of the field and remains the best study of the heritage of nuclear archaeology published to date. The text is largely concerned with documenting the birth and evolution of nuclear structures in the built landscape with a focus on military and industrial complexes. It stands alone as the best and only large scale survey of the archaeology and heritage of nuclear installations and is a breathtakingly thorough analysis of the effect that nuclear science had on the military-industrial complex and consequently the archaeology of the Cold War.

In terms of NRMs specific to this chapter, time and afforded space disallow an exhaustive history of Scientology (being the most complex and deliberately confusing NRM in existence and a focus of this chapter). Several significant histories of Scientology exist, most notably Jon Atack's (1990) *A Piece of Blue Sky: Scientology, Dianetics and L. Ron Hubbard Exposed*.

The Church of Scientology – history, the future and preserving the *homo novus*

L. Ron Hubbard first introduced his 'science of thought', 'Dianetics' in a piece he called 'Dianetics: The Evolution of a Science' for the May 1950 issue of *Astounding Science Fiction* magazine and later that year as a stand-alone publication (Hubbard, 1950). Hubbard was renowned for championing the use of the E-Meter™, a relatively rudimentary skin resistivity meter, in his *Dianetics* (Hubbard, 1950), and consequently, it was encultured as a sacred and unchallengeable artefact within core processes in the Church of Scientology (Hubbard, 1952), which we will consider in greater length shortly. In Hubbard's metaphysics, thought has mass in the way matter has mass, and the human operator aims to rid themselves of their 'reactive mind', an element of the self which Dianetics claims is the source of all mental illness and the catalyst for physical disease (Hubbard, 1952). The E-Meter™ and the act of 'auditing' are the ways this is achieved.

On the one hand, auditing sessions are directed, therapeutic sessions during which a Scientologist interacts with both the staff of the Church and the sacred artefact, the E-Meter™. On the other hand, this is also a very effective method by which the organisation may collect sensitive information on the individual which would, it appears, have the potential to be used against them.

Dianetics was, as Hubbard initially described it, a method so the individual could rid themselves of trauma, issues or negative thoughts through this process known as auditing (Hubbard, 1952). This is done by a technician known as an auditor, and sessions are performed using the CoS's patented E-Meter™ (http://www.xenu.net/archive/books/tsos/sos.html), a religious technology that can be calibrated and controlled by the auditor using a series of controls. Metal 'cans' are held by the Scientologist and their responses to questions recorded. Negative experiences in the past are interrogated over and over again in more and more detail until the negativity associated with that event or trauma 'blows', indicated to the auditor by a wild swing of the E-Meter™ needle to the right. Auditing sessions can last for multiple hours and cost in the thousands of dollars to complete (http://www.xenu.net/archive/books/tsos/sos.html). Suffice it to say that auditing, as a process of personal interrogation and as a system of control and organisation, remains at the core of Church of Scientology behaviour to this day (see Lewis and Hellesøy 2017 for discussion). Regardless of historical challenges to or proofs of the ineffectiveness of the auditing process, it remains a strongly-held Scientology tradition and a pivotal methodology.

Hubbard was a science fiction author and romantic futurist, so it is natural to find these themes as being central to Scientological belief and cosmology. Emergent 20th-century technologies were seen as 'futuristic' and written into the Xenu narrative (http://www.xenu.net/archive/ot/) – the central creation myth of CoS belief and only revealed during OT III, an upper-level of Scientology which many believers fail to reach. Hydrogen bombs, spacecraft, alien species and movie cinemas are all mentioned in the Xenu narrative, stated to have been in existence 27 million years ago, when the planet was a penal colony known as Teegeeack (http://www.xenu.net/archive/ot/).

As spectacular and unique as the Xenu myth may be, one important observation that many other critics fail to take into account is the Scientological focus on reincarnation – an extremely common trait held by many world religions and philosophies of belief. In Scientology, individuals consist of an etheric or astral body known as a Thetan (Atack, 1990). This etheric self is plagued by particles of spiritual matter, fragments of conscious, self-aware souls atomised during the Xenu narrative, known as 'body thetans' (Atack, 1990). These body thetans are the material which the auditee is expected to locate, audit and 'blow' during the upper OT levels of the organisation. The self is a holographic element in CoS cosmology. Each individual contains a self which contains other selves, et cetera. Thus, everyone is connected on a spiritual level, throughout the cosmos, and it is the requirement of the Scientologist to bring everyone on Earth to a plum-level zero point, a neutral, unencumbered position of CoS-affirmed 'effectiveness' known as 'Clear' (Atack, 1990).

When L. Ron Hubbard died in 1986, he left behind an organisation with a mission to, in its very essence, convert the planet to Scientology. This could only be achieved if the original works of the founder could be secured into the generations against any perceived threat. The Church of Scientology is, in fact, a trademarked organisation owned and run by the Church of Spiritual Technology (CST) (www.cs.cmu.edu). Scientology is known for its myriad umbrella compa-nies, trademarks, side companies and education and 'addiction-recovery'-based organisations. Most, if not all, are owned or operated by entities who trace their authority back to the CST. In a time of crisis, the Church can cede control of CoS to CST and enact a series of measures to ensure the survival of Scientology materials. To do this, CST built the complex at Trementina, New Mexico (www .cs.cmu.edu). Construction of the vault system began at Trementina Base in 1986 and is believed to have been completed in 1992 (Lewis and Hammer, 2007).

Trementina – the archaeology of a secret

The structures associated with Scientology at Trementina are, for the most part, deliberately underground, buried beneath restricted airspace and surrounded by privately owned and security-patrolled property with a private airstrip. Scientology holds that the base 'stands as a symbol of the timelessness of Hubbard's texts and as a three-dimensional manifestation of the purity of Hubbard's legacy' (Lewis and Hammer, 2007: 25) and in a very real sense, they are typologically correct. The 'Trementina Base' is known to house, or has housed at one time, the collated works of Hubbard in the form of documents transcribed onto stainless steel plates, films, audio recordings and other ephemera, all of which are housed within titanium, blast-proof containers. This hoard of artefacts is believed to include every scrap of written material left behind by the founder and each piece a holy relic requiring security, protection and safe passage into the future. Other underground vaults are believed to exist at Trementina, Rim Forest and possibly Gold Base near Hemet, California (Ortega, 2012a).

Any vault at Trementina (or elsewhere) would also act as a nuclear bunker and shelter in case of nuclear crisis and was built with the purpose of ensuring against nuclear detonation and/or contamination by being below ground with a blast-proof door and frontage. The subterranean nature of the complex also fosters privacy and concealment. Very few outsiders have ever been allowed onto the property and none have been given unfettered access. Until its recent demolition (for unknown reasons), the entrance to the vault complex looks very much like a domestic structure; it is a deliberate rouse, a camouflaging of infrastructure as a domicile or similar building. The house, however, clearly abutting a cliff face at the rear, indicates it is an entrance to a potentially large underground complex. That structure, what is commonly known as the 'ventilation building', is being replaced with another construction, though at the time of writing its purpose, and that of the entire project, is completely unknown.

The Trementina complex also bears another archaeological feature of note, apart from and separate to the structures above or below ground, an earthwork in the landscape, visible only from the air, first publicised in the *Washington Post* in 2005 (Leiby, 2005). The earthwork is the logo of the CST: two circles interlock-ing with diamonds at the centre of each circle. This logo bears a very striking resemblance to the logo for Kool cigarettes, a brand of cigarette Hubbard was devoted to smoking for the majority of his adult life. Access to the earthwork or anywhere else on the Trementina Base is not permitted and even speaking about the base is believed to be enough to warrant punishment within the organisation. After being found in New Mexico, other CST earthwork logos have been identified in the northern Californian town of Petrolia and at a ranch near the town of Creston, also in California (Ortega, 2012b). According to journalist and critic Tony Ortega, during a conversation with Dylan Gill, a contractor who worked on the CST complexes, Gill stated: 'that's where LRH [L. Ron Hubbard] is supposed to go, when he returns.' Once Hubbard adopts a new body, he is expected to make his way to one of the CST bases. 'That's where he's supposed to be raised and be taken care of,' Gill says. 'So the symbol is a way for a spirit to find its way back to where it belongs' (Ortega, 2012b).

This earthwork is interesting archaeologically, in that it is a true and unique religiously-oriented earthwork that dates to the 20th century. In terms of global earthworks visible from the air (the Nazca Lines being another obvious example), the CST logo is a very singular and incisive work of archaeology wherever it appears – it is agency of a purely semiotic nature. It is a symbol of belief and of branding. It is a product of its time in the most intriguing way.

Another feature of the typical secret Scientology structural complex is the Hubbard House or LRH House. As Hubbard is not technically 'dead' in terms of Scientological belief (he is in 'an exterior state'), a series of Hubbard Houses have been constructed at various Scientology bases, such as Rim Forest, a compound in the San Bernardino Mountains which ex-Scientologists refer to as Twin Peaks (Ortega, 2016). Another is located on a ranch in Creston, California, another again at Gold Base – the Church of Scientology's proxy headquarters (Ortega, 2016). When Hubbard reincarnates into human form, these houses are intended to be ready for him, should he appear, at any point. They are kept with beds and bedding, stationery, slippers, novels and other assorted items of which Hubbard was known to be fond. These houses are shrines to the belief that the Commodore may, one day, return. So long as Scientology can survive the apocalypse, in whatever form that may take (Remini, 2017).

Secrecy was, is and always will be at the heart of Scientology methodologies; information is compartmentalised and revealed by degrees as an individual 'progresses' within the organisation. The security of information is paramount. Trementina, Rim Forest, Petrolia, Creston; all are expressions of the crucial value afforded to secrecy and highly restricted access to information. It would be fair to say that most Scientologists probably do not even know most of these locations exist. It is one enormous secret, built to ensure secrecy, hierarchy, and the continuation of Scientology beyond an envisioned armageddon. In that sense, it might be said that scientology is a religion paranoid by nature (see Urban 2017 for discussion), and so it holds that this paranoia will translate into the material and associative heritage left by Hubbard and the formative period of the organisation in the 20th century.

By 'clearing' a person, within Scientology it is believed that person is rendered changed on a cellular level, going from *Homo Sapiens* to *Homo Novus* (http://www.xenu.net/archive/ot/), the New Human, clear of past trauma and ready to embrace the upper levels of Scientology. The Trementina complex is entirely about the concept of the future, as perceived by the Church and other Scientology organisations, at the time of the founder's death. It is an expression of a period of perceived threat, a crisis and a need to secure information into an uncertain future. It is a complex built during a time of uncertainty, both physically and spiritually, as insurance against a hostile future.

Preserving the works of Hubbard, constructing elaborate vault systems and earthworks, building empty-yet-complete houses – non-places of non-habitation – Scientology betrays itself in its sites, structures and archaeology, from the E-Meter™ to the underground vault.

A heritage of fear

In a broad sense, the field of NRMs is a goldmine of heritage-related information and an asset to humanity as a whole. The flourishing and variety of NRMs during the Cold War period is a testament to the widespread uptake of a modernist concept of the self, an individual understood as an agent of change, able to question the socially accepted institutions of religion and social organisation. NRMs empower the individual in the way that the emergence of the bicycle empowered individuals, particularly women, to navigate society alone and unchaperoned by another. They offer the individual the ability to choose which belief system they align with, or enact one of their own, in order to get from a conceptual A to a conceptual B. Whether that is a valid exercise is not the question of this chapter. It is the fact that the bicycle exists that matters, not where it is going. The agent of change, when encultured by the individual in society, becomes a vehicle for social fluidity. This increase in fluidity has the potential for a consequential increase in social complexity as a direct result. This is a specific point of interest in the field of NRMs.

Just as Eastern philosophy had a massive impact upon the belief systems inherited by the NRMs of the Cold War (concepts of reincarnation, meditation, yoga, breathing exercises, communalism, polytheism, naturism, urban monasticism and mantras are just some of the expressions of contact and Eastern influence), the contemporary influence can be seen in the enculturation of nuclear science, electronics and the military and political atmosphere. The uptake of technology and science by emergent systems of belief had a direct impact upon the physical landscape and the heritage of the period. The structures and bunkers of groups like the CST ask us to remember a time when we felt threatened on an atomic level. We felt the very real and imminent threat of nuclear war and everything else that entailed. The likelihood of death in such an outcome would be extremely high, and the quality of life negligible. This fear of total annihilation, or worse, being left to die in a radiation-scorched landscape was much more present in popular thought and culture of the 1980s than it is today, even with the advent of the internet and other telecommunications technologies. The threat of nuclear war during the Cuban Missile Crisis was staggeringly high, just as it was during the Soviet False Alarm event of 1983. As the superpowers had nuclear warheads loaded and ready to strike upon request, the atmosphere was substantially tenser then than now.

The emergence of nuclear science is perhaps one of the most remarkable turning points for our species, and it would suggest that a significant amount of time and effort should go into investigating the impact of nuclear science upon human society during the first decades of discovery. It is clear that we have participated in an uptake of a technology without a total working knowledge of its potential impacts upon us. What gets lost, however, is the archaeology and heritage of nuclear armageddonism that marked the Cold War as a period of intense fear and social unease unlike any that preceded it.

While the popular conception of the 1980s is now one of colour and pop music and hairspray, the lived experience of the Cold War is one filled with much more trauma and a foreboding about the future. The future was bleak and frightening. It was a place filled with death, loss, radiation, cancer and social disarray. It was a world that we would produce through the behaviours of war, enacted by the science of nuclear physics, upon the entire planet, and the only thing one could do was prepare. The heritage of the future in the context of the Cold War is, to put it mildly, depressing, and could be as much of a psychological toxin as the material itself is a physical one. Regardless, the period deserves more attention than it has received to date. Perhaps with time, social change and a new approach, the nuclear fears of the Cold War can be seen to be productive elements of the contemporary past rather than a topic to be avoided or forgotten. The sites and artefacts of the nuclear threat are important indicators of social psychology and prevailing attitudes toward global politics, industry, science and technology. Just as any artefact is a product of its period, context and material, the nuclear armageddonism of the Cold War period can be seen to be of significant unique value in its material, contextual and chronological specificity. It is a window into the contemporary past that we still find troubling. The wastelands depicted in movies like *Threads*[1] and *The Day After*[2] were potential real-world outcomes for the viewer. These nuclear apocalypse films are perhaps the most telling artefacts of the period, for they truly envisage the world that was perceived to be just around the corner. Suburbs rendered uninhabitable for thousands of years, families destroyed, cities obliterated. These nightmares of total annihilation and social collapse were far from distant possibilities.

Today, we again find ourselves in a period of global uncertainty. The shadows of the Cold War loom large over current socio-political trends, and the relationship between Russia and the USA is complicated, to say the least. In light of the 2016 election of Donald Trump as US President, much conversation covered social media and indeed media of all forms. There is widespread fear, based on the possibility of an unheralded, spontaneous nuclear exchange. In an age of intercontinental ballistic missiles, the immediacy of social media and the penchant of the US President for using Twitter as a valid platform for advocacy and political statements, it may be that we are now, in the 21st century, even closer to nuclear apocalypse than we were for the vast majority of the 20th century.

Perhaps as the world fears it is entering headlong into a Second Cold War or worse, a Third World War, we can re-evaluate the artefacts of the Cold War. A Trump Presidency may force us to look back on our crisis of going forward. We may be able to look at these artefacts from a more comfortable place and see them as indicative of our social health, both physical and psychological. They are the only repository of such information – a unique assemblage of places, things and behaviours that show that discoveries in the field of science have a heritage-related impact upon society. They shape the future we choose to enter.

Science and belief are not polar opposites. Science is often used as a prop for religious belief. It may, in the case of the E-Meter™, become a religious artefact in and of itself. Given enough time, all technology will be encultured as a tool of self-expression, spiritual expression or some other form of individualism. The field of science and the phenomenon of faith are not necessarily at odds with each other, at least not from the position of the believer. For the believer, technology is a tool to be used to change themselves, to evolve and become more intellectually fluid. This is a human phenomenon as much as archaeology is a human phenomenon; it is the process of enculturation.

It is our capacity to question, penetrate and analyse that which allows us to move forward. The objects and landscapes we leave behind us speak not to the recorded histories and orthodox chronologies of the recent past. Rather they are our only true relics of the world that we saw coming. They are the pieces of ourselves we left behind in the landscape as testament to our fears for the future. They are, perhaps more than anything else, a repository for the lived experience of the Cold War 20th century, in all its facets. We lived for the present and prepared against the future.

Notes

1 Jackson (dir.), 1984.
2 Meyer (dir.), 1983.

References

Arnold, L., 1992. *Windscale 1957 – Anatomy of a Nuclear Accident*. London: Macmillan Press.

Arnone, P., 1990. *The Farce Revealed – Church Universal and Triumphant in Scholarly Perspective*. https://www.apologeticsindex.org/a106a.html. Last accessed 20/1/2017.

Atack, J., 1990. *A Piece of Blue Sky: Scientology Dianetics and L. Ron Hubbard Exposed*. London: Lyle Stewart.

Boyer, P., 1985. *By the Bomb's Early Light- American Thought and Culture at the Dawn of the Atomic Age*. New York: Pantheon.

Cocroft, W. and Thomas, R.J.C., 2004. *Cold War – Building for Nuclear Confrontation 1946–1989*. London: English Heritage.

Cooksey, R.J. 1968. Pine Gap. *The Australian Quarterly* 40(4), 12–20.

Harvey, D., 2005. *Deadly Sunshine – The History and Fatal Legacy of Radium*. Stroud: Tempus.

Hubbard, L.R., 1950. *Dianetics: The Modern Science of Mental Health*. New York: Hermitage House.

Hubbard, L.R., 1952. *A History of Man*. Phoenix: Scientific Press.

Jacobs, R. (ed.)., 2010. *Filling the Hole in the Nuclear Future – Art and Popular Culture Respond to the Bomb*. Plymouth: Lexington Books.

Leiby, R., 2005. A Place in the Desert for New Mexico's Most Exclusive Circles. *Washington Post*, 27/11/2005.

Lewis, J. and Hammer, O., 2007. *The Invention of Sacred Tradition*. Cambridge: Cambridge University Press.

Lewis, J.R. and Hellesøy, K. (eds.), 2017. *The Handbook of Scientology*. Brill Handbooks on Contemporary Religion, volume 14. Boston: Brill.

Maxwell, R., 2015. The Claw: A Song of Electrons. In: S. Brown, A. Clarke and U. Frederick, eds. *Object Stories: Artifacts and Archaeologists*. San Francisco: Left Coast Press; pp. 147–153.

Maxwell, R., 2016. The Radium Water Worked Fine Until His Jaw Came Off: The Changing Role of Radioactivity in the 20th Century. In: U. Frederick and A. Clarke, eds. *That Was Then, This Is Now: Contemporary Archaeology and Material Culture in Australia*. Newcastle-Upon-Tyne: Cambridge Scholars Press; pp. 84–100.

Operation Clambake Presents the OT Levels. http://www.xenu.net/archive/ot/ (last accessed 0/11/2015).

Ortega, T., 2012a/2/6. Scientology's Secret Vaults: A Rare Interview with a Former Member of Hush-Hush 'CST'. http://www.villagevoice.com/news/scientologys-secret-vaults-a-rare-interview-with-a-former-member-of-hush-hush-cst-6704625 (last accessed 20/1/2017).

Ortega, T., 2012b/2/16. Scientology's Secret Ranch: Where LRH Will Reincarnate? http://www.villagevoice.com/news/scientologys-secret-ranch-where-lrh-will-reincarnate-6670291 (last accessed 10/1/2017).

Ortega, T., 2016/09/14. DRONE FLYOVER: Scientology's Secret Base Where David Miscavige Keeps Wife out of Sight. http://tonyortega.org/2016/09/14/drone-flyover-scientologys-secret-base-where-david-miscavige-keeps-wife-out-of-sight/ (last accessed 10/01/2017).

Remini, L., 2017/1/17. *Leah Remini: Scientology and the Aftermath: Ask Me Anything Part 2*. A&E TV.

Swainson, M., 2017. The Price of Freedom: Scientology and Neoliberalism. In J.R. Lewis and K. Hellesøy (eds.), *The Handbook of Scientology*. Brill Handbooks on Contemporary Religion, volume 14. Boston: Brill, 200–223.

'The High Cost of Scientology' by Paulette Cooper at Operation Clambake: The Scientology Resource Archive. http://www.xenu.net/archive/books/tsos/sos.html (last accessed 10/11/2015).

Urban, H.B., 2017. 'Secrets, secrets, SECRETS!' Concealment, Surveillance, and Information-Control in the Church of Scientology. In J.R. Lewis and K. Hellesøy (eds.), *The Handbook of Scientology*. Brill Handbooks on Contemporary Religion, volume 14. Boston: Brill, 279–299.

Zoellner, T., 2009. *Uranium – War, Energy and the Rock That Shaped the World*. London: Viking.

9

FUTURE VISIONS AND THE HERITAGE OF SPACE

Nostalgia for infinity[1]

A dialogue between Alice Gorman and Sarah May

Introduction

Since the late 19th century, outer space and spacecraft have been symbols of the future, and indeed, futurist symbols. In the 1950s, space technology was seen as the solution to the human condition, the locus for new utopias – and dystopias. The future was shiny, metallic, robotic, orderly, the province of science and reason.

The reality has been far less dramatic, but perhaps far more transformative, as daily life on the planet is now structured by access to GNSS (global navigation satellite systems) and PNT (positioning, navigation and timing). Yet most people rarely give any thought to the satellites that provide them with such essential services. Only some spacecraft stick in the popular imagination: Vanguard 1, Telstar 1, the Skylab space station, Pioneer 10 and 11, Voyager 1 and 2 and the Tesla Roadster sports car.

These spacecraft are powerful representations of the ultimate heritage. In space, they are not subject to the unruly organic and geological processes that cause human artefacts to decay on Earth. The Pioneers and Voyagers were deliberately designed to last beyond human time scales. As heritage, they are not just what we want future generations to remember, but what we want alien species to understand about life on Earth. To this end, both the Voyagers and the Pioneers were sent into interstellar space bearing cultural symbols. The Pioneers had engraved plaques, and the Voyagers, the famous Golden Records containing sounds, greetings and music of Earth. In terms of the cultural choices they represent, these iconic spacecraft are as much messages to our future selves than to any putative alien species 40,000 years hence, when Voyager 1 nears the star system Gliese 445.

They are time capsules, inaccessible to be sure, but preserved against the ravages of organic decay under Earth's surface. We may never know how non-humans interpret these messages, but we can revisit them through their extensive documentation and make our own interpretations of the past.

In the interstellar time frame of the Voyagers and Pioneers, what might remain in the more domestic setting of Earth orbit? The proliferation of spacecraft debris could be likened to lithic 'debitage'. To the observers of the future, the earliest human spacecraft such as Telstar 1 and Vanguard 1 may appear as 'primitive' as the once-controversial eoliths or 'dawn stones' (O'Connor 2003) – barely recognisable as technology. Twenty-first-century humanity will need as much decoding as any alien message from the stars.

Utilising 'space-age' satellite technology, Alice Gorman spoke with Sarah May over a Skype call between her home in Australia and Sarah's home in the UK. Starting from the ideas in the introduction above, the conversation tacked between the practical and political materialities of contemporary spacecraft and their aesthetics, which still hold a 'future' place in many imaginations.

Future aesthetics

Sarah: Why do people think of space in relation to the future?

Alice: People are quite heavily invested in that notion because leaving space in the future also leaves it in the realm of possibility. To move it into any other temporal zone leads to disappointment. This shows in the aesthetics. The early spacecraft were very different in comparison to contemporary spacecraft. Contemporary spacecraft really are kind of work-a-day, lacking the space-age shininess of popular culture visions of the future. Space in the present tense is less aesthetically pleasing than space futures or space heritage.

There is a Russian science fiction novel from 1924, Yevgeny Zamyatin's *We*, which is really about heritage in a sense. The main character falls in love with someone from a social class he's not allowed to have access to. And she takes him to a sort of museum that preserves all of the chaos and messiness from the past, and not the glass and metal artefacts of the present (Figure 9.1). So the novel is very much juxtaposing that future of the clean vertical lines of metal and glass, with the round, knobbly, coloured decaying objects in the museum. The whole plot then turns on how the main character encounters and processes the notion unknown to him until that point – that life can be just incredibly messy.

I found it really, really interesting because it's an aesthetic of the future, written long before anyone had built a spacecraft or conceived a future where there are no plants or animals left. Now there are many, many visions of that future, where everything is artificial. Zamyatin is making an argument about how you understand, how you compare the past and the present. I've been thinking about this book in terms of how we see space. These objects, satellites and space ships relate to that kind of vision of the future, which is a non-biological vision effectively, particularly as these

FIGURE 9.1 Illustration by Kit Russell for We, 2018.

objects are robots. I mean, people don't think about satellites as robots, but they are technically a robot.

Satellites as symbols

Sarah: We talk about the grand ventures of spacecraft sent beyond the solar system, but there are these less dramatic things to do with global navigation, satellite systems and positioning, navigation and timing. It really strikes me that this is the stuff that actually makes a difference in peoples' lives. We're even relying on this now-mundane technology, you and I right now, to allow us to talk.

Alice: [Laughs] Yes.

Sarah: When you and I started in archaeology, this particular thing that we're doing, talking across continents for so long, would not have been possible. So, there's a way in which we look away from the things that have actually come to pass. Perhaps that disappointment that you mentioned pushes back against some of the wonder that we could have for the way that our lives are.

Alice: This is a really interesting thing isn't it? They just introduced a National Broadband Network in Australia which is meant to make everyone's internet speeds faster, and we've got a couple of satellites that are hooked into that network. It's been a big disaster for a whole bunch of political reasons, but people get really upset at the thought that their internet speed might be slower than other places. There's lots of comparisons; in fact, this is interesting now that I'm thinking about it. In the same way that in Australia people would often say, 'We don't have a space agency. Even Nigeria has a space agency!', there's a kind of outrage that an affluent, colonial nation should be on the same level as a so-called 'developing' country. [Note: an Australian Space Agency was established in 2018, after this discussion].

Sarah: 'Oh, we should be better than Nigeria!'

Alice: Yes, that's exactly it! People are saying, 'No, you know, our internet speeds are slower than the Philippines!' In exactly that sort of way, this stuff is all about national identity in the present. There's a few frameworks you can place around people's understanding of this. Some of them are around ideas of invisible technologies or transparent technologies. And satellites have certainly become invisible. The early satellites were almost works of art. They were scientific pioneers, one-offs, doing things that had never been done before. These days, navigation and telecommunications and other satellites are just like cookie-cutter objects that come off the factory floor, and they all look similar. A lot of telecoms satellites are manufactured by Boeing or similar companies, and you just order one and then it's launched. There's not even anything nationalist about that, although nationalism is a massive theme in space.

Sarah: Can we think about a space future, which isn't a nationalist space future? But we could have a whole conversation just about that topic.

Alice: This is one of those aspects of the space industry that people tend not to look at: telecommunication satellites rolling off a production line at Boeing or Orbital ATK, in one country, and being purchased and launched by another country. People aren't particularly inspired by that level of industrial production and launch. But there are stories that show how nationalism is still a driver.

One of my favourite satellites is Palapa A1, launched by Indonesia in 1976. It was manufactured by Boeing Hughes, as it was then, and it's identical to a whole bunch of other satellites. These are cylindrical satellites, as opposed to the earlier spherical satellites, and they've got little dish antennas attached to them.

Palapa A1 (Figure 9.2) was explicitly intended to unite the culturally and linguistically diverse Indonesian nation of over 3,000 islands. So, even though it was one of those satellites just like any other, when it was launched, it was positioned as a symbol of unifying a nation. Achieving that for a modern, political entity that has such incredible differences across all of the islands was hard to imagine. This satellite was not only providing

FIGURE 9.2   Palapa A1 satellite. Image credit: ieee.ca

telecoms to all of these places but was above them, so, in that position from Earth orbit, it can't be corrupted by anyone else. It oversees all, those 3,000 islands, and it becomes the perfect symbol of a united nation, and with that comes the future, so it's a promise. Everybody's going to get access to the same technology, the same television, the same telephone capacities. But it also means an erasing of differences. If everybody has access to the same data, it's a way to homogenise cultural difference across a place.

Faye Ginsburg has talked about satellites as a sort of a silent colonialism. She argues satellite telecommunications can actually work to reduce diversity and overlay existing societies or cultures with a homogenised capitalist, more globalised view (Ginsburg 1991).

Also, satellite-based telecommunications are very heavily regulated, and a lot of that stuff is, again, really boring. Every time we use a telephone, we don't want to read through all the various bits of legislation and policy. Space telecommunication is regulated by the International Telecommunications Union and access to parts of the spectrum are very heavily contested, but people who use satellite services generally don't pay much attention to this. At the end of the day that hardware is only in space because it receives or transmits within a particular band of the spectrum.

It's not the physical satellite that is the key asset; it is actually the band. Those are literally invisible because you cannot see the spectrum. The satellite is a physical representation of that part of the spectrum.

The power of junk

Sarah: Earlier, we spoke about the aesthetics of space hardware and what people expect it to look like and how that relates to the future. Contrast that with the nitty-gritty of political negotiations around bandwidth and power relations around particular bands. The way that heritage acts to conceal inequalities and power relations is through a focus on aesthetics. It seems the same thing is happening in space. There is substantial political negotiation about resources and control that is, as you say, actually quite boring. But it's also quite contested, yes? It's having quite an impact on people's lives, but that's hidden behind a continuing imaginary of Sputnik and antennae and shiny spheres. So that operates in the same way that heritage operates in other circumstances.

Alice: Oh, yes, that's an interesting analogy. I'm just thinking now of contemporary spacecraft that are a focus of imagination and I've had many of these conversations on Twitter in recent times. Many people got very, very, angry about what I said about the sports car. Elon Musk's test launch of the Falcon Heavy rocket in 2018 carried a Tesla sports car as a payload (Figure 9.3). We both published articles on it (Gorman 2018; May 2018). I pointed out the phallic symbolism and the role of the sports car in toxic male imaginaries. I've found that people don't like it if you start to unpack all those other meanings within a technology. Or, if you dig down into

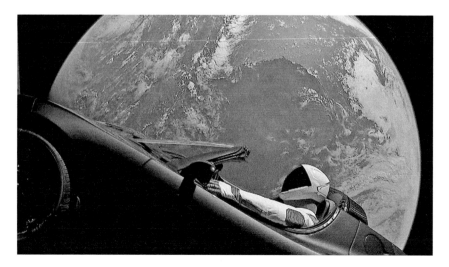

FIGURE 9.3   Elon Musk's Tesla Roadster in space. Image credit: SpaceX.

those geopolitical realities that are behind it, that disrupts – definitely disrupts – what people think about the possibilities of human future existence in space.

Distance protects the future, distance protects the quality of the future in certain spacecraft and preserves that for people to focus on. So Palapa 1 is the perfect example of that, isn't it? It's like the Golden Records (the Sounds of Earth records, carried on the Voyager spacecraft); the further away they travel the more they can be the repository of all of those hopes and dreams. They become the ultimate symbol of space hardware as something benign and peaceful and hopeful. They're *so* far away and people still focus on them. So, they're in a sense a mask for the near-Earth orbit junk, as well.

Sarah: That's a very interesting point isn't it, that the more that we send things further out, the more that we cannot look at the cloud of things that are in front of our noses because the imaginary is always following those distant ones.

Alice: Yes, I think there is something in that and the other contrasts we make. There's this word 'junk', which is often used about human space artefacts. Occasionally the term is applied to stuff left on the Moon, but it's more common to call this trash, rather than junk.

People still talk about what the Apollo missions left behind as potential pollution of the lunar environment, another example of humans buggering up the environment and leaving their garbage, not junk, behind. How do you imagine that? You say 'trash' and the kinds of things that you imagine are often the classic metal garbage can with a lid, and that's associated with that term in people's minds. Or you might think of 'junk' as in a scrap yard or a rubbish tip.

The people who own the stuff see it differently. There's visualisations by NASA and ESA [European Space Agency] that show the tracked bits of junk as little white dots (Figure 9.4). It's a particular kind of map that's usually shown in relation to Earth. Earth is in the centre of it, and I think that's important. It's not just, 'Well here we are, and this is the location'. It strips out that image of the junkyard. It's modelled in that classical way where each catalogued item is a point or a sphere. It's all reduced to that point, and that point is called the junk.

These images get rid of any necessity to engage with the material, which is of course, what I spend a lot of my time doing. I'm trying to put personality back onto the thing that's just the dot. The image enables a narrative which runs: this is junk, this is bad, junk has to be removed to return space to natural black. And that's fine as far as it goes, except it's a scenario of inaction. Environmental clean-up movements on Earth have resulted in various sorts of direct actions people can take. We've seen this more and more with the emphasis on recycling and using less. But people talk about space junk and in fact, there's nothing you can do. There's no solution that's

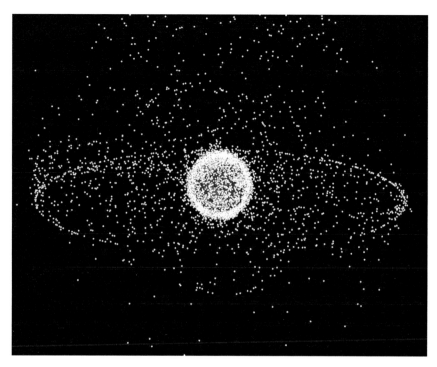

FIGURE 9.4   Space junk in Earth orbit. Image credit: NASA.

accessible to regular people. I think it's a mirror opposite to what we were talking about earlier. It's about the future being ruined before our eyes.

Sarah: Yes. That's really interesting and that ties in with the work that Jenny Morgan and Sharon McDonald are doing in the heritage futures project about profusion and the way that we send selected things into the future (Morgan and McDonald, 2018). We've determined that these particular things ought to go to the future. That's good for the future, that's a gift, that's fantastic, but if you send too much to the future, then that's ruining the future, as you say. So, you can't be sending a whole lot of stuff because that's terrible, but you have to send something because otherwise, the future will be bereft.

Alice: Yes, that's really interesting and true, isn't it?

Sarah: Yes. So the junk is the profusion, but then spacecraft that go out beyond Earth's orbit are gifts? The location determines the meaning of the thing.

The sports car in space

Sarah: Let's come back to the Tesla Roadster, the dreaded mid-life crisis in space, which you've written about (Gorman 2018). The red sports car is a widely understood symbol of masculine rejection of domesticity and longing for youth (Freund and Ritter 2009; Gatling et al. 2014). It's about speed and sex. The spacecraft sports car didn't exist when this book was proposed, because it's so new. When it launched, many people said, 'We're living in the future! We're living in the future!' It's interesting that immediately, as soon as they saw the launch, people were talking about the car on its journey towards Mars, rather than the actual innovation, which was the re-landing of the boosters. Old rocket boosters or rocket bodies left in orbit are a major contributor to orbital debris, so the technology developed by Elon Musk's company SpaceX to return them to Earth is a major development. That didn't catch much interest at all outside of the space sphere.

Alice: Yes, it's curious, isn't it? I mean, obviously, the space nuts were pretty much focused on that aspect as well as the Tesla Roadster. I suppose, for the space crowd, the vulgarity of the sports car was balanced or diminished by the booster re-landings and the other technical successes.

Sarah: They were prepared to put up with it. It ties into Shirtgate too, doesn't it? Shirtgate was a controversy over an inappropriate shirt worn by a member of the Rosetta spacecraft team at a press conference, and the way it demonstrated sexism in space science (see Plait 2014). The scientist in question described Rosetta in sexualised terms, and then wore the notorious shirt, made from fabric depicting semi-naked women offered up for the male gaze. Until the television cameras broadcast it to the world, it seemed no-one had thought through the implications of this fabric.

Alice: That, yes, yes! I think you're absolutely right; it does tie so closely. When the Roadster was launched few people made this connection in the media – perhaps they were too afraid to open old wounds or had genuinely forgotten about Shirtgate. But in both instances, there were depths of gendered symbolism around space objects.

Sarah: There was a sense of 'Don't be ruining this wonderful, technical, clean, pure, shiny, Sputnik moment, with your awful maleness'. You know. [Laughs]

Alice: God! Yes. Wasn't it terrible? I mean, the whole Tesla Roadster thing is just so blatant. I suppose what's surprised me is how little critique there has been of it. Despite my reservations, for many, that car is an aspiration. I think of it as both these things at once. It's the rich man's toy, the symbol of elite wealth, but also one that many hope to own. So, it's both exclusionary and inclusionary simultaneously.

Sarah: Yes, because it's not a unique object, like the Voyager discs, it isn't singularised, it's still something that is purchasable.

Alice: Yes, and people can dream of having one, and sometimes they do get to have one, or they get to drive their mate's, or they read about it in magazines or they watch the advertisements on television. So, the idea of it is accessible and what it means is accessible. One of its symbolic meanings is success, and that is something that people can aspire to. That's part of the reason why it resonated so strongly with the public.

It's very much about the individual, the capitalist body – literally the body, as a space-suited dummy rode inside the car – and it's a very strong message that private corporate space is here. So it's a radical, radical break with the idea of spacecraft representing all humanity or it's representing all humanity in a completely different way.

Sarah: The metonymy is 'flash car = successful man'. That's a message for today. The successful man is living in the future. The way in which *we* might relate to the *future* hasn't been considered; there's no interest. But these objects are time capsules whether or not we send them out deliberately as such. Whether we're sending Golden Records or messages to Mars (Lomberg 2013), or even when we just launch a weather satellite, our interactions with space are always time capsules.

Alice: When the last believer dies, so does that God die. As long as people are talking about that bloody Roadster then it is performing the function for which it was launched. So, in that sense, it's got, at least in human terms, a potentially endless function. It subverts the idea of what junk is and what death is.

The signs of death

Alice: I'm writing something at the moment about satellite death (Gorman 2019). It's an analogy between the signs of death in the human body and how we determine when a satellite is 'junk'. The signs of human death are, in fact, very difficult to determine. In the 18th and 19th centuries, people built mortuary waiting houses, where corpses had bells on their toes, in case they woke up. There was a tremendous fear of being buried alive. There's the death of the body, and there's brain death. If someone's brain is dead but their organs function, then their organs are available to be harvested and given to the next person. But, it's really difficult to tell when the brain is actually dead.

I've been thinking about this in relation to satellites. To be classified as junk, they have to die. There's the moment when the fuel runs out, or the batteries run out, and you can't communicate with it anymore. That's a sort of satellite death.

There's also the end of the mission. The spacecraft might have enough fuel left, you might be able to talk to it, but the mission is technically over. All of the staff are reassigned to something else. The software and the hardware that are used to support the mission are moved over to the next project. The satellite can still talk and hear, but nobody's listening. So it becomes junk because it's not serving that purpose, but it's not because the satellite itself is actually dead.

Or you have a satellite that's been damaged, and we've had a few cases of this as well, but someone mucks about with the software and manages to get it back online. So, death can be a temporary state; it's not a permanent state.

FIGURE 9.5 A typical satellite explosion. Image credit: ESA.

Or there's a satellite in the process of breaking up, as many of them are (Figure 9.5). When a satellite or a rocket body explodes from residual fuel or plasma arcing, I suppose you could say it's dead then. The bits individually can no longer do anything; it needs to be together and operating as a unit to be functional for its original purpose. So that's a form of death. But then what if it's just a little bit dead? At what point do you draw that line? Like the Knight in *Monty Python and the Holy Grail* (1975) who keeps fighting when all his arms and legs have been chopped off.

Sarah: [Laughs] Yes.

Alice: Where is that line? When do you say this satellite is actually dead? If something is still being used, it's in its technical context rather than archaeological and so not, according to some, really up for study. But it's just not as easy as that in life; it's not easy to classify.

Sarah: But it's interesting that you're talking about death for the objects of our study. In UK legislation a building can't be taken into state guardianship as heritage if it is still functioning. This is one of the reasons why, post-war, a lot of those stately homes got their roofs taken off them, because they couldn't be given to the state, to take care of them, whilst they still had roofs on. They took the roofs off so they could get rid of them. They couldn't, legally, be taken into the heritage sphere until they were beyond use.

Alice: Wow, I'm quite astonished. I didn't realise that. That's not very good for the buildings.

Sarah: Well, no, it's been a real problem for them. English Heritage pushed back against this a lot because a building without a roof is much more difficult to care for (see Keay, 2004). But people did deliberately take the roofs off a number of them post-war in order to be able to take them into guardianship. We define things as heritage by putting them beyond use, and being beyond use is part of their definition.

But the notion of them being dead also makes me think of terror management theory (Sani et al. 2009: 244). Heritage as a future-focused activity, ensuring objects continue to 'live' beyond our lifetimes, is a method of dealing with the terror of death. As Elon Musk said on Twitter, 'I love the thought of a car drifting apparently endlessly through space and perhaps being discovered by an alien race millions of years in the future' (Musk 2018).

Alice: Both those things relate to the old story ending of 'Riding off into the sunset to live happily after'. And it's also what you said before, I think, taking it beyond. You take it far beyond anything that we've known, far beyond where humans have managed to reach yet, which isn't very far at all in galactic terms. So, the space object becomes insurance against death, like some religious beliefs. It's the aspiration to immortality as well. The idea of heritage damping down the rising force of terror at our own mortality is really on the money. Yes.

The hidden technology

Sarah: Let's go back to the beginning of this conversation when we spoke about what we want our space hardware to look like. The aesthetic desire persists that our space hardware ought to be shiny and have antennas and be curved and space-age. It is literally reflective of our desire. It's function is hidden. So we focus on its symbolic function, which can be accessed without having to get involved in any of that messiness, which only reminds us that it will actually decay.

Alice: The interior of the spacecraft is concealed from view, and that's an interesting thing in itself. Because the space environment is so harsh, instruments and fuel systems are hidden behind shielding. There's always that threat that they're a weapon as well. I would estimate that defence-based hardware is probably at least 50% of everything that's up there. The exterior surface also contains a veiled threat.

Sarah: The messy physical realities of spacecraft are behind shielding. That shielding also tidies up the messy political realities of those spacecraft. What's more, shiny, smooth spacecraft are part of the future, so not available for contemporary critique.

Heritage does this tidying job too. When heritage tidies up fears and inequalities, it can also – whilst it's at it – do a great job of just tidying up bits and pieces that powerful people don't want you to look at in the present moment. While we think about the heritage issues in space, we don't count how many satellites have defence functions.

Because it's such a good tidying-up mechanism, it can do shielding for the powerful as well. Which is, to a certain extent, what we were talking about with the Tesla. If everybody is looking at the symbolic message and the space nuts – as you say – looking at the technical, virtuosity of the re-landing, then the political questions are shielded. Who gets to operate in space? Who gets to make decisions about what happens in space? Where does the money come from? What's the purpose of the activity? All those questions just get side-lined. We are culturally and technically dazzled.

Alice: Yes, yes. Absolutely right and I think we've really seen that to such a large degree, haven't we? And so much of it is also premised on the cult of personality around Musk. A distraction.

Sarah: Putting our eyes into the future, that takes our eyes away from the present.

Alice: So we don't look at things like the United Nations treaties, such as the Outer Space Treaty of 1967, or the Moon Agreement of 1979. The private corporations are gunning for the treaties at the moment because they are based on the principle that space is the common heritage of humanity. This is antithetical to the capitalist desire to exploit the resources of space, such as minerals and orbits. Such distractions make it more difficult to resist the erosion of these principles. These kinds of implications tend to get forgotten in the excitement about the successes and the quirky playfulness of the car.

Sarah: This may be a place to finish. The pairing of space and the future is a key component of space heritage. In space, as on Earth, heritage can function as distraction, something to draw attention from ways in which decisions get taken. Space heritage refocuses us on the present, on the decisions and politics that are entangled with the material we have sent into orbit.

Note

1 *Nostalgia for Infinity* is the name of a famous starship in the works of Alastair Reynolds.

References

Freund, A., and Ritter, J., 2009. Midlife crisis: A debate. *Gerontology* 55(5), 582–591.
Gatling, M., Mills, J., and Lindsay, D., 2014. Representations of middle age in comedy film: A critical discourse analysis. *Qualitative Report* 19(12), 1–15.
Ginsburg, F., 1991. Indigenous media: Faustian contract or global village? *Cultural Anthropology* 6(1), 92–112.
Gorman, A., 2018. A sports car and a glitter ball are now in space – What does that say about us as humans? *The Conversation.* http://theconversation.com/a-sports-car-and-a-glitter-ball-are-now-in-space-what-does-that-say-about-us-as-humans-91156 (accessed 1.12.19).

Gorman, A., 2019. *Dr Space Junk vs the Universe. Archaeology and the Future.* Cambridge, MA: MIT Press.

Keay, A., 2004. The presentation of guardianship sites. *Transactions of the Ancient Monuments Society* 4, 7–20.

Lomberg, J., 2013. Messages to mars. *Ke Ola Magazine*, July 15. https://keolamagazine.com/science/messages-to-mars/ (accessed 27.4.2019).

May, S., 2018. How does heritage work when we're 'Living in the future'? *Heritage Futures.* https://heritage-futures.org/heritage-work-living-future/ (accessed 1.12.19).

Morgan, J., and Macdonald, S., 2018. De-growing museum collections for new heritage futures. *International Journal of Heritage Studies* (online first). doi:10.1080/13527258.2018.1530289.

Musk, E., 2018. Twitter account, 24 June. twitter.com/elonmusk/status/1011083630301536256 (accessed 27.04.2019).

O'Connor, A., 2003. Geology, archaeology, and 'the raging vortex of the "eolith" controversy'. *Proceedings of the Geologists Association* 114(3), 255–262.

Plait, P., 2014. Shirtstorm: Casual sexism and the inevitable horrid backlash when it's called out. *Slate Magazine.* https://slate.com/technology/2014/11/casual-sexism-when-a-shirt-is-more-than-a-shirt.html (accessed 1.12.19).

Sani, F., Herrera, M., and Bowe, M., 2009. Perceived collective continuity and ingroup identification as defence against death awareness. *Journal of Experimental Social Psychology* 45(1), 242–245.

Zamyatin, Y., 1924. *We.* New York: E.P. Dutton.

10

WHAT LIES AHEAD?

Nuclear waste as cultural heritage of the future

Cornelius Holtorf and Anders Högberg

Introduction

One of the societal challenges of our time is to design, build and operate repositories for the safe disposal of long-lived nuclear waste. As material remains of a future past, these repositories and their content are part of the cultural heritage of the future. This particular legacy of our time has specific properties about which the people today want future generations to know. In this chapter, we are considering the question of how to manage transmissions of essential records, knowledge and memory concerning final repositories for nuclear waste across long time periods. We are taking a heritage futures perspective.

Heritage futures are concerned with the roles of heritage in managing the relations between present and future societies, e.g., through anticipation or planning. We argue that it is helpful to consider in this context the significance of perceptions of the future and analyze their impact on how people plan for what lies ahead – both literally in the repositories and metaphorically in the times to come. Our discussion concerning repositories of nuclear waste will also feed back into how we perceive and manage more ordinary cultural heritage. The chapter builds on our long-standing research on this topic (e.g., Holtorf and Högberg, 2014a; 2014b; 2015a; 2015b; 2016; Högberg et al., 2017; Wollentz et al. 2020).

Final repositories for nuclear waste

Civil uses of nuclear power have until now resulted in more than 250,000 tonnes of high-level nuclear waste (IAEA 2018), with an estimated 12,000 tonnes being added every year. How much military uses of nuclear power contribute additionally is unclear. Most nuclear waste originates from the world's more than 600 nuclear power plants providing energy in many countries

(World-nuclear.org, 2017). Medicine, science and industry also contribute nuclear waste but to a lesser extent. All radioactive waste is toxic and must be safely kept away from humans and nature until it has decayed to levels of radiation that are equal to, or lower than, variation in natural background radiation, often thousands of years ahead (Chapman and McCombie, 2003). In Sweden, the regulations state that repositories have to be safe for 100,000 years, in the US, the equivalent figure is 10,000, and in Germany even 1,000,000 years (Jensen, 1993; Trauth et al., 1993; Herrmann and Röthemeyer, 1998; Elfwing et al., 2013).

Deep geological repositories are currently planned or already being built at specific locations in several countries, including Onkalo in Finland, Forsmark in Sweden, and Bure in France (Swedish National Council for Nuclear Waste, 2019; see Figure 10.1), to facilitate safe final disposal of long-lived nuclear waste. These consist of mined tunnels drilled into stable geological formations several hundred metres below the surface. In the US, the Waste Isolation Pilot Plant (WIPP) at Carlsbad, New Mexico, is already in use for the disposal of nuclear waste left from the research and production of nuclear weapons for the next 10,000 years (Schröder, 2019; see also Buser et al., this volume).

Most stakeholders in the nuclear waste sector agree today that it is important to empower future generations to make informed decisions during any kind of

FIGURE 10.1   Image of the planned final repository for spent nuclear fuel at Forsmark in Sweden. Once in operation, it will take more than 80 years before this deep geological repository is expected to be sealed. Source: Swedish Nuclear Fuel and Waste Management Company (SKB). Courtesy of SKB. Photo: Lasse Modin. Illustrator: Phosworks.

interaction with the repository to avoid inadvertent intrusion or facilitate safe retrieval of any part of the content. Today, society is therefore charged with the task not only of building repositories for the safe disposal of nuclear waste but also of ensuring future memory and active knowledge on the basis of accurate records, for thousands if not hundreds of thousands of years to come (see also Trauth et al., 1993; van Wyck, 2005; Andrén, 2012; Moisey, 2012; Schröder, 2019).

Never before in the history of humankind has any comparably complex information been communicated across comparable time periods. Any building or physical marker at the location will struggle to exist over such long time periods, given the expected impact of major environmental changes including the next ice age during which massive layers of ice will abrade the surface of the land. Physical archives are kept all over the world, but we cannot guarantee that they will survive long enough either. Moreover, we know neither which written languages will be understood in the long-term future nor whether pictograms or symbols will be interpreted in the way we meant them. In fact, we cannot even be sure that the hominids interacting with deep geological repositories in the future will belong to the species *Homo Sapiens*, which is circa 300,000 years old (Schlebusch et al., 2017) and may not exist in the same form a few hundred thousand years ahead. Ergo, the task at hand is complex, on the verge of unresolvable. Still, it needs to be done. The waste is here and will not disappear quickly. It needs to be handled safely and responsibly, now and for the future.

For tackling such a complex task, we need creative ideas and a good deal of innovation. We argue here that it is helpful to perceive and discuss nuclear waste as cultural heritage and to build up competency based on a particular kind of future consciousness.

Nuclear waste as cultural heritage

The long-term preservation of nuclear waste and the legacy of the nuclear age are not only technical and historical concerns but deeply cultural. They have inspired the visual arts, science-fiction literature, ethics and semiotics, among other fields; they also raised important issues about communication, concepts of time, and indeed our own future legacies and heritage (Posner, 1990; Moisey, 2012, 2017, Musch, 2016, Carpenter, 2016; see also Figure 10.2).

Nuclear waste has more in common with cultural heritage than one might think. In fact, nuclear waste may be seen as a particular form of cultural heritage. This is partly because the planned geological repositories and their content will help future generations recall important aspects of 20th- and 21st-century human civilization in advanced technological societies. As the Australian contemporary archaeologist Robert Charlotte Maxwell (2016: 100) noted, "[i]t is not radioactivity itself, but our attitudes *towards* it that become visible in the archaeological record" and thus help us to understand better the story of the nuclear age. At these sites, people will be able to learn about "atomic culture" and the global history of nuclear power and the nuclear industry, the changing relations between (nuclear)

FIGURE 10.2   Erich Berger and Mari Keto's installation *Inheritance* consists of a box to be passed on as an heirloom and heritage from one generation to the next, containing, among other things, jewellery incorporating radio-active stones. The jewellery can be worn as soon as the accompanying radiograph indicates that the stones are safe to use. *Inheritance* is thus also a repetitive ritual and intangible inheritance. Seamlessly connecting the natural world, science, and technology with human values, rituals, and behaviour, this work of contemporary art implies a future of risk but also of appreciation and change. Part of the exhibition Perpetual Uncertainty, curated by Ele Carpenter and held at Malmö Art Museum in Malmö, Sweden, 24 April–26 August 2018. Photograph by Daniel Lindskog.

technology and society, and indeed about the emergence of the environmental movement and its impact (Zeman and Amundson, 2004; Storm, 2014).

At the same time, nuclear waste kept in repositories is a special case of cultural heritage, also in a more general sense. Those managing heritage and waste sites are equally dealing with places and things but ultimately care for people and their wellbeing; in a certain way, they value what remains from past civilizations and are eager to provide benefits for future generations. One of their joint challenges is the need to manage both tangible and intangible properties while balancing parameters linked to culture/society with others that are determined by nature/physics. Whereas choosing overall strategies for managing nuclear waste and cultural heritage depends on interpretation and values, implementing them in practice requires specialist knowledge. In each realm, the job is to take care of legacies that contain both risks and benefits for very long time periods ahead, and there are legal requirements specifying to some extent how to do that. But preserving objects and associated information always requires resources, the availability of which constrains specific choices.

Heritage negotiates people's understanding and a society's relationship between past, present, and future. This applies to nuclear waste to the same extent as to other forms of cultural heritage. But whereas archaeologists, historians, geographers, anthropologists, and many other specialists in cultural heritage have often looked backwards asking how the past and its remains have been understood, represented, and used in various ways up to the present day, nuclear engineers and safety experts are looking ahead and constructing future repositories for what will remain from our time. This distinction requires some more discussion.

Future consciousness

The ability to understand the present as a consequence of change over time and the future as something possible to imagine and plan for distinguishes humans from other species (Suddendorf and Corballis, 2007). Thus, the way we make sense of pasts and futures is important for how we cognize ourselves in the present. Depending on variation in personal knowledge, skill, and mindset, there are, however, differences in how individuals perform this ability. To a large extent, this is not linked to an individual's character but depends on variation in skill and knowledge related to future thinking. Hence, even though the ability to imagine and plan for the future is deeply human, the way it is performed can be enhanced by knowledge. One way to encourage the capacity of future thinking is to flesh out the complexity in processes involved in how relations between past, present, and future can be understood.

Historical consciousness refers to the underlying thought structures that generate meaning when a particular historical perspective is given significance, informing the way we look at the present and the future (Rüsen, 2004). However, particular perspectives on the future can generate meaning in a similar way, with consequences for how we see the past and the present. We argue, therefore, that when shifting attention from the past in the present to the future in the present, historical consciousness turns into future consciousness. Both historical consciousness and future consciousness create meaningful relations between past, present, and future. Just as historical consciousness manifests itself in uses of the past, future consciousness manifests itself in perceptions and uses of the future.

A graphic (Figure 10.3) illustrates how we can understand future consciousness as human processing of past and future in the present (see also Sandford and Cassar, this volume). Each of us lives in the *now*. This *now* is the present moment in which past and future are perceived based on certain assumptions about pasts and futures. Human beings are capable of imagining a great many events and processes that are *possible* to have happened in the past. After research and reasoning about the available evidence, some events and processes, however,

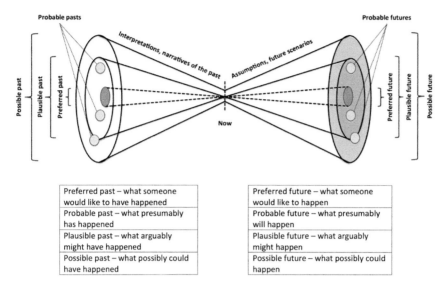

Preferred past – what someone would like to have happened	Preferred future – what someone would like to happen
Probable past – what presumably has happened	Probable future – what presumably will happen
Plausible past – what arguably might have happened	Plausible future – what arguably might happen
Possible past – what possibly could have happened	Possible future – what possibly could happen

FIGURE 10.3 Future consciousness: schematic illustration of how human interpretations and narratives of the past are transformed through the needle's eye of *now* into assumptions and future scenarios. Crucially, this is a "rolling now" constantly moving along the axis of time as the future becomes present and the present becomes past. The grey tone in the future part of the figure marks the fact that even though past and future are conceptually closely linked, there are differences in how they are perceived. Figure by Anders Högberg, inspired by graphics of Stephan Magnus (see also Dunne and Fiona 2013).

appear to be more *plausible* to have happened than others. Among such plausible pasts, some pasts are more *probable* than others in a given historical scenario. For example, it is certainly possible that extraterrestrials visited Earth in the past, but from an academic perspective it is not particularly plausible, given the lack of direct evidence; for most people, it is even less probable, given the existence of more convincing accounts of what presumably happened in the human past. Finally, in any given present context, there may be one particular past that one or more people, for example, politicians, would like to have happened for some reason. This preferred past does not require any reasoning based on evidence or counter-evidence, but it can gain in persuasiveness when it even seems probable, plausible, or at least possible.

By the same token, in any specific context, people may have a *preferred future*. But even when they would like something to happen, this does not mean that it presumably will happen and is therefore *probable*. Indeed, there are arguably many different futures that are *plausible* enough to happen, within a wide spectrum of *possible* future events and processes that can be imagined by people in any *now*. To stay with the example from above, many of us may be able to imagine that extra-terrestrial life forms will one day try to make contact with humans on Earth, but there is not much evidence for arguing that this plausibly might happen; there are few scenarios of probable futures where such contact is likely to occur (Hawking, 2018), no matter how much anybody might prefer this to happen.

These pasts and futures all have to be processed in our present, the *now* in Figure 10.3. This processing includes social processes such as learning, educa-tion, and contestation that influence our perceptions. Nonetheless, as sand in an hourglass has to flow from one container to another through a narrow passage, time is constantly flowing through an ever-changing present. As that narrow passage moves onward in time, the needle's eye comprising our present, pasts, and futures constantly moves and with that perceptions change. Consequently, through time, the spectrum of preferred, probable, plausible, and possible pasts and futures will keep changing, but the model represented by the figure will stay the same. Every past and every future present have specific possibilities and limits of how people understand their own *now* in relation to how they perceive past and future. Even though we speak here about a singular *now*, there may be vari-ous *nows* and multiple presents, but the point is that our graphic applies to each of these (Högberg and Holtorf, 2016).

Perceptions of the past and the future shape human thought and action in the present. There is, however, one crucial difference between our perceptions of past and future in relation to the world today. No matter how we perceive the past, we cannot affect what has already happened and have to live with the social and material consequences of the past today. Yet however we perceive the future, we will have to face the consequences of our actions in the future. How we shape the future today is driven by particular human emotions linked to what we love and what we abhor, what we fear and what we hope for, what we dare to do and what we choose not to risk – all informing human engagement in the present, whether in the form of action or lack of action (see also Holtorf and Högberg, chapter 4 this volume).

Let us have a look at how variation in future perceptions, together with techno-logical development, have contributed to changes in the history of nuclear waste.

Future perceptions in relation to nuclear waste

Today, it is generally accepted that nuclear waste will have to be stored for very long time periods, safely away from humans and nature. This has not always been the case.

During the 1950s and 1960s, transforming uranium into energy was opti-mistically regarded as a reliable source of energy for a nearly infinite future (Storm, 2014). Although the risks of human exposure to radioactive substances were known, it was thought that innovative future nuclear power plants could reduce the remaining waste to virtually nil. According to the modern trust in technological progress, nuclear material was perceived as a resource rather than as waste (Anshelm, 2006). The emphasis was on possible and preferred futures that were also perceived as plausible and indeed probable.

From the 1960s onwards, nuclear waste was increasingly perceived as a liability in some, at that time, very plausible futures. A radical increase in volume, increased knowledge about the radioactivity of some substances, and difficulties in reprocessing the waste turned earlier optimism into uncertainty. Ambitions to reprocess spent fuel were stopped due to concerns about the global availability of plutonium that could be used in nuclear weapons (Carter, 1977). It became clear that there were significant amounts of nuclear waste that required final repositories safely away from humans and nature (Anshelm, 2006), effectively altering which futures were considered most plausible and probable.

At the start of the 1990s, a new future emerged as plausible, involving the new transmutation technology that could generate energy from spent nuclear fuel while leaving behind very small amounts of residual waste that would decay in less than a thousand years (Nakajima, 2015). As a form of recycling in the nuclear energy sector, this became a preferred future at that time. Again, technological developments had resulted in an expanded range of possible and plausible futures. As doubts about the viability of transmutation technology grew and its plausibility vanished, the present thinking emerged that nuclear waste might best be stored indefinitely in deep geological repositories (Anshelm, 2006; Andrén, 2012) and a new probable future had been created (Schröder, 2019).

We see in this example how the future of nuclear waste has been perceived differently over time. Such a pattern of changing perceptions over time applies generally in human history (Ricoeur, 1988, chapter 10) and has important implications for how we should manage processes of transmitting records, knowledge, and memory to future generations. We can assume that future societies, too, will have their own perceptions of the future (and indeed of the past) and that they will shape their own present and create new futures on the basis of these perceptions, just like we do. Future consciousness thus fosters an awareness of the mutability of human perspectives and perceptions over time. As a proverb states, "nothing ages faster than the future, and nothing is more difficult to predict than the past." Much simpler, every present has its own past and future. The "rolling now" manifests the rolling course of human history.

The question at hand is not, therefore, how to create a long-term strategy based on our own perspectives and perceptions of the challenges ahead. Instead, we need to remember the "rolling now" of future consciousness and create a long-term strategy that appreciates what will happen in future *nows*. In these future *nows*, people will act as creatively and innovatively as we do, having generated perspectives and perceptions that we cannot even imagine today. This insight changes the nature of planning from working towards futures as we perceive them today to finding ways of working that allow for, and expect, futures to create their own pasts, presents, and futures based on their own premises. From this perspective, future changes of perspective are not a problem to be eliminated from our own strategies of preserving records, knowledge, and memory but a basic condition of human development over time that we need to understand and accommodate in our long-term plans. Planning for the future thus requires a new approach. This approach is not about predicting the future but about creating capacity in order to deal with a world that is – and will be – continuously changing.

Mutual benefits: lessons to be learned

Understanding nuclear waste as cultural heritage opens up for perspectives that promise benefits and innovations for both realms. Perceiving nuclear waste as cultural heritage invites us to see the former in the light of insights and knowledge already gained about the latter, in particular concerning the mutability and politics of heritage over time. These insights are in line with the notion of future consciousness according to which, we will, in the long term, need to reckon with futures that in significant ways differ from the present and cannot be sufficiently predicted or controlled by us. This lesson is derived from learning that the history of heritage is not about conservation, continuity, and reconstruction but about loss, change, and renewal.

The example of European megalithic tombs shows how people's interpretations of their meanings and significance have varied and changed drastically over time, from the Neolithic period up until today (Holtorf, 2000–2008). Along the way, many of these imposing structures were completely destroyed or put to entirely new uses. The preservation of some relied a great deal on keeping them both re-interpretable and re-usable over time (Figure 10.4). Arguably, their continued existence over up to 6,000 years relied on a certain amount of ambiguity of their significance. Therefore, divergent interpretations of the records we leave behind and thus different future knowledge about one and the same legacy do not need to be an obstacle but are also a precondition for the preservation of these records, the associated knowledge, and the memory of the site as a whole. This is the subtle insight that archaeologists can draw even from the longevity of prominent archaeological monuments like the stone circle of Stonehenge; it may be a successful marker of a location, but it was not capable of successfully preserving complex messages from antiquity to the present day, as discussed in relation to nuclear waste disposal by Maureen Kaplan and Mel Adams (Kaplan, 1986; Kaplan and Adams, 1986; see also Joyce, this volume).

Indeed, the site of Stonehenge illustrates how the social history of heritage typically features controversies, contestations, and conflicts of interests among stakeholders who value them very differently (Chippindale, 2012). As the past is renegotiated in each present, conflicts tend to arise concerning ownership (*power*), unequal distribution of economic benefits (*wealth*), and exclusionary notions of belonging (*identity*), among other issues. Such politics of heritage are best assumed to be inherent in managing legacies and heritage across long time periods, not a negative interference of such processes (Smith, 2006; de la Torre,

FIGURE 10.4   A megalithic tomb that changed its meaning, use, and significance over time, from protecting an ancient burial to framing the gate of the farm opposite Herdada Peral de Cima, near Gafanhoeir, Alentejo, Portugal. Photograph: Cornelius Holtorf, 2001.

2013; Harrison, 2013). These conflicts, therefore, are not necessarily an obstacle for the preservation of records, knowledge, and memory at nuclear waste repositories, but likewise an opportunity and maybe even a precondition for their successful transmission across generations. Social conflicts that address key issues in society such as power, wealth, and identity can make heritage (and memory) more pertinent in society and thus ultimately stronger in society rather than weaker. Moreover, conflicts and controversies mobilize people generally and thus reduce the risk of forgetting as a result of sheer irrelevance. The nuclear waste sector may need to learn more about managing and indeed facilitating a balanced amount of opposition and controversy (in relation to the government? dominant ideologies? industry?) in order to make longevity of memory and preservation of records and knowledge more likely. Such lessons from Heritage Studies can improve judgements made in designing geological repositories for nuclear waste and associated strategies of ensuring the preservation of relevant records, knowledge, and memory (Holtorf and Högberg, 2015b).

Conversely, learning about nuclear waste management prompts Heritage Studies to consider the roles of heritage in future societies, e.g., through anticipation or planning. It is frequently stated that the value of heritage implies a duty to preserve it for the benefit of future generations who will want to appreciate it too. It is thus pertinent to engage with heritage futures and study how to manage the relations between present and future societies through heritage and preservation (Holtorf and Högberg, 2014b; Högberg et al., 2017). The nuclear waste sector has demonstrated how to work with the long-term future systematically and thoroughly in international collaboration and with a multidisciplinary approach (Schröder, 2019). The heritage sector, too, needs to be concerned with what lies ahead and could work in similar ways.

When we make decisions today that are based on long-term trajectories of memory and preservation, they necessarily rely on contemporary perceptions and expectations of a particular future to come. This should not stop us from engaging with heritage futures, whether related to nuclear waste or more generally. But we need to understand too that the concept of "the rolling now" means that the futures anybody can imagine are not going to come "true" in any specific present but will keep changing. This means, among other things, that the perceived risks and qualities of nuclear waste, including its character as useless waste, is subject to change and contestation as it is transmitted to future generations. We cannot assume that our toxic waste is also the future's toxic waste. This is not because we are trivializing the toxic nature of radioactive material but because we understand the mutability and political nature of heritage.

The changing content of messages about nuclear waste addressed to the future provides a good example. As recently as during the 1990s, the best message to be sent to the future was often imagined to be a warning and to some extent an apology: "this place is not a place of honour" … "nothing valued is here" … "this message is a warning about danger" … "this place is best shunned and left uninhabited" (Trauth et al., 1993: F-49-50). The underlying reasoning was that since we know the content of the repository is dangerous, it is our responsibility to warn future generations from this embarrassing legacy so they can avoid any inadvertent intrusion of the site. Today, the international consensus in the nuclear waste sector is that any messages should not contain value judgements or warnings but best communicate factual information about the repository and what lies in it (Schröder, 2019: 2.3). Then, people in the future will be able to make their own knowledgeable decisions on what is best to do. There is a strong possibility that before the repositories are closed yet another kind of message will have been agreed, or possibly several different ones.

Conclusions

In this paper, we have been discussing how to manage relations between present and future societies, using the example of preserving records, knowledge, and memory concerning final repositories for nuclear waste across long time periods. We approached nuclear waste as cultural heritage, suggesting that both realms are concerned with closely related societal challenges to do with material and immaterial legacies, human wellbeing, and preservation for the future.

We argued that it is useful in this context to introduce the concept of future consciousness, which creates meaningful relations between past, present, and future and manifests itself in particular perceptions and uses of the future. According to our model, past and future are processed and interpreted in every present, shaping human thought and action. This present *now* is of course constantly moving over time, and with it, the way we perceive, interpret, and use the past and the future moves, too. In planning for the future, it is therefore important to realize that we need to plan not for a single, unchanging future but for multiple, changing futures. As discussed, this insight about ever-changing perceptions and possible uses is born out, not the least in the history of nuclear waste during the 20th and 21st centuries. Rather than attempting to predict the future, we need to acquire the capacity to deal with a world that is – and will be – continuously changing.

This insight corresponds with what we know from the long history of cultural heritage, which is a long sequence of loss, change, and renewal. In managing a heritage site, you can never be sure what lies ahead. Moreover, the history of heritage typically features significant controversies, contestations, and conflicts of interests that ultimately contribute to keeping cultural heritage in some way relevant and socially important. We believe that the nuclear waste sector should take this on board and get better at planning for changing futures. Preserving records, knowledge, and memory concerning repositories of nuclear waste requires a long-term strategy that allows for future presents in which human beings will be creating their own perspectives and perceptions on the basis of which they will act as creatively and decisively as we do, not seldom in conflict with others.

We cannot be certain that nuclear waste will always be seen predominantly as a hazardous substance posing a threat to humanity, nor that its radioactivity or other physical properties will always be its most significant property. Although radioactive substances are very dangerous, for example, when they enter the food chain or are used in dirty bombs, the repositories we create to house radioactive material will not forever be seen as areas of deadly threats but may, given time, be transformed into altogether different things. As mentioned before, this is not to trivialize or deny real dangers posed by radioactive material to future generations but more to look at these perceived dangers in the present from a different perspective on their possible future meaning. The relevant bodies in society need to think carefully how to design deep geological repositories of nuclear waste that will become a contested and mutable heritage to last for many thousand years, transforming itself in line with every new future present. We believe that the best chance to transmit knowledge in the long term under changing circumstances may be to keep records, knowledge, and memory alive, inviting future generations to interpret and use these sites in their own way.

At the same time, the heritage sector can benefit from working on its own efforts to manage the relations between present and future societies. Experiences from ongoing work in the global nuclear waste sector show how it is possible to improve joint strategies for the preservation of records, knowledge, and memory across generations. Managing nuclear waste for the long term should, therefore, be considered as a very important case study for heritage futures; it can act as a catalyst for heritage managers to better address the long-term future implied in their work. We hope that many more exciting collaborations between the two sectors lie ahead!

Acknowledgements

Our research was supported by the Swedish Nuclear Fuel and Waste Management Company (SKB) and benefitted from discussions within the AHRC-funded Heritage Futures research programme led by Rodney Harrison, UCL. Parts of the present chapter are based on a manuscript submitted to a forthcoming volume entitled *Toxic Immanence* (ed. Rodica-Livia Altaras).

References

Andrén, M., 2012. *Nuclear Waste Management and Legitimacy: Nihilism and Responsibility.* New York: Routledge.

Anshelm, J., 2006. *Bergsäkert eller våghalsigt? Frågan om kärnavfallets hantering i det offentliga samtalet i Sverige 1950–2002.* Lund: Arkiv förlag.

Carpenter, E. (ed.)., 2016. *The Nuclear Culture Source Book.* London: Black Dog.

Carter, J., 1977. Nuclear Power Policy Statement on Decisions Reached Following a Review, April 7, 1977. Online by G. Peters and J.T. Woolley, *The American Presidency Project.* Available at http://www.presidency.ucsb.edu/ws/?pid=7316. Accessed 25 February 2017.

Chapman, N.A. and McCombie, C., 2003. *Principles and Standards for the Disposal of Long-Lived Radioactive Wastes.* Waste Management Series 3. Amsterdam: Pergamon.

Chippindale, C., 2012. *Stonehenge Complete.* 4th edition. London: Thames and Hudson.

De la Torre, M., 2013. Values and Heritage Conservation. *Heritage and Society* 60(2), 155–166.

Dunne, A. and Fiona, R., 2013. *Speculative Everything. Design, Fiction, and Social Dreaming.* Cambridge, MA and London: MIT Press.

Elfwing, M., Evins, L.Z., Gontier, M., Grahm, P., Mårtensson, P. and Tunbrant, S., 2013. *SFL Concept Study. Main Report.* Technical Report TR-13-14. Stockholm: Svensk Kärnbränslehantering AB.

Harrison, R., 2013. *Heritage: Critical Approaches.* Abingdon and New York: Routledge.

Hawking, S., 2018. *Brief Answers to the Big Questions.* New York: Bantam Books.

Herrmann, A.G. and Röthemeyer, H., 1998. *Langfristig sichere Deponien. Situation, Grundlagen, Realisierung.* Berlin: Springer.

Holtorf, C., 2000–2008. *Monumental Past: The Life-Histories of Megalithic Monuments in Mecklenburg-Vorpommern (Germany).* Electronic monograph. University of Toronto: Centre for Instructional Technology Development. Available at http://hdl.handle.net/1807/245.

Holtorf, C. and Högberg, A., 2014a. Nuclear Waste as Cultural Heritage of the Future. *WM2014 Conference Proceedings*, Atlanta, GA. Available at https://www.diva-portal.org/smash/get/diva2:718845/FULLTEXT01.pdf.

Holtorf, C. and Högberg, A., 2014b. Communicating with Future Generations: What Are the Benefits of Preserving Cultural Heritage? Nuclear Power and Beyond. *The European Journal of Post – Classical Archaeologies* 4, 315–330.

Holtorf, C. and Högberg, A., 2015a. Contemporary Heritage and the Future. In: E. Watson and S. Watson, eds. *The Palgrave Handbook of Contemporary Heritage Research.* New York: Palgrave Macmillan; pp. 509–523.

Holtorf, C. and Högberg, A., 2015b. Archaeology and the Future: Managing Nuclear Waste as a Living Heritage. In: *Radioactive Waste Management and Constructing Memory for Future Generations.* Nuclear Energy Agency, no 7259. Paris: OECD; pp. 97–101.

Holtorf, C. and Högberg, A., 2016. The Contemporary Archaeology of Nuclear Waste. Communicating with the Future. *Arkæologisk Forum* 35, 31–37.

Högberg, A. and Holtorf, C., 2016. Långtidsförvaring av kärnavfall. Från samtidsarkeologi till framtidsarkeologi. *Primitive Tider* 18, 285–295.

Högberg, A., Holtorf, C., May, S. and Wollentz, G., 2017. No Future in Archaeological Heritage Management? *World Archaeology* 49(5), 639–647. doi:10.1080/00438243.20 17.1406398.

IAEA, 2018. *Status and Trends in Spent Fuel and Radioactive Waste Management.* IAEA Nuclear Energy Series No. NW-T-1.14. Vienna: International Atomic Energy Agency.

Jensen, M. (ed.)., 1993. *Conservation and Retrieval of Information: Elements of a Strategy to Inform Future Societies about Nuclear Waste Repositories.* Nordic Committee for Nuclear Safety Research, Nordic Council of Ministers. Available at http://www.iaea.org/inis/collection/NCLCollectionStore/_Public/28/038/28038113.pdf Accessed 27 February 2017.

Kaplan, M.F., 1986. Mankind's Future: Using the Past to Protect the Future. Archaeology and the Disposal of Highly Radioactive Wastes. *Interdisciplinary Science Reviews* 11(3), 257–268.

Kaplan, M.F. and Adams, M., 1986. Using the Past to Protect the Future: Marking Nuclear Waste Disposal Sites. *Archaeology* 39(5), 107–112.

Maxwell, R., 2016. The Radium Water Worked Fine Until His Jaw Came Off": The Changing Role of Radioactivity in the Twentieth Century. In: U.K. Frederick and A. Clarke, eds. *That Was Then, This Is Now: Contemporary Archaeology and Material Cultures in Australia.* Cambridge: Cambridge Scholars; pp. 84–100.

Moisey, A., 2012. Considering the Desire to Mark Our Buried Nuclear Waste: *Into Eternity* and the Waste Isolation Pilot Plant. *Qui Parle: Critical Humanities and Social Sciences* 20(2), 101–125.

Moisey, A., 2017. Permanent Negative Value: The Waste Isolation Pilot Plant. *Critical Inquiry* 43(4), 861–892.

Musch, S., 2016. The Atomic Priesthood and Nuclear Waste Management: Religion, Sci-Fi Literature, and the End of Our Civilization. *Zygon®* 51(3), 626–639.

Nakajima, K. (ed.)., 2015. *Nuclear Back-End and Transmutation Technology for Waste Disposal: Beyond the Fukushima Accident.* New York and London: Springer Open.

Posner, R. (ed.)., 1990. *Warnungen an die Ferne Zukunft: Atommüll als Kommunikationsproblem.* München: Raben.

Ricœur, P., 1988. *Memory, History, Forgetting.* Chicago, IL: The University of Chicago Press.

Rüsen, J., 2004. Historical Consciousness: Narrative Structure, Moral Function, and Ontogenetic Development. In: P. Seixas, ed. *Theorizing Historical Consciousness.* Toronto: University of Toronto Press; pp. 63–85.

Schlebusch, C.M., Malmström, H., Günther, T., Sjödin, P., Coutinho, A., Edlund, H., Munters, A.R., Vicente, M., Steyn, M., Soodyall, H., Lombard, M. and Jakobsson,

M., 2017. Southern African Ancient Genomes Estimate Modern Human Divergence to 350,000 to 260,000 Years Ago. *Science*, 28 September 2017. doi:10.1126/science. aao6266.

Schröder, J., 2019. *Preservation of Records, Knowledge and Memory (RK&M) Across Generations: Final Report of the RK&M Initiative*. Paris: OECD, Nuclear Energy Agency. Available at https://www.oecd-nea.org/rwm/pubs/2019/7421-RKM-Final.pdf (Accessed 31 December 2019).

Smith, L., 2006. *Uses of Heritage*. London and New York: Routledge.

Storm, A., 2014. *Post-Industrial Landscape Scars*. New York: Palgrave Macmillian.

Suddendorf, T. and Corballis, M.C., 2007. The Evolution of Foresight: What Is Mental Time Travel, and Is It Unique to Humans? *Behavioral and Brain Sciences* 30(3), 299–313.

Swedish National Council for Nuclear Waste, 2019. Overview of Eight Countries – Status April 2019. Swedish National Council for Nuclear Waste, Report 2019(1). Stockholm. Available at https://www.karnavfallsradet.se/sites/default/files/documents/report_2019_1.pdf

Trauth, K.M., Hora, S.C. and Guzowski, R.V., 1993. *Expert Judgement on Markers to Deter Inadvertent Human Intrusion into the Waste Isolation Pilot Plant*. Sandia Report SAND92 – 1282. UC – 721. New Mexico: Albuquerque.

van Wyck, P.C., 2005. *Signs of Danger. Waste, Trauma, and Nuclear Threat*. Minneapolis: University of Minnesota Press.

Wollentz, G., May, S., Holtorf, C. and Högberg, A., 2020. Toxic heritage: Uncertain and unsafe. In: R. Harrison, C. DeSilvey, C. Holtorf, S. Macdonald, N. Bartolini, E. Breithoff, H. Fredheim, A. Lyons, S. May, J. Morgan and S. Penrose, *Heritage Futures. Comparative Approaches to Natural and Cultural Heritage Practices*. London: UCL Press, pp. 294–312.

World-nuclear.org, 2017. Available at http://www.world-nuclear.org. Accessed 12 April 2017.

Zeman, S.C. and Amundson, M.A. (eds)., 2004. *Atomic Culture. How We Learned to Stop Worrying and Love the Bomb*. Boulder, CO: University Press of Colorado.

11

THE FUTURE IN THE PAST, THE PAST IN THE FUTURE

Rosemary A. Joyce

In this chapter, I use a contemporary experiment of imagining futures that draws deliberately on heritage monuments to question what I argue are two implicit assumptions shared by broader archaeological thought and cultural heritage development: that things recognized today as monuments were meant by their builders to last and that they were meant to communicate specific meanings. I characterize the thinking involved as a form of "common sense", building on Michael Herzfeld's (2001: 1) definition of anthropology as "the study of common sense". In the case of the mobilization of archaeology in the project I am discussing, the cultural common sense is unusually well documented because this was a government-sponsored and government-reviewed planning process to mark nuclear waste repositories to prevent intrusion in the future. Throughout this chapter, I use quotes from these government documents that illustrate what was being taken for granted by the planners, information that was stated without argument or citation, treated as not needing justification, which I argue shows it formed a body of planners' common sense about the intentions of those who originally created the assemblages that today are archaeological sites, many recognized as World Heritage monuments. The arguments presented in this chapter were developed during the writing of a book that considers the issues raised in greater detail than is possible here, including extended discussion of some of the examples of cultural heritage thinking explored below (Joyce, 2020).

Archaeological sites identified as cultural heritage, especially those singled out for listing under UNESCO guidelines, are treated as evidence of significant progress in human social life in the past or as originary locations for technologies, aesthetic works, historical events, or social arrangements that, in hindsight, can be celebrated as important roots for present-day social and cultural life (Labadi, 2013: 32–36). Much of this cultural heritage framework has been subjected to critique, including from within the heritage community (Harrison, 2013). In particular, critiques of the role of heritage making in creating a peculiar kind of temporality are central to this chapter. As Anne Eriksen (2014: 142) puts it, heritage creation is a "strategy... to create historical time", in which the past "is seen from the position of *somebody's* present".

Archaeology, as a contemporary practice, shares this common-sense framework of creating historical time from the present with cultural heritage thought. I have argued that places privileged in heritage thought as sites of intentional commemoration of events that lend themselves to being treated as if they had been created with an eye to a future are privileged by archaeological emphasis on the monumental (Joyce, 2006). Archaeologists may treat monumental sites as messages meant to endure into the future of their builders, even when the evidence fails to support this inference (Joyce, 2004).

What makes the case I am discussing interesting is that the past of the builders of specific heritage sites is represented as analogous to our present in order to allow designers of nuclear waste markers in the present to assert that a deliberately created heritage site will endure and be an intelligible signal into our future. My view of the temporality involved differs slightly from the vision offered by Cornelius Holtorf and Anders Högberg (2015) in their parallel exploration of nuclear waste marking schemes drawing on archaeology in Scandinavia. They propose that humans occupy a "rolling now" from which they view all pasts as converging on the present and see a range of futures opening out. While I agree with them that "the way humans make sense of pasts and futures in the present is important for how we understand ourselves and our present time" (Holtorf and Högberg, 2015: 98), I do not see any singular way of imagining past-present-future that is inherent in the condition of being human. Thus, I seek in the words and actions of the planners whose project I am examining their representation of the past-present-future relationship. That temporality I understand using the work of anthropologist Michael Herzfeld (1991; 2001) on what he called social and monumental time, and what he later clarified were simply two different kinds of social time, each with its own characteristics.

To understand better the common-sense assumptions contemporary archaeologists may be using when we try to understand archaeological sites that have endured for long periods of time, I turned my attention to a modern, well-documented project to design a simulacrum of an archaeological site intended to convey meanings thousands of years into the future: the marker system for the US Waste Isolation Pilot Plant (WIPP) in Carlsbad, New Mexico. In the pages that follow I first introduce this project and relate it to Herzfeld's discussions of temporality. I then walk through in detail the specific discussions of archaeological sites and show how the language used by planners reveals assumptions they made about the intent and durability of these monuments. I then discuss the overlap between the sites drawn on by planners and UNESCO World Heritage in order to make clearer the parallel common sense that underwrote the nuclear waste planning project and World Heritage designation. Finally, I come back to archaeological practice itself, arguing that archaeologists not only provide the fodder for this common sense but rely on it as well, in ways that we need to revisit and question.

Monumental expectations

The United States Department of Energy (DOE) was charged with developing the WIPP as a "research and development facility to demonstrate the safe disposal of radioactive wastes resulting from the defense activities and programs of the US exempted from regulation by the Nuclear Regulatory Commission" (Hora, von Winterfeldt, and Trauth, 1991: I-5). Drilling for the WIPP project began in 1981 (WIPP, 2007). By 1989, the DOE completed construction of underground storage. The US Environmental Protection Agency (EPA) certified WIPP for use in 1998, and in 1999 shipments of radioactive waste began to arrive (WIPP, 2007).

To be licensed, the WIPP project had to fulfill a set of EPA expectations for the design of a marker system (Hora, von Winterfeldt, and Trauth, 1991: I-8). This needed to indicate locations where nuclear waste would be concentrated, and communicate that the location, and especially digging at the location, was dangerous, for up to 10,000 years (DOE, 1996). An equation of the proposed marker system with heritage sites was made explicit in a 1993 document describing design proposals that said the marker system would "convey the message that the entire area *enclosed by the monument* should not be disturbed" (DOE, 1996: 5–6; emphasis added). The planners proposed to create the kind of setting that today is commonly nominated as World Heritage: a prefabricated archaeological site, built as a ruin, modeled on known archaeological ruins of global significance.

The required marker system would be based on "historical analogues of structures, media and messages that have *withstood the test of time*" (EPA, 1996: 36; emphasis added). It is my contention that the phrase "test of time" embodies an assumption, part of the "common sense" on which this project relies, that things that have survived did so at least in part because they were *meant* to last by their builders, and that they did so in the face of challenges thrown up by "time". In this passage, the EPA employs an understanding of temporality like that used by participants in the creation of cultural heritage sites today. UNESCO World Heritage guidelines seek to portray cultural heritage sites as stable points of reference that maintain some fundamental significance (Labadi, 2013: 114–125). As heritage for the future constructed in its past, our present, the marker system design was modeled on sites in our present recognized as heritage conveyed from our past: things meant to last that conserved meaning on at least some level.

The concept of "monument" that links the EPA mandate and UNESCO World Heritage guidelines involves projecting a sharp break between what Herzfeld (1991) called social time, and what he labeled monumental time. Monumental time, he initially argued, is "reductive and generic"; it freezes things in unchanging form to signify a transcendent value, creating "collective predictability" (Herzfeld, 1991: 10).

In an interview 20 years after the publication of this influential characterization, Herzfeld expanded on his concept of monumental time, clarifying that it is itself a particular form of social time, social time created by and for the state:

> monumental time is also social time. It has its own rhythms, they're slower, and that slowness is what the state cultivates to its own advantage.
>
> *(Byrne 2011: 150)*

One of my arguments in this chapter is that the stability asserted for monuments in both the nuclear waste marker plan and in the kind of cultural heritage thought critiqued by many scholars (among others, Erikson, 2014; Harrison, 2013; Labadi, 2013) is a product of adopting the perspective of monumental time, thinking in "well-defined periods" that are "always retrospective" (Herzfeld, 1991: 6, 14). This is thinking in the social time of the state. The social time of the state is made through the repeated hearings and documents that have reproduced virtually the same assertions over a period of going on 40 years, even as the archaeological sites and monuments involved continue to change both in recognized form and posited meaning. It is recognizable in the claim that the monuments used as models lasted for periods of thousands of years, which can only be made by ignoring what changes over those same periods of time.

A ruin can become a cultural heritage monument because, although decayed to some extent, it is understood as relatively stable from the perspective of monumental time. It is viewed as a product of its history with any further change to be avoided as a source of inauthenticity and to be countered by preservation efforts. In ruins transformed into monuments, the retrospective vision of monumental time, the social time of state apparatuses that establish and monitor heritage, sees the history of the site as ended. While the physical assemblage may endure, it is supposed to do so without change. From the perspective of the monumental time of cultural heritage, the monument has no unfolding future, just a past that delivered it to a timeless present.

I argue that monumental time, as retrospective, thus contradicts common-sense ideas of monuments as products of future-oriented thought. Monuments are created retrospectively through processes such as inscription as heritage sites. Their intended persistence and signaling is created post hoc. My view is that the WIPP project can be seen as a process of creation of a future for the present, achieved by asserting that monuments used as warrants for the project were built in the past for an intended future audience. The future of the builders of cultural heritage monuments is our present in which these past projects have become ruins and cultural heritage sites. By building a ruin today that will, in theory, be remembered for thousands of years, the WIPP project sought to structure the future reception of markers on the lines the planners justified through their common-sense understanding of the origins of present-day ruins, monuments, and cultural heritage sites.

Engineering a heritage monument for the future

The conscription of things as warrants for the survival of human intentions in the marking of nuclear waste disposal sites is documented exhaustively for the WIPP project due to its emergence from government planning. We can distinguish four stages in the development of explicit arguments linking archaeological sites to the proposed design: proposals developed by an archaeological consultant (Kaplan, 1982; Kaplan and Adams, 1986); reports from two experts teams published in 1993 (Trauth, Hora, and Guzowski, 1993); a design based on these sources offered by the Department of Energy in 1996 for review by the Environmental Protection Agency (DOE, 1996); and response by the EPA to the DOE design proposal (EPA, 1996). By 2004, the implementation plan for the marker system no longer included any mention of archaeological models (Hart and Associates, 2004).

I do not attempt in this chapter to exhaustively discuss all the documents available. Instead, what I want to do is show the ways common-sense understandings of archaeological sites as heritage were mobilized, assumptions exposed through the choices of language used in the various reports, and what this tells us about what people in the US—including archaeologists—take for granted about archaeological sites and heritage monuments.

The marker system proposal submitted by the DOE was dominated by three large-scale installations (Figure 11.1) with three less spatially extensive elements reinforcing the communication of intended messages (DOE, 1996). The perimeter of the marker system was to be defined by two concentric lines of granite monoliths inscribed with diagrams and texts. One would surround the basic footprint of the core zone of waste disposal, and another would delimit a wider zone around the central core to "*convey the message* that the entire area enclosed... should not be disturbed" (DOE, 1996: 5–6; emphasis added). An explicit analogy with Stonehenge provided the warrant for an estimated lifespan of at least 4,000 years for the proposed monoliths. The proposal suggested that the endurance of Stonehenge could be bettered through the selection of material the experts asserted would be more durable:

> Monoliths made out of natural stone have survived for 3,500 years at Stonehenge, quite a wet climate. At the WIPP site, monoliths are very likely to survive at the site for 10,000 years if bedded properly and left undisturbed.
>
> *(Trauth, Hora, and Guzowski, 1993: F-98)*

> Eighteen of the original... monoliths of the Sarsen Circle of Stonehenge have been standing for 3,500–4,000 years... *There is reason to assume* that large, granitic stones—which are harder and more durable than sandstone—purposely shaped and positioned to remain upright for 10,000 years, would last longer than Stonehenge.
>
> *(Trauth, Hora, and Guzowski, 1993: G-41; emphasis added)*

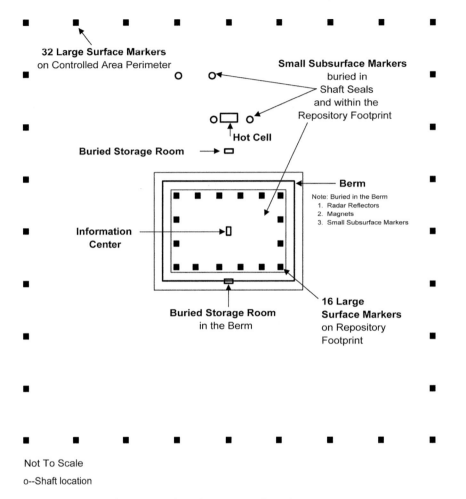

FIGURE 11.1   Plan for proposed marker system (from https://www.wipp.energy.gov/
fctshts/PICs.pdf).

An earthen berm was the third large-scale element of the design. Originally proposed to be made of "local earth and caliche", a calcium carbonate that forms in
soils in the local environment, it "would be spiked with materials with properties
anomalous to the naturally occurring ones", "for detection by aircraft or satellite
equipment" (Trauth, Hora, and Guzowski, 1993: 3–9). The original proposals
estimated that earthworks of the scale proposed would have the potential to last
for 500 to over 5,000 years, again citing earthworks that form part of Stonehenge,
but adding mounds in the United States, in particular at the Cahokia site in southern Illinois, as shorter-term warrants (Trauth, Hora, and Guzowski, 1993: G-37).

   By 1996, the specific analogues offered to justify the lifespan estimate for this
part of the design were changed to Stonehenge and Serpent Mound. Serpent

Mound, located in Ohio, had been part of an earlier exploration of elements for a marker for nuclear waste sites by an archaeologist who also participated in the WIPP expert panel exercise (DOE, 1996: 5–5; Kaplan, 1982: 34–35). By substituting Serpent Mound for Cahokia, the expert group ignored her argument that Serpent Mound was an example of a monument whose unique features impede its interpretation, and thus made it an example of a bad commemorative marker:

> the Serpent Mound is an example of what *not* to do. Obviously, the serpent form meant something to the builders, but the meaning has been lost to us... The Serpent Mound has no parallel in the United States. Likewise, there may be only one high-level waste repository in this country. Developing a unique symbol for a possibly unique high-level waste repository could be futile, since the symbol would have no points of reference or comparison for its future viewers.
>
> *(Kaplan and Adams, 1986: 52–53)*

Why was Serpent Mound replaced by Cahokia in the 1993 report? There is one key difference between Serpent Mound and the Native American site selected in its place, Cahokia Mounds. The latter site was recognized as a World Heritage site in 1982. In contrast, Serpent Mound was not even nominated for listing until 2008. If we take nomination as a World Heritage site as an endorsement of what otherwise is the common sense of the individual planners, then Cahokia has the advantage of being recognized for having survived as a meaningful, significant place. The expert panel shifted from an archaeological warrant that was first proposed to be an example of what not to do, because it was unintelligible as a message, to a historically and culturally related site that could more easily be equated with Stonehenge. Cahokia exemplified the combination of physical endurance and continued intelligibility that was demanded for the marker design, characteristics that form part of the logic supporting the designation of some remains of past projects as cultural heritage monuments while others do not qualify, are not nominated, or may not even be recognized as remains of a past project.

At the center of the marker system, granite slabs would form a structure, also inscribed with messages on its surfaces (Trauth, Hora, and Guzowski, 1993: 5–9, F-102). Buried rooms with similar inscribed surfaces were also proposed (Trauth, Hora, and Guzowski, 1993: F-104). The central "message chamber" to be built above ground was originally estimated to have a likely life span of over 10,000 years based on the assumption that it would improve on European megalithic chamber tombs including Newgrange, cited as having endured for 5,000 to 5,500 years (Trauth, Hora, and Guzowski, 19931993: Figures 4-4.7 and 4-4.8). Three years later, although the buried rooms continued to be supported by comparison with Newgrange and tombs in Egyptian pyramids, the message chamber—renamed the Information Center—was compared to the Acropolis in Athens and to Australian rock art (DOE, 1996: 5–10 to 5–16).

This change in associated archaeological warrants appears to reflect a shift in emphasis from the mere physical persistence of the chamber and the focus of comments on Newgrange in the 1993 report to the continued existence and intelligibility of the messages that would be inscribed on its walls. The estimated lifespan of 2,400 years reached for the Information Center was primarily based on the Acropolis.

The 1996 DOE proposal concluded that the carved stone elements of the Acropolis "have endured the weather and the ravages of war, and although damaged, much of their original materials of construction and their overall configuration remain" (DOE, 1996: 5–11). This conclusion about the material persistence of the Acropolis was complemented by the observation that written documents about the construction of the Acropolis have been durable in their own right:

> Information documenting much of the history of the Acropolis has survived more than 2,400 years in a region of the world that has experienced much conflict and occupation by armed foreigners... sufficient information remains at the site to convey configuration of the structures and enough records have survived to convey their meaning... the history of conflicts in the Mediterranean area that did not destroy either the physical artifacts or their purpose and meaning for more than 2,400 years... provides a credible argument for confidence in the marker system's ability to survive many centuries and convey the intended warnings.
>
> *(DOE, 1996: 5–12)*

The Acropolis occupied pride of place in the common-sense model employed by the authors of the DOE report, allowing them to argue that the marker system would survive and transmit its intended meaning 2,400 years into the future or more if physical preservation was improved by using different kinds of stone.

The forthright nature of this argument contrasts remarkably with the discussion of Australian rock art, the second analogue offered in support of the Information Center design in 1996. After first stating that "this rock art is estimated to be approximately 25,000 years old and possibly 35,000 years old", the report suggests that the placement of WIPP messages on granite surfaces will allow for "maximum durability" and thus result in endurance for longer spans than "the relatively fragile media of Australian painted and pecked rock art". The proposal ends without stating an explicit temporal span for the survival of the Information Center based on Australian rock art: "the performance of the Information Center will be *at least as good* as the endurance of Australian rock art and will be recognizable for the entire regulatory period" (DOE, 1996: 5–10; emphasis added).

The original experts' report and the DOE proposal for the Information Center contrast sharply in their use of early rock art as a warrant. The experts did not mention Australian rock art at all; instead, they cited "Spanish Levantine rock art" dating to 12,000 years before the present, specifically to justify the continued intelligibility of iconic messages over that long term. Inscribed as World Heritage in 1998 under the name "Rock Art of the Mediterranean Basin on the Iberian Peninsula", rock art from the Spanish Neolithic was represented by the experts as offering still intelligible messages today, on certain conditions. They wrote that this group of works

> still speaks to those *willing and imaginative enough* to reconstruct depicted narrative scenes of human hunting parties pursuing prey animals. Thus, there is a better than even chance that message designers consciously working to preserve iconicity and to enhance the narrative significance of pictographic messages could send recognizable meanings across the 10,000-year span.
>
> *(Trauth, Hora, and Guzowski, 1993: G-48; emphasis added)*

The "better than even chance" of controlling the construal of meaning over 10,000 years envisaged by the expert panel was ignored in the final proposal, even as rock art as a category was retained as a generalized warrant for material endurance of iconic messages. By 1996, the ability to transmit recognizable meanings was reserved to the Acropolis by virtue of the existence of documents using an interpretable writing system located apart from the monument itself.

The Acropolis, on which so much of the 1996 proposal rested, was not discussed by the experts in their 1993 report. Its inclusion revived material from the earlier proposal to design markers for nuclear waste disposal sites using archaeological information (Kaplan, 1982; Kaplan and Adams, 1986). In this work, six assemblages of archaeological materials called "archaeological markers" were discussed: the Great Pyramids of Egypt, Stonehenge, the Nazca Lines, Serpent Mound, the Great Wall of China, and the Acropolis (Table 11.1). The global coverage was deliberate, intended to "indicate that the making of monuments and their survival is not keyed to a particular culture".

The slippage here—equating archaeological sites of diverse origins and uses with each other as both "monument" and "marker"—demonstrates that these selected examples were being viewed retrospectively in their current state as ruins and as heritage sites. Emphasis was placed on identifying a date of construction, the identity of particular people responsible for the construction, and a rationale for the construction of the features. Together, these facts established the moment of origin and original significance of each monument.

The 1996 proposal for the WIPP marker system incorporated word-for-word material on the Acropolis from this earlier report. Yet there were selective omissions. Not integrated into the 1996 document was a critical sentence from the 1982 document explaining the importance of the Acropolis as "an example of an area with its monuments for which we *can follow the history* in some detail for over two millennia" (Kaplan, 1982: 43; emphasis added). This way of writing about archaeological sites, in which their dynamic histories are acknowledged,

TABLE 11.1 World Heritage status of archaeological analogues

Archaeological analogue	Kaplan, 1982	Trauth, Hora, and Guzowski, 1993	DOE, 1996	World Heritage status
Great Pyramids of Egypt	x	x	x	inscribed 1979
Stonehenge	x	x	x	inscribed 1986
Acropolis	x		x	inscribed 1987
Serpent Mound	x		x	nominated 2008
Great Wall of China	x			inscribed 1987
Nazca Lines	x			inscribed 1994
Newgrange tomb		x	x	inscribed 1983
Cahokia Mounds		x		inscribed 1982
Spanish rock art		x		inscribed 1998
Australian rock art			x	inscribed 1981 (Kakadu National Park)
Rock of Behistun			x	inscribed 2006

exemplifies archaeological thinking. It does not lend itself to the project of using archaeological sites as examples of stability of meaning and success of the intentions of an original generation of builders. It is thus not surprising that the official proposal represents the Acropolis, and other archaeological analogues, as atemporal. Each archaeological warrant had a presumed moment of creation in which its meaning was established, and the decay of the physical form and its meaning were the only way change could occur. Holtorf and Högberg (2015) similarly criticize this kind of static conception, arguing instead for a concept of "living heritage" as the most likely way knowledge about places might be preserved. Their "living heritage" is closely related to Herzfeld's (1991) original contrast of monumental time with social time.

Temporality did enter into the discussions of the expert teams and crept into the DOE proposal in a novel feature, "small buried markers" (DOE, 1996: 5–19 to 5–20). These were to consist of thousands of objects, each with an inscribed warning. The expert panels had provided a general basis for this feature, described by one team as "time capsules" of ceramic, glass, or durable forms of metal that "would have information inscribed on the outside" (Trauth, Hora, and Guzowski, 1993: 3–10). As proposed by that team, "salting the site with small markers" was meant to allow them to "work their way to the surface via erosion or surface excavation... to remind the potential home builder or farmer that they really do not want to be there" (Trauth, Hora, and Guzowski, 1993: F-17). The warning messages would be inscribed on the surface of what this team imagined as disks of fired clay or glass. The vision offered is of a site undergoing constant change rather than of a place frozen in time with its form and meaning available for decoding.

The second expert team described small buried markers, which it also proposed as "likely to be decoded by less developed societies in the future, and decoded and chronologically dated by as-advanced and more-advanced societies" (Trauth, Hora, and Guzowski, 1993: G-14). This team developed explicit estimates of the durability of these small buried markers, ranging from 500 to 10,000 years, based on the recovery in North American Paleoindian archaeological sites of "stone projectile points, bone needles and bison teeth" and "camel teeth and bones", and in the arid environment of Egypt, of naturally mummified human tissues (Trauth, Hora, and Guzowski, 1993: G-42 to G-43). Most of these occur in archaeological sites that project members recognized did not result from intentions for either preservation for the future or communication to it. It is perhaps not surprising that the stone projectile points, bone needles, animal bones, and natural mummies disappeared from discussion after this, eventually to be replaced by a category of portable objects that could be treated as intentional messages for future audiences: cuneiform tablets.

What binds the slightly different proposals for small buried markers by the two teams is the citation by each team of archaeology, a practice of digging deliberately for historical purposes, as an imagined activity in the future. As the overall report put it, these objects "would be placed to be found by those beginning to intrude upon the site—e.g., by archaeologists" (Trauth, Hora, and Guzowski, 1993: 3–10). Nothing could make it clearer that the teams were designing not a commemorative monument but an archaeological site.

In keeping with its mandate, by 1996, the DOE had developed its own arguments for its proposed use of small buried markers. These emphasized persistence of meaning rather than changing form (DOE, 1996: 5–19 to 5–20). Entirely new warrants were provided with a focus on meaning being conveyed intact: the Code of Hammurabi and "Mesopotamian Artifacts", specifically, "fired clay tablets written in cuneiform script" (DOE, 1996: 5–19). Neither had been mentioned in the 1993 experts' reports. The 1982 design proposal briefly touched on the topic of clay tablets in a discussion of the durability of inscribed messages to be deposited in a central "vault", the precedent for the "message" or "information" center of later proposals (Kaplan, 1982: 66–67). The description of Mesopotamian clay tablets there was more detailed than the 1996 DOE proposal:

> Everyday texts such as lists of commodities and private and business letters were on unfired, but sun-dried tablets; royal annals and literary works were often fired to enhance their survival. Fired tablets are much like potsherds; they may break but they are otherwise extremely durable.
>
> *(Kaplan, 1982: 66)*

The temporality of Mesopotamian clay tablets, a social time of business, trade, and governance, disappears and is replaced by the monumental time of sheer endurance in the DOE proposal:

One of the other materials being considered for the buried markers is fired clay. Based on evidence found in the Mesopotamian tells, the DOE asserts that buried clay markers will last for 5,000 years, with a high probability of enduring for the entire regulatory period.

(DOE 1996:5–20)

With one last archaeological analogue, newly emphasized in the 1996 proposal, it becomes clear that the design for the nuclear waste site involves systematically monumentalizing features of enduring objects by ignoring their engagement in shorter-term temporalities in the past. In the discussion of the likely survival of stone monoliths, the DOE in 1996 cited not only Stonehenge but also the Rock of Behistun. This archaeological analogue appeared in one expert team's report about the persistence of written messages (Trauth, Guzowski, and Hora, 1993: G-42).

The discussion of this analogue in the 1996 DOE proposal echoed the emphasis on writing seen in the discussion of the Acropolis and cuneiform tablets. In some ways, it went further, claiming that the text on this monument

was inscribed *for the purpose of reaching generations to come*... the sculpture has endured longer than the common use of the languages it contains, but the essence of its message remains interpretable by modern day scholars. *It is an example of an authority creating a message for future generations to learn of the deeds of an earlier generation.*

(DOE, 1996: 5–8; emphasis added)

None of these claims were made by the expert teams. Scholarly research on the Rock of Behistun (today, Bisitun or Bisotun) does not support the characterization by the planners that this was a message intended for "future generations". Instead, these statements included by the DOE in its justification for the project reflect the common sense assumptions these planners felt were self-evident. The Rock of Behistun is legible now, and that showed, *as the planners wrote*, that it "was inscribed for the purpose of reaching generations to come".

Instead, researchers believe the patron of the monument, the Achaemenid emperor Darius who had usurped the throne, was concerned with establishing legitimacy for his model of rulership and arguably had as primary audience the god who was his patron (Finn, 2011). The inscription is one of a series of Achaemenid depictions visually and discursively creating a new concept of "subjects as *co-operating* with their emperor" (Kuhrt, 1984: 157; emphasis original). The Rock of Behistun is seen as a product of intentions of the Achaemenids to "directly relate themselves to earlier traditions" (Kuhrt, 1984: 158). It used a Babylonian inscription to signify a connection to preceding generations, Elamite, to relate to the people of the locality where it was placed, and Persian as a sign of the new imperium founded by Darius (Huyse, 1999: 57–58). It was not created all at once, but rather, was added to in various stages (Huyse, 1999: 55–57).

Only near the end of the inscription does Darius add a few lines enjoining those who see the monument not to destroy it and invoking the blessings of his god on those who did not do so. To take those admonitions, which in context are clearly to a near, not distant future, as evidence that the Rock of Behistun was created for "future generations" is a reworking of the original inscription to make it fit a modernist idea of the cultural heritage monument.

This passage in the DOE report is followed immediately by a claim that the use of multiple languages on the Rock of Behistun provides a model for the proposal to inscribe messages on the monoliths of WIPP in multiple languages, "to inform future generations of the existence of the WIPP and the risk of intruding". The real future-orientation of the WIPP project overwhelms the intentions of Darius, and retrospectively grants to his monument the intention of communicating to a specific "future generation", us.

Cultural heritage in ruins

As an archaeologist, my reaction to this deliberate plan to create present-day ruins, a pre-made cultural heritage site to be transmitted to future generations, has always been skeptical. The sites selected to support claims of endurance all have dynamic histories of change, intrusion, and reworking. The assertion that modern technology will improve on ancient analogues betrays a progressivist bias. Archaeology tells me that the behavior of actual assemblages will exceed the intentions of builders, as it has in the past (Joyce, 2004; 2016; 2020). I wonder why the planners believed that the places they used as warrants for the effectiveness of various elements ever had intended, singular meanings. How have archaeologists failed to convey even to other academics the reality that the places we make into heritage sites were not designed and imbued with meaning at a single point in time but rather accrued and continue to unfold different kinds of relations, including relations of meaning, throughout complex histories of emergent form? In order to address that question, I want to identify the cultural common sense involved in developing the WIPP proposal. Much of this, I argue, matches the framework of World Heritage.

At different points in 1982, 1993, and 1996, overlapping but not identical sets of archaeological sites were used as evidence that a marker could be designed that would last for thousands of years and under certain circumstances would continue to convey clear messages. Of the archaeological ruins proposed as warrants for the performance of the proposed marker system, Stonehenge, Serpent Mound, the Egyptian pyramids, and the Acropolis came from the initial archaeologist consultant report (Kaplan, 1982). Stonehenge and, to a lesser extent, the Egyptian pyramids were cited by the experts convened by the DOE, who also introduced new analogues such as Newgrange (Trauth, Hora, and Guzowski, 1993). Australian rock art, included in the 1996 DOE proposal, clearly replaced the Spanish Levantine rock art cited by experts in their discussions (Trauth, Hora, and Guzowski, 1993), perhaps because of the longer time spans associated with

Australian rock art. The Code of Hammurabi and cuneiform tablets mentioned by the DOE gave more precision to previous references to enduring artifacts as precedents for small buried markers proposed by the expert teams (Trauth, Hora, and Guzowski, 1993).

The group of sites used in these different reports shares one characteristic: they all were inscribed as World Heritage or have subsequently been nominated (Table 11.1). As described in the UNESCO convention, to achieve listing, cultural properties must either be monuments which exemplify "outstanding universal value from the point of view of history, art or science" or groups of buildings that "because of their architecture, their homogeneity or their place in the landscape, are of outstanding universal value from the point of view of history, art or science" or sites that "are of outstanding universal value from the historical, aesthetic, ethnological or anthropological point of view" (http://whc .unesco.org/en/convention/).

Much criticism of World Heritage concepts has centered on the concept of universal value (Harrison, 2013: 110–118; Labadi, 2013). While universalism is clearly part of the framework of the WIPP expert consultants and the DOE, the UNESCO convention also conveys an implicit temporality, indexed by the repeated citation of "point of view". This is a reminder that these places are heritage from the perspective of the present. This is the point of view of "monumental time", "reductive and generic", providing a physical form of "collective predictability" (Herzfeld, 1991: 10) or perhaps better, collective retrodictability. The mobilization of the selected sites as warrants for a predicted future rests on the common-sense understanding on the part of the planners of today about the future orientations the builders of these sites had in our past.

Cultural heritage is only a past from the perspective of "*somebody's* present" (Eriksen, 2014: 142). The present in which the WIPP markers and World Heritage converged most closely in the planning process can be narrowed to 1991 when the panels of experts made their arguments for specific markers. Kaplan (1982) had employed an archaeological sense of sites as having histories. Her ultimate conclusion was that historicizing practices using texts would be necessary for a marker to convey anything more than a general "we were there" message. For Kaplan, the selection of sites used as analogues was not dictated by or even closely related to World Heritage status; of her examples, only the Great Pyramids were listed when she wrote.

With the convening of the expert teams, cited analogues for the marker system converged with World Heritage sites. Expert Team B, which most closely specified the building of a modern ruin in its proposal, is particularly clear in its imagination of the marker system as a future heritage monument. These experts specified the audience for the marker in "any conceivable culture or future society" as explicitly including "future archaeologists" (Trauth, Guzowski, and Hora, 1993: G-9 to G-10). They argued that the design's success would require a future social world that would recognize the markers as a "human monument worth preserving (e.g., like Stonehenge)" (Trauth, Guzowski, and Hora, 1993: G-38).

This they judged likely, commenting that "human curiosity regarding ancient earthworks, and creative thoughts about what their patterns signify" should last for millennia (Trauth, Guzowski, and Hora, 1993: G-43). The team universalized monumentality as a criterion of value "the monumental configuration of large, shaped stones would connote, 'Something *important* is here'"(Trauth, Guzowski, and Hora, 1993: G-44; emphasis original). They argued that "with age the monoliths could become recognized as a preservable, historical resource" (Trauth, Guzowski, and Hora, 1993: G-45). Ultimately, they collapsed the future-orientation they projected onto builders of past archaeological sites with their own expectations about the future, writing that while

> a monument designed by 20th–21st century humans will present something of a mystery to future generations, we assume our descendants will respond to the challenge as eagerly as 20th-century men and women have responded to questions and enigmas posed by ancient monuments.
>
> *(Trauth, Guzowski, and Hora, 1993: G-64)*

The warrants cited by the DOE only partially overlapped World Heritage sites. The DOE included Serpent Mound (not yet nominated as a World Heritage site) and the Rock of Behistun (only inscribed in 2006). Mention of Australian rock art in the proposal is non-specific and in no way references Kakadu National Park, listed in 1981. Yet the DOE also incorporated a common sense about past, present, future, and cultural heritage sites similar to that more richly illustrated by the expert panel report. The DOE explicitly defined assumptions it recognized it was making, arguing that "people will continue to be interested in their past history" (DOE, 1996: 3–2). It was the DOE that described the Rock of Behistun as "an example of an authority creating a message for future generations to learn of the deeds of an earlier generation" (DOE, 1996: 5–8).

Unintended consequences

The "questions and enigmas posed by ancient monuments" cited by expert Team B exist only when monuments, groups of buildings, or sites are seen as relics from the past set before us to decipher: messages in a landscape-scale bottle. In order to plan the marker system, the experts projected their own task onto past makers of sites today recognized as heritage, and the DOE embedded that assumption in its proposal. Both the expert team and the DOE treated archaeological sites whose actual audiences and intentions were part of present- and past-making of former times as if they were oriented toward a distant future, which we now occupy. They imagined successor societies in the future as if their own concerns with past and present will inevitably continue our contemporary concern with connecting to pasts seen as signs for us to understand.

All of this can be seen as common sense informed by contemporary heritage thinking. Archaeologists operate inside this contemporary common sense.

When we come to think of what heritage will be like in the future, just as when we try to project the intentions of builders of monuments in the past, we operate with the assumption that people are universally concerned with their futures, including distant ones. Identifying the common sense in which we participate can be transformative for how we think about both things being made for the future and those things that have endured long periods from their making into our present.

Possible unintended consequences of the proposed WIPP marker system, although one focus of expert modeling, have yet to be reassessed without reliance on cultural heritage common sense. When they are, it should be by using archaeology not as a form of cultural heritage logic that assumes things survive because they were designed to convey sentiments to a distant future, but by exploring how people and materials together create effects, with the expectation that these effects will always exceed and often subvert expectations.

References

Byrne, D., 2011. Archaeological Heritage and Cultural Intimacy: An Interview with Michael Herzfeld. *Journal of Social Archaeology* 11(2), 144–157.

DOE, 1996. Title 40 CFR Part 191 Compliance Certification Application for the Waste Isolation Pilot Plant: Appendix EPIC: Effectiveness of Passive Institutional Controls in Reducing Inadvertent Human Intrusion into the Waste Isolation Plant for use in Performance Assessments. United States Department of Energy, Waste Isolation Pilot Plant, Carlsbad, NM, June 4, 1996, accessed October 24, 2014. http://www.wipp.energy.gov/library/CRA/CRA-2014/References/CCA/Appendix_EPIC.PDF

EPA, 1996. Compliance Application Review Document No. 43: Passive Institutional Controls. Compliance Application Review Documents for the Criteria for the Certification and Re-Certification of the Waste Isolation Pilot Plant's Compliance with the 40 CFR Part 191 Disposal Regulations. Washington, DC: Disposal Regulations. US Environmental Protection Agency. October 29, 1996, accessed October 24, 2014. http://www.epa.gov/rpdweb00/docs/wipp/card43.pdf

Eriksen, A., 2014. *From Antiquities to Heritage: Transformations of Cultural Memory.* Oxford: Berghahn.

Finn, J., 2011. Gods, Kings, Men: Trilingual Inscriptions and Symbolic Visualizations in the Achaemenid Empire. *Ars Orientalis* 41, 219–275.

Hart, J. and Associates., 2004. Passive Institutional Controls Implementation Plan. United States Department of Energy, Waste Isolation Pilot Plant, Carlsbad, NM. DOE/WIPP 04-2301, August 19, 2004, consulted October 24, 2014. http://www.wipp.energy.gov/library/PICsImplementationPlan.pdf

Harrison, R., 2013. *Heritage: Critical Approaches.* London: Routledge.

Herzfeld, M., 1991. *A Place in History. Social and Monumental Time in a Cretan Town.* Princeton, NJ: Princeton University Press.

Herzfeld, M., 2001. *Anthropology: Theoretical Practice in Culture and Society.* Malden, MA: Blackwell.

Holtorf, C. and Högberg, A., 2015. Archaeology and the Future: Managing Nuclear Waste as a Living Heritage. In: *Radioactive Waste Management and Constructing Memory for Future Generations.* Nuclear Energy Agency, no. 7259. Paris: OECD; pp. 97–101.

Hora, S.C., von Winterfeldt, D. and Trauth, K.M., 1991. Expert Judgment on Inadvertent Human Intrusion into the Waste Isolation Pilot Plant. Sandia Report SAND90-3063. Albuquerque, NM. Sandia National Laboratories.

Huyse, P., 1999. Some Further Thoughts on the Bisitun Monument and the Genesis of the Old Persian Cuneiform Script. *Bulletin of the Asia Institute* 13, 45–66.

Joyce, R.A., 2004. Unintended Consequences? Monumentality as a Novel Experience in Formative Mesoamerica. *Journal of Archaeological Method and Theory* 11(1), 5–29.

Joyce, R.A., 2006. The Monumental and the Trace: Archaeological Conservation and the Materiality of the Past. In: N. Agnew and J. Bridgland, eds. *Of the Past, for the Future: Integrating Archaeology and Conservation*. Los Angeles, CA: Getty Conservation Institute, 13–18.

Joyce, R.A., 2016. Failure? An Archaeology of the Architecture of Nuclear Waste Containment. In: M. Bille and T. Flohr Sørensen, eds. *Elements of Architecture: Assembling Architecture, Atmosphere, and the Performance of Building Space* London: Routledge; pp. 424–438.

Joyce, R.A., 2020. *The Future of Nuclear Waste: What Art and Archaeology Can Tell Us About Securing the World's Most Hazardous Material*. Oxford: Oxford University Press.

Kaplan, M.F., 1982. Archaeological Data as a Basis for Repository Marker Design. ONWI-354. Technical Report Prepared by the Analytic Sciences Corporation for the Office of Nuclear Waste Isolation. Columbus, OH: Batelle Memorial Institute.

Kaplan, M.F. and Adams, M., 1986. Using the Past to Protect the Future: Marking Nuclear Waste Disposal Sites. *Archaeology* 39(5), 51–54.

Kuhrt, A., 1984. The Achaemenid Concept of Kingship. *Iran* 22, 156–160.

Labadi, S., 2013. *UNESCO, Cultural Heritage, and Outstanding Universal Value*. Lanham, MD: AltaMira Press.

Trauth, K.M., Hora, S.C. and Guzowski, R.V., 1993. Expert Judgment on Markers to Deter Inadvertent Intrusion into the Waste Isolation Pilot Plant. Sandia Report SAND92-1382. Albuquerque, NM. Sandia National Laboratories.

WIPP, 2007. WIPP Chronology. Updated February 5, 2007, accessed October 24, 2014. http://www.wipp.energy.gov/tctshts/Chronology.pdf

12

RADIOACTIVE HERITAGE OF THE FUTURE

A legacy of risk

*Marcos Buser, Abraham Van Luik†,
Roger Nelson and Cornelius Holtorf*

Introduction

This conversation is based on manuscripts submitted by Marcos Buser and by
Abraham Van Luik and Roger Nelson for this volume. One section is derived
from an interview by Cornelius Holtorf and Anders Högberg with Abraham
Van Luik conducted on 11 March 2014 and approved by Van Luik on 19 June
2015. The final version of this text was edited and approved by Marcos Buser
and Roger Nelson.

Marcos Buser is a geologist and social scientist at the Institute for Sustainable
Waste Management, Zürich, Switzerland. He worked for decades in the clean-
up of large dump sites and was a member or chair of several commissions in the
field of nuclear waste disposal. His expertise in the field of marker projects is even
internationally widely recognised.

Abraham Van Luik (†2016) worked on siting studies for the US during the
1980s as a geochemist analysing candidate deep geologic repository options
in multiple rock formations across the US. He joined the US Department of
Energy (DOE) Office of Civilian Radioactive Waste Management in the early
1990s, as the repository site at Yucca Mountain was legislatively selected by
the US Congress as the only site that would be studied. He worked on the
Yucca Mountain Project in various capacities until 2011, when he joined the
Department of Energy's Waste Isolation Pilot Plant (WIPP) as manager of international programmes. There, he championed efforts to develop international
standards for informing future generations about radioactive waste repositories
around the world.

Roger Nelson recently retired from the US Department of Energy's Waste
Isolation Pilot Plant, where he served as the project chief scientist. He focused on
the repository licence application in the 1990s, and when it opened, his efforts

turned to broadening its waste acceptance criteria, with emphasis on separated and surplus plutonium from nuclear weapons production during the Cold War. Prior to his WIPP contributions, he served as the project manager for the Uranium Mill Tailings Remedial Action Project, which cleaned up and created 19 engineered, shallow subsurface disposal cells across western states in the USA.

Waste as cultural heritage

Question: Thank you for joining us for this conversation. Marcos Buser, you have for some time been exploring the connections between cultural heritage and toxic waste (e.g., Buser, 2015), why do you see toxic waste as heritage?

Buser: In terms of general perceptions in society, waste is just waste, and it won't be of any special interest to future generations. This is the most common view. But we also have the view of professionals who are in one way or another working with waste, whether they are managing the risks and hazards posed by waste or whether they are involved in art, architecture or archaeology. They know that contemporary waste, just like ancient waste, can tell us an enormous amount of things about humans and their intellectual and philosophical concepts, about ethics as well as about the structure of societies, about history and about artistic work.

From an anthropological point of view, waste exists only from the perspective of the beholder and his/her value system that structures concepts of hygiene and patterns of order (Douglas, 1966; see Figure 12.1). These ideas have been later elaborated by Michael Thompson (1979) in his account of "Rubbish Theory" and since then in numerous other works (e.g., Fassler, 1991; Hauser, 2001; Wagner, 2008).

Two fundamental findings on the cultural importance of waste follow from these considerations. The first, waste can be recycled, becoming

FIGURE 12.1   Cultural significance of waste. Left: paleo-littering (bones) at the Palaeolithic site of Laténium Hauterive, Switzerland; photograph by R. Zurbuchen, reproduced by permission. Right: contemporary littering after a public party in Zürich (2012); photograph provided by Entsorgung + Recycling Zürich, Switzerland, reproduced by permission.

"waste material". People have long been re-using material which they considered to be valuable. Examples include the use of spolia in architecture (Poeschke, 1996) and of pre-existing objects in modern art, from Dadaism and Surrealism to the "nouveau Realists" and modern waste art. What humans once created, has often, in some form, been re-used later.

I am convinced that all waste, as an anthropogenic product, should also be regarded as a form of cultural heritage. Toxic waste is special insofar as it primarily carries negative traits and in fact, represents a burdensome heritage. This is an onerous legacy of the industrial age, which is clearly in contrast to the great cultural achievements of humankind we are proud to extol, yet like any other heritage, it reflects human behaviour and cultural activities.

Hazardous waste: a legacy of risk

Question: What are the implications for heritage management of the fact that this particular form of modern heritage is toxic?

Buser: Problems with waste dumps of settlements or the heaps of ore deposits started already in ancient times (Rathje and Murphy, 2001; Rebrik, 1987; Thüry, 2001). But it was not until modern times that highly hazardous industrial waste and bulk waste from daily consumption, such as plastics, were created, posing a new category of threat not only in terms of its wide distribution and the sheer amount of waste left behind but also concerning the length of time during which the waste will remain a threat to future generations. Today, there is not one spot on Earth which is not directly confronted with problems of civilisation wastes.

Two categories of waste pose particular challenges for the future in terms of environmental management and also heritage management: chemo-toxic hazardous wastes from industrial manufacturing and processing as well as radioactive wastes, especially those produced for electricity generation in nuclear plants. Hazardous chemical waste is little-present in the public perception, in contrast to the radioactive wastes, which have achieved a true cult status when it comes to the refusal by society in general and many concerned site locations for permanent disposal in particular (see also Wollentz et al. 2020).

Nelson/Van Luik: Living generations are aware of and sensitive to the needs of their immediate succeeding generation and their offspring, and perhaps one or two additional future generations after them. Present generations typically intend to be good stewards of resources for the sake of their successors and hope to leave a positive legacy in terms of a clean environment, not a negative one of imposed environmental risks (Figure 12.2).

It is inevitable though that every living generation also imposes a legacy of risk on future generations. Being alive and consuming resources and creating wastes inevitably imposes risk on others, both currently alive and

FIGURE 12.2   Contact–handled waste emplacement in the WIPP, near Carlsbad, New Mexico, scheduled for decommissioning and sealing in 2055. Photograph: Roger Nelson.

in the future. At the same time, being alive is a prerequisite to there being a future generation. The point is that there is risk in all we do, for ourselves as well as our offspring. We will all die, that risk is certain, but the quality and length of life available to any particular generation ought not to be seriously affected by risks imposed by predecessor generations.

It is inevitable that the waste products of each generation find their way into the air and water and be buried in the ground. So there is a particular problem with toxic waste which we need to deal with.

Question: So what are we going to do in the light of these problems?

Buser: The task that presents itself to us and the hundreds of generations that come after us, is enormous considering the mountains of toxic waste of the industrial society. The liberty of the use of industrial resources is associated with a duty to avoid the socialisation of risks and hazards over long periods of time, i.e., the shifting of risks onto subsequent generations. In other words, benefits and risks of technologies should not be spread over time. The beneficiaries also have to bear the risks, as William Kapp recognised decades ago (Kapp, 2000).

With the radioactive wastes, this equation is unfortunately not adding up. Considering the current state of science and technology, it is hardly possible to tread another path than to banish these long-lived hazardous

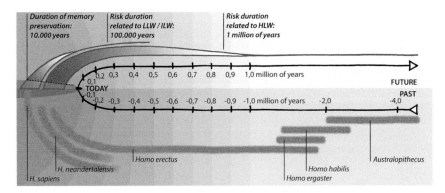

FIGURE 12.3 Time spans for radioactive waste disposal. Copyright: Marcos Buser, 2017.

wastes from the environment of human life. The quantities are relatively small, between 300,000 and 400,000 tonnes of highly radioactive waste from the world's nuclear plants, but the biological hazard of radioactive and toxic waste is unanimously regarded as unique. In most nuclear-energy-using countries, it is assumed that the waste must be kept from the biosphere for hundreds of thousands of years (Figure 12.3). This corresponds to tens of thousands of generations. These are time periods that go beyond any previous understanding of culture.

But we face a real dilemma here. Not only do we have to protect the people from the repositories but also the repositories from the people. We will probably have no other choice than to go forward with good intentions trying to develop the best possible stewardship and marking systems designed to protect people in the future. With this plan, we relieve ourselves, at least morally. But the uncertainty of the success of such programmes will prevail, no matter how much we resist this fact.

Ethical obligations

Question: You mentioned morals. What are the particular ethical challenges concerning toxic wastes? Roger Nelson and Abraham Van Luik, you have been thinking a great deal with such issues in relation to your work at the WIPP.

Nelson/Van Luik: Ethically, living generations need to minimise and mitigate the risks they bury in the ground for the sake of future generations, in terms of municipal, industrial, chemical and radioactive toxic wastes. Mitigation usually means moving the more toxic wastes, or the longest-lived wastes, deeper under the surface of the Earth to reduce the probability of gradual release and likelihood of inadvertent human intrusion. In contrast, an argument could be made, and sustained, that this is generally not being done well for many chemically toxic waste streams, whose toxicity lasts forever. As Marcos Buser mentioned earlier, the one waste stream that is being given much attention in terms of reducing risk to future generations is the higher level of radioactive waste from nuclear power plants and other nuclear facilities. By definition, all radioactive elements have half-lives; hence their risk from exposure reduces over time and eventually is negligible in comparison with all of life's other risks.

Arguments have been made that the attention focused on the radioactive waste issue in terms of avoiding future generation risk is resulting in unethically high costs to current generations. Ethics comes into the picture when a current generation is asked to forego vital health and wellbeing support against real threats to their lives so as to be able to pay to protect hypothetical future generations from an uncertain exposure resulting in an uncertain risk. Sunstein (2001) speaks of impoverishing the present for the sake of the future, which is perhaps a little more dramatic than warranted for a repository information-preservation problem, but there is a very real ethical question as to what ought to be taken from current and near-term generations facing multiple, real risks to protect the far future from a single and uncertain, localised and likely minimal risk. Present generations are facing many risk-laden challenges in real-time, and using their resources to attempt to warn far-future generations of a potential risk to a hypothetical intruder takes these resources away from other projects that may benefit future generations more.

To make this type of ethical judgement still harder, there is uncertainty about the likely health effects of a chronic low dose intake of radioactivity in a case where someone or some small community is drawing contaminated water from a well or several wells. Below a sizeable exposure rate, no deleterious health effects have ever been conclusively demonstrated. At low doses, the risks seem low. Yet national regulatory bodies typically impose annual dose limits from nuclear facilities (including geologic repositories) to the public that are actually smaller than the natural variability in regional background radiation. This makes doing a health-consequence to health-consequence comparison between the present and the far future so uncertain as to be meaningless since projected potential exposures are unlikely to have identifiable health consequences.

These are valid arguments. Nevertheless, the nuclear waste management community around the world is acutely aware that they are ethically obliged to do what is practicable and reasonable to protect future generations from the risks they are burying very deep underground. Practicable and reasonable are key terms of art, but they mean different things to different people.

Buser: The dropping of the first two atomic bombs on Japan in August 1945 shook the opinion of many contemporaries. Many nuclear physicists at the forefront of research and development were stunned and did not believe that such a bomb could be built. In philosopher Günther Anders' book, *The Nuclear Threat* (1972), he postulated theories on the nuclear age and already scourged the blindness to the apocalypse of our society by revealing the discrepancy between the production capacity of human technology and the limited capacity to evaluate its consequences: "We are actually inverted utopians: while utopians cannot produce what they imagine, we are unable to imagine what we produce" (Anders, 1972, p. 96). Anders thus addressed something extremely fundamental, namely the fact that we can hardly fathom the impact of our future actions. As he argued elsewhere (Anders, 1987, p. 262–263), our emotional and empathic system fails above a certain dimensional threshold. This difficulty also applies to nuclear waste.

Question: What do you consider to be practicable and reasonable to do in order to protect future generations from the risks contained in the radioactive waste we leave behind? What has been done already, and what is being done now?

Buser: The unusually long periods during which waste must be kept from humans and the environment reflect themselves in the concepts and projects of waste management (Figure 12.4; Organisation for Economic Co-operation and Development (OECD), 2013, p. 18). While grotesque-looking waste management solutions were proposed at first with regards to nuclear waste

FIGURE 12.4 Field of Thorns landscape, one of the more ominous markers suggested by Trauth et al. (1993, Figure 4.3-1).

– such as the dilution of waste in the oceans, shooting it into outer space, or introducing it into the ice sheet of Antarctica (EKRA, 2000, p. 13; WNWR 2019; Buser et al. 2020) – the projects focused more and more on the concentration of the waste in the bedrock of the continents. Today, the strategy to dispose of radioactive wastes in the host rocks of the geological bedrock at 500-metres to 1000-metres depth has become the international standard. It remains to be seen how these concepts will be implemented. So far, projects of underground storage of high-risk waste have been accompanied by problems and accidents, for example in the repositories of Asse and Morsleben in Germany since the 1980s, or in the final storage facility for chemo-toxic waste, StocaMine in France, since 2002. Basic failures in safety culture lead even to accidents in the disposal facility for transuranic military waste at the WIPP in New Mexico in 2014 (DOE 2014a, 2014b, 2015; Klaus, 2019). Despite these failures, however, the strategy of final storage in the deep underground is being pursued internationally.

Nelson/Van Luik: The vision of the current radioactive waste management community around the world is that every nation, or perhaps region, will dispose of the more highly radioactive wastes in deep geological structures, typically by way of a repository, although very deep boreholes may also come into use at some point in time. So several generations from now, there ought to be dozens of working repositories in the world for these types of radioactive wastes. Isolation from the biosphere and avoiding inadvertent human intrusion are key components of the site selection process and safety design of these systems. In some instances, the only credible way that releases can occur from repositories in very tight host rock is via the human intrusion pathway either bringing waste to the surface or degrading the natural or engineered barrier systems of a well sited and built repository.

Present generations are paying much attention to this issue, and it has risen to the attention of the international organisations dealing with the technical and safety assurance aspects of future radioactive waste repositories. The International Atomic Energy Agency (IAEA) in Vienna, the Nuclear Energy Agency (NEA) in Paris and the European Commission's (EC's) Research Directorate in Brussels have all launched projects dealing with the human intrusion issue. Both the IAEA and the NEA have also done work on coming up with a consensus view of what is ethical, yet practicable and reasonable, in terms of creating systems that inform future generations of the radiological risks that have been buried.

Assuring continued safety after a repository is closed requires a technical approach based on good siting and engineered closure and sealing systems, as well as messages of various types (records, markers, etc.) to inform, and hopefully deter, potential inadvertent intruders. Radioactive wastes in a repository present a range of potential risks, depending on their half-lives, their physical and chemical form as extracted and their use or management when brought to the surface during a far-future (and hypothetical) drilling operation. Also, a far-future drilling operation should not be allowed to compromise the engineered or natural barriers that assure continued containment. Therefore, it is important to inform, and hence warn, the future of the possible risk of intrusion.

Comprehensive studies were performed in the 1980s and 1990s to suggest ways of warning the future through massive and peculiar monuments and buried archives on-site and off (Trauth et al., 1993). Those early efforts focused on warnings as well as information that would help future potential intruders understand the risk of intrusion. They were based on the premise that risks from exposure to these wastes were great and that the monuments and information they contained must survive intact for deep time. This premise justified the allocation of substantial present-day resources to build such massive and robust structures.

Today, as several repositories in Europe and the US begin to look at meeting their regulations' requirements for assuring there is communication into the future about the location and nature of the radioactive waste deep underground, an international effort is underway to take advantage of progress in the various disciplines that can aid the design of a future-informing system (OECD-NEA, 2013; Schröder 2019). Some of the recommendations from the earlier work done in this area are likely impracticable, technically, or unreasonable from a fiscal point of view. Fiscal infeasibility brings into play intergenerational ethics as an issue.

In environmental legal cases in the United States, there has been sufficient case law to derive an accepted set of principles for judging the feasibility (technical) and reasonableness (cost versus benefit) of risk mitigation regulatory requirements. Although this case law refers exclusively to environmental regulatory requirements that apply to industries, there are several principles that would also logically apply to judge the practicability and reasonableness of requirements for informing the future of a potential risk (Sunstein, 2001). The warning system needs to be practicable from a technical point of view, reasonable from an investment point of view and ethical from an intergenerational equity point of view.

Nuclear semiotics

Question: There have been some concrete suggestions in the past concerning warning systems in relation to the WIPP. How do you look at them from today's perspective, several decades on?

Buser: The marking studies in the US relating to the WIPP recognised the need to preserve the contemporary knowledge over many generations. For this purpose, various ways of passing information through time were considered. In this context, the book *Warnings to the Distant Future* (Posner, 1990) was an early and broad attempt to consider the complex issues of what has become known as nuclear semiotics.

In 1972, Alvin Weinberg, the former director of Oak Ridge National Laboratory (USA), one of the leading laboratories in the history of nuclear technology, proposed the creation of a body of nuclear scientists, who should be responsible for the long-term monitoring of the nuclear waste (Weinberg, 1972; 1994). Weinberg was referring to the drama *Faust* by the German poet, Wolfgang von Goethe, when he spoke of a "Faustian bargain": for the unlimited magical energy that the society received, it had to ensure the vigilance and longevity of social institutions. Weinberg's article on this Faustian bargain sparked off a debate in society that continues to the present day.

Weinberg's Faustian bargain and his "atomic priesthood" as leaders of a future nuclear community were seriously questioned due to doubts about the persistence of religious institutions in society but also due to the anti-democratic nature of a knowledgeable elite unaccountable to anybody. Other scientists proposed similar bodies for the long-term stewardship of nuclear wastes (Sebeok, 1990), and they were criticised for similar reasons (Blonsky, 1990; Hauser, 1990). Subsequently, new models and terminology were proposed. Some authors suggested "news guards", others talked about the "happy few" bearers of knowledge of closed repositories (Buser, 2010; Voigt, 1990). Even a scientific variety of millennialism was brought into play (Weinberg, 1999; Minois, 1996; Cohn, 1961).

Key findings from this debate continue to have an effect up to this day. One of them concerns the role that institutions have to play in the future to pass information on to future generations and to ensure the protection of the concerned populations over long periods of time. The guardian-ship of waste has been replaced by a guardianship of knowledge over long periods of time. Over the last couple of decades, the scientific community has tended to favour such a relay system to be re-implemented every 100 years or so, also known as "long-term stewardship"(Sprenger, 2007; Tonn, 2001). Although the approach of constantly renewed recoding of information bears the risk of erroneous coding and loss of information, steering committees at the US Department of Energy and at the Nuclear Energy Agency of the OECD are developing strategies for an active, socially supported relay system that involves local communities (Pastina, 2004; Pescatore and Mays, 2008; Schröder 2019).

Nelson/Van Luik: The previous efforts at guiding the US Department of Energy on its plans for marking and preserving the memory of its WIPP nuclear waste repository for transuranic defence-wastes near Carlsbad, New Mexico, suggested fanciful, unworkably complex and expensive monuments such as the famed "Field of Thorns", dark metallic spikes over the repository area to create a sense of foreboding (Figure 12.4). One of its suggested messages was an apology to the future for having produced weapons-related wastes:

"This is not a place of honor" – an attempt to affect the future emotionally. Today we think that expressing opinions about what was done during the Cold War are as unreasonable as attempts to strike fear into the hearts of future generations (see also Holtorf and Högberg, chapter 10 this volume). The goal of communications into the future ought to be to convey facts, not to transmit current emotions and affect future ones. Acute radiation exposure is detectable and treatable today and will be in the future if technology remains at a similar level. Those who drill into a repository are using rather sophisticated technology.

This is not to suggest that the work using interdisciplinary teams of experts reported in Trauth et al. (1993) was not useful. Recommendations in that report directly contributed to the so-called "passive institutional controls" now proposed for both the WIPP and the proposed Yucca Mountain repository in Nevada (see also Joyce, chapter 11 this volume).

Figures 12.5 and 12.6 give a look at artists' renditions of the proposed surface marker structures for both the WIPP and Yucca Mountain repositories, both reflecting recommendations in Trauth et al. (1993).

Proposing designs with complex structures, such as those pictured in Figures 12.5 and 12.6, has given the US Department of Energy, in particular its Carlsbad Field office which has the WIPP repository under its

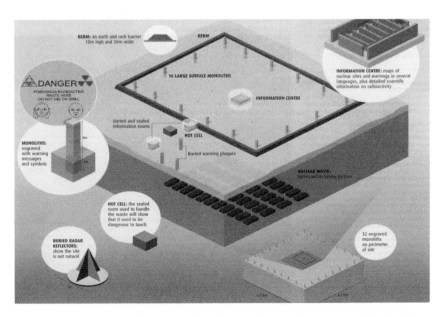

FIGURE 12.5   Conceptual design of surface markers and structures for the Waste Isolation Pilot Plant repository near Carlsbad, New Mexico, USA. Image prepared by *Los Angeles Times* (3 May 2006) and subsequently released for use by US DOE.

FIGURE 12.6   Conceptual design of surface marker structures for the proposed Yucca Mountain repository in Nevada, USA.

purview, the motivation to join the OECD-NEA initiative on Records, Knowledge and Memory Preservation (RK&M) for an international discussion, perhaps leading to a consensus view on this future-messaging challenge faced by all radioactive waste management organisations, their regulators and stakeholders (OECD-NEA, 2014a; Schröder 2019).

Communicating with future audiences

Question: But can knowledge and memory really reliably be transmitted over many thousands of years, whether directly or from one generation to another? Are there any historical precedents?

Buser: This is a very good question. What are the lessons learned and the knowledge gained with regards to structures from the past surviving over very long periods of time? Can methods and approaches on how to ensure sustained stewardship over administrative and safety structures for long-term monitoring be derived from past experience at all, or are we better off with our own theoretical considerations? What are the challenges and risks for the relay systems? Can we really link long-term memory to stewardship over such long time spans? The task is colossal and still lacks a basic outline.

The debate among scientists and the nuclear community repeatedly proposes institutions like the Vatican or monastic orders to assume the task of providing evidence for structural longevity and continuity. But these examples are a poor choice and can – especially in terms of ensuring continuity – easily be disproved. Communities and their institutions, especially those with ideological content, are rather prone to change, as illustrated by numerous historical examples. The creation of solid social structures presumes the development and implementation of normative rules and cultural codes. The implementation of such norms and codes over time by a specific institution requires canonisation of information and hence of language, form and content. And this is exactly where long-lasting religious institutions, such as churches, experience problems since the canons and codes are likely to be outdated by the time they are transferred to a new value system. Conveying of information through millenary structures is thus doomed to fail.

Technical infrastructure, however, may provide a far more reliable and successful way of implementing the required tasks, as they are specialised in archiving, in water supplies, care and maintenance of dams, bridges, aqueducts or the management of forests. Good historical examples document the continuity of action in difficult situations and the longevity of technical institutions. The Cloaca Maxima in Rome, at least 2,500 years old and still in operation (Thüry, 2001, pp. 48–49), the water supply of Eupalinos in Samos, all Greek, Roman and Arab aqueducts (Grewe, 2010), which remained in service over thousands of years, bear witness to the fact that at least some essential infrastructures can be continuously maintained and preserved for long periods (Figure 12.7). Some information might also be transmitted by rituals, legends, myths and folklore. They may, therefore, all be good examples demonstrating that long-living cultural heritage can be associated with a task that sets its goal to protect future generations from toxic wastes.

FIGURE 12.7 Aqueduct of Segovia, Spain, in active use until the 19th century. Photograph: Marcos Buser.

Nelson/Van Luik: The transmission of information across long time periods has to deal with several major challenges.

Firstly, who is the audience? Defining the audience of the future has to be based on present experience. The types of people who work in local or regional governmental units and define and enforce land-use regulations are not nuclear scientists, engineers or regulators. They are "lay" in the sense of being a non-technical audience with no specialised scientific knowledge regarding the topic at hand, which is a local or regional deep geologic repository. This means that the frontline agents defending a repository from potential intrusion are likely to be laypersons who are not familiar with the science and higher math used to construct a case for a repository's long-term safety. The document that needs to be available for the successions of persons performing such land-use control duties, therefore, ought to be in plain language and to the point, not unduly complex or lengthy.

Away from the frontline, so to speak, there may be an expert audience: academics and other researchers working on behalf of governments or industries who want to know more about a repository in terms of its potential value, or risk, in their time. Perhaps they would like to use its behaviour, as determined through sampling its environment, as an analogue for making a safety case for a planned new disposal facility. To address this expert audience, it is foreseen that the detailed scientific documents prepared for licensing, and the regulations being addressed in the licence proceedings, are the appropriate information vehicles. It is primarily for this audience that a regional, or national, or even international archive may be utilised. If in the course of an informed investigation of this nature there is an intrusion, it is a purposeful intrusion, not an inadvertent intrusion. Current generations are not concerned with such informed intrusive activities or their consequences. The ethical requirement is to do what is practicable and reasonable to prevent inadvertent human intrusion.

Suggestions have been made to cause collective community memory of a repository to be maintained as if it were some sort of great ever-threatening natural disaster that ought to be continually feared and prepared for. School curricula and community pageants and even the creation of new religious traditions have been proposed to help preserve the memory of the facility in a society. However, whereas the community governing body should remain aware of subsurface and perhaps other land-use restrictions that need to be maintained, the remainder of the community need not worry or fret over the deeply buried risks presented by a repository in the region that is designed to be passively safe.

As far as the question of how to construct any marker is concerned, we have to remember that there is no dialogue possible with the future; hence this is a one-way communication exercise. These communications need to take on a variety of forms to have a hope of being effective in the longer term. Again, we assume that what is valid for humans today can be safely assumed to be valid in the future. Large permanent markers from our own past still survive, but warning messages they contain may be ignored by future generations who see these warnings as reflecting a more primitive time. Small artefacts intended to convey art and religious concepts also survive, but the concepts they reflect in their form may have changed meaning with time.

Regardless of form, messages to the future must accomplish four things to be effective.

First, the message must survive the ages. Climate change, freeze-thaw cycles, harsh exposure to an oxidising environment and ultraviolet light will all erode the effectiveness of a message to the future. The message must be made with durable materials.

Second, the message must be found by the intended recipients prior to intrusion. This can be in direct conflict with the first requirement. One might attempt to bury the message to protect it from the ravages of time, but that also reduces the likelihood the message will be found. Of course, signs are for honest people. By making the message visible, the possibility that it will be vandalised or removed increases. In this context, it is worth noting that marker materials should be selected that are durable yet not commercially attractive or likely to become more scarce and expensive in the future. In that vein, the use of small ceramic discs or other materials or shapes as buried markers above the repository, once their presence becomes known in society at large, can have the opposite of the intended warning effect: it can lead to collectors disturbing the site. It may also be an advantage for a message to be transferable to new media that may come into vogue in the future without a great deal of effort.

Third, the message must be read and understood. Languages evolve. Old English from as recent as 400 years ago cannot be understood by the average English reader today. However, as the Rosetta Stone demonstrated, it is possible for messages to include methods for scholars to decipher them, embedded within the message itself.

Fourth, the message must be believed. It will do no good for a message to have survived, been found and deciphered if the reader doesn't believe it and intrudes into a repository anyway. This fourth requirement is the one that past messages to current generations have failed. Messages from our antiquity generally appealed to fear of punishment to the intruder, whether from a deity or the reigning authority of the time. Over the ages, tomb raiders didn't believe these threats, and neither did modern archaeologists. To convince a would-be intruder to avoid going further requires that the message convince the intruder of the message's veracity. Messages based on alarm and warning will likely be ignored. Only a message with enough information and sincerity has a chance of being heeded. How much is enough? Unfortunately, the first three requirements may severely limit how much information can be conveyed, and more extensive records in archives may survive into the far future but not be consulted.

Question: What are the lessons of the tsunami marker stones in Japan?

Nelson/Van Luik: The Japanese tsunami marker stones are a sobering lesson from the present (Figure 12.8). Tsunamis in Japan are a real risk to present generations so severe that all of the recommended methods of knowledge preservation have been used. Monuments and markers have been built and inscribed and clever site-naming ploys have been used. In addition, community and family traditions have been built up over time to warn of this specific and very deadly risk: great earthquakes and what follows them in certain parts of the world, the killer waves called tsunamis (OECD-NEA, 2014b).

The 2011 tsunami disaster was a real disaster, and it followed a string of such disasters back in the past. Previous generations attempted to warn future generations. They built monuments and markers. They gave towns and regions names that recalled the tsunamis of the past. In some locales, schools did tsunami drills teaching kids where to run without stopping after they felt the earth shake. Wherever these warnings were heeded, people survived.

The message was understood and believed, but in most locales, the embedded warnings were ignored because of the busyness of daily life and

FIGURE 12.8   "High dwellings are the peace and harmony of our descendants. Remember the calamity of the great tsunamis. Do not build any homes below this point". Giant Tsunami Stone from 1933, at Aneyoshi Village, Miyako, Iwate, Japan. Photograph by T. Kishimoto, licensed under CC BY-SA 4.0.

trust in new technology, sea-walls, caused there to be no fear of tsunamis in the current generation. Hence, no one survived in these areas built below the warning markers. These markers warn against a real and re-occurring threat that in 2011 killed tens of thousands of people. A repository's risk, in comparison, is negligible. Even active nuclear installations that were damaged and destroyed by the tsunami did not kill anyone.

Managing legacies

Question: As the nuclear industry, nuclear testing and indeed tsunamis enter history, they do not only leave a legacy of continuous risk of exposure to toxic waste and radiation but also a legacy of science, technology, human behaviour and governmental intervention, among others, connected to specific places. Are there ways of combining these legacies for the benefit of future audiences?

Van Luik: A good example is the Gnome site, about 40 miles outside of Carlsbad, New Mexico, and 8.7 kilometres away from the WIPP site. In December of 1961, the Gnome site was chosen as an experiment to see if a nuclear detonation in salt would store enough energy to make it a useful source for producing electricity and heat for an extended period of time. The blast was a three kiloton device put 1,216 feet, which is about 370 metres, underground in bedded salt. The experiment did not produce the result that was desired, partly because it unexpectedly vented – radioactive steam rose out of the ground and drifted over the area including over spectators that were nearby to feel the shock and see the earth move up and down with the blast.

The marker at the Gnome site is a historical marker (Figure 12.9). The function is, as the small print says down below, do not dig, do not use this place within certain areal and depth boundaries. Implicit in this warning is that there may be residual radioactivity underground. The marker is part of the way that the US Department of Energy's Office of Legacy Management office administers all of the US' radioactively contaminated, but no longer used, sites. They are in charge of all the used nuclear sites including mine tailing sites, formally utilised waste management sites, formally utilised nuclear production sites – all of those sites, once they're cleared and cleaned to the degree agreed to between the DOE and the host states. Basically, passive sites like this are not given much attention because they're not exactly tourist attractions.

The marker has been shot at by people checking their ammunition to see what kind of damage it does to concrete and bronze. And so there are several pits. There used to be something glued on top of the marker; I have no idea what it was, we can see the residual glue. It's probably received enough gunshots to knock it off its pedestal. All this is caused by people having fun with their guns in the desert. I don't think this is malevolent; I

FIGURE 12.9   The Gnome site historical marker near Carlsbad, New Mexico, USA. Top: Abraham Van Luik at the Gnome site. Photograph: Cornelius Holtorf, 2014. Bottom: prohibition message at the bottom of the marker: "No excavation and/or drilling is permitted…". Photograph: Cornelius Holtorf, 2014.

think this is just carelessness and stupidity on the part of people that carry guns into the desert.

I think the idea of the DOE Office of Legacy Management caretakers is that if a marker becomes unreadable or defaced they will replace it because their charge from the federal government is to manage these sites in perpetuity, which is a very strange language to use when you realise that government entities tend not to survive in perpetuity.

However, we know that that's not really going to happen, and so in our regulations that we have for WIPP for example, we are supposed to maintain markers as long as practicable and at the same time, the risk after that

time from human intrusion for oil and gas drilling mainly is to be accepta-
bly low and meet the expectations of the Environmental Protection Agency
for up to 10,000 years. They will only give us credit for a hundred years of
making sure that there's no drilling on the site. So the regulation that we
work under for a repository is different from the regulations that govern
these Legacy Management sites, where basically they're looking at taking
credit for having a presence on-site or a monitoring function in perpetuity.

We, at WIPP, are looking at managing this site for probably, at least several hundred years after closure. The long-term perspective is that things
are just left alone. And the Office of Legacy Management is working in the
medium term. When they say, "in perpetuity", it basically means "as long
as your institutions, your government institutions are alive and well and
managing". This is not to belittle their effort, in fact, the key to longer-
term oversight is local importance and involvement, something that the
Office of Legacy Management is well aware of and implements successfully
through the creation of local partnerships.

The Office of Legacy Management works very closely with their host
states, New Mexico, in this instance, and with their host counties. This
restricted-use land area named on the marker is on the registry in the
county and the state, so anyone that wants to use this land has to go to the
registry to get permission to use this land, and then they will be told of
these restrictions. So there are different safeguard levels, even though there
is no one present at the site at any given time.

The future

Question: How do you see the future of managing our radioactive heritage?

Nelson/Van Luik: We believe that the age of deep geologic repositories for long-
lived radioactive waste has arrived. As more countries strive to meet their
sustainable energy needs, nuclear power generation and their inevitable
radioactive waste stockpiles will continue to grow. Deep geologic repositories will eventually be developed around the globe. International standards
for radioactive waste disposal have been developed, and many countries
are developing repository programmes consistent with these standards. An
international consensus on the need and standards for informing future
generations of their presence and their portent is a worthy goal to pursue.

Buser: No one really knows where the journey goes. At the moment, the concept
of deep geological storage with the option of retrievability of radioactive
waste seems to have been established in the industrialised world as the best
solution. Elsewhere – for example on former military test grounds or in the
uranium mining areas in the "Global South" – a certain degree of radioactive contamination is accepted in daily life. Money for comprehensive pro-
tective measures or clean-up actions is missing. There is a lack of discussion
on the environmental consequences of human action, as can be seen in the

case of the dumping of chemo-toxic waste in old mines. In these waste-producing societies, what happens afterwards, and what it could mean for future generations, is not considered. Over decades, poisonous and radio-active wastewaters have been discharged into the ground or injected deep underground through old boreholes. The problem of marking old disposal sites of toxic waste will, therefore, have to be addressed in the future. From this perspective, I use the metaphor of the "pigsty earth" to indicate how widespread and how deep the pollution of the environment is through human technology.

The question of keeping records and characterising and marking dangerous sites does not arise solely for nuclear technology, and it does not arise solely for rich industrialised countries. It is likely to have a universal significance the more people and societies become aware of the dangerous side effects associated with the production of hazardous substances. Therefore, an open-minded engagement and an open discussion of such problems are of great importance; a long-term dialogue is needed, which must also involve the local populations. For whatever the value of waste may be as heritage of the future, human safety must come first.

Acknowledgements

Marcos Buser would like to acknowledge support by Riemer Knoop, Reinwardt Academy, Amsterdam, Netherlands. We would all like to thank Anders Högberg for comments about a penultimate version of this chapter.

References

Anders, G., 1987. *Die Antiquiertheit des Menschen. Über die Seele im Zeitalter der zweiten industriellen Revolution.* München: Beck'sche Reihe.

Anders, G., 1972. *Die atomare Drohung. Radikale Überlegungen zum atomaren Zeitalter.* München: Beck'sche Reihe.

Blonsky, M., 1990. Wes Geistes Kind ist die Atomsemiotik. In: R. Posner, ed. *Warnungen an die ferne Zukunft. Atommüll als Kommunikationsproblem.* München: Raben-Verlag.

Buser, M., 2010. *Literaturstudie zum Stand der Markierung von geologischen Tiefenlagern.* Bern: Bundesamt für Energie, May 2010.

Buser, M., 2015. *Rubbish Theory: The Heritage of Toxic Waste.* Reinwardt Memorial Lecture, 18 March 2015. Amsterdam: Reinwardt Academy, Amsterdam University of the Arts.

Buser, M., Lambert, A. and Wildi, W., 2020. Deep Geological and Chemical Waste Disposal: Where We Stand and Where We Go. *atw – International Journal for Nuclear Power* 65 (6/7), 311–316.

Cohn, N., 1961. *The Pursuit of the Millenium, Revolutionary Millenarians and Mystical Anarchists of the Middle Ages.* Oxford: Oxford University Press.

DOE, 2014a. Accident Investigation Report, Underground Salt Haul Truck Fire at the Waste Isolation Pilot Plant on February 5, 2014, Department of Energy (DOE), Office of Environmental Management, March 2014.

DOE, 2014b. Accident Investigation Report, Phase 1, Radiological Release Event at the Waste Isolation Pilot Plant on February 14, 2014, Department of Energy (DOE), Office of Environmental Management, April 2014.

DOE, 2015. Accident Investigation Report, Phase 2, Radiological Release Event at the Waste Isolation Pilot Plant on February 14, 2014, Department of Energy (DOE), Office of Environmental Management, April 2015.

Douglas, M., 1966. *Purity and Danger.* London: Routledge.

EKRA, 2000. *Disposal Concepts for Radioactive Waste.* Bern: Federal Department for the Environment, Transport, Energy and Communication, 31 January 2000.

Fassler, M., 1991. *Abfall – Moderne – Gegenwart. Beiträge zum evolutionären Eigenrecht von Gegenwart.* Gießen: Focus.

Grewe, K., 2010. *Meisterwerke antiker Technik.* Mainz am Rhein: Verlag Philipp von Zabern.

Hauser, S., 1990. Bisherige Erfahrungen mit der Kommunikation über radioaktiven Abfall. In: R. Posner, ed. *Warnungen an die ferne Zukunft. Atommüll als Kommunikationsproblem.* München: Raben-Verlag; pp. 195–258.

Hauser, S., 2001. *Metamorphosen des Abfalls.* Frankfurt am Main: Campus Verlag.

Kapp, K.W., 2000. Social Costs of Business (Private) Enterprise 1963, Spokesman. http://www.kwilliam-kapp.de/documents/SCOBE_000.pdf

Klaus, D.M., 2019. What really went wrong at WIPP: An insider's view of two accidents at the only US underground nuclear waste repository. *Bulletin of the Atomic Scientists,* 75, 197–204.

Minois, G., 1996. *Histoire de l'avenir des Prophètes à la prospective.* Paris: Fayard.

OECD-NEA, 2014a. Foundations and Guiding Principles for the Preservation of Records, Knowledge and Memory across Generations: A Focus on the Post-Closure Phase of Geological Repositories. A Collective Statement of the NEA Radioactive Waste Management Committee. Paris: OECD-NEA. https://www.oecd-nea.org/rwm/rkm/documents/flyer-A4-rkm-collective-statement-en-2014.pdf

OECD-NEA, 2014b. *Preservation of Records, Knowledge and Memory across Generations (RKandM) ---Markers - Reflections on Intergenerational Warnings in the Form of Japanese Tsunami Stones,* NEA/RWM/R(2014)4. Paris: OECD-NEA. https://www.oecd-nea.org/rwm/docs/2014/rwm-r2014-4.pdf

OECD Nuclear Energy Agency (NEA), 2013. *Preservation of Records, Knowledge and Memory Across Generations (RKandM), A Literature Survey on Markers and Memory Preservation for Deep Geological Repositories.* NEA/RWM/R(2013)5. Paris: OECD-NEA. https://www.oecd-nea.org/rwm/docs/2013/rwm-r2013-5.pdf

Pastina, B., 2004. Implementing Long-Term Stewardship: A National Challenge. Pdf Paper for the Board on Radioactive Management, the National Academies, 16 March 2004. www.cistems.fsu.edu/PDF/pastina.pdf

Pescatore, C. and Mays, C., 2008. Geological Disposal of Radioactive Wastes: Records, Markers, and People. An Integration Challenge to Be Met over Millennia. [Nuclear Energy Agency], *NEA News* 26, 26–30. www.oecd-nea.org/pub/newsletter/2008/Geological%20Disposal.pdf

Poeschke, J., 1996. *Antike Spolien in der Architektur Des Mittelalters und der Renaissance.* München: Hirmer-Verlag.

Posner, R., 1990. *Warnungen an die ferne Zukunft. Atommüll als Kommunikationsproblem.* München: Raben-Verlag.

Rathje, W. and Murphy, C., 2001. *Rubbish. The Archaeology of Garbage.* Tucson: University of Arizona Press.

Rebrik, B., 1987. *Geologie und Bergbau in der Antike.* Leipzig: VEB.

Schröder, J., 2019. *Preservation of Records, Knowledge and Memory (RK&M) Across Generations: Final Report of the RK&M Initiative.* Paris: OECD, Nuclear Energy Agency.

Sebeok, T., 1990. Die Büchse der Pandora und ihre Sicherung: Ein Relaissystem in der Obhut einer Atompriesterschaft. In: R. Posner, ed. *Warnungen an die ferne Zukunft. Atommüll als Kommunikationsproblem.* München: Raben-Verlag.

Sprenger, F., 2007. *Atommüllager: Medien, Zeit und Raum eines Kommunikationsproblems.* Unpublished master's thesis, Fakultät für Philologie, Ruhr-Universität Bochum, Germany.

Sunstein, C.R., 2001. Cost-Benefit Default Principles. *Chicago Working Paper Series Index.* http://chicagounbound.uchicago.edu/cgi/viewcontent.cgi?article=1141&context=law:and_economics

Thomson, M., 1979. *Rubbish Theory: The Creation and Destruction of Value.* Oxford: Oxford University Press.

Thüry, G.E., 2001. *Müll und Marmorsäulen. Siedlungshygiene in der römischen Antike.* Mainz am Rhein: Verlag Philipp von Zabern.

Tonn, B., 2001. Institutional Design for Long-Term Stewardship of Nuclear and Hazardous Waste Sites. *Technological Forecasting and Social Change* 68(3), 255–273.

Trauth, K.M., Hora, S.C. and Guzowski, R., 1993. Expert Judgement on Markers to Deter Inadvertent Human Intrusion into the Waste Isolation Pilot Plant. SAND92-1382. Albuquerque, New Mexico: Sandia National Laboratories. http://prod.sandia.gov/techlib/access-control.cgi/1992/921382.pdf

Voigt, V., 1990. Konzentrisch angeordnete Warntafeln in zunehmend neueren Sprachformen. In: R. Posner, ed. *Warnungen an die ferne Zukunft. Atommüll als Kommunikationsproblem.* München: Raben-Verlag.

Wagner, A., (ed.)., 2008. *Abfallmoderne, zu den Schmutzrändern der Kultur.* Berlin: Lit-Verlag.

Weinberg, A., 1972. Social Institutions and Nuclear Energy. *Science* 177(7), 27–34.

Weinberg, A., 1994. *The First Nuclear Era. The Life and Times of a Technological Fixer.* Woodbury NY: American Institute of Physics Press.

Weinberg, A., 1999. Scientific Millenniarism. *Proceedings of the American Philosophical Society* 143, 531–539.

WNWR, 2019. *The World Nuclear Waste Report, Focus Europe.* Berlin: Heinrich Böll Foundation and Partners.

Wollentz, G., May, S., Holtorf, C. and Högberg, A., 2020. Toxic heritage: Uncertain and unsafe. In: R. Harrison, C. DeSilvey, C. Holtorf, S. Macdonald, N. Bartolini, E. Breithoff, H. Fredheim, A. Lyons, S. May, J. Morgan and S. Penrose, *Heritage Futures. Comparative Approaches to Natural and Cultural Heritage Practices.* London: UCL Press; pp. 294–312.

13

SUSTAINABILITY, INTERGENERATIONAL EQUITY, AND PLURALISM

Can heritage conservation create alternative futures?

Erica Avrami

A primary aim of the heritage enterprise is to identify and manage those places that have the highest potential for incurring social and environmental benefits in the future, by protecting tangible heritage resources (products) and engaging communities in dialogues (processes) about how and why those places matter. While the heritage field has evolved to include much more robust practices of participatory decision-making in post-colonial and increasingly pluralistic socie-ties, current heritage policies prioritize the longevity of the resources over the continuity of engagement. The fundamental bequest is still the heritage product.

Through listing and designation, the heritage field creates a growing stock of protected resources, thereby privileging the physical past over future constructs in the interest of intergenerational equity. In an era when the sustainability of the planet and its inhabitants compels significant changes in the way we create and manage the built environment, the ongoing accumulation of heritage resources, particularly in growing urban areas, can limit options, create burdens, and effec-tively destroy alternative futures.

If, in fact, the field acknowledges that heritage conservation fundamentally seeks to preserve the values that people ascribe to places and spatialize within par-ticular built forms – and that values are constantly changing over time – one might argue that the more important bequest is heritage as a process. That is to say, how do we afford future generations the potential to engage and re-engage over time in decision-making about what places matter and why? In light of the need to ensure a more sustainable built environment, how can heritage conservation empower future generations to be agents of change rather than stewards of the past?

Places and stories

An inherent aim of heritage conservation is to provide a canvas for storytelling and narratives about the past in the built environment. By reifying the concept of heritage in structures, sites, and landscapes, the conservation field has promulgated the notion that the societal benefits of its efforts are embodied in the conserved place – or material *product*. Therefore the listing, and thus long-term protection, of historic places has emerged as paramount in professional heritage practice and institutional missions, so as to ensure the physical survival of historic fabric.

Such listing or designation of heritage has generally been viewed as an act of stewardship. Vestiges of former times are considered a bequest from past generations to present ones, who take on (and pass on) the responsibility of ensuring their survival into the future. Through expert opinion and community interaction, a given resource is identified as having some significance and placed under regulatory protection so as to ensure against demolition or alteration. Theories and traditions of connoisseurship underpin a curatorial approach to such inventory and management of cultural resources (Stanley-Price, Talley, and Melucco Vaccaro, 1996). In keeping with the modernist paradigm of designing and controlling the environment to engender social order, the heritage field has effectively branded its expertise as curatorial managers of the built world (Fitch, 1998). More recent scholarship has recognized that designation is not a neutral process of discerning some sort of intrinsic, historic, or aesthetic value. Rather it is a creative process of valorizing a given resource or element within the built environment for the purpose of perpetuating particular ideas or narratives about a place.

"Place" itself, however, is a concept that transcends the purely physical and extends beyond the realm of heritage. Evolving theoretical discourse in the urban planning field has explored the concept of place and its relationship to people (Hayden, 1995; Tuan, 1977; Lynch, 1972). Key aspects of this discourse derive from the work of Habermas (1984) and other social theorists who challenged the rationalist tradition and elucidated the function of deliberation and the free exchange of ideas in social action. Developments regarding the duality of structure and human agency (Giddens, 1984; Sewell, 2005) and the modern/postmodern transformation (Harvey, 1989) likewise informed understanding of the political relationships and elements that can empower or constrain social change. Further scholarship on the social construction of knowledge (Minnich, 1990), power relationships and the role of experts (Friedmann, 1987), and the potential for communicative action (Forester, 1989; 1999) have served to transform planning and management of the built environment into a more socially- and contextually-responsive endeavour.

Arguing how the manipulation of the built environment can perpetuate dominant culture, foster exclusion, and create bias toward the "architectural legacy of wealth and power," Hayden (1995, p. 8) suggests that "place" has the potential to support greater diversity, inclusion, and cultural citizenship through participatory processes of place-making and memory preservation. Sandercock (2003) similarly uses memory and storytelling as both a metaphor for understanding the past and an operative tool for the potential management of "place," as a way of connecting communities to the larger urban narrative. Sandercock contends that efforts to preserve memory, and to collectively shape both the past and future, can empower a multicultural citizenry to "connect through engaging in activities together" (2003, p. 144), thereby enabling an always "contested engagement with and continually redefined notion of the common good and the shared destiny of the citizens of the city" (2003, p. 151). Thus, through the concept of "place," the city fabric becomes both pallet and canvas for layered memories and storytelling by multiple publics.

If, as Sandercock suggests, "memory locates us" (2003, p. 221), the tools by which communities interpret and transmit the past become increasingly significant. What to conserve and how to conserve, for whom and by whom, raises new issues with regard to pluralism, inclusion, and social equity. At its core, it suggests that the heritage enterprise may engender benefits that have less to do with places or heritage products themselves (fabric) and more to do with the way in which heritage enables participatory dialogue.

This growing awareness of conservation decision-making processes as vital civic engagement has helped to elucidate the role of values in the heritage enterprise. Values about what to preserve and how to preserve are derived from the stories that people ascribe to buildings, sites, and landscapes, and are constructed among individual, institutional, and community actors. Values may change over time or as a result of contextual dynamics. Thus, the multiplicity and temporality of values or "cultural significance" in the conservation process have become increasingly salient topics within the literature (Lipe, 1984; Tainter and Lucas, 1983; Tomlan, 1998; Avrami, Mason, and de la Torre, 2000).

Within heritage practice, this has promoted broader non-expert participation, challenged "top-down" expert-driven models, encouraged the recognition of social difference, improved understanding of the different ways in which knowledge is created and transmitted, and given voice to historically underrepresented stakeholders (Lee, 2003, 2004; Kaufman, 2009; Dubrow, 2003). Research dealing with cultural landscapes – which fundamentally incurs close connections between place, nature, communities, and local development – has also helped to advance thinking (Sabaté and Warren, 2015), as has scholarship from the field of anthropology, which has examined the relationship of heritage and human rights (Hodder, 2010; Meskell, 2010; Silverman and Ruggles, 2007).

Heritage policy has begun to incorporate values-based approaches, such as Australia's Burra Charter (Australian ICOMOS, 2004), as well as rights-based approaches, such as the European Union's Faro Convention (2005). However, most legislative frameworks and policy infrastructure, which have largely been based on earlier theoretical paradigms, make change challenging. The place-bound nature of the conservation field – and its preoccupation with identifying ever more historic places through processes of listing – still reinforce a practical adherence to fabric (products) as the critical element of the heritage enterprise:

> It is commonly accepted now that the values attributed to a heritage place are not an immutable constant, but rather that they evolve in respect to

both time and space … Given the constantly shifting nature of values, how can we consider statements of values or even of a Statement of Outstanding Universal Value in the context of the World Heritage Convention as more than a snapshot taken at a given moment? The truth is that values can be neither protected nor preserved. In the context of heritage, values are a vaguely shared set of intangible concepts that simply emerge from and exist in the ether of the communal public consciousness … If we analyze what has guided the conservation endeavor, it becomes clear that heritage professionals have never really protected or preserved values; the task has always been protecting and preserving the material vessels where values have been determined to reside.

(Araoz, 2011, pp. 58–59)

So while stakeholder values and community engagement have become part of the general rhetoric of conservation practice, how cultural difference, multiple knowledges, and deliberative dialogue translate to a new set of processes for heritage policy remains largely uncharted territory.

Sustainability and the accumulation of heritage

This challenge of balancing products and processes – of creating heritage places and engaging memory through place – is compounded by broader social and environmental concerns regarding sustainability. While the concept of *place* may simply be a trope for how people physically, intellectually, and emotionally interact with and within the spaces they create and occupy, *space* is both real and limited. Earth is a finite system, and growth of the built environment – increasing human occupation of space on the planet – is taxing that system. UN-Habitat estimates that, globally, urban areas consume between 60 and 80 per cent of energy and emit between as much as 70 per cent of greenhouse gases (UN-Habitat 2011). The built environment plays a significant role; in the US, for example, the building sector consumes 40 per cent of all energy. On average, land consumption in urban areas around the world is expanding at two times the rate of their populations (Seto, Güneralpa, and Hutyrac, 2012). If current urban construction and land-use trends in the US continue, it is estimated that by 2030, more than 27 per cent of the buildings that exist today will be replaced and 50 per cent more will be constructed (Urban Land Institute, 2005). Given these conditions, the built environment plays a critical role in overall sustainability.

While the concept of sustainability is complex, multidimensional, and the subject of wide debate, its common definition is attributed to the 1987 Brundtland Commission Report, *Our Common Future*, which described sustainable development as meeting "the needs of the present without compromising the ability of future generations to meet their own needs" (World Commission on the Environment and Development (WCED), 1987, p. 43), thus codifying its emphasis on intergenerational equity.

To facilitate understanding of its scope, sustainability has been reduced to what is familiarly known as the three pillars: *economy*, *society*, and the *environment*. Various models (Figure 13.1) have been used to visually represent the three pillars (Moir and Carter, 2012), and over time their interrelationship has been more fully recognized through what is referred to as a nested dependency – or "bull's eye" – model. Rather than simply characterizing these three spheres as interconnected, there is a shift in thinking from an anthropocentrically-focused environmental paradigm to an ecological paradigm that places humankind within a more complex system of bio-dynamics. In short, economy exists in service to society and both are constrained by the environment because the planet is a closed or finite system – neither the economy nor society can exist without it (Giddings, Hopwood, and O'Brien, 2002).

Recent advocacy and research efforts explore the concept of culture as a fourth pillar of sustainability (Dessein et al., 2015; Soini and Birkeland, 2014; Hawkes, 2001), and much of this discourse derives from the notion of culture as a basic human right. But "culture" is a socially constructed concept with myriad historical definitions, such that it has been invoked as "something which both differentiates the world and provides a concept for understanding that differentiation" (Mitchell, 1995, p. 103). At once a system of interrelation, an explanatory concept of distinction, and an attribute of bounded social entities, the malleable concept of culture is used "to turn differences into something orderly, mappable and controllable" (Mitchell, 1995, p. 107), thereby precluding a more robust examination of how the concept of culture is a vehicle for power and dominance. Culture may be viewed as the driver of many forms of oppression and violence, from slavery to genital mutilation. So are only some aspects of culture considered a right while others are not? That is not to suggest that culture is *not* an integral aspect of sustainability, rather one might view culture as cross-cutting or transversal, influencing – and integrally linked to – all of the dimensions of sustainability: environmental, social, and economic.

A great deal of the dialogue about the fourth pillar derives from a community of heritage-oriented professionals and scholars seeking to protect places and practices from loss. This differentiation of a fourth pillar in many respects mirrors the way in which the heritage profession seeks to differentiate certain structures, sites, and landscapes from the rest of the built environment. By valorizing and listing places of significance, they are intended to be protected from the political and market forces of destruction, thereby endowing them with a certain right to survival over other elements of the built environment.

This differentiation of heritage from the built environment can be problematic, in the same way that the evolution of the built environment, distinct from our understanding of ecological systems and interrelationships, has contributed to contemporary sustainability challenges. Recognizing the planet as a closed or finite system, the built environment essentially functions as a sub-system. Applying, albeit superficially, a systems-thinking lens (Meadows, 2008), buildings and sites may be viewed as physical *stock*. Society and nature create flux

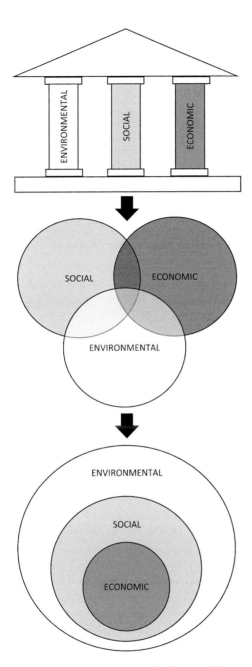

FIGURE 13.1   Evolving model of sustainability. Diagram by author.

within the built environment, meaning that new structures are built and others demolished, and forms, patterns, and uses change. Population growth and variations in the way people occupy space (i.e., increased per capita land use) can cause the stock to increase, as can market conditions that encourage real estate speculation and development as a profit-generating enterprise. Land-use regulations, building and demolition codes, zoning, and other such planning devices help to control stocks within a given range of values, that is to say, they serve as tools for managing the built environment. As indicated previously, trends in the growth of the built environment compel increased management, so as not to over-consume the planet's resources.

An essential function of contemporary heritage conservation is to save particular places as permanent stock. The process of listing or designating sites creates the cadre of historic structures, sites, and landscapes that constitute built heritage. By helping to determine which places should not be demolished or significantly altered because of the meanings and values ascribed to them by society, it effectively red flags or prohibits, depending on the regulatory framework, the outflow of particular places from the built environment stock. In this sense, conservation may be viewed as a means of minimizing (embodied) energy consumption and material flows, or of maintaining the values of past capital investment in the built environment. The heritage community may view this as a positive form of control, in that it prevents the loss of irreplaceable stock and helps to stabilize the built environment, and thus communities. However, some regard conservation, like many land-use regulations, as a negative influence that can simply push new construction (increased stock) elsewhere, sometimes contributing to sprawl and social exclusion (Talen, 2012). Within a framework of spatial economics, heritage protection might also be characterized as a response or a contributor to over-accumulation – a social reinvestment in physical capital that complicates the cycles of creative destruction (Harvey, 2001).

Conservation, particularly through the process of listing, effectively creates an endless inflow of constantly increasing heritage stock, which does not correlate to an equivalent decrease in new construction. Nor is the ever-accumulating stock of heritage itself capped. The US National Register of Historic Places includes over 1.4 million resources; the World Heritage List is over 1,000 and growing. Not all forms of designation provide explicit legal protection against demolition, but both destruction (intentional and unintentional) and delisting are comparatively rare once a property has been designated as heritage through regulatory channels. So while there is a need to check the growth of stocks writ large within the built environment, the growth of heritage stocks remains unchecked.

By continually adding to the stock of built heritage resources, conservation sees itself as saving resources for future generations. However, the constant accumulation of built heritage, particularly in urban contexts, creates burdens and inflexibility for future generations. In terms of the social cost, cultural economist Benhamou (1996) argues that productivity gains in the conservation sector do not keep pace with the permanent expansion of listed heritage, thereby necessitating increased government subsidies, more private sector support, and/or delisting to stabilize the system. In terms of environmental cost, as part and parcel of the larger built environment, heritage cannot be viewed as a neutral player in the aforementioned consumption of land, energy, and resources. While the heritage community makes claims about the environmental sustainability of conservation, research and policy to date do not conclusively substantiate that position (Avrami, 2016).

Much like the concept of biodiversity and the protection of endangered species, the accumulation of heritage is often viewed as a means of maintaining diversity within the stock of the built environment and thereby ensuring intergenerational equity – preventing loss so as to ensure the right of future populations to experience a variety of places. This argument derives from the idea that heritage is a nonrenewable resource (Holtorf, 2001; Throsby, 2002). Nonrenewable, a term co-opted from the field of environmental conservation, suggests that the resource cannot be replenished or recovered at a rate that exceeds consumption or destruction. But by continually valorizing places through designation, society creates more and more heritage, as evidenced by growing lists. Heritage as a process is renewable. As more time passes and definitions of heritage widen, there is more history; there are potentially more stories to tell through the built environment. The conservation field, with its emphasis on the fabric or vessels through which those stories are told or values represented, perpetuates an unbridled physical accumulation – endless stories, endless places.

However, one can question whether a boundless quantity of heritage products ensures diversity when it comes to the values, narratives, and stakeholders that are involved in heritage processes. Nearly half of the sites on the World Heritage List are in Europe. Of the more than 2,500 National Historic Landmarks in the United States, 24 per cent are concentrated in three states: New York, Massachusetts, and Pennsylvania (Figure 13.2). More than one-quarter of the property lots in Manhattan are under some form of landmark regulation (Figure 13.3). The other four boroughs of New York City have far fewer landmarks, ranging from 0.3 per cent of their property lots, in the case of Staten Island, to 4.5 per cent in Brooklyn (Gould, McCabe, and Stern, 2016). If an unlimited quantity is intended to facilitate inclusion and thus ensure diversity, the distributional characteristics of lists do not bear out this aim. And by failing to check this growth, future generations inherit our biases and the burden of sustaining them.

That is not to say that the process of listing heritage is inherently flawed or bad for society. Rather, *unchecked* listing is problematic in the long-term, because it limits flexibility within and potentially contributes to growth of the built environment writ large. The system of the built environment cannot grow endlessly because the planet cannot support it. Sustainability concerns will more and more control the overall growth of the built environment, impelling many buildings to be replaced or renovated to accommodate higher density and spurring infill development in urban areas. If heritage conservation has virtually no outflow, meaning

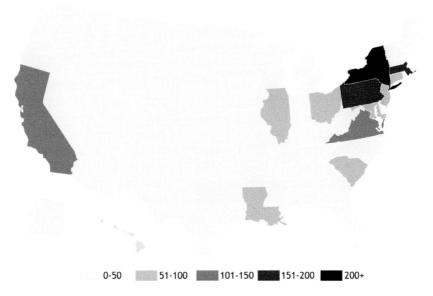

United States of America
National Historic Landmarks per State

0-50   51-100   101-150   151-200   200+

FIGURE 13.2   Geographic distribution by State of US National Historic Landmarks (NHLs). Nearly one quarter of all NHLs are concentrated in three northeastern states, raising questions about the effectiveness of such designations in representing a diversity of publics and narratives. Data source: US National Park Service Database of National Historic Landmarks (accessed August 31, 2016).

it just keeps expanding its stock, this stock escalation will only create conflict with the larger built environment system and sustainability interests in the future. Much like the nested, bullseye model of sustainability, the long-term viability of conservation hinges on aligning its goals toward those of the larger built environment, rather than trying to differentiate heritage from it (Figure 13.4).

In short: we cannot keep collecting old buildings. The system has to change.

Changing the system

At least three factors are driving the need for change within the heritage enterprise:

- the environmental imperative to adapt the built environment and to mitigate climate change through the reduction of land, energy, and resource consumption, while also accommodating growing populations in urban areas;

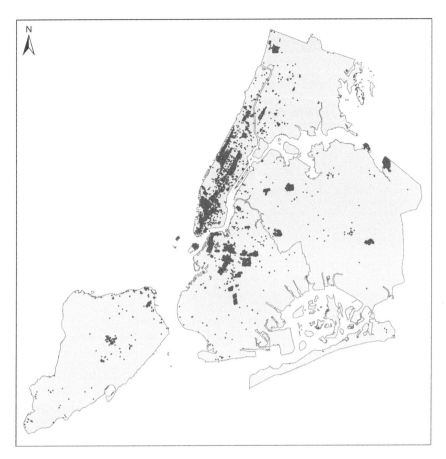

FIGURE 13.3 Geographic distribution of New York City Landmarks and Historic Districts. Data source: NYC Landmarks Preservation Commission. Diagram created by Jennifer Most (GIS research associate to the author).

- a paradigm cum infrastructure of heritage policy that emphasizes fabric and orients management toward physical conservation;
- the need for robust participation of multiple publics over time in heritage deliberation and decision-making.

Environmental imperative

Sustainability concerns compel changes in the way we design, construct, and manage the built environment. Cities, in particular, face acute challenges. In addition to the egregious energy and land consumption outlined above, the world's urban population has grown from 746 million in 1950 to 3.9 billion in 2014 and is expected to increase by another 2.5 billion by 2050 (UN, 2014).

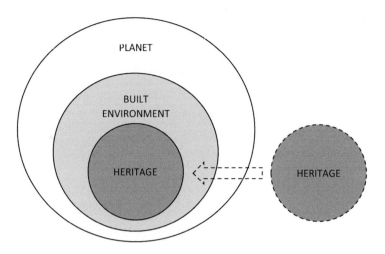

FIGURE 13.4 Bullseye model of heritage. Diagram by author.

This growth of cities will put increasing pressure on urban built environments to accommodate more inhabitants. Accommodating more people without consuming more land and resources will impact the capacity to accumulate and sustain physical heritage places.

This tension will be exacerbated by the need to adapt the built environment of cities to be more resilient. For example, at the land-use level, recent projections now model a sea-level rise of nearly two metres by 2100 if current greenhouse gas (GHG) emissions are not cut (DeConto and Pollard, 2016). This will potentially force significant geographic shifts in low-lying cities around the globe in the coming century, requiring major transformations in infrastructure and buildings. How will heritage professionals anticipate and contribute positively toward these large-scale spatial relocations? Is it the role of the field simply to protect the heritage products it has designated or should it strive to translate and apply heritage processes so as to inform adaptation and resilience? The former suggests that the heritage field pursue its current avenues of advocacy to protect significant places from the effects of climate change. The latter suggests a transformation in the way in which heritage professionals study, analyze, and evolve sites and structures, by placing increased emphasis on the way in which people engage with and use spaces, and less on the original fabric of particular places. This position fundamentally asserts that heritage has an affirmative obligation to prevent and mitigate climate change and to help make communities more resilient in the face of inevitable change. Loss of physical heritage will likely be unavoidable, but the preservation of the values ascribed to it will not. Will the heritage field adapt its policies and practices now to anticipate these challenges, or will it take a sandbag approach and try to hold its ground while the waters rise?

At the building and material level, design for disassembly (DfD) trends within the sustainable design and construction sector likewise raise profound questions about the long-term stewardship of historic places. There is growing regulation regarding the recyclability and reuse of building materials, and an increased need for flexibility in construction to enable nimble approaches to change in and resilience of the built environment. Per data from the 2007 US Census American Community Survey, the average American will move more than 11 times in their lifetime (US Census 2007). Factories and businesses likewise must adapt and often relocate in the face of technological advances and environmental challenges. Rapid change and increased mobility, combined with the need to reduce energy, resource, and land consumption, suggest that the significant places of the future will have been engineered for deconstruction and the recovery of materials and components. How will the conservation of built heritage (fabric) function when structures are more and more designed and constructed to be impermanent?

Fabric-oriented heritage policies

As noted previously, the emphasis on preserving the physical fabric of places through time has pervaded heritage policy, despite advances in knowledge regarding the social construction of heritage and its associated values. These policies inherently privilege the "authentic" material past over other ways of codifying collective memory. Leo (2016, p. 108) notes that the contemporary heritage enterprise works largely within what Ogilvy (2002) characterizes as an "Enlightenment paradigm of strategic planning, where the field's decision-makers start with a preferred outcome … and plan toward that end." While the heritage field has made stronger claims to managing rather than preventing change in recent years (Araoz, 2008), its focus on a strategic aim of conserving the heritage product stifles open-ended decision-making and the exploration of alternative heritage futures.

In exploring Ingold's (2010) theories regarding loss aversion, Holtorf (2015) asserts that physical loss does not necessarily curtail the functioning of cultural heritage. If we accept that the societal benefits of heritage conservation can emerge through creative processes of engagement and not simply through fabric, managing heritage – or more specifically managing change through heritage – poses a much broader range of future scenarios. Leo (2016) contends that the use of scenario planning has the potential to more effectively incorporate multi-stakeholder values in heritage decision-making without *a priori* defining outcomes, thereby exploring a range of ways in which values and their associated narratives might be spatialized within the built environment beyond the retention of original fabric. As futurist Schwartz notes:

> Scenarios are only stories after all. They are not ideologies or matters of faith. They are simply ways of exploring possibilities. Scenarios provide

a way of having a more imaginative and coherent conversation about the future. And since there are more than one plausible scenario, scenario planning enables a conversation that does not end with one side winning and the other losing. Indeed the differences among us are among the most important tools for creating a diversity of possible futures, giving real meaning to human freedom.

(Schwartz, 2002, as cited in Leo, 2016, p. 100)

As Giaoutzi and Bartolomeo (2013, p. 4) note, the value of futures research is in "opening minds to consider new possibilities," thereby changing the policy agenda through better decision-making processes that compel us to anticipate change. But, as Holtorf and Högberg (2014) pose, can such a shift in both thinking and practice be achieved in the realm of heritage conservation?

Participation, deliberation, and listing

Coupled with urban population growth is an increase in urban diversity in many parts of the world. In North America, more than 40 per cent of the population of some of its largest cities – namely Vancouver, Toronto, and Los Angeles – are foreign-born. Six out of ten New Yorkers are now immigrants or children of immigrants. If, as Sandercock (2003) suggests, we are to "wrest new possibilities from space" (p. 10), how will the interests of these increasingly plural publics be included in decision-making about the urban built environment? How do we recognize and incorporate difference and different ways of knowing in place-making and heritage creation? And how are conflicting values and memories reconciled?

Stories are made up of multiple layered stories, memories of multiple layered memories. In cities with a multiplicity of people and difference, this is ever more poignant. As Glassberg (2001, pp. 116–117) argues, collective memories ascribed to places "emerge out of dialogue and social interaction," but are likewise the consequence of "conflicts with political implications over the meanings attached to places." A shared destiny does not compel a shared past, nor a shared vision for the future. Racial, ethnic and cultural groups that do not adhere to prevailing cultural heritage theories (which are based largely on Western European experience) are at a clear disadvantage in the participatory process. From a Marxist perspective, the listing or designation of certain elements of the built environment as "heritage" can easily be viewed as a tool of cultural hegemony, with certain values being ascribed to places through the structures and institutions of an expert cum elite class that seeks to promulgate particular narratives. Aspects of conservation history and practice, indeed, do not effectively contradict such views, be it the dominance of theories emerging from Western Europe in the professional discourse or the disproportionate number of Western European sites on the World Heritage List, for example. The fundamental policy of listing is rife with tensions between pluralistic and "universal" values. The generalization resulting from the listing of heritage at global, national, and municipal levels has helped to inspire collective agency and promote ideas of common values and shared stewardship. At the same time, in creating universal narratives, conservation steps away from the messy, multiplicity of stories and stakeholders at the heart of the heritage-creating process.

The unchecked capacity to continually add more and more heritage to the rosters is not effectively engaging an increasingly plural society, nor contributing robustly to a sustainable built environment, nor ensuring intergenerational equity. Delisting, hierarchical listing, and attempts at capping lists do not provide sufficient controls to keep expansion manageable. Nor do existing listing approaches, for the most part, incorporate criteria or processes that fully examine the social, economic, and environmental consequences of protection. As a socially constructed process, heritage and the values ascribed to it are not absolute; they are relative to the context, to time, and space. While no one wants to make conservation a hostage of relativism, there are limited provisions within the system to accommodate changing and conflicting values given the relative permanence of listing and its focus on preserving physical fabric.

An unchecked process of listing will ultimately make heritage an unwieldy and evermore contentious enterprise, jeopardizing not only the sustainability of the broader built environment but also conservation's own survival. Revisiting actual listings or the listing process, in general, would provide an important opportunity for checks and balances within the system, whether through simply slowing listing rates, making listing more stringent or hierarchical, or creating improved information flows and tools for measuring the social, economic, and environmental efficacy of conservation.

Conclusion

A refocus on heritage processes rather than on heritage products can give voice to multiple publics, encourage dialogue, champion local knowledge, empower communities, and anticipate change. The values involved in such processes are often contentious and conflicted, the narratives layered and discordant. Politics and power may dominate in negotiations about heritage, but the conservation process should serve to mediate these relationships in an effort to find a shared vision for the future through a collective past. In doing so, there is what Uffe Jensen (2000, p. 43) refers to as a "deference to an ideal of human flourishing" that transcends the particular and the local. It is precisely this ideal that epitomizes the universality of heritage conservation: through difference and deliberation, we seek shared understanding.

Mason (2009, pp. 247–248) contends that the existing heritage enterprise – forged over a century of scholarship, debates, and professional development – is a tremendous asset. Indeed, it has fostered a public dialogue and social convention around heritage and its protection. It has established strong legal foundations and institutional arrangements to undertake its mission. However, it is precisely the strength of the existing system and its dominant culture that may prevent the possibility of change.

The policies and practices of today's heritage enterprise are formalized and embedded within a weighty infrastructure of institutions and legislation and professionals. These authorities offer educated opinions about what places to preserve and how to preserve them, prescribed through typified building inventories, guidelines, and charters. While many valued sites and structures have been saved from the wrecking ball, one might argue that the creative processes of codifying collective memory in the built environment have been effectively squelched by this infrastructure. How might alternative processes, voices, stories, and outcomes be incorporated into this infrastructure?

Listing, because of its gatekeeper function, is at the crux of many national and local heritage systems in that it often triggers legal protection; in many places, like the United States, it can also trigger design review, incentive eligibility, code waivers, and more. What if listing were provisional? After a probationary period of ten, twenty, or more years, the social, economic, and environmental benefits of both the heritage product and processes might be assessed to inform a decision regarding permanent listing. Such assessment could engage broad publics and multidisciplinary stakeholders – expert and non-expert – by essentially providing a forum for continued storytelling, deliberation, and re-valorization. This would entirely change the set of criteria against which heritage is evaluated and designated, creating an imperative for agency and ensuring that conservation ultimately serves the greater good of the population and the planet. By emphasizing processes of heritage dialogue and their outcomes, it would compel the field to look beyond the simple physical rescue of a place and to contextualize conservation within a broader built environment and societal dynamic over time. It could also encourage creativity and alternative approaches beyond material conservation by affording future generations the opportunity to change narratives, values, and fabric/form.

Or what if listing were temporary or term-based, requiring renewal every quarter-century or more using similar social, economic, and environmental assessments and deliberative discourse? If indeed conservation is premised on notions of intergenerational equity, it seems a fairer course of action would be to allow future generations to decide if they want to continue to steward some heritage resources or not, rather than simply burdening them with a growing stock. This would more fully acknowledge the concept of heritage as a social construction influenced by time, values, and other contextual factors. It would also shift the focus of the heritage enterprise from simply saving places to generating information flows and feedback loops that foster accountability for listing across generations. While these are hypothetical suggestions, they speak to the important need to revisit the values ascribed to a place and to ensure that processes are inclusive and allow for different kinds of knowledge to be brought to bear on heritage.

By revisiting listing, time becomes a much more critical factor, and one that can facilitate more robust participation and storytelling, of and by multiple publics. Just as it may take time for society to appreciate certain styles of architecture or the historical importance of past events, it likewise takes time to fully realize the social potential of a heritage place and society's engagement with it. But it is precisely because of such time lags that revisiting the stories and values ascribed to heritage may be warranted. If indeed those properties designated as landmarks or given similar status are the places with the most significance and potential to tell stories about the past, should not listing provide an iterative process for both promoting and assessing their effectiveness in this regard?

Conservation is not merely an act of stewardship that privileges the past over the present; it is a creative destruction of alternative futures. A successful and sustainable vision for the future hinges on motivating human action through broad public participation and accessible discourse. Heritage conservation has the potential to provide a means to such ends, not simply because of the resources it safeguards, but because of the civic engagement it can engender, now and in the future.

Translating theory to practice and adapting institutional policies and arrangements for more democratized and creative decision-making poses significant challenges. However, they also prompt a call to action with regard to heritage and its role in society. Some of the most challenging issues we face today transcend the local: large-scale environmental sustainability, urban growth and migration, increasingly diverse populations. There is a need to recognize that part of the work of the heritage enterprise should be to inspire *agency*, at many scales, for just purposes – even though we cannot ensure that the outcomes will be just, and right, and good for all. Premised on the principle that we are all equal, we all have an equal responsibility to act, to be agents of change. Harnessing agency means, at times, envisioning a whole that is more than the sum of its parts that amalgamates many knowledges, but at the same time reinforces the link between the particular and the universal, between the local and greater good. The greatest challenge in contemporary heritage conservation is to help create a force for change, to reinforce the undeniable need to act, and to instil a hope that collective agency will indeed make the world a better place.

References

Araoz, G.F., 2008. Heritage Classifications and the Need to Adjust Them to Emerging Paradigms, The United States Experience. In: A. Tomaszewski, ed. *Values and Criteria in Heritage Conservation*. Florence: Edizioni Polistampa; pp. 167–182.

Araoz, G.F., 2011. Preserving Heritage Places under a New Paradigm. *Journal of Cultural Heritage Management and Sustainable Development* 1(1), 55–60.

Australia ICOMOS, Marquis-Kyle, P. and Walker, M., 2004. *The Illustrated Burra Charter.* Sydney, NSW: ICOMOS.

Avrami, E., 2016. Making Historic Preservation Sustainable. *Journal of the American Planning Association* 82(2), 104–112. doi: 10.1080/01944363.2015.1126196.

Avrami, E., Mason, R. and de la Torre, R., 2000. *Values and Heritage Conservation*. Los Angeles, CA: J. Paul Getty Trust.

Benhamou, F., 1996. Is Increased Public Spending for the Preservation of Historic Monuments Inevitable? The French Case. *Journal of Cultural Economics* 20(2), 115–131.

DeConto, R.M. and Pollard, D., 2016. Contribution of Antarctica to Past and Future Sea-Level Rise. *Nature* 531(7596), 591–597. doi: 10.1038/nature17145.

Dessein, J., Soini, K., Fairclough, G. and Horlings, L. (eds.), 2015. *Culture in, for and as Sustainable Development. Conclusions from the COST Action IS1007 Investigating Cultural Sustainability*. Finland: University of Jyväskylä.

Dubrow, G.L., 2003. Blazing Trails with Pink Triangles and Rainbow Flags. In: G.L. Dubrow and J.B. Goodman, eds. *Restoring Women's History through Historic Preservation*. Baltimore, MD: Johns Hopkins University Press; pp. 281–299.

Faro Convention, 2005. Council of Europe Framework Convention on the Value of Cultural Heritage for Society Council of Europe Treaty. Series - 199, Faro 2005 27.X.2005.

Fitch, J.M., 1998. *Historic Preservation: Curatorial Management of the Built World*. Charlottesville, VA: University of Virginia.

Forester, J., 1989. *Planning in the Face of Power*. Berkeley, CA: University of California Press.

Forester, J., 1999. *The Deliberative Practitioner: Encouraging Participatory Planning Processes*. Cambridge, MA: MIT Press.

Friedmann, J., 1987. *Planning in the Public Domain -- From Knowledge to Action*. Princeton, NJ: Princeton University Press.

Giaoutzi, M. and Bartolomeo, S., 2013. Search of Foresight Methodologies: Riddle or Necessity. In: M. Giaoutzi, and S. Bartolomeo, eds. *Recent Developments in Foresight Methodologies*. New York: Springer; pp. 3–9.

Giddens, A., 1984. *The Constitution of Society: Outline of the Theory of Structuration*. Cambridge: Polity Press.

Giddings, B., Hopwood, B. and O'Brien, B., 2002. Environment, Economy and Society: Fitting Them Together into Sustainable Development. *Sustainable Development* 10(4), 187–196. doi: 10.1002/sd.199.

Glassberg, D., 2001. *The Place of the Past in American Life*. Amherst, MA: University of Massachusetts Press.

Gould, E.I., McCabe, B. and Stern, E., 2016. Fifty Years of Historic Preservation in New York City. Furman Center, New York University, March 2016. Retrieved from http://furmancenter.org/files/NYUFurmanCenter_50YearsHistoricPresNYC_7 MAR2016.pdf

Habermas, J., 1984. *The Theory of Communicative Action*. Boston, MA: Beacon Press.

Harvey, D., 1989. *The Condition of Postmodernity: An Enquiry into the Origins of Cultural Change*. Cambridge, MA: Blackwell.

Harvey, D., 2001. *Spaces of Capital, Towards a Critical Geography*. New York: Routledge.

Hawkes, J., 2001. *The Fourth Pillar of Sustainability: Culture's Essential Role in Public Planning*. Melbourne, VIC: Common Ground.

Hayden, D., 1995. *The Power of Place: Urban Landscapes as Public History*. Cambridge, MA: MIT Press.

Hodder, I., 2010. Cultural Heritage Rights: From Ownership and Descent to Justice and Well-Being. *Anthropological Quarterly* 83(4), 861–882.

Holtorf, C., 2001. Is the Past a Non-Renewable Resource? In: R. Layton, R. Stone, J. Thomas and M. Hall, eds. *Destruction and Conservation of Cultural Property*. London, England: Routledge; pp. 286–297.

Holtorf, C., 2015. Averting Loss Aversion in Cultural Heritage. *International Journal of Heritage Studies* 21(4), 405–421. doi: 10.1080/13527258.2014.938766.

Holtorf, C. and Högberg, A., 2014. Communicating with Future Generations: What Are the Benefits of Preserving Cultural Heritage? Nuclear Power and beyond. *European Journal of Postclassical Archaeologies* 4, 343–358.

Ingold, T., 2010. No More Ancient; No More Human: The Future Past of Archaeology and Anthropology. In: D. Garrow and T. Yarrow, eds. *Archaeology and Anthropology*. Oxford: Oxbow; pp. 160–170.

Jensen, U.J., 2000. Cultural Heritage, Liberal Education, and Human Flourishing. In: E. Avrami, R. Mason and M. de la Torre, eds. *Values and Heritage Conservation*. Los Angeles, CA: J. Paul Getty Trust; pp. 38–43.

Kaufman, N., 2009. *Place Race and Story: Essays on the Past and Future of Historic Preservation*. New York: Routledge.

Lee, A., 2003. The Social and Ethnic Dimensions of Historic Preservation. In: R. Stipe, ed. *A Richer Heritage*. Chapel Hill, NC: University of North Carolina Press; pp. 385–404.

Lee, A., 2004. Historians as Managers of the Nation's Cultural Heritage. *American Studies International* 42(2–3), 118–136.

Leo, C., 2016. 'When I'm Dead, Demolish It'. Contradictions and Compromises in Preserving Values at Lee Kuan Yew's Oxley Road Home, Singapore. Master thesis, Columbia University.

Lipe, W.D., 1984. Value and Meaning in Cultural Resources. In: H. Cleere, ed. *Approaches to the Archaeological Heritage, A Comparative Study of the World Cultural Resources Management Systems*. New York: Cambridge University Press; pp. 1–11.

Lynch, K., 1972. *What Time is this Place?* Cambridge, MA: MIT Press.

Mason, R., 2009. *The Once and Future New York, Historic Preservation and the Modern City*. Minneapolis, MN: University of Minnesota Press.

Meadows, D.H., 2008. *Thinking in Systems, A Primer*. Diana Wright, ed. White River Junction, VT: Chelsea Green Publishing.

Meskell, L., 2010. Human Rights and Heritage Ethics. *Anthropological Quarterly* 83(4), 839–860.

Minnich, E.K., 1990. *Transforming Knowledge*. Philadelphia, PA: Temple University Press.

Mitchell, D., 1995. There's No Such Thing as Culture: Towards a Reconceptualization of the Idea of Culture in Geography. *Transactions of the Institute of British Geographers*. New Series 10(1), 102–116.

Moir, S. and Carter, K., 2012. Diagrammatic Representations of Sustainability: A Review and Synthesis. In: S.D. Smith, ed. *Proceedings of the 28th Annual ARCOM Conference*, 3–5 September 2012, Edinburgh, UK. Association of Researchers in Construction Management; pp. 1479–1489.

Ogilvy, J.A., 2002. *Creating Better Futures, Scenario Planning as a Tool for a Better Tomorrow*. New York: Oxford University Press.

Sabaté, J. and Warren, M., 2015. Cultural Landscapes, Heritage Preservation as a Foundation for Sustainable Regional Development. In: M. Albert, ed. *Perceptions of Sustainability in Heritage Studies*. Boston, MA: De Gruyter; pp. 147–158.

Sandercock, L., 2003. *Cosmopolis II: Mongrel Cities of the 21st Century*. New York: Continuum.

Schwartz, P., 2002. *Foreword in J.A. Ogilvy, Creating Better Futures, Scenario Planning as a Tool for a Better Tomorrow*. New York: Oxford University Press.

Seto, K.C., Güneralpa, B. and Hutyrac, L.R., 2012. Global Forecasts of Urban Expansion to 2030 and Direct Impacts on Biodiversity and Carbon Pools. *Proceedings of the National Academy of Sciences of the United States of America* 109(40), 16083–16088.

Sewell, W., 2005. *Logics of History: Social Theory and Social Transformation*. Chicago, IL: University of Chicago Press.

Silverman, H. and Ruggles, D.F., 2007. Cultural Heritage and Human Rights. In: H. Silverman and D.F. Ruggles, eds. *Cultural Heritage and Human Rights*. New York: Springer; pp. 3–18.

Soini, K. and Birkeland, I., 2014. Exploring the Scientific Discourse on Cultural Sustainability. *Geoforum* 51, 213–223.

Stanley-Price, N., Talley. Jr., M.K. and Melucco Vaccaro, A. (eds.)., 1996. *Historical and Philosophical Issues in the Conservation of Cultural Heritage*. Los Angeles, CA: Getty Conservation Institute.

Tainter, J.A. and Lucas, J.G., 1983. Epistemology of the Significance Concept. *American Antiquity* 48(4), 707–719.

Talen, E., 2102. *City Rules, How Regulations Affect Urban Form*. Washington, DC: Island Press.

Throsby, D., 2002. Cultural Capital and Sustainability Concepts in the Economics of Cultural Heritage. In: M. de la Torre, ed. *Assessing the Values of Cultural Heritage*. Los Angeles, CA: J. Paul Getty Trust; pp. 101–117.

Tomlan, M. (ed.)., 1998. *Preservation of What, for Whom?: A Critical Look at Historical Significance*. Ithaca, NY: National Council for Preservation Education.

Tuan, Y.F., 1977. *Space and Place: The Perspective of Experience*. Minneapolis, MN: University of Minnesota Press.

UN-Habitat, 2011. *Cities and Climate Change: Global Report on Human Settlements*. London: Earthscan.

United Nations, 2014. *World Urbanization Prospects, 2014. Revision*. New York: United Nations.

Urban Land Institute, 2005. *High Density Development: Myth and Fact*. Washington, DC: Urban Land Institute.

US Census, 2007. Calculating Migration Expectancy Using ACS Data. Available at: https://www.census.gov/topics/population/migration/guidance/calculating-migration-expectancy.html#:~:text=Using%202007%20ACS%20data%2C%20it, one%20move%20per%20single%20year

World Commission on the Environment and Development (WCED), 1987. *Our Common Future*. London: Oxford University Press.

14

PALLIATIVE CURATION AND FUTURE PERSISTENCE

Life after death

Caitlin DeSilvey

A lighthouse stands on the North Sea's Suffolk coast—a thirty-metre tapered column of red and white painted masonry, capped by a trellis-glazed lantern. Orford Ness, where the structure is located, is a ten-mile-long shingle spit connected to the mainland by a narrow land bridge at its northern end. By the time this chapter appears in print, the lighthouse may no longer be standing. The story I tell here begins with a brief history of the structure and then narrates a sequence of events that occurred between 2012 and 2016 when the fate of the lighthouse became the topic of intense debate. Because the lighthouse is on the front line of a changing landscape, on a constantly shifting shingle spit, much of this debate focused on strategies for coping with change and uncertainty in the short- to medium-term future. In the years that have passed since the events I describe took place, the story has, inevitably, moved on. The shape of the long-term future that I speculate about in the chapter that follows has become clearer, and some of the key actors in the story have shifted their positions. Perhaps this is one of the peculiar challenges of writing about cultural heritage and the future— the future always lies in wait, ready to rewrite your conclusions and undermine your well-crafted arguments. I have resisted the impulse to include new material in this chapter, but offer this narrative instead as speculative reflection anchored in a particular moment in time, which explores the interval between presence and absence, and considers the ways in which the lighthouse may persist into the future after its apparent demise.

Beginnings and beacons

The first documented aids to navigation on Orford Ness were two wooden towers, built in the middle of the seventeenth century. The doubled light allowed sailors to align the beacons to locate themselves off the coast for safe passage through treacherous offshore shingle and sandbanks. These towers were unstable and vulnerable to undermining by processes of longshore drift, which continually lifted the shingle and transported it farther down the spit. Although one of them was eventually replaced by a masonry structure, by the late eighteenth century, the need for major improvement of the beacon system was evident.

The landowner, Lord Braybrooke, commissioned the building of a new beacon set well back from the shoreline, constructed of brick with a lantern lit by fourteen oil lamps set in silver-plated reflectors. For a while, after the new light came into use in 1792, one of the former beacons remained in place as the "low light." They were both present in the 1820s, when William Daniell featured them in an etching on his coastal circumnavigation of Great Britain and when J.M.W. Turner painted them from the vantage of a stormy sea. In 1887, the low light was decommissioned, and the high light was altered to compensate for the loss with the installation of an occulting main lantern (English Heritage, n.d.).

In 2012, when I first visited Orford Ness, the 1792 lighthouse was still in operation, though Trinity House (the authority responsible for the provision and maintenance of navigational aids in England and Wales) had recently determined that the lighthouse was no longer required as an aid to navigation. The background to this decision was the inexorable erosion of the bank where the lighthouse stood. The span from lighthouse base to beach crest was only fifteen metres, and with average annual erosion on that section of the spit estimated at three and a half metres, the structure did not seem to have much time left. The standing beacon was at the eleventh hour on a slow-motion seascape clock, with the old low light already passed, and the interval between each former beacon measuring centuries, rather than hours [Figure 14.1]. The National Trust owned most of the land surrounding the lighthouse facility and managed it as a National Nature Reserve (with an incongruous inholding of ruined and restored structures dating to the site's use for military research and testing during much of the twentieth century) (DeSilvey, 2014).

Decision and intervention

When Trinity House decided to decommission the lighthouse, they consulted with the National Trust about a possible transfer of ownership or a lease agreement. In these discussions, the Trust made it clear that if they accepted responsibility for the structure, they would take no measures to defend it, and would follow the guidance set out in the 2010 Shoreline Management Plan, which recommended "no active intervention" on this stretch of coastline (Environment Agency, 2010). Eventually, the lighthouse—which English Heritage had listed in 2008 as a Grade II building of "special architectural or historic interest"—would cede its ground to the sea (English Heritage, n.d.). Some voices within the National Trust were of the opinion that the organisation should take on responsibility for the structure and use it as a "test case" for developing imaginative and

FIGURE 14.1 Orfordness Lighthouse, 2012 (photo by author).

proactive coastal adaptation strategies; ultimately, uncertainties about liability and expense swayed the decision, and the Trust decided not to seek acquisition.[1]

Trinity House decommissioned the light in June 2013, and the BBC marked the occasion with a headline reading, "Orfordness lighthouse gets switched off and left to the sea" (BBC, 2013). In an unexpected twist, a London lawyer with a second home near Orford purchased the structure from Trinity House in September and promptly formed the Orfordness Lighthouse Company (Fletcher, 2014). The stated aim of Nicholas Gold's new company was "preservation so far as possible" of the beleaguered lighthouse, "until such time as it may fall victim to the sea and waves" (Orford Ness Lighthouse Company, 2014). As the autumn storms began to batter the Suffolk coastline six months later, it became clear that the time might be closer than anyone had imagined. Each successive storm event brought the base of the lighthouse closer to the waves, and the newly-formed company devised a hasty plan to temporarily stabilise the beach crest with a fifty-metre long barrier of geotextile bags filled with beach pebbles (Suffolk Coastal District Council, 2013). The National Trust expressed concerns about the proposal, and pointed out that when Trinity House announced the decision to decommission the lighthouse in 2010, they had collaboratively agreed a position based on the recommendations in the Shoreline Management Plan, "that we would allow natural forces to dictate the future of the building." They also noted that sea defences might inadvertently accelerate erosion elsewhere on the spit, and "cause unacceptable damage to what is a fragile habitat of international importance" (National Trust, 2014a). In a subsequent statement the National Trust acknowledged that, given the urgency of the situation, temporary stabilisation measures might be necessary to "allow time to remove the principal features and fittings from this historically important building" (National Trust, 2014b). Some of those who commented on the planning proposal seemed not to appreciate the temporary nature of the solution. One local resident opined, "All efforts should be made to *prolong the life* of this historic building" (Suffolk Coastal District Council, 2013). Meanwhile, other residents of Orford and the surrounding community were making their own plans: they wanted to hold a "wake" for the dying lighthouse. The group of concerned local residents sought to recognise the emotions stirred up by the decommissioning and eventual loss of the lighthouse and began to seek funding for an extended programme of community events.

Palliative curation

Although the idea of holding a wake for a building may seem odd, the impulse to understand the deterioration of built structures by drawing parallels with our own corporeal vulnerability, and eventual mortality, is a very old one. If we accept that our buildings have lives then we also must accept that they, like us, have deaths. Rose Macauley (1953) diagnosed the "realization of mortality" as the dominant emotion inspired by ruined and transient architectures, and David Lowenthal (1994, p. 43) observed, "objects and structures that display the erosions and accretions of age seem conformable with our own transient and ever-changing selves."

Michael Shanks (1998) pushes this argument further to make "a plea for pathology." "Death and decay await us all, people and objects alike," he writes, "In common we have our materiality." For Shanks, recognition of our common lifecycles is a precondition for an awareness of the "symmetry of people and things," a symmetry that works to "dissolve the absolute distinction between people and the object world" (Shanks, 1998, p. 17). Shanks's insights find common ground in recent work in geography, which has also sought to question the exceptionalism of human life. We are linked through our "shared finitude," writes Pepe Romanillos (2011), and when we extend our ethical response to non-human subjects, both organic and inorganic, we find ourselves in a relation of care and compassion for all vulnerable "mortal" subjects (Romanillos, 2011). When these vulnerable subjects are structural, rather than biological, the extension of care can be a way of casting the memory of these structures into the future and allowing them to persist despite the dissolution of their discrete material form.

But what kind of care should we extend to a subject whose death is imminent? In clinical contexts, the term "palliative" has come to refer to end-of-life care that seeks to relieve or soothe the symptoms of a disease or disorder without effecting a cure. Palliative care of a terminally ill patient involves minimal intervention, only that necessary to ensure comfort and dignity. I once heard an interview on BBC radio with a palliative care consultant who explained that the aim of palliative care is to "help people cope with uncertainty—in the movement between life and death."

The idea of extending palliative care to buildings and to artefacts is one that was first mooted by a friend in Montana who shared with me the perplexity of finding the appropriate treatment for the derelict structures on the Montana homestead where I carried out my doctoral work (DeSilvey, 2006; 2007a; 2007b). When we took on responsibility for the site, many of the buildings were so far gone that the only sensible thing to do seemed to be to allow them to continue going and to document their gradual demise. We can call it "palliative curation," he suggested, which is not as absurd as it sounds. The root of the word "curation" is the Latin *curare*, to tend or to care. The contemporary meaning, to arrange or to assemble, came later. As curators of the homestead, we sought a way of respectfully and attentively easing the terminal structures into their next phase of existence, and unsettling the assumption that they would be "lost" to the future by encouraging people to understand their passing as a process that had meaning and value in its own right.

In *Building Lives*, Neil Harris (1999) proposes that we need "life stage rituals" for buildings as well as people. Such rituals should acknowledge "the powerful emotions raised by the expiration of a structure's time on earth" (Harris, 1999, p. 117) and recognise that "disintegration and dissolution are part of the natural building cycle" (Harris, 1999, p. 157). Some of the existing, implicit, rituals of leave-taking include exhaustive documentation, such as the early photographic surveys studied by Elizabeth Edwards (2012), which sought to create a visual record of threatened and deteriorating architectural features. Edwards argues that the documentary impulse functions to assuage our "entropic anxieties" about disappearance and loss. Such acts of recognition and revaluation can also be understood, in a more positive sense, as "life-affirming" gestures for terminal structures (Harris, 1999). Kevin Lynch highlights more expansive possibilities:

> Since... the destruction and death of environment may be as significant a point in its process as its creation, why not celebrate that moment in some more significant way?... There could be a visible event and a suitable transformation when a place 'came of age' or was about to disappear.
>
> *(1971, p. 178)*

But any form of palliative care involves a series of decisions, and these decisions can be fraught and emotionally complex, especially if the carers are not in agreement. Precisely such a conflict over end-of-life care developed on Orford Ness in the stormy season of 2014. Both the National Trust and the Orfordness Lighthouse Company wished to extend care and compassion to the lighthouse in its final days, they just had different ideas about how this should be done, and the appropriate rituals of retreat. The company and its supporters wished to use artificial means to provide the equivalent of architectural life-support. Their temporary defences did not promise a miracle cure, but they did seek to prolong the life of the structure "so far as possible," which may have meant months, or, more optimistically, years. The position held by National Trust, and supported by the Shoreline Management Plan, aspired to the clarity of a "do not resuscitate" order, which accepted the loss of the lighthouse as part of a natural process of erosion and landscape change. In March 2014, the district council approved the proposed defences, granting a permit for a maximum period of five years. The decision letter stressed the "non-permanent nature" of the engineering works and noted that future options included either "controlled demolition or dismantling" or "retention of the lighthouse structure" on another site (Suffolk Coastal District Council, 2013). The lighthouse would be supported with the apparatus of intensive care, but only temporarily, it seemed.

The bags were filled with pebbles and placed on the eroding edge of the bank in front of the lighthouse. The Orfordness Lighthouse Company hosted a series of public tours over the course of the summer, bringing to the Ness a steady stream of well-wishers coming to pay their last respects to the structure. The spit is usually accessible only by the National Trust ferry, but permission was granted for a limited number of additional journeys (on a vessel named *Regardless*). As the summer went on conflicts arose between the National Trust and the company over the increased number of visitors on the site (with associated public safety risks due to the presence of unexploded ordnance in the shingle) and concerns about disturbance to the fragile protected habitats.

On retention and relinquishment

In the months and years after the temporary defences were approved and installed, the tension between the different positions did not perceptibly ease. By the end of the 2016 storm season, the base of the lighthouse lay only a few metres from the beach crest, and a few sections of the pebble-bagged defences had been stripped away. As the threat to the structure became more immediate, the position taken by the Orfordness Lighthouse Company seemed to become more entrenched. In 2014, Nicholas Gold was willing to concede that,

> Long term I cannot stop nature. The sea will come in, I recognise that. It would cost a fortune to make it last fifty or a hundred years that was why Trinity House had to bail out, but in the short term I can slow things down.
> *(ITV Anglia, 2014)*

Two years later, the tone had shifted, and news coverage suggested that the company was seeking a "long-term solution," involving the installation of steel sheet piling to protect the lighthouse and its outbuildings (BBC News, 2016; Tonkin, 2016). A post on the company's website explained that the temporary defences were intended to buy time while they "make plans for a more permanent preservation of Orfordness Lighthouse" (Orfordness Lighthouse Trust, 2016). An appeal for funds to repair the defences damaged during the winter storms provoked a counter-response from a local expert on coastal processes:

> I think anything done to try to protect the lighthouse will be an absolute waste of time, unless you spend millions of pounds on rock defences right away along the edge of Orfordness … If you put steel piling in, the sea would go round it and the lighthouse would become an island and still be lost. The best answer would be to move it backwards away from the edge to give it more life.
>
> *(Cornwall, 2016)*

At this moment in time, there appeared to be many possible futures for the lighthouse. One trajectory would have involved accepting the inevitability of coastal erosion to "allow natural forces to dictate the future of the building" (National Trust, 2014b). Another might have involved "controlled demolition or dismantling," with elements of the structure salvaged for conservation and displayed as symbolic remnants. Relocation and retention of the lighthouse structure on another site was a third option, though the expense of such an undertaking would have been prohibitive. The final option—"permanent preservation" *in situ*—had the air of an impossible proposition. All of these apparent options made different assumptions about the desired future, and the place of the lighthouse in that future; they could also all be identified as emerging from different stages of the grieving process.

Elisabeth Kübler-Ross described the emotions associated with our experience of grief as "denial, anger, bargaining, depression, and acceptance," but she was careful to point out that the progression through these stages is not necessarily sequential (Kübler-Ross and Kesslar, 2007). As ecologist Richard Hobbs (2013) observes, when people are caught in different phases of the grieving process, conflict can arise—and this applies equally to our experience of landscape change or species loss. It is not difficult to diagnose an element of denial in the proposals that would have the lighthouse preserved for posterity in its current location. Salvage of selected features aligns more closely with a bargaining mode, which tries to hedge against future losses through consideration of trade-offs and adoption of short term measures to provide temporary stability. Others, who have accepted the inevitability of change, may be more willing to work on finding ways forward in the new circumstances. Kathryn Yusoff, also referring to species extinctions, observes, "Loss requires mourning and grieving for the destruction of a relation and those subjects that are constituted through that relation" (Yusoff, 2011, p. 590). Yet, on the other side of loss, there is always the possibility that new relations, and new subjects, will emerge. Jes Wienberg (2014) has explored a similar dilemma which is playing out in relation to threatened coastal structures in Northern Jutland, Denmark. He proposes the concept of "creative dismantling" as a compromise between preservation and destruction, which seeks to generate new knowledge through acts of salvage, displacement, and re-use (Wienberg, 2014). As Tim Flohr Sørensen (2014) points, however, this model still stops short of realising the radical potential for a "sacrificial" heritage logic, which sees the process of decay and disappearance as having value in its own right.

In 2016, the most likely outcome for the Orfordness Lighthouse, given restrictions around further intervention in coastal processes and the highly protected status of the vegetated shingle landscape inland of the current site, seemed to be that the future of the building would ultimately be dictated by "natural forces." But how this process would play out remained unknown. There was no real possibility of standing back and allowing for the uncontrolled collapse of the structure as the sea undermined the ground it stood on (not least because the collapse of the lighthouse tower *in situ* could have created an artificial groin, with the potential to alter coastal process along the whole of the spit).[2] And yet, given the vulnerability of the structure, the time available for planning a gradual, staged deconstruction effort was shrinking. Perhaps because of the ongoing disagreement about the lighthouse's fate, no one had articulated the practical steps that would have needed to be taken to allow the erosive process initiated by the sea to be completed by deliberate acts of human intervention and remediation.

Other cultural traditions may provide models for how retention and relinquishment can be brought into a productive relation. East Asian architectural philosophy, in particular, tends to privilege the transmission of spiritual significance across many generations, rather than the material permanence of a built structure (Chung, 2005; Ito, 1995). The dissolution and decay of structural material, and its cyclical repair and replacement, are given meaning through grounding in traditions that embrace impermanence, renewal, and rebirth. The elusive Japanese concept of *wabi-sabi*, described as, "an aesthetic sensibility that finds a melancholic beauty in the impermanence of all things," values transience as a reflection of the irreversible flow of life and matter (Juniper, 2003, p. 51). The anxiety about impermanence that characterises Anglo-European heritage practice is alien to many other cultures. David Lowenthal cites a comment offered by the inhabitant of a damaged house in Santa Clara Pueblo, "It has been a good house; it had been taken care of, blessed and healed many times in its life, and now it is time for it to go back to the earth" (as cited in Gillette, 1992, p. 45). While we cannot, as Lowenthal (1989) warns, simply shed our obsession with material preservation to try on borrowed cultural practices, awareness of "different modes of defining and preserving pasts... may help us to extend the forms and functions" of our own (p. 77).

The Ise Shrine in Japan has been rebuilt every twenty years, for many centuries. The interval aligns with that of a human generation but also corresponds to the lifecycle of the deities that inhabit the structure and the onset of decay in the temple's supporting columns (Ito, 1994). An analogue understanding could frame the Orfordness Lighthouse as a structure that is also, similarly, continually renewed, though at two-hundred-year, rather than twenty-year, intervals, to correspond with rates of coastal erosion. In the most recent iteration of the cycle, the chain of material beacons at this site is broken—replaced by the ethereal (though no less material, at its sources) technological warning system of GPS and the strengthened beam at nearby Southwold light.

Persistence over preservation

We need to "think of a world not of finished entities... but of processes that are continually carrying on," asserts Tim Ingold, and to "think of the life of the person, too, as a process without beginning or end, punctuated but not originated or terminated by key events such as birth and death, and the other things that happen in between" (Ingold, 2010, pp. 163–164). How does our perspective shift when we try to understand the lighthouse as a process, rather than a thing? Ingold points out that our convention is to pinpoint age to the moment of the "making" of an object or structure, as with the birth of an individual person. But what if we allow the lifecycle of the lighthouse to scroll out into the pre-history of its construction in 1792, and seek to tell the life stories of its constituent materials as well? The iron, brick, and concrete that make up the bulk of the structure have biographies of formation, extraction, and transformation that precede their assembly in the ostensibly coherent shape of the lighthouse, and these constituent materials also have a future, which will play out after the structure loses its current form—perhaps through incorporation in other structures. We are willing to accept that the integrity of the shingle spit endures, despite its continual reshaping and reassembly, pebble by shifting pebble. Why not extend this sense of dynamic, distributed identity to the lighthouse as well, and, as Ingold suggests, locate meaning in "persistence, not preservation" (Ingold, 2010, p. 164)? Such a shift in perspective would allow us to focus not on the material persistence of the heritage object in its original structure and form, as explored by Tim Cresswell and Gareth Hoskins (2008), but the persistence of the matter incorporated within it, as it is drawn into other systems and processes (Cresswell and Hoskins, 2008).

Some of the systems and processes through which the lighthouse persists into the future may be physical and material. Others will be cultural and social, and these forms of persistence may actually be more enduring and influential in the long term. Over the past several years, rituals of leave-taking for the lighthouse (many of them supported by the National Trust in its status as interested neighbour) have demonstrated the role that art and creative practice can play in helping people assimilate change and construct new forms of heritage that draw energy and inspiration from transience. Simon Read, a painter who lives on a barge not far from Orford Ness, used the predictions of coastal erosion and sea-level rise in the 2010 Suffolk Shoreline Management Plan to depict the lighthouse as a red dot bobbing in the surf off the new coastline, sending out a ghosted halo of lost light. Thomas Dolby, a nearby resident, produced a film entitled *The Invisible Lighthouse*, which filters the lighthouse's future through a dark rendering of destructive energies held within the wider landscape of the Ness. Liz Ferretti, director of the Orfordness Lighthouse Project (which developed out of the early conversations about the need for a lighthouse wake), hosted a short story competition that encouraged people to address the uncertain future of the symbolic structure. In autumn 2015, she worked with local schoolchildren and other artists to create a "cycle of lighthouse songs," inspired by the structure's history and looking to its future, which was performed in Orford Church (in association with an exhibition of recovered artefacts and related artwork) (Ferretti, 2015). These activities allowed people to examine their emotional response to the loss of a loved local landmark, but to do so in an imaginative and oblique way, that sidestepped the fraught negotiations over its immediate fate.[3] They also laid the foundation for the future heritage of the structure. By extending an ethic of palliative curation to terminal structure, they made it possible to imagine a future in which the lighthouse persists in memory, image, and imagination, its potency altered but not necessarily diminished. The lighthouse will also persist in the proliferation of media coverage that it has attracted over the last several years— each sensational headline predicting its imminent surrender to the sea—and in the more measured musings of academic publications like this one. If one still desires a material souvenir, it is possible to order a scale model that faithfully reproduces the lighthouse and its outbuildings in printed paper (Figure 14.2).

FIGURE 14.2   Orfordness Lighthouse paper model. Image courtesy of David Hathaway/ Paper Shipwright. Assembled version of a card model/kit available from www.papershipwright.co.uk

In conclusion, I would like to suggest that the powerful emotional response generated by the imminent demise of the lighthouse suggests that we may be more inclined than we would like to admit to think about the objects we share our lives with as living entities (Jones, 2006). Paradoxically, however, our impulse to seek material protection can work to disrupt, rather than extend, the lifecycle by effectively embalming a living thing. As this discussion has illustrated, a heritage practice that privileges persistence over preservation allows the threatened heritage object to remain relevant and resonant, beyond the point of apparent disintegration. Central to such an approach is a willingness to acknowledge and attend to the uncertainty that arises in the negotiation of the transition between life and death—and to understand palliative care not (only) as an ending, but (also) as an opening into many possible futures.

Acknowledgement

A version of this chapter previously appeared in C. DeSilvey, *Curated Decay: Heritage Beyond Saving* (Minneapolis: University of Minnesota Press, 2017).

Notes

1 Personal communication with Phil Dyke, Coast and Marine Advisor, 4 June 2015.
2 Personal communication with Phil Dyke, Coast and Marine Advisor, 19 November 2014.
3 Personal communication with Liz Ferretti, Director of the Orfordness Lighthouse Project, 29 April 2015.

References

BBC News, 2013. Orfordness lighthouse gets switched off and left to the sea. 28 June. Available from: http://www.bbc.co.uk/news/uk-england-suffolk-23091214 [Accessed 16 July 2015].
BBC News, 2016. Orfordness lighthouse 'perilously' close to falling into sea. 5 January. Available from: https://www.bbc.com/news/uk-england-suffolk-35231897 [Accessed 26 February 2016].
Chung, S. J., 2005. East Asian values in historic conservation. *Journal of Architectural Conservation* 11(1), 55–70.
Cornwall, R., 2016. Moving Orfordness Lighthouse is 'the only answer' to save it *East Anglian Daily Times*, 7 January.
Cresswell, T. and Hoskins, G., 2008. Place, persistence, and practice: Evaluating historical significance at Angel Island, San Francisco, and Maxwell Street, Chicago. *Annals of the Association of American Geographers* 98(2), 392–413.
DeSilvey, C., 2006. Observed decay: Telling stories with mutable things. *Journal of Material Culture* 11(3), 317–337.
DeSilvey, C., 2007a. Art and archive: Memory-work on a Montana homestead. *Journal of Historical Geography* 33(4), 878–900.
DeSilvey, C., 2007b. Salvage memory: Constellating material histories on a hardscrabble homestead. *Cultural Geographies* 14(3), 401–424.

DeSilvey, C., 2014. Palliative curation: Art and entropy on Orford Ness. In: B. Olsen and T. Petursdottir, eds. *Ruin Memories: Materialities, Aesthetics and the Archaeology of the Recent Past.* London: Routledge; pp. 79–91.

Edwards, E., 2012. *The Camera as Historian: Amateur Photographers and Historical Imagination, 1885–1918.* Durham, NC: Duke University Press.

English Heritage, n.d. Orfordness Lighthouse, List Entry Number 1392631. Available from: https://historicengland.org.uk/listing/the-list/list-entry/1392631. [Accessed 11 November 2019].

Environment Agency, 2010. *Suffolk Shoreline Management Plan 2, Sub-cell 3c, Policy Development Zone 6 – Orford Ness to Cobbold's Point.* Suffolk: Suffolk Coastal District Council/Waveney District Council/Environment Agency. Available from: suffolksmp2.org.uk [Accessed 23 June 2015].

Ferretti, L., 2015. The Orfordness Lighthouse project. *EADT Suffolk Magazine.*

Fletcher, M., 2014. Slipping away: Row threatens centuries-old lighthouse." *The Telegraph,* 12 January. Available from: https://www.telegraph.co.uk/news/10566068/Slipping-away-row-threatens-centuries-old-lighthouse.html.

Gillette, J., 1992. On her own terms. *Historic Preservation* 44(6), 26.

Harris, N., 1999. *Building Lives: Constructing Rites and Passages.* New Haven, CT: Yale University Press.

Hobbs, R., 2013. Grieving for the past and hoping for the future: Balancing polarizing perspectives in conservation and restoration. *Restoration Ecology* 21(2), 145–148.

Ingold, T., 2010. No more ancient, no more human: The future past of archaeology and anthropology. In: D. Garrow and T. Yarrow, eds. *Archaeology and Anthropology: Understanding Similarity, Exploring Difference.* Oxford: Oxbow Books; pp. 163–164.

Ito, N., 1995. Authenticity' inherent in cultural heritage in Asia and Japan. *Nara conference on authenticity in relation to the World Heritage Convention. Proceedings,* pp. 35–45.

ITV Anglia, 2014. The Race is on to Save an Iconic Lighthouse. ITV Report, 21 May. Available from: https://www.itv.com/news/anglia/2014-05-21/the-race-is-on-to-save-an-iconic-lighthouse/ [Accessed 26 February 2016].

Jones, S., 2006. The growth of things and the fossilisation of heritage. In: R. Layton, S. Shennan, and P. Stone, eds. *A Future for Archaeology: The past in the Present.* London: UCL Press; pp. 107–126.

Juniper, A., 2003. *Wabi-sabi: The Japanese Art of Impermanence.* Tokyo/Rutland, VT: Tuttle Publishing.

Kübler-Ross, E. and Kesslar, D., 2007. *On Greif and Grieving: Finding the Meaning of Grief through the Five Stages of Loss.* New York: Scribner.

Lynch, K., 1971. *What Time is this Place?* Cambridge: MIT Press.

Lowenthal, D., 1989. Material preservation and its alternatives. *Perspecta* 25, 67–77.

Lowenthal, D., 1994. The value of age and decay. In: W. Krumbein, P. Brimblecombe, P. D. Cosgrove, and S. Staniforth, eds. *Durability and Change: The Science, Responsibility, and Cost of Sustaining Cultural Heritage.* Chichester: Wiley and Sons; pp. 39–49.

Macaulay, R., 1953. *The Pleasure of Ruins.* London: Thames and Hudson.

National Trust, 2014a. The National Trust's position on the Orford Ness Lighthouse. 12 January 2014. Available from: http://ntpressoffice.wordpress.com/2014/01/12/national-trusts-position-on-the-orford-ness-lighthouse/ [Accessed 25 November 2014].

National Trust, 2014b. National Trust, east of England blog, 3 February 2014 blog post. Available from: https://eastofenglandnt.wordpress.com/2014/02/03/orford-ness-lighthouse/[Accessed 25 November 2014].

Orford Ness Lighthouse Company, Available from: http://www.orford.org.uk/community/orfordness-lighthouse-company-2/ [Accessed 25 November 2014].

Orfordness Lighthouse Trust, Available from: http://www.orfordnesslighthouse.co.uk/ [Accessed 6 February 2016].

Romanillos, P., 2011. Geography, death and finitude. *Environment and Planning. Part A* 43(11), 2533–2553.

Shanks, M., 1998. The life of an artifact in interpretive archaeology. *Fennoscandia Archaeologica* XV, 15–42.

Sørensen, T., 2014. Transience and the objects of heritage: A matter of time. *Danish Journal of Archaeology* 3(1), 86–90.

Suffolk Coastal District Council, 2013. Planning application DC/14/0206/FUL and public comments. Available from: https://publicaccess.eastsuffolk.gov.uk/online-applications/ [Accessed 11 November 2019].

Tonkin, S., 2016. Lighthouse that has guarded treacherous coastline for 224 years could topple into the sea. *The Daily Mail*, 5 January. Available from: http://www.dailymail.co.uk/news/article-3385316/Suffolk-lighthouse-guarded-treacherous-coastline-224-years-topple-sea.html /[Accessed 2 February 2016].

Weinberg, J., 2014. Four churches and a lighthouse: Preservation, 'creative dismantling' or destruction." *Danish Journal of Archaeology* 3(1), 68–75.

Yusoff, K., 2011. Aesthetics of loss: Biodiversity, banal violence, and biotic subjects. *Transactions of the Institute of British Geographers* 37(4), 578–592.

15

THE FUTURE, ATEMPORALITY, AND HERITAGE

"Yesterday's tomorrow is not today"

Paul Graves-Brown

The episteme of the "future"

In this chapter, I argue that the future is an episteme – it is an integrated set of ideas or metaphors, a *Weltanschauung* that is historically circumscribed and contingent (Foucault, 1970; 1972). As such, the future has an origin, a beginning in terms of historic and cultural contexts – specifically, the future was invented or "discovered" (Wells, 1902) in the late 19th century. To say that the future was "invented" might seem a little curious, yet as Van Creveld (1991) points out, the idea of invention was itself only invented in the 19th century. Subsequently, the future has developed and mutated, periodically flourishing, waning and being (apparently) reborn. The future has probably arrived, and according to some may well already be over.

When it comes to heritage, the future constitutes a problem, perhaps more than one. Firstly, in a seemingly oxymoronic sense, the future, like modernity, already has a past. Yet throughout this history, the future has had an uneasy relationship with the past; indeed, as a trope, it may be defined in terms of a rejection of the past. The future (usually written with a capital "F"), like its cognates Futurism and Modernism, treats the past as an obstacle to its accomplishment; the "Homeric cheeses and legendary wool winders" with which Marinetti (2005) lambasted John Ruskin. In order to inhabit the future, do we need to "erase the traces" (Hatherley, 2008) of the past and, by implication, heritage? Conversely, does a future which attempts to carry the past along with it end up in a kind of limbo, described by William Gibson (2012: 44) as "a sort of endless digital Now, a state of atemporality enabled by our increasingly efficient communal prosthetic memory"?

Let's try to find out...

Not the future

The future bears a tropic resemblance to the "Golden Age." This situation is made more complicated by the fact that at least some cultures have envisioned the Golden Age as being *in* the future. Generally, though, the Golden Age is one of purity and perfection that has been lost, both in the cosmic terms of Greek or Hindu mythology and in the more mundane sense that we now talk of "the Golden Age" of motoring or rock and roll. In Judeo-Christian thinking, the loss of this pristine situation is a fall from grace, an expulsion from Eden or Paradise.

It is in this equivocal religious/mythic context that we see the emergence of various utopias (and dystopias), not least Thomas More's (1516) eponymous locale. Although the idea of a "utopian future" is commonplace, I want to suggest that the idea of utopia is quite distinct from the future. At the very least, despite that fact that More's word "U-topia" or "Ou-topia" means "no place," utopia is, as often as not, a place, in More's case an island in the Atlantic, which is said to exist contemporaneously with the account thereof (Jameson, 1977). In this sense, utopias are like the paradise represented on the Hereford Mappa Mundi – an inaccessible and yet physically existing region. Throughout the period from the 16th to the 19th century, utopias were almost invariably defined by their spatial isolation from contemporary society, either for didactic or satirical reasons (Jameson, 1977; 2005). Yet what is notable is the shift of "utopian" thought from space to time in the late 19th century. Bellamy's *Looking Backwards: 2000–1887* (1889) and William Morris' riposte *News from Nowhere* (1890) are often cited in the utopian canon, yet what is notable is that their setting is the future, to which the protagonist is transported through sleep and or trance into a socialist society (Bellamy and Morris, in turn, drew heavily on the likes of Fourier, Owen and Saint-Simon). I would argue that this transition is both significant and timely (!), marking the beginning of the future episteme. Three years after Morris' novel was published, American historian Frederick Jackson Turner presented his seminal "The significance of the frontier in American History" to the American Historical Association at the Chicago World's Columbian Exposition. Arguing that American culture had been defined by the frontier since colonial times, Turner declared that era at an end. A century later, in his search for "Pirate Utopias," Hakim Bey (1991) observes; "'the closure of the map.' The last bit of Earth unclaimed by any nation-state was eaten up in 1899. Ours is the first century without terra incognita, without a frontier" (but see below).

It follows, then, that the ideal society can no longer be imagined in the now because all available terra incognita has been swallowed by imperialism and capitalism. However, in the process, I suggest, the future becomes something more malleable than utopia; the spatial utopia or Eden tends to be static, unchanging, but the very temporal placement of the future renders it irredeemably in flux.

Equally, the future cannot be equated with progress. If utopia is a destination, usually spatial, latterly temporal, where on arrival there is nowhere else to go, then progress is, by contrast, a matter of open-ended, incremental betterment. The future shares this sense of betterment but is usually defined in terms of specific trajectories with accessible objectives – the future has a plan. This is its essential antinomy: something that looks like a destination in the utopian sense, but which has the potential to be unattainable or surpassed – like a desert mirage, when you get there it is not there. Indeed, the fact that, in recent decades, it has been claimed that the future is either here, or already over, underpins the idea that it can be considered as a temporally constrained episteme. How did this come about?

The political economy of the future

The future is framed by three key concepts, affluence, planning and novelty, arising from the rapid developments in agriculture, industry, technology, science and transportation since the late 18th century. These elements of the future episteme were embraced by political regimes of both left and right in the first half of the 20th century, but, as we shall see, with varying degrees of enthusiasm.

The importance of affluence is typified in the work of Simon Patten (a lesser-known contemporary of Thorsten Veblen) whose *New Basis for Civilisation* from 1907 replaces the economics of scarcity, epitomised by Malthus, with an economics based on abundance. Patten recognised that technological change could create an affluent society driven by consumption rather than the struggle to produce sufficiency. And, in fact, this was already becoming the case – in 1907 United States' car production was around 36,000 and by 1914 the figure was nearly 500,000. By the 1920s, business leaders, particularly in the United States, had come to see consumption as the key to future prosperity, as the onus had shifted from production to promotion of goods through advertising and marketing (Ewen, 2001).

The second strand is that of planning, often in relation to infrastructure, which Galbraith (1958) saw as still lacking in Eisenhower's USA. Industrial "progress" was and is chaotic, which is perhaps why the analogy is drawn with natural selection. Yet inevitably, the needs of an urban-industrial society began to require some level of planning. Thus, for example, despite the chaos of "railway mania" in the UK in the 1840s, the rail network did become integrated and acted as a force for social/cultural integration, best illustrated by the advent of "railway time." Similarly, the investment in public health that began in the mid-19th century in cities such as London, Bazelgette's sewerage system or the new cemeteries, were a function of necessity but none the less involved a planned approach. Thus, by the end of the 19th century, the idea of urban planning became established through, for example, Ebenezer Howard's Garden City movement or Charles Booth's work in London in the 1890s, leading to the kinds of integrated modernist city envisioned by Le Corbusier, the Futurama exhibit at the 1939 New York World's fair or indeed Jellicoe's Motopia (1961). For Banham (1976: 62) "New York... has been the model for Futuropolis since around 1900," and here as Willis (1986: 169–170) observes,

> The importance of zoning as a catalyst for a new conception of the city of the future cannot be underestimated. Indeed, it can be argued that the

concept of the city rationalised by planning was an outgrowth of the country's first comprehensive zoning law, the New York statute of 1916.

Finally, the future is defined by its rejection of the past and the embrace of novelty. In a sense, this can be traced back to the questioning of tradition in the renaissance and the enlightenment,

> modernity as a new way of conceptualizing time that emerged around the sixteenth century, specifically the perception of the present as distinct from the past: the break with tradition.
>
> *(Lucas, 2004: 109)*

but is brought to a head by the scientific and technological changes of the latter half of the 19th century and here modernity and Modernism/Futurism are not the same thing. With modernity "[a]ll that is solid melts into air, all that is holy is profaned" (Marx and Engels, 1848). Yet Modernists and Futurists, unlike earlier moderns, see nothing in the past that *is* holy, and celebrate the profanation of the ancient and venerable – a cultural year zero. In this I can see no clear distinction between the future, Futurism and Modernism. Modernism in architecture from Louis B. Sullivan or Adolf Loos onwards was based on the rejection of tradition in favour of a truth to new materials and methods. Something similar could be said of the art of Picasso and Braque or the novels of Thomas Mann. Marinetti's (2005) Futurism involved embracing the romance of new technology in the face of the stifling weight of the past which haunted Italy and Rome,

> what you love in our dear peninsula is exactly the object of our hatreds. Indeed, you crisscross Italy only to meticulously sniff out the traces of our oppressive past, and you are happy, insanely happy, if you have the good fortune to carry home some miserable stone that has been trodden by our ancestors.
>
> *(Marinetti, 1915, as cited by Rainey, 2005)*

Although as Hatherley (2008:24) points out, the future sensibility, as represented by Sinclair Lewis and the Vorticists, was already long established in the more industrialised Great Britain.

Politically, the fate of Futurism exemplifies the broad but inconsistent embrace of the future. In 1918, Marinetti attended the inaugural meeting, in Milan, of Mussolini's fascist party (Rainey, 2005), yet at the same time, Futurism was becoming one of the major ideological and cultural forces in the early development of the Soviet Union. For the most part, Mussolini's Italy did not share Marinetti's Futurist enthusiasm, choosing a more traditional trajectory with classical Rome as its model. Though, as Schnapp (2005) discusses, there were those such as Gaetano Ciocca who promoted a more modernist approach, following Gropius and particularly Le Corbusier who, after a fashion, himself admired classical Rome. Ultimately the trajectory of the Soviet Union was similar; although Shukhov's radio tower was constructed between 1920 and 1922, Vladimir Tatlin's famous Monument to the Third International was never built. As Hatherley (2008) describes, the early Soviet years saw a considerable flowering in Constructivist (=Modernist/Futurist) design and architecture, so much so that prominent German modernists such as Bruno Taut fled there, and Gropius and Van der Rohe fled to the USA. Yet by 1930, leading Futurist Vladimir Mayakovsky had committed suicide, and under Stalin, art and architecture became highly conservative; most public buildings in the period 1933–1955 adopted what has been termed a Stalinist Empire or Stalinist Gothic style, which was also exported to Soviet satellites (c.f. the Warsaw Palace of Culture). Although somewhat eclectic, Soviet architecture was largely neo-Classical (perhaps reflecting the era of Catherine the Great) and/or a version of Art Deco, Constructivism having been largely rejected by Stalin. In art and literature, the parallel style of Socialist Realism became official policy after the First Writers Congress in 1934. Stressing "proletarian" values, Socialist Realism rejected anything that the workers would, supposedly, not understand, and hence the novelty of Modernism and other avant-garde styles were rejected as "decadent" in favour of highly conservative modes of representation.

What is ironic is how closely this trajectory is paralleled in Germany – following the flowering of Bauhaus under the Weimar Republic, the Nazi approach to art and architecture became increasingly conservative, culminating in the Entartete Kunst exhibition in Munich in 1937. Architecturally, Hitler, like Stalin, favoured a form of neo-classicism, as delivered by Albert Speer; the planned Welthauptstadt *Germania* incorporated a simplified monumental classicism that can still be seen in the Berlin Olympic Stadium. Perhaps the key to all of these trajectories lies in Speer's concept of ruin value; that authoritarians of both left and right were aiming not at change but at stasis, a thousand-year Reich or as Orwell (1949) puts it: "If you want a picture of the future, imagine a boot stamping on a human face — forever." Here, as Edgerton points out in *The Shock of the Old* (2006: 75), the two most famous 20th-century dystopias, *Brave New World* and *1984*, "were not revolutionary or progressive, even technologically. These are worlds of order without change."

Nevertheless, liberal democracy did little better. Although generally said to originate with the 1925 Exposition Internationale des Arts Décoratifs et Industriels Modernes in Paris, Art Deco can be seen to have earlier origins in the Art Nouveau and Cubism of the pre-1914 period. Although the term seems to have been coined by Le Corbusier, it did not gain currency as a distinct cultural trope until 1968. What connects Art Deco with other contemporary trajectories is its continued reference to the past in ancient Egyptian, Greek, Roman and Mesopotamian stylistic elements. In the USA, which perhaps embraced Art Deco more thoroughly than anywhere else, these were supplemented with styles borrowed from the Maya, Inca and Aztecs. Indeed, one might characterise Art Deco as a form of *Modernism Lite*, a novelty of form and materials domesticated by constant reference to the past. Only in the mid to late 1930s do we see the emergence of the "streamlined moderne" approach to design, typified by the work of Henry Dreyfuss, Walter Dorwin Teague and Norman Bel Geddes, which is more overtly modernist and eschews the trappings of the past. It is perhaps not surprising that it was the work of these three designers that predominated at the 1939 World of Tomorrow in New York. Yet even here, at least in retrospect, the Gernsbackian future of Futurama and Democracity hints at "the sinister fruitiness of Hitler Youth propaganda" (Gibson, 1986:47).

Politically, then, virtually all societies have embraced the idea of an affluent society, which was to see its full flowering in the West in the 1950s and 1960s and spread with advanced industrialisation to Japan, Korea and latterly to China and India (and many other places). Other aspects of the future episteme have not fared so well. Whilst Banham's Futuropolis of Modernism can be seen replicated in London, Singapore or Shanghai, the broader idea of a planned world has not materialised. In the 1960s, left liberals such as Jane Jacobs (1961) opposed the futuristic visions of the likes of Robert Moses, a strand of localism that developed into the environmental activism of the 1970s and 1990s (see e.g., Tyme, 1978). Ultimately, libertarians of both left and right have come to oppose the "oppressive" will of the very planners who were supposed to deliver the future. Equally, for regimes of all political persuasions, the embrace of novelty and rejection of past values has proved too threatening. In effect, the desire for a future year zero has been frustrated by a, small "c," conservative desire to retain the past, epitomised by the fact that the very concept of a planned world has come to incorporate planned conservation of "heritage." This reluctance to fully embrace the future is already evident in the future-lite represented by Art Deco, but has continued and ramified as the idea of the future failed to deliver on its promises.

When was the future?

> The myth of the golden past gave way to the myth of the golden future but, for a short time in the 90s and then in the 1960s we enjoyed the myth of the golden present.
>
> *(Moorcock, 1977: 218)*

"Yesterday's tomorrow is not today" (Alloway, 1956) and yet, somehow, tomorrow seems to have arrived. Despite some rapid technological advances, the future probably seemed somewhat remote in 1914 even though, ironically, the impending war was to bring it closer. In the interwar period, visions such as Lang's *Metropolis* (1927) or Korda's *Things to Come* (1936) still seem to imply that the future is some way off, yet by 1939, New York could host an International Exposition on the theme of the World of Tomorrow. Indeed in the first issue of *Amazing Stories* (in his rather cumbersome style) Hugo Gernsback (1926: 3) had already observed that "New inventions pictured for us in the scientifiction [sic] of today are not at all impossible of realization tomorrow."[1] According to the brochure for the World's Fair *Democracity* exhibit (Seldes, 1939):

> This isn't "the city of the future." It isn't a blueprint of a dictated city. It's a symbol of a way of living – not meant to be followed in detail. Yet you can start to build this city tomorrow morning. There are no trick materials, no imaginary machines.

Indeed the multi-lane highways of the General Motors' *Futurama* pavilion were already taking shape as the Nazi's *Autobahnen*, although Eisenhower's Interstate Highway System (inspired by the Autobahnen – Petroski, 2006) was not begun until 1956 and the first UK motorway not opened until 1959.

By 1956 things had again changed. The exhibition, This is Tomorrow staged by the Independent Group at the Whitechapel Gallery seemed to proclaim that tomorrow was indeed here (Massey, 1995). Creating as it did the first Pop art in the UK, it was a celebration of what Pountain and Robins (2000) call Popular Modernism, summed up in Richard Hamilton's famous poster-collage "Just What Is It that Makes Today's Homes So Different, So Appealing?" The "House of the future" imagined by the Smithsons (members of the Independent Group) for the Ideal Home Exhibition in 1956 would be, above all, "glamourous" (Hatherley, 2008: 31). The "golden present" that Moorcock sees as emerging in the 1960s has its roots in the fact that Modernism, a trope of the avant-garde since the early 1900s, was now very much part of the mainstream; it was being built in the architecture of the Smithsons and Erno Goldfinger (Massey, 1995). Moreover, the future that does become apparent in the 1960s is very much a function of what is termed "cool capitalism." As originally recognised by Patten in 1907, the key to the future is a transition from the emphasis on production to that of consumption; an affluent society in which choices can be made based upon style and fashion (McGuigan, 2012; Pountain and Robins, 2000). Not only was this period the high point of the Madison Avenue "Mad Men," it was also one in which the more uniform and staid (not to say regimented) model that the future had often taken on gave way to a playful and ultimately post-modern diversity (not planned prosperity), perhaps signalling that this future contained the seeds of its own demise.

Yet the 1960s were to see another significant, perhaps terminal shift in the history of the future episteme. At the Democratic National Convention in 1960, John F. Kennedy (1960) announced:

> We stand today on the edge of a New Frontier—the frontier of the 1960s, the frontier of unknown opportunities and perils, the frontier of unfilled hopes and unfilled threats... Beyond that frontier are uncharted areas of science and space, unsolved problems of peace and war, unconquered problems of ignorance and prejudice, unanswered questions of poverty and surplus.

Whilst this ostensibly looks like the aspirations of Bellamy or Patten, the metaphor of the frontier brings us full circle to Turner's speech of 1893. Outer space, in particular, offers what appears to be a new frontier where utopia, or in Kennedy's case Camelot, *can* exist. Indeed, as far back as Wells' *War of the Worlds*, space had been imagined in terms of colonialism (except in Wells case *we* were on the receiving end). Moreover, space seems to offer the ultimate frontier, in Roddenberry's words a "Final Frontier" – in fact, *Star Trek* had been specifically imagined as the transfer of NBCs TV series *Wagon Train* to space (Worland, 1994). It is not entirely fanciful, as some have done, to note that James Kirk shares the same initials as Kennedy. Star Trek promoted/promotes the same liberal values as did the Kennedy administration in terms of gender and race relations, the absurdity of the Cold War, etcetera. It has, perhaps, come to epitomise an unfulfilled aspiration for the future (see below). But more than this, perhaps, the final frontier partially reverses the dynamic of the future, it offers the illusory promise that the closed map of 1893 or 1899 can be reopened as a map of the stars.

One thing we can be certain about is that, as Alloway (1956) suggests, yesterday's tomorrow is never today. H.G. Wells firmly believed that there would be a world government by the 1960s, and whilst in the early 1940s, Roosevelt, and Wilkie (1943), had imagined this as a possibility, the Cold War had shown otherwise. Similarly, as he freely admits, Gibson's imagined future of the "Sprawl" novels (e.g., *Neuromancer*, 1984*)*, which introduced us to the concept of cyberspace, had the fatal omission of a lack of cell phones (Gibson, 2012). Whatever the future that had been imagined, the future we got is quite different. As Reynolds (2011: 364) observes:

> in lots of ways, we're in the future – but it infiltrates our lives in a low-key fashion. There have been astounding advances in medicine and surgery, but you don't really *see* them… The most remarkable transformations have occurred in the realm of computing and telecommunications … Trouble is micro *looks* so much less impressive than macro.

This is true – the future has been insidious because there are, as yet, no colonies on the Moon nor a tunnel under the Atlantic. Moving walkways or pavements have been the transport of the future since their debut at the Chicago World's Fair of 1893. In the imagination of Isaac Asimov (1954), they became the arteries of megacities. In reality, they exist but are confined to airports and railway stations (Wilson, 2007). These are the limits of the planned future.

Meanwhile, the rise of the micro from 1988 to 2000 represented another "golden present" in which cyberspace offered yet another return to the frontier (Graves-Brown, 2009; 2013). As Berardi (2011) points out, the Italian Futurists' love of technology had been bound up with speed, and the internet offered a fresh experience thereof. More, it offered community, knowledge and power, even, to some, a mystical or religious experience (Pesci, n.d.; Porush, 1998;

Rheingold, 1994; Reid, 1997) and a potentially infinite space to explore. Yet in retrospect, the euphoria of 1995–1996 has a certain pathos; the Dot-Com bubble, and as many have suggested 9/11, revised the Euro-American world's enthusiasm for the electronic frontier. Equally, in the light of the failure of the Arab Spring, one might feel a certain scepticism as to the power of the internet and social media to create the "One World" envisaged by Wilkie (1943).

One small step for man: the end of the future

> A vista into a world of wondrous ideas, signifying Man's achievements... A step into the future, with predictions of constructed things to come. Tomorrow offers new frontiers in science, adventure and ideals. The Atomic Age, the challenge of Outer Space and the hope for a peaceful, unified world.
>
> *(Walter E. Disney, 17 July 1955)*

There is as Dawdy (2010: 764) says, "self-proclaimed exceptionalism of modernity" in archaeology that somehow places the modern world outside of the ravages of time. Yet modernity and Modernism, however defined, have a long and growing past, as does the episteme of the future. One might almost suggest that the future described here by Disney ended when he died in December 1966. Others (Banham, 1976; Reynolds, 2011) see the slightly later landing of Apollo 11's lunar module as the key turning point. The monorail future, Disney's future, was in Banham's vivid phrase "crushed under Neil Armstrong's boot," whilst Reynolds calls the section on the Moon landings in his *Retromania* (2011) "The Closing of the Frontier" pointing out that "the lay-offs began at NASA whilst Armstrong and Aldrin were still on their victory tour." Significantly, he also notes that the first Moon landing took place shortly before Woodstock, another event that marked the highpoint, not to say apogee of a trend, only to fall back to Earth with the disillusion of Altamont.

Disney's House of the Future attraction closed in 1967 and in recent years the entire Tomorrowland element of the various Disney parks has been restyled as a retro-future, clockpunk or, as O'Rourke (2008) has it, "Jules Vernacular." As O'Rourke goes on to say, "Disney's Tomorrowland is deeply, thoroughly, almost furiously unimaginative. This is not the fault of the 'Disney culture'; it is the fault of our culture. We seem to have entered a deeply unimaginative era."

Bernardi sees the crucial date as 1977 when the Sex Pistols declared there was "no future." The truth is more that people had begun, since the early 1970s, to realise that we are already in a version of the future and that much of what had been imagined to be the stuff of such a future was never going to be realised. The deregulation of the Reagan-Thatcher era and the 1990s' dive into cyberspace created fresh bursts of enthusiasm for the horizon, but I believe that it has gradually sunk into our culture that the lineal trajectory of time implicit in the future episteme is illusory. If the future is indeed an episteme, then it can have an end.

An endless now: the future as heritage
– heritage as the future

Although he was the Professor of the History of Architecture at University College London, Reyner Banham *loved* Los Angeles (Banham, 1971; Cooper, 1972). Driving its freeways, he saw a new, cool version of the future – Brutalism and Autopia – a kind of optimistic version of J.G. Ballard. If his views became temporarily unfashionable, it was because the future was already here, and looking a little ragged in the wake of the 1973 oil shock, the US evacuation of Saigon and the cancellation of the Apollo programme, a situation that he regretfully acknowledged, "No wonder future Home Improvements of Willesden has gone out of business. There's no future home to improve" (Banham, 1976:63). With nowhere left to go, the Western world began to bury its head in the past through heritage, and in this context, the future itself became a retro-future.

It is no accident that the rise in rescue archaeology and buildings preservation during the 1960s and 1970s – the creation of a heritage "industry" (Hewison, 1987; Lowenthal, 1985; 2015; Wright, 1985) coincides with a loss of faith in the future. As Reynolds (2011) argues, in the absence of something new to do, our society can only obsessively archive and recycle its past. This creates what Gibson (2012: 45) has termed "atemporality";

> This new found state of No Future is... a very good thing. It indicates a kind of maturity, an understanding that every future is someone else's past, every present someone else's future. Upon arriving in the capital-F future, we discover it to be the lower-case now.

Will Self (2015) recently described the future as "a vast and prosthetic present," but, as he argues, there is and only ever has been a now within which the past resides (see Olivier, 2013). Here it may seem that we "look at the present through a rear-view mirror. We march backwards into the future" (McLuhan and Fiore, 1967) perceiving "one single catastrophe which keeps piling wreckage upon wreckage" (Benjamin, 1999: 249). But this assumes, as Benjamin does, that "the storm is blowing from Paradise" – presumably a biblical golden age – and we *might* choose to turn away from the wreckage and look forward, as Futurists have done since the 1880s.

Ironically, the preservationist heritage ethos is confronted by the same forces that undermined the future. As DeSilvey (2012: 33) describes, the UK National Trust's aim to preserve the past "forever, for everyone" is, on occasion, thwarted by environmental change, and destruction has to be conceded. In any case, the past is all too often represented by "contrived dereliction" (Oakley, 2015), monumental ruins that are arrested in a kind of frozen state of decay. The future, by contrast, cannot live in the past: "The notion of a modern monument is veritably a contradiction in terms: if it is a monument it is not modern, and if it is modern, it cannot be a monument" (Mumford,

1938). Heritage sits well with the naturalised mythologies described by Barthes (1993), but the future and perhaps modernity, in general, are constitutionally at odds with this:

> History should be the name of a future oriented *project*: history-which-is-to-be-made rather than stately history-which-is-already-made and demands only veneration in what it also dismisses as an abjectly inferior present.
>
> *(Wright, 1985: 236)*

The era of atemporality suits both traditional and neo-conservatives because "if anything goes, everything stays" and heritage becomes a static utopian past. But "atemporality is a philosophy of history with a built-in expiration date … It's not going to last forever" (Sterling, 2010). By archiving the future we seem to accept the abandonment of its aspirations, yet it remains dangerous; there will always be "others" who want to "vandalise" the past (Merrill, 2011), as Marinetti did.

Hatherley rages that (2008:3):

> We have been cheated out of the future, yet the future's ruins lie about us hidden or ostentatiously rotting … Can we, should we, try and excavate utopia? To do so might be a final, bitter betrayal of Modernism itself.

Hatherley's solution is not to "erase the traces" but to go "Forward (Not Forgetting)." I am not sure this is entirely a viable proposition. As a person born in the golden now of the 1960s I share the sense articulated by John Lydon – "ever get the feeling you've been cheated?" – but the sleight of hand is actually that we *did* get the future, or at least *a* future. The problem is, where now? As suggested at the beginning of this chapter, the future, modernity and Modernism do not sit easily with the concept of utopia, because in its stasis utopia is as dead as "contrived dereliction." Indeed, and again ironically, punk's nihilistic declaration of "no future" demands a kind of anti-heritage where the traces do not matter one way or another (Graves-Brown and Schofield, 2011).

The dilemma is neatly expressed by Rem Koolhaus,

> the arrogance of the modernists made the preservationist look like a futile, irrelevant figure. Postmodernism, in spite of its lip service to the past, did no better. The current moment has almost no idea how to negotiate the coexistence of radical change and radical stasis that is our future.
>
> *(As cited by Stoppani, 2011: 101)*

Comparing the two editions of Lowenthal's *The Past is a Foreign Country* (1985; 2015) it is striking how the past has become increasingly contested and subject to widely varying interpretations, the very basis for any encounter with the past being deconstructed. This, according to Bruce Sterling (2010) is a function of the networked nature of our times – "There is no single authoritative voice of history" – or as Varnelis (2011) puts it "we no longer seem capable of framing our time" because the possibility of a narrative, a delineable trajectory, is lost in the atemporality of an endless now. If we are already in the future, where is there left to go? And hence, perhaps, the past as guarantor of the future becomes irrelevant.

One might object that, as Gibson says, the future has just become a lower case now, and other futures can arise. Perhaps, but if the narrative of futurity is inevitably entrained in the episteme of the future and of modernity, if the idea of history has become a function of the project of modernity, then, in a sense, they are mutually dependent. As Sterling (2010) says, Fukuyama's "End of History" (1989) ended because the stasis of the neoliberal new world order fragmented into an entropy of events, but perhaps, in this entropic state, History (capital H) ends with the future? Certainly, environmental debates and climate change suggest that if the further diffusion of the future is not curtailed, it will destroy us. Thus when Heritage England introduces an annual review with the perennial phrase "conserving heritage for the future" (Heritage England, 2015), one might ask what exactly this future is? Who, if anyone, will benefit from the effort of conservation, and how?

I would prefer an approach to heritage that is "future-oriented," in that it is only interested in the past to the extent that it contributes to society now (following Wright, 1985, quoted above, see Graves-Brown, 2015; Orange, 2015). In this context, the obsessive desire to curate every minute aspect of the past seems futile; for decades archaeologists have opted to "preserve in situ" but for whom? All of us and everything around us are the culmination of "the past," and hence the cloying weight of preservation becomes the "oppressive past" rejected by Marinetti and the Futurists in the early years of the last century. Samuel (1994: 221) observed that "Today … the past is seen not as a prelude to the present but as an alternative to it," to escape this we need to concentrate on how, if and when the past facilitates the present and constrains future possibility. Ultimately, the era of atemporality represents the failure of the future, thus far, to escape the clutches of the past. The archetypal future human was going to be the engineer or scientist, "[a] subject who would supposedly be the absolute origin of his own discourse.." (Derrida (1978: 280), but even the discourse of the future has lapsed into a bricolage of the past.

Acknowledgements

Thanks to Anders and Cornelius for their editorial efforts.

Note

1 Science fiction, particularly since George Lucas' *Star Wars*, now tends to be seen mainly in terms of entertainment. But in earlier decades, it was taken entirely seriously and many significant developments, such as nuclear weapons or communication satellites, appeared first as sci-fi speculations.

References

Alloway, L., 1956. Introduction. *This is Tomorrow*. (Exhibition Catalogue, Reprinted 2014). London: Whitechapel Gallery.

Azimov, I., 1954. *The Caves of Steel*. New York: Doubleday.

Banham, R., 1971. *Los Angeles The Architecture of Four Ecologies*. New York: Harper and Row.

Banham, R., 1976. Come in 2000... Your Time is Up. *New Society*, 8 January, 62–63.

Barthes, R., 1993. *Mythologies*. London: Vintage.

Bellamy, E., 1889. *Looking Backward: 2000–1887*. New York: Houghton Mifflin.

Benjamin, W., 1999. *Illuminations*. London: Pimlico.

Berardi, F., 2011. *After the future*. Edinburgh: AK Press.

Bey, H., 1991. The Temporary Autonomous Zone, Ontological Anarchy, Poetic Terrorism. http://hermetic.com/bey/taz_cont.html

Cooper, J., 1972. Reyner Banham Loves Los Angeles *One Pair of Eyes*. BBC. https://vimeo.com/22488225 (accessed 04/11/19).

Dawdy, S.L., 2010. Clockpunk Anthropology and the Ruins of Modernity. *Current Anthropology* 51(6), 761–793. doi: 10.1086/657626

Derrida, J., 1978. *Writing and Difference*, trans. Alan Bass. London: Routledge.

DeSilvey, C., 2012. Making Sense of Transience: An Anticipatory History. *Cultural Geographies* 19(1), 31–54. doi: 10.1177%2F1474474010397599

Edgerton, D., 2006. *The Shock of the Old*. London: Profile.

Ewen, S., 2001. *Captains of Consciousness: Advertising and the Social Roots of the Consumer Culture. 25th Anniversary Edition*. New York: Basic Books.

Foucault, M., 1970. *The Order of Things: An Archaeology of the Human Sciences*. London: Tavistock Press.

Foucault, M., 1972. *The Archaeology of Knowledge*. London: Tavistock Press.

Fukuyama, F., 1989. The End of History? *The National Interest* (16): 3–18.

Galbraith, J.K., 1958. *The Affluent Society*. New York: Houghton Mifflin.

Gernsback, H. 1926. Introduction. *Amazing Stories* 1:1, 3.

Gibson, W., 1984. *Neuromancer*. New York: Ace.

Gibson, W., 1986. The Gernsback Continuum. In: *Burning Chrome,* 39–55 . London: Harper Collins.

Gibson, W., 2012. Talk for Book Expo, New York. In: W. Gibson, ed. *Distrust that Particular Flavor*. London: Penguin Viking; pp. 41–48.

Graves-Brown, P., 2009. The Library of Babel: Origins of the World Wide Web. In: J. Schofield, ed. *Defining Moments: Dramatic Archaeologies of the Twentieth Century* (BAR S2005). Oxford: Archaeopress; pp. 123–134.

Graves-Brown, P., 2013. Archaeology of the Internet. *Encyclopedia of Global Archaeology*. London: Springer.

Graves-Brown, P., 2015. Re-animation or Danse Macabre? In: H. Orange, ed. *Reanimating Industrial Spaces*. Walnut Creek: Left Coast Press; pp. 235–247.

Graves-Brown, P. and Schofield, J., 2011. The Filth and the Fury: 6 Denmark Street (London) and the Sex Pistols. *Antiquity* 85(330), 1–17. doi: 10.1017/S0003598X00062128

Hatherley, O., 2008. *Militant Modernism*. Winchester: Zero Books.

Heritage England, 2015. 3 December. Available at: http://www.facebook.com (Accessed: 3 December 2015).

Hewison, R., 1987. *The Heritage Industry*. London: Methuen.

Jacobs, J., 1961. *The Death and Life of Great American Cities*. New York: Random House.

Jameson, F., 1977. Of Islands and Trenches: Neutralization and the Production of Utopian Discourse. *Diacritics* 7(2), 2–21.

Jameson, F., 2005. *Archaeologies of the Future: The Desire Called Utopia and Other Science Fictions*. London: Verso.

Jellicoe, G., 1961. *Motopia: A Study in the Evolution of Urban Landscape*. London: Studio.

Kennedy, J.F., 1960. Speech to Democratic National Convention, 15 July 1960. John F. Kennedy Library and Museum. https://www.jfklibrary.org/Asset-Viewer/AS08q5oYz0SFUZg9uOi4iw.aspx

Lowenthal, D., 1985. *The Past is a Foreign Country*. Cambridge: Cambridge University Press.

Lowenthal, D. 2015. *The Past is a Foreign Country* (Second revised edition). Cambridge, UK: Cambridge University Press.

Lucas, G., 2004. Modern Disturbances: On the Ambiguities of Archaeology. *Modernism/Modernity* 11(1), 109–120.

McGuigan, J., 2012. The Coolness of Capitalism Today. *TripleC: Communication, Capitalism and Critique* 10(2), 425–438. www.triple-c.at.

McLuhan, M. and Fiore, Q., 1967. *The Medium is the Massage*. Harmondsworth: Penguin.

Marinetti, F.T., 2005. Futurist Speech to the English. In: L. Rainey, ed. *Modernism. An Anthology*. London: Oxford University Press; pp. 6–9.

Marx, K. and Engels, F., 1848. *The Communist Manifesto*. London: Workers' Educational Association (*Kommunistischer Arbeiterbildungsverein*).

Massey, A., 1995. *The Independent Group: Modernism and Mass Culture in Britain, 1945–59*. Manchester: Manchester University Press.

Merrill, S., 2011. Graffiti at Heritage Places: Vandalism as Cultural Significance or Conservation Sacrilege? *Time and Mind* 4(1), 59–75. doi: 10.2752/175169711X12893985693711

Morris, W., 1890. *News From Nowhere*. London: Kelmscott Press.

Moorcock, M., 1977. *The Condition of Muzac*. London: Allison and Busby.

Mumford, L., 1938. *The Culture of Cities*. New York: Harcourt Brace.

Oakley, P., 2015. A Permanent State of Decay: Contrived Dereliction at Heritage Mining Sites. In: H. Orange, ed. *Reanimating Industrial Spaces*. Walnut Creek: Left Coast Press; pp. 49–71.

Olivier, L., 2013. Time. In: P. Graves-Brown., R. Harrison and A. Piccini, eds. *The Oxford Handbook of the Archaeology of the Contemporary World*. Abingdon: Oxford University Press.

Orange, H. (ed.)., 2015. *Reanimating Industrial Spaces*. Walnut Creek: Left Coast Press.

Orwell, G., 1949. *Nineteen Eighty-Four*. London: Secker & Warburg.

O'Rourke, P.J., 2008. future Schlock. *The Atlantic*, 1 December. http://www.theatlantic.com/magazine/archive/2008/12/future-schlock/307151/

Pesce, M., n.d. *Cybersamhian Ritual*. http://hyperreal.org/%7Empesce/samhain/ (accessed 04/11/19).

Petroski, H., 2006. On the Road. *American Scientist* 94(5), 396–399.

Porush, D., 1998. Telepathy: Alphabetic Consciousness and the Age of Cyborg Illiteracy. In: J. Broadhurst Dixon and E. Cassidy, eds. *Virtual futures*. London: Routledge; pp. 57–94.

Pountain, D. and Robins, D., 2000. *Cool Rules. Anatomy of an Attitude*. London: Reaktion Books.

Rainey, L. (ed.), 2005. *Modernism: An Anthology*. London: Blackwell.

Reid, R., 1997. *Architects of the Web. 1,000 Day that Built the Future of Business*. Chichester: Wiley.

Reynolds, S., 2011. *Retromania: Pop Culture's Addiction to Its Own Past*. London: Faber and Faber.

Rheingold, H., 1994. *The Virtual Community: Finding Connection in a Computerised World*. New York: Secker and Warburg.

Samuel, R., 1994. *Theatres of Memory*. London: Verso.

Schnapp, J.T., 2005. Excavating the Corporativist City. *Modernism/Modernity* 11(1), 89–104.

Seldes, G., 1939. *Text of "Your World of Tomorrow" Brochure. New York World's Fair*. New York: Rogers-Kellogg-Stillson.

Self, Will, 2015. The Nature of Time. A Point of View. BBC. *Radio 4*, Friday 6 March 20.50 pm.

Sterling, B., 2010. Atemporality for the Creative Artist (Speech at Transmediale 10, Berlin, 6 February 2010). *Wired*. http://www.wired.com/2010/02/atemporality-for-the-creative-artist/ (accessed 25/02/10).

Stoppani, T., 2011. Altered States of Preservation: Preservation by OMA/AMO. *Future Anterior* 8(1), 96–109.

Tyme, J., 1978. *Motorways versus Democracy*. London: MacMillan.

Van Creveld, M., 1991. *Technology and War*. New York: Free Press.

Varnelis, K., 2011. History after the End. *Cornell Journal of Architecture* 8 http://cornelljournalofarchitecture.cornell.edu/read.html?id=4

Wells, H.G., 1902. *The Discovery of the future. A Discourse Delivered to the Royal Institution on 24 January, 1902*. London: T Fisher Unwin.

Willis, C., 1986. Skyscraper Utopias. Visionary Urbanism in the 1920s. In: J.J. Corn, ed. *Imagining Tomorrow. History, Technology and the American future*. Cambridge: MIT Press; pp. 164–187.

Wilkie, W., 1943. *One World*. New York: Simon and Schuster.

Wilson, D.H., 2007. *Where's My Jetpack*. London: Bloomsbury.

Worland, R., 1994. From the New Frontier to the Final Frontier: Star Trek From Kennedy to Gorbachev. *Film & History: An Interdisciplinary Journal of Film and Television Studies* 24(1–2); 19–35. https://muse.jhu.edu/article/395001

Wright, Patrick, 1985. *On Living in an Old Country*. London: Verso. doi: 10.1086/ahr/91.4.932

16

HERITAGES OF FUTURES THINKING

Strategic foresight and critical futures

Richard Sandford and May Cassar

Introduction: heritage futures

Heritage has a necessary relation to the future. Without some idea of the future, the practice and concept of heritage are both without meaning. Heritage is a fundamentally anticipatory practice, not simply in the way that any social practice is but because it is through heritage that we reflexively equip ourselves with the cultural resources necessary for future anticipation, establishing the future's relationship to the past not simply through necessity but through an axiological process of choosing and discarding. The recognition of the impermanent nature of heritage objects and the need to understand better how to manage and accept change and loss of heritage underpin a growing understanding that those working within heritage need to attend to the relationship between heritage and the future.

Within heritage studies, this necessary concern with the future has begun to be explored through the kind of critical attention represented in this volume. The transient character of heritage and the consequences of change and loss have also been central concerns for the fields of sustainable heritage (e.g., Barthel-Bouchier, 2016; Sabbioni, Brimblecombe, and Cassar, 2010) and heritage science (Strlič, 2018; Brown, Lichtblau, Fearn, and Strlič, 2017). As yet, however, within heritage studies there has been little engagement with the nature of the future and the mechanisms through which it might shape and be shaped by heritage and heritage practice. Yet the stances society adopts towards the future and the futures that are imagined as a result will ground any decisions about what should be passed on to succeeding generations or choices about what should be left or lost. Heritage scholars and practitioners have a need to elaborate the different ways in which futures are produced within society, and the ways these intersect with, shape, and constrain ways of thinking about heritage (Högberg, Holtorf, May, and Wollentz, 2017).

Other fields of practice and scholarship have been engaged with the question of the future for some time, and attending to their responses is valuable as the field of heritage develops its own relation to the future. This chapter is a step towards placing heritage in dialogue with some of these other fields, introducing a range of concepts and theoretical stances to illustrate the degree of attention that has already been given to the topic of the future within them. It suggests, as well, that these fields might themselves benefit from heritage developing its own, distinct stance towards the future, one that is able to think about how changing things can still persist over time.

What follows is organised around three broad tasks. First, we describe some of the fields that have addressed the future and its production, and propose, for the convenience of this chapter's argument, an organisation of these fields into two clusters of intellectual activity. These two clusters represent, broadly, the study of the future and the study of the social production of the future. Second, we offer for each cluster an account of its strengths and limitations and what it might offer heritage. Finally, we discuss some of the ways in which heritage and futures fields might enrich one another, better equipping each to address the challenges facing the world.

The future plays some part in every domain of human experience and within every academic field. Within this chapter, however, our intention is to concentrate on fields of study and practice that have directly addressed the nature of the future and its place in society. That means that we will not, here, discuss (for example) the contributions of scholars working in memory studies, education, or geography that consider the future as it relates to their fields, relevant though these are to heritage studies. Nor will this chapter consider disciplines that focus on forecasting and prediction in a purely mathematical sense, such as data science or economics, since much of the work we consider here aims to go beyond the limited kinds of future that modelling or projection are able to produce, valuable though these approaches are in the right context.

Instead, we focus on two related clusters of work that have each developed tools and resources for considering the nature of the future and what it might contain, and for making visible the relation between society and the future.[1] The first, concerned primarily with the study of the future itself, might be thought of as practical futures work, methods, and stances towards exploring the future developed largely in the context of corporations and governments, which for the purposes of this chapter we gather together here under the general term of 'strategic foresight'. The other, driven largely by a desire to understand the ways in which societies imagine futures and the work of these future imaginaries within society, develops a perspective that we name here 'critical futures'. Work in this cluster emerges from 'futures studies' (Bell, 2003) alongside work from across the academy concerned with the future more generally. What follows, then, is intended to signpost a range of different ideas and literature within these two clusters, offered as a jumping-off point for researchers with an interest in engaging with the future.

Strategic foresight

There are three broad strands of work that we are clustering together here under the banner of 'strategic foresight'. One strand represents an instrumental approach towards managing the future developed during the Second World War: the probabilistic methods of the newly-developed 'operational research' were employed in peacetime by the RAND[2] organisation alongside the 'scenario planning' developed by Hermann Kahn to generate many multiple possible futures in which an organisation might have to operate (Bradfield, Wright, Burt, Cairns, and van der Heijden, 2005). The practice was adopted by the multinational energy corporation Shell and credited with that organisation's anticipation of the oil crisis in the 1970s. Through this example, and the work of consultancies such as the Global Business Network (GBN), scenario planning has become a cornerstone of corporate strategy amongst private companies, non-profits, and international organisations. Shell's model, developed by Pierre Wack, tempered the probabilistic approach of RAND with the more normative approaches to the future developed by Gaston Berger and de Jouvenel (e.g., de Jouvenel, 1967) in France (Wilkinson and Kupers, 2013). This second strand, forged in European post-war reconstruction efforts, emphasised the need for human society to develop positive 'images of the future' (Polak, 1973) and actively work to bring those futures into being through, for example, the 'futures workshops' developed from the mid-1960s by Robert Jungk and Norbert Müllert (Jungk and Müllert, 1987). Where the foresight of RAND and GBN was technocratic and strategic, this European tradition was more focussed on peace and transition to a just and sustainable world. The third strand, emerging like the other two in the 1960s and 1970s, was a disparate mix of academics and professionals with a common interest in understanding the future in order to shape it. The 'sociology of the future' Bell and Mau called for in 1971 (Bell and Mau, 1971) failed to emerge (Bell, 1996), instead, the field of 'futures studies' (Bell, 2003) gathered together forecasters, philosophers, anthropologists, technologists, systems analysts, economists, and others in groups like the World Future Society (founded in 1966) and the World Futures Studies Foundation (founded in 1973). At the time Bell introduced readers to 'futuristics' (Bell, 1983), the field was still new enough that fields and interests that look, from 2019, very different, could be grouped happily under one roof.

Public policy has engaged with these approaches in various forms. For example, in the UK, the government built on its own internal approach to anticipation through policy analysis, first, by making extensive use of computer simulations and exploring systems dynamics in the 1970s (Turnbull, 2018), and second, by drawing on scenario planning and other futures methods to supplement modelling with more qualitative approaches.[3] These exercises bring emerging issues to the attention of policy teams, sensitising them to their potential impacts. Other governments, notably Sweden, the Netherlands, Finland, and Singapore (Andersson, 2006; 2018; Andersson and Keizer; 2014; Habegger, 2010; Nováky and Monda, 2015), have been through similar trajectories in establishing a place for strategic foresight in their policy processes. This place is not unchallenged. There are tensions between the horizons necessary for long-term planning and the diminishing horizons for action within administrative and political domains (O'Hara, 2015) that can make it hard for policy teams to engage with the outcomes of strategic foresight. And the recent growth of 'design labs'[4] and 'what works'[5] approaches within governments, which focus on iterative experimentation and immediate solutions over structured speculation and long horizons, offer policy teams alternative sources of ideas about the future.

'Strategic foresight', as we use the term here, represents a linked but heterogeneous set of practices that emerged from the post-war military-industrial complex and exists principally today in the space shared by governments and corporations. It encompasses forecasting and simulation, systems dynamics, scenario planning, and other tools (such as morphological analysis) that are intended to illustrate a wider range of possibilities and outcomes than those imagined in day-to-day life and applied across a wide range of domains by a variety of actors. Despite this diversity, there are some central principles that are regularly espoused by consultants and researchers working in the field (set out by Bell in his 2003 introduction to the field, and repeated in many locations since).

The underpinning ontological assumption for futurists is the asymmetry of time; time's arrow moves in one direction, "progressively and irreversibly through time from out of the past toward the future" (Bell, 1983). This future is open, not predetermined, and contains within it things that have not previously existed. Futurists, therefore, concern themselves with multiple possible futures rather than a single future or with making predictions. People and groups can intentionally shape these futures through their actions, though without knowledge of possible consequences or being aware of possibilities in the first place, it is difficult to do this. The task of a futurist, then, is to help provide knowledge of the future, despite the future being fundamentally unknowable; they are to identify "possible, probable and plausible futures" (Amara, 1981) to help organisations and societies prosper.

These principles are commonly represented in the 'futures cone', a diagram that has shown itself to be an adaptable tool for thinking futures. Originally employed as the 'cone of plausibility' in 1988 by Taylor (1993) for the US Army War College, some version of the diagram popularised by Joseph Voros is more usually seen in futures work (Figure 16.1). Variations tend to focus on shading the cross-section to illustrate qualitative differences in possible futures or extending the cone back in time, following Taylor's lead (Figure 16.2).

The futures represented within the cone are described as being produced through the actions of 'trends' and 'driving forces', two terms used widely, though not always consistently. In general, 'trends' are clear patterns of activity operating within shorter horizons that may be reversed and 'driving forces' are clusters of many different trends forming deeper dynamics that work over a longer horizon; these are slow to form, slow to recede, and unlikely to be

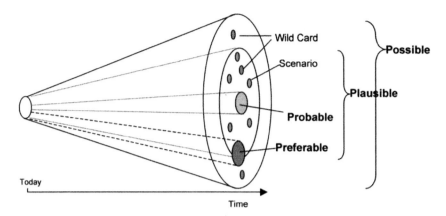

FIGURE 16.1   The 'futures cone' (used with permission of Joseph Voros).

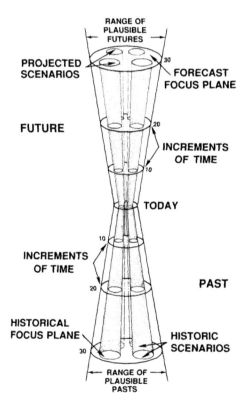

FIGURE 16.2   The Cone of Plausibility: Past and Future. Reproduced with permission from the United States Army War College. *Alternative World Scenarios for a New Order of Nations*, by Dr Charles W. Taylor, 1993.

reversed. Demography and climate change are canonical examples of driving forces; technology and politics are categories that are also often employed in this way. Part of the promise of foresight is the detection of 'weak signals', the precursors of coming change and emerging trends that are revealed through 'horizon scanning' or sifting through data from many different sources to find indicators of change. Fostering a sensitivity to these weak signals is an important aspect of foresight practice, as is, at the other extreme, an appreciation that the past is not always a guide to the future, and that 'wild cards' and discontinuities are always possible. These surprises may be understood, ontologically, as emergent events arising from the complexity of the systems under consideration, or epistemologically, as areas that have been unexamined, unintentionally or wilfully (Heffernan, 2011). Epistemological sources of surprise are regularly divided into 'known unknowns' and 'unknown unknowns'. The work of strategic foresight is to uncover the unknown unknowns, since managing known knowns and unknowns are already the objects of administration and risk assessment. Žižek (2006) reminds us that a fourth category is another source of surprise, the 'unknown knowns', or the "disavowed beliefs" that underpin action, though working with these is often more challenging for foresight practitioners since this is where the politics of foresight are made most apparent.

The narratives of possible futures that emerge from combining these elements are traditionally presented as 'scenarios' (Urry, 2016), often developed with different internal and external stakeholders to ensure they represent a range of perspectives. These are then used as tools within policy and strategy teams to test assumptions or explore consequences. Using these tools well requires practitioners to develop an appreciation of when and where their use is most appropriate and a sensitivity to the issues they raise, a capacity often referred to as 'futures thinking' by practitioners. Within organisations, this is valued as a way of avoiding the 'business as usual' thinking that is seen as a vulnerability in a world often represented as 'VUCA' – volatile, uncertain, complex, and ambiguous (Johansen and Euchner, 2013).

Strategic foresight, as briefly characterised here, represents a way of relating to the future that, while far from mainstream, has a place within governments and in organisations, and is part of the way that actors within those groups form their ideas of the future. It often aims to be inclusive and participatory, works with a wide range of evidence (and so understands that there are multiple ways of knowing the world), and seeks to trouble established understandings in order to better perceive possibilities of change. These possibilities are not regarded as predetermined, but the changes their fulfilment would usher in are real, with real consequences and opportunities. Within the field, however, there is a tendency to treat this real world 'out there' uncritically. As much a craft and practice as an academic discipline, foresight lacks theory beyond the ontological categories of trends and drivers sketched above (Wilkinson, 2013; Poli, 2010) and so can lend itself to instrumental futures that leave fundamental ideas about the future and social change unexamined. For a field so ready to think big, the futures it produces can sometimes lack conceptual depth.

What might such an approach towards the future offer heritage? It offers a practical way of thinking about possible future events that goes beyond the contingency planning of risk management (e.g., Ashley-Smith, 1999), supporting heritage managers and practitioners to consider long-term futures that span longer periods than projections are able to describe. It draws attention to the potential interactions between different trends necessary for considering the complex causal relationships across multiple domains that give rise to heritage objects. It highlights, too, the way that the categories used to describe heritage can make some possibilities inaccessible to an organisation's view, increasing the risk of being surprised by events. These features may make strategic foresight helpful in responding to changes in the nature of heritage and its role in society and for imagining actions to take as well as simply recognising emerging threats. However, it may not be sufficient as an approach for heritage in working with the future from a critical perspective: for example, working with futures of dissonant or difficult heritage or heritage from marginalised or oppressed groups (MacDonald, 2015; Robertson, 2008) requires ways of recognising multiple, contested worldviews and differences in power that may be inaccessible to the uncritical, naive realism often found in strategic foresight. Developing a critical heritage perspective towards the future requires an awareness of the strategic foresight approach since it represents a particular historical stance towards the future, one that is still current within some areas of public policy and planning, and one that provides a starting point for critique. But there are other approaches towards the future that pay more attention to theory.

Critical futures

Later work within futures studies attempts to develop just this kind of critical stance, while outside future studies, disciplines with a more recent interest in the future offer access to a rich set of theoretical principles that provide new perspectives and support. In this section, we want to highlight the ways in which this work directs researchers' attention to the ways in which 'the future' is produced socially and to offer a heuristic framework for distinguishing between different ways in which 'the future' might be produced.

Future studies initially was developed 'more off than on campus' (Bell, 1996, p. 39), resulting in a field lacking coherence, with inconsistent notions of quality, and with a tendency to reinvent approaches to social research (Slaughter, 1999). In response, Slaughter and others set out to develop a 'critical futures studies', attending to issues of power and representation, recognising non-Western stances towards the future, questioning the categorisations through which the field makes the world known, and encouraging a greater degree of reflexivity amongst practitioners (see also Ahlqvist and Rhisiart, 2015). Where strategic foresight concentrated on the fortunes of sponsoring organisations, developing tools to help achieve the ends of a particular group, this critical approach built on the ideas of Polak (1973), Flechtheim (1971), Boulding (1990), and others to examine the interconnected global issues of social justice, resource depletion, ecological collapse, political leadership, technological acceleration, and other elements of what Slaughter calls the 'global problematique' (Slaughter, 2004, ch. 2). Rather than producing specific narratives of the future, critical futures studies examines the ideas of the future at large in the present and seeks ways to produce alternatives that can support hope and optimism in the face of entrenched inequalities and systemic threats; it is 'critical' insofar as it takes social transformation as a necessary goal.

This critical stance within futures studies has been valuable in problematising the largely positivist ontological and epistemological assumptions implicit in strategic foresight, ensuring that narratives of possible futures are recognised as products of particular social and historic contexts, and arguing for a deeper understanding of the role of theory in the discipline (Piirainen and Gonzalez, 2015). Developing a reflexive and critical stance within the field has also been necessary, as Kuosa (2011) points out, for the field to respond to the principles of self-organisation, emergence, and complexity that challenge a more simplistic ontology of 'trends' and 'drivers'. In attending to the scale of human impact on planetary systems and considering the scope of the transition necessary for humanity to continue to be sustained, work within critical futures studies presages the more recent debates around the notion of 'the Anthropocene' (e.g. Palsson et al., 2013) and so may have something to offer critical future heritage. But the field, in general, despite endorsing an interdisciplinary approach to the study of the future, has tended to address an internal audience rather than connect with other academic fields and many of its concerns are now the subject of enquiry within more traditional disciplines. Recent work in sociology, alongside related areas of the social sciences and humanities, provides one such example, exploring the ways the future is imagined and produced within society.

Sociology, notwithstanding Bell and Mau (1971), has only recently turned to the consideration of the future as an object of study in its own right, though the field has long attended to the futures of different groups or the role of 'the future' in political discourse (Tutton, 2017; Urry, 2016; Schulz, 2015). Over the past couple of decades, however, the future has been a productive subject within sociology and the social sciences as a foundational component of enquiry into areas as diverse as big data, securitisation and emergencies, anti-microbial resistance (Coleman and Tutton, 2017), as a cultural product that exerts a particular influence (Jameson, 2005), and as a venue for exploring other ways of organising society (Srnicek and Williams, 2016; Frase, 2016). The forms and roles of different kinds of future imaginary (Cantó-Milà and Seebach, 2015) acting in society have been examined: Beckert (2013) explores the role of fictional futures in sustaining financial decision-making under conditions of uncertainty, while a sociology of expectations has been developed within science and technology studies (Borup et al., 2006) that unpicks the ways the likely or desirable futures found in discourses of scientific innovation shape patterns of investment and public understandings of science.

Underpinning these different strands of enquiry lie some well-established sociological concerns with time and risk. Earlier work on the sociology of time (e.g., Adam, 1995; Nowotny, 1994) explores the temporality of different social structures alongside individual orientations towards time and describes the production of the modern relationship between the present and the future in which time is subject to a scientific treatment that renders it linear and homogenous and in which increasing complexity and rates of change brings the horizon of the future closer to the present. For Nowotny, this results in the replacement of the category of 'future' with 'extended present', as our attempts to plan, manage, and control the systems that sustain us give rise to a series of contingencies that 'dispose of the future as if it were the present' (Nowotny, 1994, p. 52). This resonates with the compression of space and time as a consequence of technological development and rapid globalisation, the concomitant increase in uncertainty as established pasts cease to act as guides to the future, and the increasing centrality of 'risk' in configuring social and individual responses to uncertainty (e.g., Bauman, 2000; Beck, 1992).

In particular, risk and its calculation play a large role in framing sociological concerns with the future (Mythen, 2004). Massumi (2007) describes how risk can move from prevention, which deals with threats that are actual but whose consequences have not yet materialised, to preemption, which responds to threats that are yet to emerge. By organising itself around the event it wants to avoid, it 'brings the future into the present' (Massumi, 2005, p. 8) by addressing the 'affective fact' (Massumi, 2009, p. 54) of the threat rather than its potential consequences. For Amoore, preemption is a hallmark not just of the security assemblages she and Massumi explore, but of the 'data-driven' governance handed increasing responsibility for public life. Rather than engaging with the 'contingent biographies' behind data points, our behaviour and preferences are instead inferred, and these 'inferred futures' are what is acted upon (Amoore, 2013, p. 61). In a related fashion, Feher (2009) describes the way neoliberal markets value the potential future performance of individuals, who must tailor their present conduct to indicate their future marketability.

For heritage, these ideas offer ways of framing questions concerning the future that is imagined in different heritage contexts, and the work that these imagined futures do in producing these contexts. Heritage researchers are beginning to explore the way that imagined futures shape heritage. The ways of thinking about different effects of imagined futures introduced above can help to guide this exploration and locate it within wider academic enquiry into the work of the future. For example, we might ask: in what ways is the value of heritage sites bound up with ideas about the expected futures they might enable, whether framed in terms of envisaged economic returns and costs or in terms of relationships between or within communities? What futures are constructed by the various temporalities that might be acting within particular forms of heritage, and are some privileged over others by our interpretation of that heritage? When do inferred threats pre-emptively limit the uses made of heritage objects? And, in societies where rapid change means the past is no guide to the future, how might heritage provide the continuity necessary for the formation of stable identities? The distinction between the historicised 'homogeneous, empty time' of Benjamin (as cited in Eiland and Jennings, 2006) and non-linear temporalities is already familiar to heritage studies, but relating this to the work of (for example) Adam and Nowotny cited above might encourage researchers to extend the scope of these discussions to include futures alongside pasts and presents. This, in turn, would make clear how well-placed heritage is to bring other ways of understanding time into a conversation about the future, giving a place to the 'pre-modern' temporalities that Adam and Groves (2007) mention.

In doing this, in bringing the past into different kinds of relations with the present and the future, it might be useful to consider how this is done within the social subjects who give heritage its meaning. One model might be found in the pragmatist thought of Mead. The relationship between the past, present, and future is central to Mead's notion of a social self, located in a present that requires the subject to reach into the past for an understanding of the historical circumstances from which the present emerges as part of their efforts to respond to the futures they imagine arising, a 'deliberative attitude' that enables them to 'construct their pasts in anticipation of that future' (Mead, 1932, p. 76). This finds another expression in Whitehead's 'prehension', the bringing together in the present of perceived pasts and anticipated future (Whitehead, 1925, p. 91). For Whitehead, reality is a series of prehensive 'occasions' (1925, p. 89) in which past occasions and anticipated future occasions are combined to produce a new occasion, which will become part of a new prehension. Since each combining takes place from a particular perspective, what is combined in one occasion may be used differently, or not at all, in another.

Such a continual process of becoming echoes Spinoza's distinction between *natura naturans* (the unfolding of reality) and *natura naturata* (the by-products of that process). The process through which reality is constructed is not a sequential causal chain but something richer and more plural, the relationship between different occasions being closer to what Groves (2017, p. 35) describes as 'fractal', as pasts and futures reach back and forward past each other. This is a different way of thinking about 'now'. Where there is space to move amongst ideas of past, present, and future in this way, the present ceases to appear as a mathematically-thin film separating past and future, and features more as a 'thick present' (Poli, 2011), echoing Benjamin's (Eiland and Jennings, 2006) *Jetztzeit*, or 'now-time', in which "constellations" of connections with other resonant moments are apparent and are capable of interrupting sequential history to make space for past, unrealised possibilities. Multiple, thick presents, not sequential but parallel and staggered, take each other's products as starting conditions, and in turn, their products are made use of by subsequent presents.

These ideas echo recent work within heritage studies that imagines heritage objects as processes rather than products, paying attention to their fluid and impermanent natures (e.g., Harrison, 2015; 2016; Holtorf and Fairclough, 2013). Seeing the processes that constitute heritage objects as constituent elements of this kind of thick present offers the opportunity of recognising their role in constructing futures without employing a sequential notion of temporality, and, further, makes it possible to imagine heritage objects as featuring in multiple presents, depending at which point they have been brought into the prehensive moment of different social actors.

Prehension, and the notion of present occasions that have duration, form a central part of Whitehead's (1978) speculative philosophy, which, alongside the work of other pragmatists, such as Peirce on abduction (Tavory and Timmermans, 2014), and more recently Isabelle Stengers (2014; 2010), has provided a central spar for a turn towards speculative thinking in the social sciences (Wilkie *et al.*, 2017). The pragmatist notions of prehension and abduction are both concerned with what cannot be accounted for with what is already to hand. In the same way, researchers developing speculative thinking are concerned with futures and possibilities that are not available to probabilistic calculation or rational consideration, which are made possible through a "confidence that what has mattered will continue to matter in the same way" (Savransky and Stengers, 2018, p. 134). Speculation, in this sense, seeks possibilities that present modes of understanding the world cannot recognise and, in fact, must discard in order to proceed. It is concerned with the 'yet to be thought' that cannot be articulated in terms of the present, the futures that overspill the bounds of the present. In this respect, it echoes utopian concerns with the 'not yet', and the unthought perpetually immanent within the present (Levitas, 2013).

Through seeking possibilities that cannot be thought of with existing methods, then, researchers are placed in the position of developing new ways of taking hold of the world, valuing experiment and provocation over deduction and prognostication. Speculative thinking demands inventive methods (Lury and Wakeford, 2012), methods designed not to reveal what is already present but to respond to what might be made present. Within futures practice, related examples are provided by the 'speculative futures' or 'design fiction' practices (Candy and Dunagan, 2017; Bleecker, 2015; Sterling, 2013) emerging from speculative design (Dunne and Raby, 2013). In an amplification of the original aims of scenario methods, groups working at the interface of design and foresight have turned to the manufacture of artefacts and experiences intended to situate the viewer in an alternative future. Examples include Superflux's Drone Aviary (2015, http://superflux.in/index.php/work/drones/), a series of installations exploring the experience of sharing a city with different types of autonomous networked flying machines, Smithery's Time Capsule Retrieval Service (2017, http://smithery.com/making/the-time-capsule-retrieval-service/), a series of time capsules purportedly from a variety of different futures, or the Speculative Humanitarian Futures projects displaying material artefacts from imagined future responses to possible humanitarian challenges (2017, https://medium. com/phase-change/speculative-humanitarian-futures-9ce9a76dbf38). These projects aim to make imagined futures material, as a way of provoking questions and responses to issues that more traditional – discursive – ways of representing them tend not to elicit. In this respect, they might be considered inventive, insofar as they are brought into being by the problems they address, and speculative, in that they engage with affective dimensions of the future that traditional strategic foresight is not able to recognise.

If speculative approaches towards the future are becoming more prevalent within some areas of social science, how might a critical approach towards future heritage respond? On the face of it, heritage might appear to be a barrier to speculative thought. The sense that what has mattered ought to continue to matter is fundamental to heritage, and yet this continuity is precisely what speculative thought challenges. But this might be more of a risk from historical, rather than heritage, thinking, since heritage is already in the business of assessing what matters. The invitation to look again at what might matter ought to be welcomed by critical researchers concerned to rethink what we recognise as heritage. Researchers might also ask about the ways that heritage acts as a resource for speculative thought, where culture serves as a repository of ideas about the world from which arise the prehensions and speculations that form novel futures. Or perhaps we might draw from the 'inventive methods' of speculative design to create new forms of heritage research practice that offer different ways of engaging publics and offering access to heritage, building on current ethnographic approaches in the field, and bringing possible futures for heritage into the present.

More generally, what are the weaknesses and strengths, as a family, of the various currents of thought we are bringing together here as 'critical futures'? In contrast to the practical focus of strategic foresight, emphasising the connections between thinking about the future and making changes, critical futures work is more academic and perhaps concentrates more on problematising aspects of social life than it does on the practical action strategic foresight aims to support. In this respect, it is not so different to other academic endeavours, but perhaps, when the topic is the future of what is meaningful or futures in which social justice is increased, there is a greater imperative to connect academic thinking to action in the world, and the disconnect between diagnosing the problem and failing to address it is more apparent. Diagnosis, however, is a necessary first step, and critical futures work offers a wide range of intellectual resources with which to recognise and name the problems of 'the future'. For critical heritage approaches to the future, it is important to know what work has already been done, and continues to be done, outside the field; researchers thinking about the future already have a rich intellectual heritage on which to draw.

Heritage and futures

This chapter set out to put heritage studies in dialogue with other fields concerned with the future, offering a necessarily partial introduction to work from researchers in futures studies and the social sciences, and suggesting some of the ways in which this body of work might connect to the concerns of researchers in heritage studies. We have, for the purposes of this chapter, grouped this work into 'strategic foresight' and 'critical futures' in an effort to highlight the differences between work exploring the future and work exploring the way societies imagine the future. Our primary aim has been to show that 'the future' is not unexamined and that any development of a critical heritage perspective on the future will be richer for engaging with the long history of futures research in its various forms. As noted in the introduction, the description of work here is far from exhaustive. But we hope that what is presented here will spur heritage researchers interested in the future to look beyond the field. There are many ways in which heritage studies already works with concepts and interests described here (such as multiple temporalities or understandings of risk) and the many shared theoretical and methodological underpinnings of heritage studies and the social science fields mentioned above will further support engaging with futures work.

Doing so offers heritage researchers exploring the future a number of ways of enriching their enquiry. Both strategic foresight and critical futures present 'the future' not simply as a temporal category but an object of study in its own right, and model different ways of reflecting on its production. Strategic foresight approaches are useful for articulating possible long-term futures, for thinking about the interactions of factors contributing to the emergence of these futures, and for recognising the importance of developing alternative categories for describing the world. These approaches can extend existing threat and risk assessment work to explore specific future contexts for heritage, envisaging new ways for heritage practices to contribute to social wellbeing, identifying emerging novel forms of heritage, or imagining the changing role of heritage in future society. Critical futures work offers language and concepts with which to articulate questions around the future and heritage, and which also offer points of valency through which heritage studies can direct its own contributions to the study of the future, relating these to other academic fields (perhaps, in some respects, the relative lack of visibility of futures studies offers a cautionary example of the value of participating in wider academic conversations).

For researchers looking at futures and heritage, then, the ideas discussed in this chapter might suggest some specific considerations. For example, in the light of the general sociological conviction that the uncertainty brought about through communications technology and globalisation makes the past no longer useful as a guide to the future, we could consider the capacity of heritage to project some degree of continuity and stability into the future (developing the connections between risk, uncertainty, and interest in the past made by Harrison,

2013, p. 76). Work that recognises non-linear forms of temporality and complex relationships between past and present moments might make more room to discuss where the future is produced through these relationships or begin to think about a 'thick present' with duration, in which past, present, and future all play a part. Considering the role of heritage processes in thick presents and prehensive moments might help us to elaborate and better articulate the distinctive ways in which heritage is 'future-making' (Harrison, 2016, p. 170), beyond simply being a social practice that, like others, necessarily constructs social futures. Engaging with the ongoing speculative turn in the social sciences might encourage us to see how heritage, in its material, discursive, and affective aspects, serves to provide speculative thinking with the cultural and social resources it requires. We might further draw on speculative thinking as a way into developing inventive, prefigurative approaches towards researching futures in heritage. These and other considerations would deepen and support research exploring the general questions of how future imaginaries shape heritage, how heritage shapes future imaginaries, how these processes privilege some voices and experiences over others, and how critical heritage research can ensure other voices and experiences are represented in making futures.

Working with these ideas would contribute towards the development of the 'future consciousness' called for by Högberg *et al.* (2017), who suggest that those working in professional heritage management and policy settings would benefit from being better-equipped to consider the place of the future in their work. Developing this 'futures literacy' (Miller, 2007) within heritage would enable not just researchers but heritage managers and practitioners to be more aware of the different kinds of futures that feature in their work, the manner in which they are produced (through extrapolation of existing circumstances, considering possible contingent events, or through speculation), and the ways in which their work contributes to the production of particular futures: a futures-literate heritage sector would be better at imagining, describing, researching, and managing issues that arise from the future, such as working with change and loss or articulating the role of heritage in transitioning to a sustainable way of living.

Such a futures literacy would give those working within heritage the opportunity to see just how and where a heritage perspective of the future is distinctive and would provide the conceptual tools to relate this perspective to wider futures study, enriching and enlarging foresight and futures work. This has already begun in some quarters, for example, Holtorf and Högberg (2014) consider the impact of broad collections of trends and drivers on heritage, note previous (limited) work exploring futures for cultural heritage, and make a case for recognising and managing the long-term inheritances we leave future generations as cultural heritage, while Zetterstrom-Sharp (2015) describes how particular future imaginaries can shape the construction of heritage in the present. Engaging with work in other fields that has a history of considering 'futures as collectively-imagined entities' (Zetterstrom-Sharp, 2015, p. 615) would provide a firmer base for subsequent explorations of these topics and give heritage researchers room to articulate the ways in which a heritage perspective is necessary for the examination, and construction, of social futures. The field of heritage is concerned with care, responsibility, and protecting the future capacity of generations not yet present to take on these obligations. These are issues that are not yet as visible as they might be within other future-oriented fields, and yet they are at the heart of society's concern with possible futures. By engaging with these other fields, those working in the field of heritage will equip themselves to show how a heritage perspective – on time, on identity, on change, and on care – is vital to any futures practice that seeks to benefit society. Heritage is uniquely placed to develop a way of working with past and future that can focus on the potential and possibility contained in the here and now, to borrow one final time from Adam and Groves (2007), to think less about 'present futures' and more about 'future presents'.

Notes

1 For a more granular discussion of the different schools within futures studies, see Kuosa (2011).
2 The RAND organisation occupies a central place in the military-industrial complex. It was originally 'Project RAND', from 'research and development', part of the Douglas Aircraft Company, set up to link military planning with research and development. In 1948 it became an independent research institution focussed on science and public policy (https://www.rand.org/about/history.html).
3 For example, the UK Government Office for Science's Future of Cities project made use of models, consultations, and scenarios (https://www.gov.uk/government/coll ections/future-of-cities).
4 http://policy-design.org/the-uk-government-launches-a-new-policy-lab/
5 https://www.gov.uk/guidance/what-works-network

References

Adam, B., 1995. *Timewatch: The Social Analysis of Time.* Cambridge, UK: Polity Press.
Adam, B. and Groves, C., 2007. *Future Matters: Action, Knowledge, Ethics.* Leiden: Brill.
Ahlqvist, T. and Rhisiart, M., 2015. Emerging pathways for critical futures research: Changing contexts and impacts of social theory. *Futures 71*, 91–104. doi: 10.1016/j. futures.2015.07.012.
Amara, R., 1981. The futures field: Searching for definitions and boundaries. *The Futurist 15*, 25–29.
Amoore, L., 2013. *The Politics of Possibility: Risk and Security Beyond Probability.* Durham, NC: Duke University Press.
Andersson, J., 2006. Choosing futures: Alva Myrdal and the construction of Swedish futures studies, 1967–1972. *International Review of Social History 51*(2), 277–295. doi: 10.1017/S0020859006002458.
Andersson, J., 2018. *The Future of the World: Futurology, Futurists, and the Struggle for the Post Cold War Imagination.* Oxford: Oxford University Press.
Andersson, J. and Keizer, A.-G., 2014. Governing the future: Science, policy and public participation in the construction of the long term in the Netherlands and Sweden. *History of Technology 30*(1–2), 104–122. doi: 10.1080/07341512.2014.932563.

Ashley-Smith, J., 1999. *Risk Assessment for Object Conservation*. New York: Routledge.

Barthel-Bouchier, D., 2016. *Cultural Heritage and the Challenge of Sustainability*. New York: Routledge.

Bauman, Z., 2000. *Liquid Modernity* (9th ed.). Oxford: Polity Press.

Beck, U., 1992. *Risk Society: Towards a New Modernity*. London, UK: SAGE.

Beckert, J., 2013. Imagined futures: Fictional expectations in the economy. *Theory and Society 42*(3), 219–240. doi: 10.1007/s11186-013-9191-2.

Bell, W., 1983. An introduction to futuristics: Assumptions, theories, methods, and research topics. *Social and Economic Studies 32*(2), 1–64. Retrieved from http://www.jstor.org/stable/27862033 (Accessed 4th November 2019).

Bell, W., 1996. The sociology of the future and the future of sociology. *Sociological Perspectives 39*(1), 39–57. Retrieved from http://www.jstor.org/stable/1389342 (Accessed 4th November 2019).

Bell, W., 2003. *Foundations of Futures Studies: Human Science for a New Era*, vol. 1. New Brunswick, NJ: Transaction Publishers.

Bell, W. and Mau, J., 1971. Images of the future: Theories and research strategies. In: W. Bell and J. Mau, (eds.), *Sociology of the Future: Theory, Cases and Annotated Bibliography*. New York: Russell Sage Foundation; pp. 6–44.

Bleecker, J., 2015. Design fiction: A short essay on design, science, fact and fiction. Retrieved from http://drbfw5wfjlxon.cloudfront.net/writing/DesignFiction_WebEdition.pdf. (Accessed 4th November 2019).

Borup, M., Brown, N., Konrad, K. and van Lente, H., 2006. The sociology of expectations in science and technology. *Technology Analysis and Strategic Management 18*(3–4), 285–298. doi: 10.1080/09537320600777002.

Boulding, E., 1990. *Building a Global Civic Culture: Education for an Interdependent World*. New York: Syracuse University Press.

Bradfield, R., Wright, G., Burt, G., Cairns, G. and van der Heijden, K., 2005. The origins and evolution of scenario techniques in long range business planning. *Futures 37*(8), 795–812. doi: 10.1016/j.futures.2005.01.003.

Brown, N., Lichtblau, D., Fearn, T. and Strlič, M., 2017. Characterisation of 19th and 20th century Chinese paper. *Heritage Science 5*(1), 47. doi: 10.1186/s40494-017-0158-x.

Candy, S. and Dunagan, J., 2017. Designing an experiential scenario: The people who vanished. *Futures 86*, 136–153. doi: 10.1016/j.futures.2016.05.006.

Cantó-Milà, N. and Seebach, S., 2015. Desired images, regulating figures, constructed imaginaries: The future as an apriority for society to be possible. *Current Sociology 63*(2), 198–215. doi: 10.1177/0011392114556583.

Coleman, R. and Tutton, R., 2017. Introduction to special issue of sociological review on 'Futures in question: theories, methods, practices'. *The Sociological Review*, 65 (3), 440–47. doi: 10.1111/1467-954X.12448.

de Jouvenel, B., 1967. *The Art of Conjecture*. New Brunswick, NJ: Transaction Publishers.

Dunne, A. and Raby, F., 2013. *Speculative Everything: Design, Fiction, and Social Dreaming*. Cambridge, MA: MIT Press.

Eliand, H. and Jennings, M., (eds.), 2006. *Walter Benjamin: Selected. Writings 4, 1938–1940*. Cambridge MA: Harvard University Press.

Feher, M., 2009. Self-appreciation; or, the aspirations of human capital. *Public Culture 21*(1), 21–41. doi: 10.1215/08992363-2008-019.

Flechtheim, O.K., 1971. *Futurologie: Der Kampf um die Zukunft*. Köln: Verlag Wissenschaft und Politik.

Frase, P., 2016. *Four Futures*. London: Verso.

Groves, C., 2017. Emptying the future: On the environmental politics of anticipation. *Futures 92*, 29–38. doi: 10.1016/j.futures.2016.06.003.

Habegger, B., 2010. Strategic foresight in public policy: Reviewing the experiences of the UK, Singapore, and the Netherlands. *Futures 42*(1), 49–58. doi: 10.1016/j.futures.2009.08.002.

Harrison, R., 2013. *Heritage: Critical Approaches*. London: Routledge.

Harrison, R., 2015. Beyond 'natural' and 'cultural' heritage: Toward an ontological politics of heritage in the age of Anthropocene. *Heritage and Society 8*(1), 24–42. doi: 10.1179/2159032X15Z.00000000036.

Harrison, R., 2016. Archaeologies of emergent presents and futures. *Historical Archaeology 50*(3), 165–180.

Heffernan, M., 2011. *Wilful Blindness: Why We Ignore the Obvious at Our Peril*. New York: Simon and Schuster.

Högberg, A., Holtorf, C., May, S. and Wollentz, G., 2017. No future in archaeological heritage management? *World Archaeology 49*(5), 639–647. doi: 10.1080/00438243.2017.1406398.

Holtorf, C. and Fairclough, G., 2013. The new heritage and re-shapings of the past. In: A. González-Ruibal, (ed.), *Reclaiming Archaeology: Beyond the Tropes of Modernity*. Routledge. Retrieved from https://www.routledgehandbooks.com/doi/10.4324/9780203068632.ch15. (Accessed on 4th November 2019).

Holtorf, C. and Högberg, A., 2014. Communicating with future generations: What are the benefits of preserving cultural heritage? Nuclear power and beyond. *European Journal of Post-Classical Archaeologies 4*, 343–355.

Jameson, F., 2005. *Archaeologies of the Future: The Desire Called Utopia and Other Science Fictions*. London: Verso.

Johansen, B. and Euchner, J., 2013. Navigating the VUCA world. *Research-Technology Management 56*(1), 10–15. doi: 10.5437/08956308X5601003.

Jungk, R. and Müllert, N., 1987. *Future Workshops: How to Create Desirable Futures*. London: The Institute for Social Inventions.

Kuosa, T., 2011. Evolution of futures studies. *Futures 43*(3), 327–336. doi: 10.1016/j.futures.2010.04.001.

Levitas, R., 2013. *Utopia as Method: The Imaginary Reconstitution of Society*. London: Palgrave Macmillan. doi: 10.1057/9781137314253.

Lury, C. and Wakeford, N., (eds.), 2012. *Inventive Methods: The Happening of the Social*. New York: Routledge.

MacDonald, S., 2015. Is 'difficult heritage' still 'difficult'? *Museum International 67*(1–4), 6–22. doi: 10.1111/muse.12078.

Massumi, B., 2005. The future birth of the affective fact. In *Conference Proceedings: Genealogies of Biopolitics*. Retrieved from http://web.archive.org/web/20060714204250/http://www.radicalempiricism.org/biotextes/textes/massumi.pdf (Accessed 4th November 2019).

Massumi, B., 2007. Potential politics and the primacy of preemption. *Theory and Event 10*(2). doi: 10.1353/tae.2007.0066. Available at: http://muse.jhu.edu/article/218091

Massumi, B., 2009. The future birth of the affective fact: The political ontology of threat. In: S. Ahmed, B. Massumi, E. Probyn, L. Berlant, M. Gregg, and G. Seigworth, (eds.), *The Affect Theory Reader*. Durham, NC: Duke University Press; pp. 52–70.

Mead, G.H., 1932. *The Philosophy of the Present*. London, UK: The Open Court Company.

Miller, R., 2007. Futures literacy: A hybrid strategic scenario method. *Futures 39*(4), 341–362. doi: 10.1016/j.futures.2006.12.001.

Mythen, G., 2004. *Ulrich Beck: A Critical Introduction to the Risk Society*. Pluto Press. doi: 10.2307/j.ctt18fs3c4. Retrieved from http://www.jstor.org/stable/j.ctt18fs3c4 (Accessed 4th November 2019).

Nováky, E. and Monda, E., 2015. Futures studies in Finland. *Society and Economy 37*(1), 31–48. doi: 10.1556/SocEc.37.2015.1.2.

Nowotny, H., 1994. *Time: The Modern and Postmodern Experience*. Cambridge, UK: Polity Press.

O'Hara, G., 2015. Temporal governance, time, exhortation and planning in British government, c.1959–c.1979. *Journal of Modern European History 13*(3), 338–354. doi: 10.17104/1611-8944-2015-3-338.

Palsson, G., Szerszynski, B., Sörlin, S., Marks, J., Avril, B., Crumley, C. and, Weehuizen, R., 2013. Reconceptualizing the 'Anthropos' in the Anthropocene: Integrating the social sciences and humanities in global environmental change research. *Environmental Science and Policy 28*, 3–13. doi: 10.1016/j.envsci.2012.11.004.

Piirainen, K.A. and Gonzalez, R.A., 2015. Theory of and within foresight — 'what does a theory of foresight even mean?' *Technological Forecasting and Social Change 96*, 191–201. doi: 10.1016/j.techfore.2015.03.003.

Polak, F., 1973. *The Image of the Future* (E. Boulding, transl.). Amsterdam: Elsevier Scientific Publishing.

Poli, R., 2010. An introduction to the ontology of anticipation. *Futures 42*(7), 769–776. doi: 10.1016/j.futures.2010.04.028.

Poli, R., 2011. Steps towards an explicit ontology of the future. *Journal of Futures Studies 16*(1), 67–78. Retrieved from https://jfsdigital.org/articles-and-essays/2011-2/vol-16-no-1-september/articles/steps-toward-an-explicit-ontology-of-the-future/. (Accessed 4th November 2019).

Robertson, I., 2008. Heritage from below: Class, social protest and resistance. In: B. Graham and P. Howard, (eds.), *The Ashgate Research Companion to Heritage and Identity*. New York: Routledge. doi: 10.4324/9781315613031.ch8.

Sabbioni, C., Brimblecombe, P. and Cassar, M. (eds.), 2010. *Atlas of Climate Change Impact on European Cultural Heritage: Scientific Analysis and Management Strategies*. New York: Anthem Press.

Savransky, M. and Stengers, I., 2018. Relearning the art of paying attention: A conversation. *SubStance 47*(1), 130–145. Retrieved from http://muse.jhu.edu/article/689019. (Accessed 4th November 2019).

Schulz, M., 2015. Future moves: Forward-oriented studies of culture, society, and technology. *Current Sociology 63*(2), 129–139. doi: 10.1177/0011392114556573.

Slaughter, R., 1999. *Futures for the Third Millennium: Enabling the Forward View*. Sydney, NSW: Prospect.

Slaughter, R., 2004. *Futures Beyond Dystopia: Creating Social Foresight*. New York: Routledge.

Srnicek, N. and Williams, A., 2016. *Inventing the Future: Postcapitalism and a World without Work*. London: Verso.

Stengers, I., 2010. *Cosmopolitics I*. Minneapolis, MN: University of Minnesota Press.

Stengers, I., 2014. *Thinking with Whitehead: A Free and Wild Creation of Concepts*. Cambridge MA: Harvard University Press.

Sterling, B., 2013. Patently untrue: Fleshy defibrillators and synchronised baseball are changing the future. *WIRED* magazine article. Retrieved from https://www.wired.co.uk/article/patently-untrue. (Accessed 4th November 2019).

Strlič, M., 2018. Heritage science: A future-oriented cross-disciplinary field. *Angewandte Chemie International Edition 57*(25), 1433–7851. doi: 10.1002/anie.201804246.

Tavory, I. and Timmermans, S., 2014. *Abductive Analysis: Theorising Qualitative Research*. London: University of Chicago Press.

Taylor, C., 1993. *Alternative World Scenarios for a New Order of Nations* (2nd ed.). Strategic Studies Institute, US Army War College. Retrieved from https://www.jstor.org/stable/resrep11540 (Accessed: 4th November 2019).

Turnbull, T., 2018. Simulating the global environment: The British Government's response to the Limits to Growth. In: J. Agar and J. Ward, (eds.), *Histories of Technology, the Environment and Modern Britain*. UCL Press; pp. 271–299. Retrieved from http://discovery.ucl.ac.uk/10046161/1/Histories-of-Technology-the-Environment-and-Modern-Britain.pdf (Accessed: 4th November 2019).

Tutton, R., 2017. Wicked futures: Meaning, matter and the sociology of the future. *The Sociological Review* 65(3): 478–92. doi: 10.1111/1467-954X.12443.

Urry, J., 2016. *What Is the Future?* Cambridge, UK: Polity Press.

Whitehead, A.N., 1925. *Science and the Modern World*. Cambridge: Cambridge University Press.

Whitehead, A.N., 1978. *Process and reality*. (D. R. Griffin and D. W. Sherburne, eds.). New York: The Free Press (Macmillan).

Wilkie, A., Savransky, M. and Rosengarten, M., 2017. *Speculative Research: The Lure of Possible Futures*. New York: Routledge.

Wilkinson, A., 2013. Scenarios practice: In search of theory. *Journal of Futures Studies* 13(3), 107–114. Retrieved from https://jfsdigital.org/articles-and-essays/2009-2/vol-13-no-3-february/scenario-symposium/scenarios-practices-in-search-of-theory/ (Accessed: 4th November 2019).

Wilkinson, A. and Kupers, R., 2013. Living in the futures. *Harvard Business Review*. May 2013. Retrieved from https://hbr.org/2013/05/living-in-the-futures. (Accessed: 4th November 2019).

Zetterstrom-Sharp, J., 2015. Heritage as future-making: Aspiration and common destiny in Sierra Leone. *International Journal of Heritage Studies* 21(6), 609–627. doi: 10.1080/13527258.2014.973060.

Žižek, S., 2006. Philosophy, the 'unknown unknowns', and the public use of reason. *Topoi* 25(1–2), 137–142. doi: 10.1007/s11245-006-0021-2.

17

FINAL REFLECTIONS

The future of heritage

Anders Högberg and Cornelius Holtorf

> *Högberg asked: "What kind of future are you working for?"*
>
> *The person found it difficult to answer the question, saying, "We don't talk about the future in our work."*
>
> *Högberg: "If you have listed an archaeological site or a monument that you want to preserve for the future, do you talk about the future then?"*
>
> *"No, we don't, we are all well aware that there is a future, but we don't talk about it. We are not good at conducting a discussion of the future. We think short term. We are in the midst of the daily work we handle, with no opportunity to think on a deeper level."*

In an earlier study, we interviewed more than 60 experienced professionals working in the cultural heritage sector. Our results revealed a general "future illiteracy" among professional heritage experts. The short conversation above, taken from an interview with a Swedish heritage professional, is a telling example. It demonstrates a lack of future thinking. It illustrates how the future tends to remain implicit in daily heritage management, which is, in practice, operating in a continuing present. From the results of our study we concluded that although preservation is motivated by a perceived need to transmit the heritage to future generations, no shared professional strategies exist on how to deal with the future in heritage management or how to think about the future of heritage (Högberg et al., 2017). Given that heritage experts should be among those best equipped to place social practices and their underlying logics into a larger historical perspective acknowledging change over time, this is somewhat surprising.

There have been a variety of intellectual trends and socio-economic themes behind the emergence and global success of cultural heritage practices since the 19th century, including romantic nationalism, nation-building and ethno-nationalism; colonialism, post-colonialism and decolonization; citizen education supporting enlightenment; the heritage industry manifesting the experience economy; rights-based approaches and contemporary identity politics. These themes originated, developed and flourished at different times. None of them are going to persist forever, nor are the specific approaches to heritage conservation and management to which they gave rise. They all have been and are going to be subject to change. Ultimately, the very notion of heritage may be transformed so that it ceases to exist in a way that would be recognizable to us. Catherine Cameron (2010: 203) phrased the logical implication of this reasoning very succinctly, "[g]iven its boundedness in time and space, it is logical to project that heritage and its manufacture may wane or change as new social and cultural conditions unfold in the future." And, according to Paolo Ceccarelli (2017: 5), our current theories and principles of heritage preservation are "relative and dated", they may even be "expressions of a moment that went past" already and therefore require us to think more carefully about the future needs of heritage and how we may be able to meet them in the best way.

Throughout this book, many aspects of cultural heritage and the future have been addressed. There are several themes that are of particular significance and deserve to be emphasized at the end. Several authors observe that cultural heritage organizations incessantly add to the stock of heritage while maintaining that they are saving resources for the benefit of future generations. As a result, heritage keeps accumulating; there has never been as much protected heritage as today (Harrison, 2013: ch. 4). But, we actually do not know if such accumulation of heritage will eventually turn out to be a future asset or burden, if it will be wanted or unwanted. Accordingly, it may be naïve to perceive the future as a grateful recipient of the cultural heritage we preserve today. Instead, we need to go beyond business as usual.

The heritage sector would benefit from more detailed knowledge on how specific perceptions of the future inform heritage practices and how contemporary heritage management relates to those future trends that we can actually make out today (Holtorf and Högberg, 2014). Indeed, several authors in the present volume emphasize that to understand the future-related qualities of heritage and heritage practices we need to learn more about how practices of decision-making and managing cultural heritage today create and limit opportunities for future generations. This requires a better understanding of what kind of impact on the future heritage and heritage practices may actually have. Are we preserving too much or not enough of any specific sort of cultural heritage in a given area, or do we perhaps not work in the most effective way?

As mentioned elsewhere in the present volume, Gro Harlem Brundtland's UN World Commission on Environment and Development report *Our Common Future* contains the well-known definition of sustainability as "development that meets the needs of the present without compromising the ability of future generations to meet their own needs" (United Nations, 1987: para. 27). Interestingly, yet barely considered, this so-called Brundtland definition of sustainable development does not actually say that future generations will be dependent on the same resources as we are today, and in the same way, but that they need to be able to meet their own essential needs. In fact, following directly after the well-known definition it is noted that

> The concept of sustainable development does imply limits – not absolute limits but limitations imposed by the present state of technology and social organization on environmental resources and by the ability of the biosphere to absorb the effects of human activities.
>
> *(United Nations, 1987: para. 27)*

Transferred from the natural environment to the realm of heritage, this suggests that the need for the preservation of heritage, too, is not absolute but dependent on the state of technology, the social organization of heritage, and ways in which deterioration and destruction of heritage can be absorbed. Consequently, there may be futures for which the need for preservation in the present does not exist in the way we may imagine it today. Thus, a challenge lies in finding ways in which an unimagined future can successfully inform specific strategies of action in the present (Holtorf and Högberg, 2018). In order to meet this challenge with the present as a starting point, key requirements are a higher level of innovation in our thinking and a larger amount of discontinuity in our expectations.

One possible concrete strategy is to add temporality to decisions about heritage conservation. This can be achieved either by adding explicit future recipients to specific conservation projects or by setting "expiry dates". When potential benefits of preserved heritage for future generations are considered, decisions may be based on a clearer understanding of whether these future generations will live 3, 30, 300, or possibly even more years ahead. As suggested elsewhere (Holtorf and Högberg, 2015: 520), a way forward in heritage policy may be to distinguish short-term (one generation), medium-term (three generations), and long-term (ten generations?) preservation goals. Different kinds of heritage might be preserved for different timespans and a variety of future audiences and purposes (Holtorf, forthcoming). We will have to consider the significance of heritage in futures that are multiple, heterogeneous, and contradictory (Ehn et al., 2014).

This could be linked to an extension of existing practices of regularly reviewing what is protected as cultural heritage and in what way. Although existing reviews may most often be conducted in the context of damage or development that alter the character of a given site or object and may thus no longer meet the original criteria for selection, similar processes could also be used more strategically to reflect changing values, preferences, and apparent benefits of heritage. For example, the UK Good Practice Guide For Local Heritage Listing (English Heritage, 2012) mentions that a regular review of the local heritage list in Stockport, UK, was seen as "a good opportunity to reassess how [the list] could be used to recognize the contribution of locally significant heritage to the character of the town," implying that not only assessments of significance but also the character of the town may change over time, affecting the most appropriate content of the local heritage list. When the agreed time of preservation has elapsed, a new assessment could be made so that decisions about the future would be regularly updated as perceptions and values of heritage change. Heritage-related decisions could thus be conditional on a particular kind of future development in a particular area. At any time, there will also be the possibility not to go on preserving at all and instead value heritage in relation to its decay. Applying "palliative curation" to terminal heritage implies imagining a future in which heritage persists not as preserved, listed, and curated, but as deteriorating, lost, and remembered (DeSilvey, 2017).

Another possible strategy aims at directly empowering future generations. Following the principle that decisions should be made by independent experts while also involving representatives of the affected communities, we could hand power directly to future generations. This could be accomplished in two ways. One way is by including formal representatives of the future, as experts in their own right, into our decision-making processes today. As Martijn Otten (2018) argued, this could, for example, be done by allowing them via appointed representatives to veto laws that they see will have a negative impact on the future (see also Krznaric, 2019). Another way to empower future generations is to make decisions in the present that ensure not the preservation of any specific sites, artefacts, buildings, or traditions but formally regulate instead the process of future decision-making, e.g., that a particular group of future people is going to be consulted in a particular way or may even be put in charge. Maybe instead of listing a particular building, it could be determined that future decisions about it cannot be made against the will of a majority of those using it or other groups deemed to be the most appropriate decision-makers. Both ways would mean to capitalize on the insight that heritage is a set of practices and matters mostly as a process (Smith, 2006).

A final possible strategy to improve the way in which we address future generations is about education. On the one hand, it could mean that we make sure through our higher education system that future heritage managers and other relevant decision-makers have the most appropriate competence to do the job well. Today, experts in the cultural heritage sector are commonly educated in the material and physical heritage of a specific kind related to a certain period and region. If we are increasingly concerned with heritage futures, additional knowledge is needed to make sure the best decisions can be made. Considering future generations could therefore also involve the creation of a curriculum for cultural heritage experts that takes the changing needs of future users and recipients of heritage more seriously.

On the other hand, if we are committed to foreground people-centred heritage, heritage values, and the social impact of heritage, we may feel that alternative knowledge is needed among the future users and recipients of heritage. Maybe the key for future benefits of heritage lies as much in educating audiences how to think and use heritage in a way that benefits people and society rather than merely in making sure that a particular kind of heritage is physically preserved. This may not only require additional education about interpretations and possible social uses of heritage but also an increased awareness of the politics and ethics of heritage among larger sections of the population. For this reason, heritage futures are closely connected to educational futures.

In closing, it has to be said that in history, expectations for the future did not always, or even often, come true. Given the abundance of apocalyptic predictions, so much for the better. At any rate, the point of seeing the present in the light of the future is not to anticipate, predict, or control what will actually happen, but to take seriously what *could* and *might* happen. This can improve our capacity for future-making and what Riel Miller called "futures literacy" (Miller, 2011). To what extent such efforts at improving our future competence will actually turn out to be beneficial, we cannot now be certain about. In any case, considering alternative scenarios for the future helps us all to understand "that ways in which we think and act may be very different in the future and in doing so, opening up a space (or a spacetime) for critical reflection on the present," as Collins (2008: 8) put it. In other words, future thinking helps us to think – and act – outside the box in which we are so often caught in our present and which certainly does not always provide benefits to either present or future societies. Enhanced capacity for future thinking will also help us to be better prepared for the possibility of change, as and when new challenges or opportunities emerge. It will help us to deal with the range of alternative futures envisioned by people today. This is future-making as a way to change the present. And, by changing the present, a way to actually create a future that perhaps we never imagined before.

References

Cameron, C., 2010. The Unnatural History of Heritage: What's the Future for the Past? *Journal of Heritage Tourism* 5(3), 203–218.

Ceccarelli, P., 2017. Past is not a Frozen Concept: Considerations about Heritage Conservation in a Fast Changing World. *Built Heritage* 1(3), 1–12.

Collins, S.G., 2008. *All Tomorrow's Cultures. Anthropological Engagements with the Future.* New York: Berghahn.

DeSilvey, C., 2017. *Curated Decay: Heritage Beyond Saving.* Minneapolis, MN: University of Minnesota Press.

Ehn, P., Nilsson, E.M. and Topgaard, R. (eds.), 2014. *Making Futures. Marginal Notes on Innovation, Design, and Democracy.* Cambridge, MA: The MIT Press.

English Heritage, 2012. *Good Practice Guide for Local Heritage Listing.* London: English Heritage. Available at http://www.dosomethinggood.org.uk/sites/default/files/downloads/Heritage%20at%20risk%20document.pdf.

Harrison, R., 2013. *Heritage. Critical Approaches.* London: Routledge.

Holtorf, C., forthcoming. Periodization of the Future. In: Z. Simon and L. Deile, eds. *Historical Understanding: Past, Present, Future.* London: Bloomsbury.

Holtorf, C. and Högberg, A., 2014. Communicating with Future Generations: What Are the Benefits of Preserving for Future Generations? Nuclear Power and Beyond. *European Journal of Post-Classical Archaeologies* 4, 315–330.

Holtorf, C. and Högberg, A., 2015. Contemporary Heritage and the Future. *The Palgrave Handbook of Contemporary Heritage Research*. New York: Palgrave Macmillan; pp. 509–523.

Holtorf, C. and Högberg, A., 2018. Archaeology and the Future. In: C. Smith, ed. *Encyclopedia of Global Archaeology*. Cham: Springer. doi: 10.1007/978-3-319-51726-1_2792-1 (accessed April 2019).

Högberg, A., Holtorf, C., May, S. and Wollentz, G., 2017. No Future in Archaeological Heritage Management? *World Archaeology* 49(5), available in open access. doi: 10.1080/00438243.2017.1406398.

Krznaric, R., 2019. Why We Need to Reinvent Democracy for the Long-Term. *BBC. Future* (19 March 2019). Available at http://www.bbc.com/future/story/20190318-can-we-reinvent-democracy-for-the-long-term (accessed 6 May 2019).

Miller, R., 2011. Opinion: Futures Literacy – Embracing Complexity and Using the Future. *Ethos* 10, 23–38 Available at: https://www.cscollege.gov.sg/knowledge/ethos/issue%2010%20oct%202011/pages/Opinion%20Futures%20Literacy.aspx (accessed April 2019).

Otten, M., 2018. *Strong External Representation of Future Generations: Legitimate and Effective*. Leiden: Leiden University. https://openaccess.leidenuniv.nl/bitstream/handle/1887/65949/Strong%20External%20Representation%20of%20Future%20Generations%20-%20Legitimate%20And%20Effective.pdf?sequence=1 (accessed April 2019).

Smith, L., 2006. *Uses of Heritage*. London: Routledge.

United Nations, 1987. *Report of the World Commission on Environment and Development: Our Common Future*. New York. Available: http://www.un-documents.net/our-common-future.pdf (accessed April 2019).

INDEX

Pages marked in *italics* represent photos or figures, while pages in **bold** represent tables.